"There is little that is more important for an American citizen to know than the history and traditions of his country. Without such knowledge, he stands uncertain and defenseless before the world, knowing neither where he has come from nor where he is going. With such knowledge, he is no longer alone but draws a strength far greater than his own from the cumulative experience of the past and a cumulative vision of the future."

John Fitzgerald Kennedy

War Zone

World War II Off the North Carolina Coast

WAR ZONE

WORLD WAR II OFF THE NORTH CAROLINA COAST

KEVIN P. DUFFUS

Looking Glass Productions, Inc.
Raleigh

War Zone

World War II Off the North Carolina Coast

©2012 by Kevin P. Duffus

Published by:
Looking Glass Productions, Inc.
Raleigh, North Carolina, USA.
www.thelostlight.com

To contact the publisher for comments,
customer service and orders, E-mail:
looking_glass@earthlink.net

Photo title page: Steam tanker SS *Dixie Arrow* burns off Ocracoke Island on March 26, 1942. Back cover photo: Burial of Michael Cairns at Buxton by Aycock Brown courtesy Meekins family.

Book design by
Looking Glass Productions, Inc.

Library of Congress Control Number: 2012933667

ISBN 1888285427

Printed in Hong Kong
First Edition/First Printing

In Memoriam:

Lt. and Mrs. John D. Duffus,

and the untold numbers of
U.S. Armed Forces couples
who have been parted by war.

May they be together evermore.

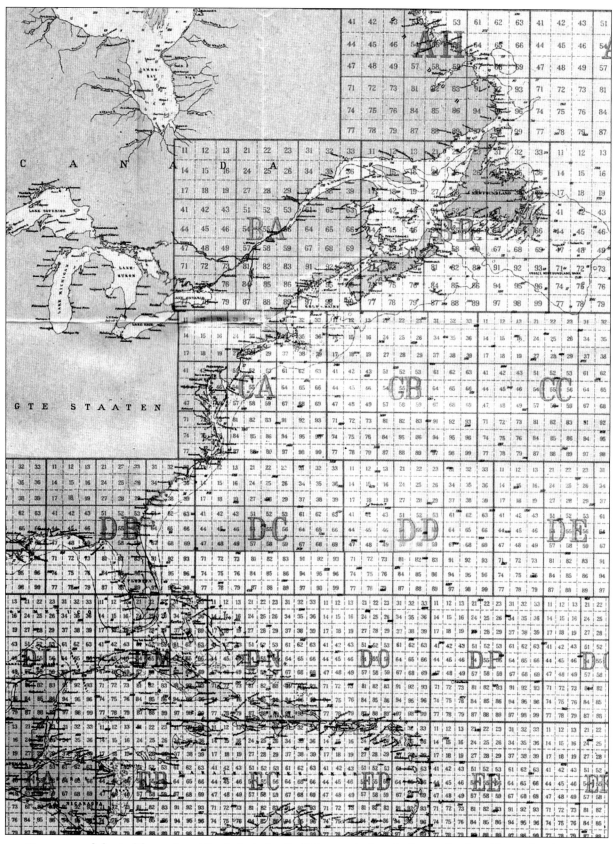

German naval chart of the western Atlantic featuring the Kriegsmarine's exclusive application of lettered and numbered squares to replace longitude and latitude. A U-boat off the NC coast might report their position as CA 8781.

CONTENTS

PROLOGUE

SS *City of New York*, pride of the Farrell family's American South African Lines.

Deliver Us From Evil

Roll on, thou deep and dark blue Ocean– roll!
Time writes no wrinkle on thine azure brow—
Such as creation's dawn beheld, thou rollest now.

George Gordon Byron

Upon the bitter dawn of March 29, 1942, the ocean 40 miles east of Cape Hatteras concealed its direful future. From horizon to horizon, the wide vista at 35.16N 74.25W was empty, save for a passing sea bird, scudding clouds, and leaping golden-crested waves. The deep and dark North Atlantic rolled onward, in one of her many beguiling moods—pleasant, pristine, peaceful, and devoid for the moment of the malevolence lurking unseen beneath the remorseless, slate-green sea.

At dawn this day it was deserted, but this vacant patch of restless ocean—about 18 acres of it—was soon to become another battlefield in the war zone off the North Carolina coast. In fact, during the early spring of 1942, the sea east of Cape Hatteras was not pleasant and pristine at all but was awash in wreckage, disgorged oil, empty lifeboats, and bloated human remains. Devastation and death there, however, were not just recent occurrences.

For five centuries, a procession of seafaring craft of countless rigs, shapes, sizes, purposes, and nationalities, traversed this position on the sea, crisscrossing every compass bearing. No one knows for certain how long this place has been feared as "a graveyard of ships and sailors." Nor is there an accurate estimate of how many vessels failed to navigate these waters unmolested. Thousands of people passed this way: dauntless explorers, anxious New World colonists, rapacious pirates, intrepid navies, impatient merchant seaman, hopeful fishermen, reliant travelers. This crossroads of the sea was no less than a moving backdrop for an endless drama of human transport and travail. And for each and every vessel that plied these waters, there were aboard mariners and passengers who fervently prayed to their Maker, pleading that they might transit the notorious Graveyard of the

Atlantic unharmed. Most did. But not on March 29, 1942. Not all prayers are answered.

On that day as the sun climbed toward its zenith, the horizon to the south was gradually altered by a growing shape flanked by white frothy spray and trailed by a plume of black smoke—a lone ship steaming her way northward. She was the 452-foot-long passenger-freighter, *City of New York*, pride of the Farrell family's American South African Lines, inbound from Cape Town via Port-of-Spain, Trinidad. From strange and exotic ports of call she had come: St. Helena, Algoa Bay, Durban, Lourenço Marques, Beira, Dar-es-Salaam, Zanzibar, Tanga, Mombasa. Nearing the end of a routine four-month voyage to the Indian Ocean ports of East Africa, the ship was little more than 24 hours from safely returning to her home berth and namesake, New York harbor.

On this particular voyage, the 8,000-ton vessel was laden with its primary cargo of South African chrome ore (which was vital to the production of stainless steel), but she also carried asbestos, wood, wool, hides, and other unspecified goods. There was also a multinational human cargo, comprised of 47 civilian passengers, 88 crew members, and nine sailors of the U.S. Navy Armed Guard. Among them were Robert Gates, a missionary's son from Rhodesia; Gifford P. Foley of Philadelphia; Ludwig and Dora Dahlberg of Germany; Sarah N. King; Jack Roy Rodriguez of Boston; and 28-year-old Desanka Mohorovicic, a blond, blue-eyed Yugoslavian woman traveling with her two-year-old daughter, Vesna. Mrs. Mohorovicic was planning to reunite with her husband Joseph, an attache of the Yugoslav Consulate in Manhattan. Entrusted to ensure the safe passage of both lives and cargo was Captain George T. Sullivan.

As Sullivan's ship knifed her way through choppy seas and a Force 6 wind out of the northwest, he nervously paced the bridge wings. He might have sensed his fate; almost assuredly he felt some apprehension. How could he not? As the *City of New York* made her way up from the eastern Caribbean and approached the North American continent, the ship's shortwave radio seemed to crackle constantly with desperate Morse code messages, "di-di-dit, dah-dah-dah, di-di-dit (SOS)," or the recently established, "di-di-dit, di-di-dit, di-di-dit, di-di-dit (SSSS—attacked by submarine)."

For two appalling weeks in March, these distress signals were broadcast, two to three times a day or more, as ships were being sent to the ocean floor off the capes of North Carolina: *Ario, Dixie Arrow, Naeco, Australia, Papoose, E. M. Clark, Acme, Atik, Atlantic Sun, Liberator, Kassandra Louloudi, W.E. Hutton, Esso Nashville, Equipoise*. Directly toward the source of these terrifying distress broadcasts was the *City of New York* heading.

Captain Sullivan's mind must have been filled with both anticipation and dread. On one hand, he was encouraged by the ship's northward progress as he plotted their position on the chart; their distance from New York harbor became shorter by the hour. But before Sullivan could squeeze his vessel through the safety of New York's Verrazano Narrows, he knew he would have to run a deadly gauntlet off the American coast, deemed by the U.S. Navy in the spring of 1942 as "the most dangerous place for merchant shipping in the world."

The *City of New York*'s captain may have thought his ship could be spared the others' fate by ordering his helmsmen to follow the thousand-fathom curve, keeping the ship 50 miles east of the most recent attacks. Their course also made the ship go faster. As the *City of New York* passed between Cape Lookout and Cape Hatteras on a heading of 33

degrees, it straddled the strongest northward flowing currents of the Gulf Stream, which added a little extra speed to the ship's 14 knots. Sullivan hoped his ship's swiftness offered them an advantage, which might explain why, for more than four hours, he had not altered course in the defensive "zigzag" pattern advised by the U.S. War Department.

Just go like hell and hope for the best! It was a tactic that worked for some but not for all.

Men of the sea were innately superstitious, and many were possessed by powerful premonitions of doom. It is not recorded what Captain Sullivan was thinking as his ship sped beyond the faintly flashing gloom of the Cape Hatteras Lighthouse and the many hulks of ships protruding from the ocean surrounding Diamond Shoals, a veritable river Styx. No doubt he kept his dark illusions to himself; for Sullivan, a sense of foreboding as he transited this graveyard of ships would have been well justified—doubly so.

Before slipping the dock lines at Trinidad, Captain Sullivan would have advised his officers and crew of the potential dangers ahead. Once underway, lifeboat drills were practiced, and the civilian passengers were briefed on what to do if the ship was somehow in distress and in danger of sinking.

As the days passed and the degrees of latitude increased, indicating their northward progress, the crew's level of anxiety likewise grew. Despite their anxiety, the officers and crew would have been circumspect about the specifics of the approaching danger, but almost everyone aboard had heard various bits of news. In the dining cabin, there were certainly frequent discussions among the passengers, some of whom had become well-acquainted with each other during the 7,000-mile journey from Cape Town. What hadn't been reported in the news about recent events off the U.S. East Coast was naturally filled in by conjecture. Whispers that a German U-boat or two had penetrated coastal defenses may have been passed among the passengers. But the rumors, no matter how imaginative, would have fallen far short of the reality. Some passengers may have even dismissed the threat and instead preferred to anticipate the excitement of their arrival at New York and being reunited with loved ones and friends. Others, less optimistic, were more likely to wonder about what they would do and what they would grab should the unthinkable happen. As the Bahama Islands passed on the port side and the Sargasso Sea to starboard, almost everyone aboard the *City of New York*, even the faithless, were by then praying for their safe deliverance.

With the sun rise on March 29, 1942, the *City of New York* was east-southeast of Cape Lookout; by noon she would be abeam of Cape Hatteras. For Christians, the day was Palm Sunday, the observance of Jesus's entry into the city of Jerusalem and the triumphant arrival of the Messiah delivering the long-awaited news of God's kingdom. But Palm Sunday for the *City of New York* in 1942 heralded not salvation but destruction; not good news borne by a donkey but bad news sent forth by evil incarnate and delivered by an exquisitely designed, 251-foot-long, steel weapon of death.

At noontime, non-denominational Palm Sunday services concluded on deck as Captain Sullivan and his second officer looked on from the bridge wings. Some passengers returned to their cabins while others strolled about the main deck awaiting the clanging of the lunch bell. A few children played a game of chase within view of their parents who enjoyed the warmth of the sun. High above, a crewman in the crow's nest on the forward mast vigilant-

Georg Lassen

ly scanned the horizon. On the aft deck, two sailors of the U.S. Navy Armed Guard stood near the ship's 4-inch gun.

Onward the *City of New York* raced. Nerves taut as violin strings, Sullivan and his men watched the sea and waited—it was all that they could do. As often happens to mariners, too much staring at the horizon will play tricks on the eyes—waves or clouds sometimes take on the very shape for which a lookout is looking. An hour earlier, excited observers on the *City of New York* had spotted two sea planes and somehow garbled the relay of information, causing Captain Sullivan to hastily issue an order to radio an SSSS along with the ship's position and heading. Soon after, the confusion was cleared up, and the radio warning was subsequently canceled. Unfortunately, it was impossible to retract their broadcast of the *City of New York*'s location.

Oberleutnant zur See Georg Lassen of the U-*160* peered at the marine haze above the southern horizon through the precision German optics of his periscope and observed the rapidly approaching northbound ship—likely the same ship that had foolishly transmitted its position and heading an hour earlier. *Right on schedule*, he may have thought. Patiently, Lassen waited at the fateful coordinates of 35.16N 74.25W. His quarry was headed directly to him.

With sparkling blue eyes and a weak, dimpled chin, Lassen had the youthful face of an accountant, or a school teacher, or a grocer. But who would have taken him for a ruthless killer? Forty-one merchant sailors of the Panamanian-flag steam freighter *Equipoise* might consider him so, since they had been killed by Lassen 48 hours earlier.

Two days before the *City of New York* arrived at Cape Hatteras, the *Equipoise* had been sunk 60 miles southeast of Cape Henry with a single torpedo fired from the U-*160* under Lassen's command.

The 36-year-old *Equipoise* was carrying 8,000 tons of manganese ore (most of which would have been used in the wartime production of 5-cent coins). Despite being named for a Depression-era champion racehorse, the *Equipoise* had been too slow to evade a German G7e electric torpedo traveling at 30-knots. The ship sank in less than two minutes. Of the 54 crew members, only 13 survived. Contributing to loss of life was the disorder of the ship's evacuation caused by the variety of languages spoken by the multinational crew of Swedes, Lithuanians, Poles, Portuguese, Danes, Brazilians, Estonians, Norwegians, Hungarians, Latvians, and Americans. The ensuing 120 seconds as the ship succumbed to the sea was described as a chaotic babel of misunderstood commands, curses, shouts, screams, and prayers.

It was the first ship kill for the recently commissioned U-*160*, under the command of its first captain, Georg Lassen—the "old man" aboard the war vessel at 26-years-old. Lassen was off to a good start.

In 1998, from his retirement home on the Mediterranean island of Majorca, a nostalgic 83-year-old Georg Lassen recalled that his time as an officer of Germany's Ubootwaffe was the happiest of his life. Despite 55 years of marriage, the widower never failed to celebrate what he described as his most memorable anniversary, the day he met his beloved mistress and assumed command of her—the U-*160*. It was on October 16, 1941. In an interview on his terrace overlooking the azure waters surrounding his island home, Lassen said that, as a sailor, he always needed to be able to see the horizon.

So it was that 56 years earlier Lassen had his baby-blue eyes focused on the horizon. The young U-boat commander shouted the order into the voice pipe from his perch at the attack periscope in the conning tower—flood bow tube, open bow cap, calculate range, bearing, enter the solution into the guidance system of the torpedo— "Los!" (Launch!) The eel was away, a 23-foot-long G7e electric torpedo with a 1,100-pound Torpex-filled warhead, speeding at nearly 30-knots at the American South African Lines' flagship, *City of New York*.

At about 12:45 p.m. ship time (1345 Eastern War Time), the eyes of the lookout in the crow's nest were suddenly diverted from the far horizon to the horrifying flash of a torpedo just below the surface, 30 feet from the port side of the *City of New York*. Instantly, the water-borne missile ripped into the No. 3 hold directly beneath the bridge, tearing a gaping hole below the waterline and at the same time smashing the No. 2 lifeboat. All electronic communications aboard the ship were disrupted, and Captain Sullivan was unable to receive damage reports or to dispatch emergency orders. Instinctively and as a result of weeks of training, the helmsman rounded the ship into the northwest wind, and the engineer shut down the engines. Crew members raced to the lifeboat stations and began to ready the davits for lowering. The telegraphist in the radio room immediately began to tap out SSSS, this time with good cause. Within 60 seconds of the torpedo strike, the U.S. Navy Armed Guard had loaded the 4-inch gun at the stern and opened fire at a periscope protruding from the surface, estimated to be about 500 yards distant. The submerged U-boat appeared to be maneuvering toward the stern of the passenger-freighter, and 12 shots were fired from the pitching and increasingly sloped stern deck of the *City of New York*. Without a word from the bridge, Sullivan's diligent preparations and endless drills were quickly put into use.

Minutes before the torpedo struck, the dining cabin's lunch bell had rung, fortuitously clearing the decks of most of the civilians and their children. Sarah King had just taken a seat and was waiting to place her order. "We heard the explosions and felt the impact, although there was not as much shaking as I had thought there would be," King recalled. The civilians aboard behaved almost as if the attack had been expected—there was little surprise, and no one panicked. Unaware of the rapid pace with which her ship was sink-

Lifeboats launched from a merchant vessel.

ing, King calmly rose from her seat and left for her cabin, where she had already organized the items she intended to take with her aboard the lifeboat, including her life preserver.

Meanwhile, passenger Robert Gates, with whom King was traveling, had been napping in his cabin when the torpedo crashed into the ship. When Gates awoke, he found himself pinned beneath his cabin's wardrobe, which had suddenly toppled over, although he did not immediately comprehend why. He extricated himself and drowsily made his way topside to find out what was going on. There he ran into King, who informed him that their ship had just been torpedoed. Shouting over the sharp crack of the deck gun that reverberated from the stern, crew members were urging everyone to get into a lifeboat. But Gates was only wearing a thin shirt and trousers and did not have his life preserver with him. Concerned, Sarah King implored him to go to her own cabin to retrieve something warm with which to wrap himself. Before Gates could do so, it became startlingly evident that there would be no time—the ship was rapidly sinking. No one recalled hearing the ship's emergency whistle or the order to abandon ship, but the need to do so was obvious.

King and Gates climbed into their assigned starboard side lifeboat, perhaps hoping that on this side of the ship they would be shielded from further U-boat assaults. Just as they were lowered into the sea, another passenger, Gifford Foley of Philadelphia, appeared with an armful of life preservers and tossed them into the lifeboat. As King reported later, without these additional preservers, some members of her group would have surely not survived.

Lowering a lifeboat was typically a dangerous and delicate operation in the best of conditions, but doing so from a steeply listing ship in Force 6 winds and choppy seas was an enormous test of skill and composure. The *City of New York*'s crew performed courageously. "I was so proud of our officer, he did such a good job of getting us lowered and launched," King said.

With her lifeboat descending on the falls, King was facing the ship's hull with her back turned to the sea, so she didn't see it coming—a second torpedo. The explosion at the waterline erupted just 20 feet away as the lifeboat precariously dangled halfway between the davits and the ocean surface. The lifeboat fell rapidly downward as a 30-foot "great geyser of water" rained down upon King, Gates, and the other occupants of the lifeboat. "We braced ourselves as it came," King said. "We were driven down into the water. As I went down, I wondered if this was really the end."

When the first torpedo struck, the Yugoslavian woman, Desanka Mohorovicic, had been quietly resting in her cabin with her daughter Vesna, awaiting the midday meal. Upon hearing the muffled rumble of an explosion, Mohorovicic grabbed some woolen blankets and led her daughter to the companionway leading to the upper deck, urging Vesna forward from behind. Halfway up the stairs, the second torpedo struck. Mohorovicic slipped and tumbled down the stairs. The young woman had good reason to be unsteady on her feet. She was pregnant and within two weeks of her due date.

For many days, Desanka Mohorovicic had prayed that she would be able to reach New York City and her husband in time for the birth of their second child. Now her ship was ominously tilting downward toward the bow at an ever increasing angle. There are those who, in such a predicament, might have thought their prayers had gone unanswered, but Mohorovicic was a woman of strong faith and character. She got up off the deck and pulled herself up the stairway, her legs badly scraped and bruised. In the mind of the expectant mother, New York City must has seemed terribly far away, but she was determined to get herself there, even if she had to swim.

Soon after emerging onto the sunlit lifeboat deck near the center of the ship, Mohorovicic was greeted by the ship's doctor, Leonard Conly, who previously had been asked by Captain Sullivan to be sure to find and stay with the pregnant woman in the event that they would have to abandon ship. Sullivan had clearly planned ahead—and had expected the worst.

Until this four-month voyage to East Africa and back, Dr. Conly had never been to sea. One can imagine that as he looked at Mohorovicic and little two-year-old Vesna, he thought of his own wife and son, one-year-old Leonard, Jr., back at Herkimer Street in Brooklyn, New York. The chance of being reunited with them suddenly seemed doubtful.

Conly rushed Mohorovicic and her daughter to lifeboat No. 4, which they boarded along with 19 others. By now, as the ship was slipping ever faster to her watery grave, composure gave way to disorder and chaos. As he hurried to board the descending lifeboat swaying wildly alongside the stricken ship, Conly slipped and fell, breaking two of his ribs. Now it was the doctor who needed medical attention, but aboard the lifeboat there was only a basic emergency first-aid kit—some bandages, gauze, and disinfectant, but no instruments and no anesthesia. No doubt, Conly had his work cut out for him.

When Sarah King rose to the surface of the ocean, all sense of order seemed to have vanished and so had her lifeboat and everyone aboard. Hope was rapidly vanishing, too. The rolling waves, which hadn't seemed so large from the deck of the ship, now lurched over the woman's head. She treaded and paddled as best as she could and was being

U-*160*

lifted and dropped with each passing wave, able only every few seconds to get her bearings and search for other survivors. A voice called out to her, asking if she could swim to the raft. *Raft? What raft? Oh, there!*

As a hedge against the possibility that lifeboats might be damaged or lost in an attack, many merchant ships also carried large muslin-wrapped balsa rafts, loosely secured anywhere there was a vacant space along the ships' decks. These cheap and lightweight rafts lacked the nautical aesthetics and maneuverability of a lifeboat but floated just the same. Most were intended to hold up to 10 passengers within a rectangular, doughnut-shaped ring. The passenger's feet, although submerged in seawater, were supported by wooden slats. Alternatively, up to 25 people could hang on the outside perimeter of the raft by holding onto what were sometimes called—and for good reason—"shark lines." One such raft had been flung from the deck of the *City of New York* by the explosion of the second torpedo attack. "It was providential," said King, "for we surely would have been lost without it."

With the help of the man who had called to her, King grabbed an oar being extended to her by survivors on the raft. As she struggled to climb aboard she was greeted by her traveling companion, Robert Gates, still clad in just his thin shirt and trousers. There were at least 13 others, either seated within the raft or in the water outside of the raft holding onto the shark lines. All were soaked and chilled by the brisk early-spring wind. "We were in the Gulf Stream, and the water was warm, but the wind was not so warm," King recalled. Weather logs from that day indicate that the water temperature averaged 72 degrees Fahrenheit, but the air temperature was about 51 degrees. The 25-knot wind would have made the air feel 10 degrees colder. Wearing wet clothes in that 25-knot wind felt even colder.

Just 15 minutes earlier, Sarah King had been comfortably seated in the *City of New York*'s dining cabin about to place her lunch order. In a bewildering, brief passage of time she was now clinging to a flimsy balsa raft heavily laden with more than a dozen strangers, 60 miles from the nearest beach. Someone shouted, and all turned their eyes toward their sinking ship, now in its final death throes, bow submerged, stern tilted skyward, surrendering fast to the call of the ocean bottom, more than 6,000 feet below. To their horror, King's group watched as one of the ship's two masts, most likely the aft mast, broke and fell, taking with it rigging and radio wires, all which toppled into the sea and nearly swamped one of the last lifeboats to be lowered. The survivors in the endangered lifeboat were saved only at the last instant when the wires snapped, averting disaster.

Even while all of this was going on, incredibly, the intrepid U.S. Navy Armed Guard had continued to fire the 50-caliber gun at the U-boat's protruding periscope as it rounded the stern of the ship and after it had launched the second torpedo. Even as the stern deck was awash and the sailors were faced with imminent peril, they continued to fire their gun. Later, the *New York World-Telegram* reported via the United Press news agency that three of the gunners were known to have died following the U-boat attack. Unfortunately, their names and the circumstances of their deaths have been forgotten in the passing of time.

About 500 yards away, Georg Lassen kept the U-*160* at periscope depth after he launched the second torpedo, even though he could see the flashes of the deck gun on the stern of the sinking ship, firing fairly accurately even as its gun platform was canted at a severe angle. Like a perverse voyeur, Lassen watched four lifeboats,

Desanka Mohorovicic

three life rafts, and some numbers of flailing swimmers tossing in the 15-foot seas. He could not have known, nor did he probably care, that among the victims were civilians: the elderly, women, children, and the eight-and-half-month pregnant Desanka Mohorovicic.

Charles Van Gorden had been a junior officer aboard his ship; now he commanded his own vessel, the *City of New York*'s Lifeboat No. 4. Aboard his boat were Ludwig and Dora Dahlberg. The Jewish couple had months earlier left their German home for the safety of America and were now probably thinking that escaping the Nazis was becoming exceedingly difficult. Near the Dahlbergs sat a North African named Khosrof Algian, and 13 others, including Desanka Mohorovicic. Not all were fluent in English—Mohorovicic spoke Serbian and some French but very little English. Most of the survivors were too stunned or scared to say anything anyway but huddled in their own private spaces in the boat and wondered what the future held. Many suffered the aches and pains of various injuries.

Van Gorden organized the merchant crewmen aboard the lifeboat, and pairs began taking turns pulling on the oars. Their first objective was to get themselves away from the dangerous debris field left by their sinking ship and to avoid those buoyant objects—masts, deck cargo, furniture—that would sometimes rocket to the surface as a ship plummeted into the deep. Van Gorden also hoped to reach those survivors not in lifeboats and soon encountered the crowded raft containing Sarah King. One survivor on the raft described their precarious state as "being piled on [the raft] like cordwood," being submerged as often as they floated. Van Gorden had a spare bundle of cotton blankets thrown over to the raft, that were eagerly distributed among its passengers who had no coats.

It was decided to transfer women and children, including King and the 8-year-old daughter of another passenger, from the raft to the relative safety of the lifeboat. The little girl, June, and her father, Richard Wrigley, were moved over first. In the high waves, it was feared that the wildly tossing lifeboat could stave the fragile balsa hull of the raft, sinking it, and further attempts were debated. Van Gorden tried once more, skillfully guiding the lifeboat by its tiller. Soon, King made it over, "jumping for all she was worth." Her friend Robert Gates made it, too.

It was something of a miracle—or a testament to their character—that the survivors clinging to the raft's shark lines restrained themselves and did not selfishly abandon the raft and grab onto the lifeboat, causing it to capsize.

By the time the additional passengers were brought aboard, a couple of the merchant sailors had rigged a small sail over the middle of the boat under which they sheltered the barefoot and pregnant Mohorovicic, who was seated on a port side bench with daughter Vesna and Dr. Conly nearby. Surely, at this point, the *City of New York* crew members glanced at one another and silently communicated their concern about the young mother, *What happens if she goes into labor?*

Up and down, they rose and fell, as waves rolled from the northwest to the southeast, pushing the survivors inexorably away from land and farther out to sea. The remaining hours of daylight seemed to pass quickly, and the three rafts and four lifeboats began to drift apart and lose contact with each other. The temperature dropped, the wind strengthened, and the crests of the waves began breaking as spray whipped through the air. Sharks had been seen circling the boats, and some had to be repelled by being struck by oars. Sometime after dark, a man on Sarah King's former life raft succumbed to his injuries and the unrelenting cold. He died, and with a brief prayer and a few who made the sign of the cross, his body was cast off into the darkness of the unmerciful sea.

Aboard Lifeboat No. 4, the first contractions came and went, and Desanka Mohorovicic did her best to ignore them and to suppress any signs of discomfort. *Ni Sad! (Not now!)* Over and over, she whispered the Serbian words of prayer for their safe deliverance—*Izbavi nas od zla (Deliver us from evil)*. By 8 p.m., however, it was no longer possible for her to hide that fact that she was having her baby. It came as little surprise to Dr. Conly, who fully expected the violent motion of the lifeboat to induce the woman's labor. Seaman Leroy Tate helped Conly arrange a section of canvas sail to help provide a little privacy for the shy young mother as she was about to give birth in the presence of 21 strangers in close quarters. "The sea was rough," Tate later said. "By the time her labor pains began, the boat was practically full of water. The woman had no shoes. She did not complain and did everything she could to make it as easy as possible for the doctor and those who attended." Neither did Dr. Conly complain, although he winced in pain on almost every lurch of the lifeboat. The physician also would have liked to have had more to work with than what was in the basic emergency lifeboat kit: hemostats, scissors, gauze, iodine, aspirin, all drenched in salt water. It would have to do.

The procedure would have been no easier if conducted in the car of a Coney Island roller coaster on a rainy dark night. It was impossible for Conly to see beneath the canvas sail; he could hardly keep from being tossed out of the lifeboat. The best he could hope for was to be ready to catch the baby at the moment of delivery, which happened at about 2:30 a.m. on Monday morning. At that time, at approximately 35-36N 74-27W, Desanka Mohorovicic delivered a healthy, 8-pound baby boy.

As often happens, remarkable historical events are made more impressive over the years by embellishments. In this case, it has since been said and often repeated that Dr. Conly nearly lost the baby overboard at the moment of delivery when an enormous wave broke over the occupants of the lifeboat. That fact can be found no where in the official records or the testimony of those who were present. In fact, the statements reflect that the baby and his mother were reasonably protected from the insults of the sea under the canvas sail in the center of the boat. Cleaning the baby, however, according to Dr. Conly, was a fairly simple matter. "The sea did that for me," Conly said. "He was wringing wet when it was all over. We all were. The worst thing about it all was having to work bent over under the sail covering without any light to work by. Mrs. Mohorovicic was lying on a water keg. While I was working over her [it] was like being on a scenic railway. We swooped up and down waves that were 15 or 20 feet high."

And so they went, borne on an invisible ocean current into the darkness of the vast Atlantic, swept ever onward toward the great mystery of their fates.

Were they headed for survival or doom?

Is it possible to imagine what must it have been like to have been there?

Were we to place ourselves in that lifeboat right now, we would hear the shrieking of the wind, the crashing of the waves, the moans and whimpering of the injured and affrighted, the murmured prayers of the faithful, and the cries of a newborn baby.

Meanwhile, back at the place where the *City of New York* was attacked and where she sank, all signs of the incident had been erased, carried away on the currents and eddies of the Gulf Stream. Yet even as the ocean returned to her natural state, elsewhere, haunting SOS signals filled the airwaves in the war zone off North Carolina's Outer Banks.

No one could have imagined it at the time (and few people know about it or fully appreciate it to this day), but the birth of Desanka Mohorovicic's son in a lifeboat 60 miles northeast of Cape Hatteras on March 30, 1942, would have a profound effect on the future of the war as it was being fought in U.S. waters. Within two weeks, retribution for Lassen's attack on the *City of New York* would be paid, in some measure inspired by the birth of "the lifeboat baby."

CHAPTER 1

A German U-boat surfaces in the North Atlantic.

A Time of Infamy

"We were all mad as hell if you want to know the truth about it, having to fight German submarines on our coast."

Chief Petty Officer Arnold Tolson, USCG

It was really not that very long ago, and there are some still living who were there when it happened—although fewer every day—the time when the greatest and most deadly war of human history came to the bucolic, sleepy shores of North Carolina.

In 1942, the United States suffered one of its worst defeats of the Second World War. Between January and July, more than 65 German U-boats waged a withering, widespread campaign against Allied merchant vessels and their military defenders. Three hundred ninety-seven ships were sunk or damaged in just half a year. Nearly 5,000 people, including many civilians, were burned to death, crushed, drowned, or vanished into the sea.

This disaster happened not in Europe nor the Pacific but within U.S. territorial waters along the nation's eastern seaboard and in the Gulf of Mexico. As forces were marshaled to foreign fronts, the enemy—unchallenged—entered America's front door.

Each day, towering columns of black smoke and orange flames from torpedoed merchant vessels filled the skies from New England to New Orleans. Explosions rattled window panes and the nerves of startled coastal residents. Beaches were littered with oil, debris, and bodies.

Mostly kept secret from the public, it was a crisis that embarrassed Washington, panicked Great Britain, and nearly changed the course of history. Within six months, the Allied war effort was in jeopardy, and the waters off the U.S. East Coast were considered the most dangerous place for merchant shipping in the world. Left unchecked, the German Ubootwaffe's ability to disrupt the vital supply chain of men and war matériel had the potential to delay, or even prevent, a future Allied invasion of Europe.

The greatest concentration of these attacks occurred in the war zone off North Carolina's Outer Banks on the approaches to Diamond Shoals, a notorious place feared for centuries as the Graveyard of the Atlantic.

On the fragile barrier islands off the mainland of North Carolina, once forgotten communities were irrevocably changed. Oil from sunken tankers washed ashore in quantities that rank among the worst environmental disasters in American history. Corpses drifted offshore and washed up on the beaches, sometimes to be found by terrified children. Adults spread stories of encounters with German sympathizers, spies, and saboteurs. The centuries-old but faltering spirit of the salvage industry was revived. And thousands of servicemen poured onto the islands of the Outer Banks, Bogue Banks, and the Cape Fear region to defend America's shores, straining public infrastructures like housing, food supplies, and postal services. It was nothing less than a war zone; the residents of North Carolina were on the front lines, and they had no choice but to watch as war was waged on their doorstop.

The stress of war so close to home—one U-boat attack occurred within seven miles of Avon village—produced panic and outrageous rumors. "There was deep concern," recalled Hatteras village real estate developer Stockton Midgett. "We would peek out our windows and see the explosions at night." On her front porch, seated on a rocking chair surrounded by a canopy of ancient live oaks on Howard Street in Ocracoke village, Blanche Joliff remembered the time vividly: "It would shake the houses, and sometimes the explosions cracked the cisterns and damaged the sheet rock and plaster in some of the houses."

Ormond Fuller was in her late teens when U-boats ravaged merchant ships within view of her Cape Hatteras home. "You could hear them; you could hear the [explosions], and you could hear the glass rattle, and the things shake when they would go off at night, and you could see the fires offshore burning," Fuller said. The horrifying reality that men were suffering and dying every time an explosion occurred was not ignored by the Outer Bankers.

"We were all mad as hell if you want to know the truth about it, having to fight German submarines on our coast," said Arnold Tolson of Manteo, a U.S. Coast Guard chief petty officer at 19 years old during the war. "I think the people on the Outer Banks saw more of the war in this country than anyone else."

There were some Outer Banks residents who saw more than just the detritus of war—men like Charles Stowe of Hatteras who one day almost came face-to-face with the enemy.

"I remember I was commercial fishing with my father," Stowe recalled. "We were going out to the M/V *Australia* that sank out there. And I was steering and was headed out there when Daddy said there was some boat up ahead. He got up [on the bow] and looked and said, 'I don't have no idea who it is.'"

Stowe pauses to explain that his father's eyesight wasn't so good in those days.

"He told me, 'just keep 'er goin,'" intending that they ignore the strange vessel ahead.

Stowe shouted to his father, "Daddy, that boat there is pretty good size!" The elder Stowe, squinting, replied, "What do you mean, pretty good size? Jus' keep 'er goin', son."

As their proximity to the unusual vessel became closer, Stowe realized what they were looking at and what they were heading toward. "I said, 'My land, it's a submarine!' And my daddy looked out there and said, 'No it ain't, hard right and turn around, we're headin' home!'"

Stowe suspected that his father didn't want to readily admit his eyesight was failing him, so it wasn't until they were well on their way back to the

Charles Stowe

harbor at Hatteras village that he acknowledged that his son was probably correct. "He said it sure was, a German submarine that had surfaced, probably to charge his batteries between here [Hatteras village] and the M/V *Australia*, and that would have been only five or six miles off this beach. That's one of the stories I remember vividly."

The first devastating action on the North Carolina coast happened in the early morning hours of January 18, 1942, commenced by U-66. Over the next few months, dozens of German U-boats followed in the U-66's wake. The result has been characterized by historians as one of the greatest maritime disasters of all time and the American Navy's single greatest defeat at sea.

Allied merchant ships became easy prey for U-boats, illuminated by brightly lit coastal towns, while Americans were kept in the dark by wartime propaganda that minimized the losses. A naïve and ambivalent nation left merchant seamen to sail in constant peril, risking their lives to deliver vital, war effort cargoes.

"I tell you, it was the damnedest thing you ever saw," said retired merchant sailor Biff Bowker at his home at Sailor's Snug Harbor in Sea Level, during an interview in 2000. "Automobiles were going by with their lights on. Down in Florida, the hotels wouldn't put their lights out. They just didn't take it seriously. I tell you, it was terrible!"

Retired Elizabeth City attorney Russell Twiford points out that U-boat successes off the beaches of North Carolina were a well-known fact among the tens of thousands of people living in the coastal region, but beyond that inland communities generally had no idea that the war was being waged in U.S. waters. "So much of it was concealed from the public, not many people knew we were having all of this carnage, damage, ships sinking, and people killed, simply because it was not publicized" Twiford said from a condominium overlooking Hatteras village harbor.

America's armed forces hastily mounted modest defenses to the marauding U-boats.

Teenage boys from the fields of the nation's heartlands were sent out into deadly waters. Against well-trained, battle-tested Germans, they bravely took up the fight with small arms, in small boats, and on small horses.

"We weren't allowed to go on the beach during the war," Blanche Joliff recalls. "The Navy patrolled the beach with horses."

Ormond Fuller and Carol Dillon, sisters living in Buxton, each had close calls with "sand pounders"—the self-named group of sailors assigned to patrolling East Coast beaches. On one occasion, Fuller remembers being reprimanded by the commander of the Cape Hatteras Coast Guard station after being caught making a late-night visit to the lighthouse. "He shook his finger in my face and said, 'Don't you know that those boys patrolling those beaches are from out West somewhere, and they've shot up everything on the beach? Everything that moves, they shoot it!' Fuller recalls.

Arnold Tolson understood why the men patrolling the beaches were trigger happy: "Everybody's emotions were high. You know, when you [patrol] the beach, hear an explosion, and then see men washing up in the surf, well... Everybody's emotions were very high. Very high."

Rumors that Germans were coming ashore ran rampant through the villages. "People were frightened to death," said Ocracoke resident Blanche Styron. "And if [the villagers] saw anything strange, any strange people, they would think that they were Germans." For the first time in memory, families in beach communities began locking their doors at night. Blanche Styron's brother, Calvin O'Neal, remembered that his sister would often check on the family at the end of the day: "My sister would come around here after dark, and the first thing she'd do is go and make sure that Momma had fastened the back door. And Momma would say, 'Blanche, why did you do that?' And Blanche would say, 'You don't know when those Germans are coming ashore!' So, we always had a sense of uneasiness."

Such are the memories of 1942, painfully and irrevocably seared into the minds of those people who survived the years when the waters off the coast of North Carolina became a war zone. It was a time of infamy, a time of irony, and a time when innocence was lost.

Gibb Gray: "Me and a friend of mine saw nine men, dead, laying on the floor with their lifejackets still on and their eyes filled with sand—that's a terrifying sight for two 15-year-old boys to see."

Arnold Tolson: "It was a bad time."

Calvin O'Neal: "We lost our innocence then."

SS *Dixie Arrow* burns off Ocracoke Island.

CHAPTER 2

National Park Service vehicle stuck in sand on "Highway 101."

ISLANDS OF INNOCENCE

"You had to be tough to live here; you had to be a tough person just to survive."

Stockton Midgett

Had you visited the North Carolina coast during the years preceding World War II, you would have seen herds of wild Spanish mustangs freely roaming the beaches, a quaint private ferry transporting cars across Oregon Inlet, or mail delivered each day by the mailboat, *Aleta*, or in the event you lived at Portsmouth, by Carl Dixon in a small, one-man skiff.

Those were the days on the Outer Banks when waterfowl hunters had no limits. Grand hunting clubs built by millionaire northern industrialists employed island men during the winter months as guides or caretakers if they weren't already employed by the government to man the chain of life-saving stations located every six miles along the beach. It was a time when an hour of clamming or oystering would fill a man's skiff, to handle seine nets laden with fish required a dozen or more strong men, and fish houses worked around the clock to ice and pack their wares for shipment to the mainland.

Old timers tell of the days when neighbors were always willing to lend a hand. If someone needed help, they never had to ask. If you needed a ride to the post office, all you had to do was wave at the next vehicle coming down the road. Groceries arrived weekly at village docks brought by freight boats like the *J.E. Sterling*, the *Annie*, the *Relief* and the long-running *Preston*. Each village had a one-room schoolhouse, a general store, and at least one gleaming-white church. Island children would spend summer days sailing small skiffs in the sound, riding ponies on the beach, or exploring the remains of shipwrecks in search of lost treasure; there is at least one recollection of a lighthouse keeper's children racing each other down the stairs by sliding on the iron handrails of their 15-story lighthouse.

Like a necklace of pearls, these were close-knit communities in an age of of innocence. It was a simpler time. Upon closer examination, however, life was not so easy.

For adults living on the Outer Banks of North Carolina, the years preceding the war had been a period of great instability. According to the late historian David Stick, "On the eve of the Great Depression, the fortunes of the Bankers had reached a new low." The age of the great hunting clubs had waned, maritime traffic decreased, shipbuilding had ceased, commercial fishing slowed, and many of the islands' young people had left to seek work elsewhere. There were worries everywhere one looked. The island's old timers noticed that the rising level of the sea seemed to increase the damage inflicted by tropical storms and winter nor'easters. Erosion of the shoreline endangered the nation's tallest brick lighthouse at Cape Hatteras, causing the U.S. Coast Guard to abandon the iconic tower in 1936. Real estate speculation, rampant during the Roaring Twenties, had swept away like an outgoing tide. The economic future of the islands looked dismal in the 1930s.

When asked what life was like on the Outer Banks during the Depression years, former Coast Guardsman and Hatteras fisherman Charles Stowe scratched the stubble on his chin and said, "Well, it didn't bother us at all. We were already depressed—how are you going to get any worse that that?"

"You had to be tough to live here; you had to be a tough person just to survive," Stockton Midgett reminisced at his real estate office in Hatteras village. "Most people's livelihood back in them days was from fishing, clamming, and oystering, and then there [were] several people who worked away on tugboats and as dock masters." Midgett was a young child during the worst of the Depression years but later his memory of the troubled decade is clear. "I always had clothes on my back, [although we] didn't have much money to spend and not too many places to spend it. We always had plenty of food on the table and plenty to eat, but sometimes we went out and caught a lot of our food. I never remember [being] without three square meals a day so I wouldn't say it was too tough." Being a child, Midgett might not have known how tough his parents thought their life was or how hard they had to work to place food on the table each day. The average, typically stoic Outer Banker simply would not have complained about their hardships, even within the privacy of their own homes, and especially not in front of their children.

On the eve of World War II, the barrier islands off the mainland of North Caroli-

na—the Outer Banks, Bogue Banks, Topsail Island, Smith Island, Oak Island, and others—were some of the most isolated and least known places in the United States. While much of America had developed through commerce, these slender islands had instead been shaped by the wind, the tides, countless storms, five wars, and the salvaged bounty of hundreds of ships that made the ocean depths or the sandy beaches their final resting place. The islands were sparsely populated, hard to get to, and hard to travel across once a visitor got there. There were no paved roads, few bridges, and only limited services such as hotels, restaurants, and refueling facilities.

Throughout its history, the Outer Banks in particular had been defined by the elements and by disaster—natural and man-made. Even though present-day tourists and vacationers rarely see the evidence, calamity and death were not infrequent occurrences. In fact, there are some people who still believe that ghosts walk these beaches, the restless spirits of the thousands who perished in shipwrecks on the coast. Shipwrecks, indeed, shaped the destiny of the Outer Banks, as much as did wind and tides.

Outer Banks historian David Stick recalled a time when driving down Hatteras Island with his father, Frank, that they passed the sun-parched remains of "wreck after wreck after wreck." A 1925 article published in *National Geographic* supports Stick's recollection—its author, on a motor-coach tour of North Carolina, described passing hundreds of skeletons of what had once been shipwrecks, even claiming to have counted 14 wrecks within 100 yards. While 14 wrecks within 100 yards is surely an exaggeration, a photo from the files of the National Park Service, clearly shows the keels of four ships in close proximity to one another. The significance of these Outer Banks shipwrecks was perhaps best described by *State Magazine* publisher Bill Sharpe who wrote in 1952, "For every mile there was a wreck, for every wreck there was a deed of heroism, and for every deed a dozen enchanting stories."

Over the years, storms and increasing numbers of shipwrecks established government bureaucracies and jobs in the Lighthouse Service, the Life-Saving Service, and the salvage industry. As a result of the many deadly and costly shipwrecks between Cape Lookout and Currituck Beach, the U.S. government built and operated some of the tallest and most beautiful lighthouses in all of North America and placed life-saving stations every six miles or so along the Outer Banks.

Lighthouses and life-saving stations notwithstanding, Mother Nature was unimpressed

with the government's efforts, and storms regularly drove ships ashore onto the submerged sand bars and onto the beaches of the barrier islands. Consequently, the salvage of shipwrecks became a huge part of everyday life on the Outer Banks. Well-attended "vendues" or public auctions of salvageable materials from shipwrecks would be held on the beaches, like one in 1899 on the beach between Salvo and Avon. At these auctions, island residents would gather to purchase unspoiled food, wine and liquor, cooking utensils, china and pottery, furniture, lamps and oil, books, clothing, canvas sails, rope, rigging, tackle, and lifeboats.

"It was an integral part of the life for this area—absolutely necessary for survival," said Stick. Houses and churches were built of salvaged timbers of shipwrecks; families were clothed and fed by the bounty from shipwrecks. Much of the livestock—horses, cows, pigs, sheep, and goats—came to the Outer Banks as a consequence of shipwrecks.

There was another product of shipwrecks thst shaped the Outer Banks: the residents themselves, many of whom could trace their lineage to an ancestor that had been washed ashore and chose to make the barrier islands their home. The result is a community with a patchwork heritage producing independent, tough, and resourceful people like Stockton Midgett and Charles Stowe.

Once marketed by tourism promoters as "The Land of Beginnings" for the early efforts of English adventurers to establish a colony in the New World, the North Carolina Outer Banks could also be called "the land of achievements." Momentous and miraculous events have happened there, but not all are sufficiently remembered for posterity.

Despite the islands being isolated and only a mile or less in width, the Outer Banks have been the stage for some of the most important, dramatic, and life-changing achievements in American and world history.

The ever-present wind and the wide-open expanses of sand and water brought great visionaries and pioneers like the Wright brothers, whose daring experiments changed the world forever. Less known is Reginald Fessenden, who conducted history's first broadcast of musical notes over the air between a transmitter at Buxton and a receiver on Roanoke Island. General Billy Mitchell came to Hatteras Island in 1923 and demonstrated the possibility for what later occurred at Pearl Harbor by sinking two decommissioned World War I-era battleships off of Cape Hatteras using only small planes dropping small bombs. And not to be forgotten: Frank Stick, a celebrated wildlife artist who first came to the Outer Banks on a hunting trip, fell in love with the islands, moved his family there, and soon after conceived the idea for a seashore park for Cape Hatteras, the nation's first National Seashore Park.

There were other luminaries who made the Outer Banks world-renown, and while these men's names don't usually appear in the history books, they were outstanding American heroes who deserve to be remembered. Malachi Corbell, Benjamin Dailey, William Gaskill, Richard Etheridge, John Allen Midgett, Patrick Etheridge, Rasmus Midgett, and Dunbar Davis were just a few of the many men of the U.S. Life-Saving Service who patrolled more than 300 miles of beaches on the North Carolina coast during the 19th and 20th centuries. Their job? Nothing less than to risk their own lives to save strangers in distress.

Time and again, the intrepid lifesavers of the North Carolina coast left the comfort and safety of their homes and life-saving stations during the most horrifying weather conditions to accomplish miraculous feats of courage. Small in stature but with enormous hearts and strength of steel, they were fearless, unassuming, and willing at a moment's notice to launch their frighteningly fragile surf boats into sea conditions that would strike many seasoned mariners with trepidation and terror.

These lifesavers routinely did heroic deeds unsurpassed in the annals of life saving and were recognized with gold medals and elaborate citations by presidents, Congresses, and the leaders of foreign nations. One such memorable rescue was summarized in the following words to the U.S. Congress: "These poor, plain men took their lives in their hands and, at most imminent risk, crossed the most tumultuous sea that any boat within the memory of living men has ever attempted on that bleak coast, and all for what? That others might live to see home and friends. Duty, their sense of obligation, and the credit of the Service impelled them to do their mighty best."

In the present, media-driven, "famous for being famous" world, it might seem odd that the lifesavers of yesteryear didn't perform their unselfish and death-defying feats of courage for recognition or media attention—they did those things because it was their job. Regrettably, despite the accomplishments of men like Rasmus Midgett, Malachi Corbell, and Benjamin Dailey, there are as yet no roadside historic markers or monuments to preserve their memory.

Even though the fortunes of many Outer Bankers had reached a new low during the Depression years, there were a number of initiatives, most of them government sponsored, to enhance the economic fortunes of the islands. Bridges were built linking Roanoke Island to Nags Head and the Currituck County mainland to the banks at Kitty Hawk. Erosion control measures had begun including erecting sand fences and planting sea oats by members of the Civilian Conservation Corps. A new outdoor drama, titled, "The Lost Colony," was created by Paul Green—the first of its kind—and performed in a natural amphitheater at Fort Raleigh. And a grand memorial was constructed at Kill Devil Hills in honor of the world's first powered flight.

Slowly but surely, connections binding the isolated sand banks to the mainland of North Carolina were being drawn tighter but only north of Oregon Inlet during the prewar years. Communities south of the inlet remained as cut off from the rest of the world as ever, except for one new device—the radio. For Hatteras, Ocracoke, and Portsmouth residents (those who could afford to own one), the radio became their bridge to the mainland and the troubled world beyond.

CHAPTER 3

Tonight the World Trembles

> *"In light of all these facts, what is there to get alarmed about?"*
>
> **John Steele, Mutual Broadcasting System**

Picture a summer's day in 1941 along a winding, live oak-canopied road in the village of Avon. Jazz tunes and white linen curtains billow out of an opened window as the sea breeze rustles the trees and rushes through the island's homes. A passerby, barefoot and plodding along in deep sand ruts, is serenaded by the pulsing buzz of seaside cicadas, the clamorous crow of a rooster, and the static of a radio broadcast of the Andrews Sisters. The song they are singing is "Ferryboat Serenade," naturally a popular tune amongst the residents of Hatteras Island.[1]

> *"I love to ride the ferry, where music is so merry."*
> *There's a man who plays the concertina, on the moonlit upper deck arena.*
> *While boys and girls are dancing, while sweethearts are romancing.*
> *Life is like a Mardi Gras, Funiculi, funicula.*

Life on the eve of WWII was hardly like a Mardi Gras. The summer of 1941 was an unsettling time for Americans, who, in the words of Winston Churchill, "looked forward with great anxiety to what would happen in the future."

The welcomed warmth of the summer sun, bright cerulean skies, and the optimistic tunes of American jazz contrasted sharply with the disquieting, dark mood that permeated the island communities along the coast of North Carolina. Like the summer humidity, anxiety weighed heavily on the population as the nation was being drawn inexorably closer and closer to war. Islanders could feel war looming like a distant hurricane

Memories of World War I

During the 1930s, Outer Banks residents had good reason to be concerned about the future. Hardly two decades had passed since the last time the tides of a world war reached their beaches. Germany's skulking weapon of war, the U-boat, had effectively proved its range and deadliness off American shores in 1918 and off the Outer Banks in particular, sinking merchant vessels with torpedoes and mines and destroying the Diamond Shoals Lightship No. *71* by gunfire.

Memories of the first U-boats have always been vivid for islanders like Ida O'Neal of Hatteras. In a 1997 interview with the author, 93-year-old Miss Ida recalled the horrifying month of August 1918 as if it had just happened. Her father, Charlie Willis, had been a crew member of the lightship when it was approached by the U-*140*. "My father was on the lightship, and the [Germans] didn't blow it up [right away]; they told him to get off, and then they blew it up," O'Neal said while in the living room of her Hatteras bungalow. Gazing upon a framed photograph of her father, Miss Ida seemed to have transported herself back in time, her voice trailing away as if she were speaking to herself. "Mmm hmm, they got in a small boat and rowed away. [The Germans] gave them the time to do it; they didn't kill them. And then they blew the lightship up." Residents in the vicinity of Cape Hatteras on that 6th day of August could hear the distant crack of the U-*140*'s deck gun, although they had no idea it was a German U-boat doing the shooting nor that their beloved lightship was the victim. Later that evening, when the 12 crewmen of the lightship came ashore in their ship's boat south of the lighthouse, everyone soon found out what happened.

The return of German U-boats to American waters was fully expected by the majority of Outer Bankers in the event that the United States would join Britain in the war against the Axis powers.

heralded by the air's leaden stillness hours before landfall; they could see war threatening like a menacing black squall rising from the far horizon.

Now, so many years later (and with so few living who can remember), it can be difficult, even impossible, for today's generations to grasp how precarious and dangerous the world must have seemed to U.S. citizens living on the precipice of World War II. These were people who had already witnessed the horror of a world-wide war that had killed more than 9 million people. They had been ravaged and humbled by the Great Depression. They had been inured to deprivation and hardship. And they had been dismayed by their vulnerability to global politics and economics over which they had no control. Unsettledness was the pervasive mood of the time, and fear about the future was its insidious shadow.

There is little wonder that the radio became American's great escape of the 1930s. By the middle of the decade, well more than half of American households owned a radio, which created a new economic opportunity for manufacturers, broadcast companies, and advertising agencies, as well as employment for program producers, writers, actors, comedians, musicians, technicians, and journalists. Often overlooked by history, the flourishing popularity of the radio contributed significantly to the nation's economic recovery.

Americans cherished their new radios made by Philco, E.H. Scott, RCA-Victor Co., General Electric, Sears Roebuck & Co., or Montgomery Wards. Industrial

and architectural design underwent a major transformation during the Depression with the emergence of the Art Deco streamline style featured in newly constructed theaters, railway stations, municipal buildings, and automobiles. Even the most humble households were able to participate in the fashion trend, simply by purchasing and proudly displaying a new radio.

The market crash of 1929 and the first few years of the Great Depression forced manufacturers to introduce lower-priced, table-top models made with cheaper cabinetry and components that were popular in urban areas among the middle-class. As the economy began to revive, top-end manufacturers began to compete to produce the most artful and powerful console sets. Some models offered the pinnacle of fidelity and opulence like Scott's All-Wave XV or Zenith's stunning and exorbitantly priced Stratosphere, considered by some modern collectors as the finest radio console of the era. Priced at $750, the Stratosphere was the cadillac of radios and nearly cost as much as the automobile made by General Motors' prestige brand.

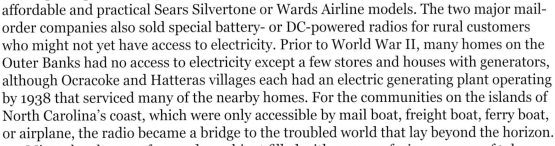

Not many families on the coast of North Carolina could afford the extravagance of a Zenith Stratosphere or the shipping costs of a Scott's All-Wave 23, but they were still able to participate in the exciting new pastime by purchasing the more affordable and practical Sears Silvertone or Wards Airline models. The two major mail-order companies also sold special battery- or DC-powered radios for rural customers who might not yet have access to electricity. Prior to World War II, many homes on the Outer Banks had no access to electricity except a few stores and houses with generators, although Ocracoke and Hatteras villages each had an electric generating plant operating by 1938 that serviced many of the nearby homes. For the communities on the islands of North Carolina's coast, which were only accessible by mail boat, freight boat, ferry boat, or airplane, the radio became a bridge to the troubled world that lay beyond the horizon.

Miraculously, out of a wooden cabinet filled with a maze of wires, a mass of tubes, speakers, and knobs, a listener on a remote island could instantly be connected to an orchestra performance or stage drama in New York, a slapstick comedy or variety show in Los Angeles, or the latest news from London, Berlin, or Rome. Those families fortunate enough to own a radio and who had some means to power it, gathered each evening in their living rooms and parlors to hear broadcasts like the "Chase and Sanborn Hour" featuring host Don Ameche and special guests like Edger Bergen & Charlie McCarthy. Other popular radio stars of the 1930s included Bob Hope, George Burns, W.C. Fields, Judy Garland, Tallulah Bankhead, Dorothy Lamour and many more. For a few minutes or hours each day, listeners could forget the unsettling times in which they lived and be entertained by an amazing assortment of entertainment programs. Despite the cheerfulness of the Andrews Sisters' harmonies or the comedy of Amos 'n' Andy or Fibber McGee, however, sobering news broadcasts punctuated the fun and reminded listeners of "the gathering storm" abroad.

If one were to ask today's senior citizens who were children living on the coast of North Carolina during the pre-war years, they would tell you that the men didn't waste their time with silly entertainment programs. Instead they were particularly intent on following the daily news and commentary broadcasts featuring names like H.V. Kaltenborn, Walter Winchell, Bob Trout, Lowell Thomas, Gabriel Heatter, and Edward R. Murrow.

Each day along the coast, just as in the mainland's rural communities, men gathered at general stores and barber shops at the end of the workday to discuss the latest news. They'd share what they had heard and discuss the merits of the latest pronouncements from the Washington politicians. Many a friendly discussion or heated disagreement was had around a store's wood-burning stove or icebox filled with soda pop. More often than not, the prevailing attitude amongst the islanders was that they just wished to be left alone, although they knew that was unlikely to happen. Even on the best days, most of the news they were hearing in the 1930s was ominous; as each week passed, the headlines in the papers and on the radio broadcasts grew more alarming.

National Socialist Party Wins Control of the German Government

Adolph Hitler Rises to Power

Germany Rearms

Germany Reoccupies the Rhineland

Rome and Berlin Form Axis Alliance

Japan Invades China

Civil War Ravages Spain

German Munitions Factories Operate at Maximum Capacity

February 12, 1938: Hitler Threatens Austria

In Washington, D.C., a debate raged between isolationists in Congress, like Republican senators Gerald Nye and Arthur Vandenberg, and interventionists led by President Franklin D. Roosevelt, with those in favor of keeping out of the world's spreading political upheavals winning the majority of the public's support. In an October 1937 speech, Roosevelt warned Americans with these prescient words: "Let no one imagine that America will escape, that America may expect mercy, that this Western Hemisphere will not be attacked."

Meanwhile, pacifists and a few radio commentators like the Mutual Network's London correspondent John Steele did their best, albeit naïvely, to allay the public's concerns about the latest troubling events in Europe.

> Mutual Broadcasting System newscast, February 20, 1938: "We take you now to London, England."
>
> (Voice of John Steele) "Good evening. I am going to talk to you now about the European situation as it has been affected by the events of the last two days. And the first thing I am going to say to you is, stop worrying.
>
> I've not the slightest doubt that you've been reading a lot of alarmist cables from Europe. You've been told the Second World War, which, of course, you've been lead to believe is inevitable, is just around the corner, that Hitler is ready to march—just in what direction, of course, doesn't matter—and that Mussolini drained the Mediterranean and has captured the British Fleet with his cavalry. Nothing of the sort has happened. I'm sorry that I can't be more thrilling, but there it is. Hitler's legions are still goose-stepping in Berlin. And the British Fleet is still afloat with plenty of water under it in the Mediterranean.
>
> But enough of this fooling as a British Prime Minister once said in Parliament. Let's get down to a consideration of just what has happened. Hitler has made a deal with Austria—at the point of a pistol, it is true, but without fighting. Mussolini has offered to begin conversations to improve Anglo-Italian relations.
>
> In light of all these facts, what is there to get alarmed about? No one has hit anyone yet, and no one seems likely to start the free-for-all that the logical pessimists have been predicting for nearly 20 years.
>
> The truth is that no one in Europe wants to fight. Several nations and their leaders do want to readjust their territory or power or prestige, but they have not the means to compel these changes by force."

Just three weeks later, Hitler's legions were no longer limiting their goose-stepping to Berlin, and, despite commentator Steele's 'Pollyanna' assurances, there was indeed a great deal to worry about. On March 13, Hitler annexed Austria, marching thousands of troops into the country and taking possession if its capital, Vienna.

On the coast of North Carolina at places like Bogue Banks, Ocracoke Island, Kitty Hawk, and Oak Island, radios crackled with the announcement no one wanted to hear, "Tonight the world trembles, torn by conflicting forces."

> Bob Trout, CBS Radio, March 13, 1938:
> "Throughout this day, event has crowded event in tumultuous Austria. Meanwhile, the outside world, gravely shaken by the Austrian crisis, moves cautiously through a maze of diplomatic perils. Since German troops have crossed the Austrian border on the historic invasion last Friday, news has flowed across the Atlantic in a steady stream. The German Chancellor now winds his way through the conquered nation in a parade of triumph to end in a tremendous spectacle in Vienna. As German

troops swarm across frontiers since their first offensive since 1914, momentous decisions are being reached in capitals outside Germany."

With Austria now part of Germany's expanding territory, Hitler quickly turned his attention to Czechoslovakia and its Sudetenland, a border region populated with a majority of ethnic Germans. In a September 26, 1938, Berlin speech, Hitler announced that the Sudetenland "is the last territorial claim I have to make in Europe." Four days later in Munich, Great Britain, France, Italy, and Germany signed an agreement allowing Hitler to annex Czechoslovakia's border province. The Czechoslovakian government had no say in the matter, and many Czech citizens referred to the accord as the "Munich Dictate." British Prime Minister Neville Chamberlain, a believer in acquiescing to Hitler's ambitions, returned to England satisfied that he had secured a lasting peace. Chamberlain said before a crowd of admirers gathered at the airfield upon his return:

> "We [Chamberlain and Hitler] regard the agreement signed last night and the Anglo-German Naval Agreement as symbolic of the desire of our two peoples never to go to war with one another again."

Later that day outside of his Downing Street office, Chamberlain added:

> "My good friends, this is the second time in our history that there has come back from Germany to Downing Street peace with honor. I believe it is peace for our time. We thank you from the bottom of our hearts. And now I recommend you to go home and sleep quietly in your beds."

And a few days later, Chamberlain addressed Parliament and shared this note of optimism:

> "It is my hope and my belief, that under the new system of guarantees, the new Czechoslovakia will find a greater security than she has ever enjoyed in the past."

No security was found and enjoyed by the new Czechoslovakia. Nazi Germany occupied the remainder of the country by March 1939. Poland would be next, then Denmark, Norway, Holland, Belgium, Luxembourg, and France. At the end of one of the most tumultuous decades in history, all that stood in the way of Hitler's total conquest and domination of Europe was the ever-isolated island nation of the United Kingdom.

A year earlier, when Britain's Neville Chamberlain celebrated the triumph of the Munich Accord, an ardent critic of Chamberlain's appeasement strategy stood across the aisle from the Prime Minister in the House of Commons and minced no words. Winston Churchill said:

> "We have suffered a total and unmitigated defeat... you will find that in a period of time which may be measured by years, but may be measured by months,

Czechoslovakia will be engulfed in the Nazi régime. We are in the presence of a disaster of the first magnitude... we have sustained a defeat without a war, the consequences of which will travel far with us along our road... we have passed an awful milestone in our history, when the whole equilibrium of Europe has been deranged, and that the terrible words have for the time being been pronounced against the Western democracies: 'Thou art weighed in the balance and found wanting.' And do not suppose that this is the end. This is only the beginning of the reckoning. This is only the first sip, the first foretaste of a bitter cup, which will be proffered to us year by year unless, by a supreme recovery of moral health and martial vigor, we arise again and take our stand for freedom as in the olden time."

Winston Churchill

Perhaps more than any other event, the diplomatic maneuvers and negotiations over the fate of Czechoslovakia's sovereignty culminating in the Munich Pact commanded the American public's attention, due in great measure to radio's live broadcasts of the speeches of Chamberlain, Churchill, Adolph Hitler, Italian dictator Benito Mussolini, and others.

Since 1933, President Roosevelt had been addressing the American public by radio in a series of informal "fireside chats," initially to ease their fears caused by the national banking crisis that coincided with his first inauguration. Six years later on September 3, 1939, and just two days after 56 German Army divisions and more than 1,500 German aircraft had begun the invasion of Poland prompting Britain and France to declare war, Roosevelt again took to the airwaves to speak to the American people. His delivery was measured and deliberate, but his voice was noticeably weary. On the slender islands off the coast of North Carolina, families surrounded their radios, in some cases with ears pressed against the speakers.

"My fellow Americans and my friends, tonight my single duty is to speak to the whole of America. Until four-thirty this morning I had hoped against hope that some miracle would prevent a devastating war in Europe and bring to an end the invasion of Poland by Germany.

For four long years, a succession of actual wars and constant crises have shaken the entire world and have threatened in each case to bring on the gigantic conflict, which is today unhappily a fact.

We have certain ideas and certain ideals of national safety, and we must act to preserve that safety today, and to preserve the safety of our children in future years.

That safety is and will be bound up with the safety of the Western Hemisphere

"Highway 101" leading into Hatteras Village ca. 1942.

and of the seas adjacent thereto. We seek to keep war from our own firesides by keeping war from coming to the Americas. For that we have historic precedent that goes back to the days of the administration of President George Washington. It is serious enough and tragic enough to every American family in every State in the Union to live in a world that is torn by wars on other continents. Those wars today affect every American home. It is our national duty to use every effort to keep them out of the Americas.

I hope the United States will keep out of this war. I believe that it will. And I give you assurance and reassurance that every effort of your government will be directed toward that end. As long as it remains within my power to prevent, there will be no black-out of peace in the United States."

Churchill, of course, was right. Roosevelt, of course, was wrong, at least regarding his belief that the United States could remain on the sidelines. The days and hours were rapidly counting down when the tides of war would engulf the world and wash upon the shores of North Carolina's tranquil barrier islands.

So it was that during the 1930s the world trembled. As the years passed, the radio steadily gathered Americans together and gave them a front row seat before the tumultuous stage of world politics for the opening act of the second world war. By the summer of 1941, adults of the coast of North Carolina did their best to go about their daily routines—fishing, keeping lighthouses, building sand fences, and ferrying mail and freight on and off the islands. Encumbered as they were with their ever-increasing sense of foreboding, islanders all hoped and prayed that the nation's leaders knew best. Then they turned their attention back to the Andrews Sisters.

> *"I love to ride the ferry, where music is so merry.*
> *There's a man who plays the concertina, on the moonlit upper deck arena.*
> *While boys and girls are dancing, while sweethearts are romancing.*
> *Life is like a Mardi Gras, Funiculi, funicula."*

CHAPTER 4

The Midgett Brothers' Manteo-Hatteras Bus.

The Wildest Bus Ride in America

"Riding in the bus was like a roller coaster ride."

Pat Williams Stevens

With his left hand seesawing the steering wheel and his right hand firmly working the long shift lever, Theodore Stockton (Stocky) Midgett, Jr., peered intently over the hood of the '38 Ford station wagon. The powerful flat-head eight-cylinder engine roared angrily as its tires spun, gaining and then losing traction in the sand. Ahead, clouds of seagulls and oystercatchers parted like a Broadway stage curtain to make way for the huge oncoming vehicle, gears grinding and barely inflated tires bouncing as it sped along the hard-packed beach at about 45 miles per hour.

The passengers in the back seat of the Ford were at once terrified, virtually helpless, and extremely anxious to reach the paved road at Whalebone Junction 50 miles up the beach. They had each purchased a $2.50 trip on Hatteras Island's only means of public transportation for the six-hour journey from Hatteras village to the county seat at Manteo. So far, they were getting more their money's worth.

With hands gripping door handles, window posts, or anything that offered a stable purchase, the riders dared to watch in disbelief as their 'bus' pitched and yawed over sand dunes, spun and slewed and splashed through small ponds, and raced along the ocean's edge as the surf greedily grasped at its speeding wheels.

The year was 1938, and behind the steering wheel was one of three professional drivers for the Midgett Brothers' Manteo-Hatteras Bus Line. Stocky was 10-years-old, which might explain the anxiety shared by the passengers in the back seat and why their bus driver was seated atop a large pillow.

What does an adult passenger talk about with a kid bus driver who can barely see over the hood of his bus? Not much, as it turned out, because Stocky wasn't a very talkative kid. He let his driving do the talking, and he was a good driver. In fact, he was a better driver than most adults on the island and far better than the typical mainlander whose maiden attempts to venture onto the sands of Hatteras in their own cars often ended in disaster. In many cases, those cars are still buried on the beach or out in the surf somewhere. Stocky always got his bus and his customers to their destination. Almost always.

Of all the possible tales to tell, the story of Stocky Midgett and his brothers best personifies the innocence of the islands of the Outer Banks on the eve of the second world war. The story, which has been told often, begins with Stocky's father.

As a surfman for the U.S. Coast Guard, Theodore Stockton Midgett, Sr., routinely scanned the ocean's horizon for ships in distress, but he was also always on the lookout for better ways to provide income for his wife and four children. Midgett had keen vision. In the early-'30s, he wisely purchased a dump truck that was frequently hired by the state for various transportation-related projects on the upper half of Hatteras Island. In 1936, he opened a general store near his home in Rodanthe to provide provisions for the Civilian Conservation Corps camps installing erosion-control measures on the island. And in 1938, the forward-looking father happened upon a promising enterprise for his three sons; a franchise to operate a much-needed car-for-hire business to transport people and packages from each of the seven villages of Hatteras Island to Manteo and back. He purchased the franchise and a car and planned to gradually incorporate his three sons into the business as they matured. Harold, 18, was the eldest; Anderson was 13, and Stocky, Jr., was 10. But before their 44-year-old father was able to return home after securing the franchise and filing the proper paperwork, he collapsed and died of a heart attack in Manteo.

Unexpected loss and tragedy were sad but familiar parts of life on the Outer Banks. When confronted with the death of a loved one, few Outer Banks families could afford to spend much time mourning. To survive, it was necessary to move on quickly. Consequently, it was not unusual that the Midgett brothers, led by Harold, decided to keep their father's dream alive, although they didn't have the luxury to wait until Anderson and Stocky, Jr., matured. In the fall of 1938, after a few trial runs with the family's brand-new Ford station wagon, the boys began the Manteo-Hatteras Bus Line, sometimes also known as the "Sea-going Bus Line." (Alternatively, perhaps, it might have been called the "Sand-going Bus Line.")

If the Midgett boys knew anything, it was sand. Sand shaped their lives, and it was everywhere they turned. It was in their houses, in their shoes, in their hair, and in their blood. "There's not many grains of sand on this island that my brothers and I haven't had in our hands at one time or another," Stocky, Jr., once said. Driving on sand was as natural to them as piloting a boat on water. Their first "bus"—a '38 Ford costing $827—was not as well-suited to sand as were its drivers. The boys "wore-out" the station wagon in their first eight months of beach driving. Of course, the salt-infused environment and resulting rust had much to do with the car's demise, too.

The business proved to be successful, however, so the Midgett brothers added other vehicles, including what they called the "old blue goose," a Ford truck with a wooden

box-like body made in Philadelphia with bench seats along the sides. They wore that one out, too, and it didn't provide a very scenic view for the passengers. Over the 26 years of operating their bus line, the Midgett brothers reckon they purchased and wore-out as many as 45 vehicles, including Jeep-like commando cars and 20-passenger buses in the early years and then, later, buses that carried up to 35 passengers.

Each day, year-round, the "Sea-going Bus Line" departed Hatteras village at 8 a.m. for its run north and stops to collect riders, mail, and packages at Frisco, Buxton, Avon, Salvo, Waves, and Rodanthe before catching the ferry across Oregon Inlet. At Manteo, riders (salesmen mostly) could continue their journey by connecting with the Virginia Dare Bus Line that passed through Elizabeth City and on up to Norfolk. Depending on the weather, wind, and tides, the timetable was somewhat variable, so riders at designated bus stops had to be both patient and alert to quickly jump aboard when they heard the horn honk on the days when it was running a little late. When the tide was high or in storm conditions, the bus would have to navigate the inside route, on the sound-side of the dune line where a myriad of tire tracks seemed to lead in a myriad of directions. The freshest set of tracks were the ones inexperienced drivers were usually advised to follow, regardless of where the tracks seemed to lead. If the ruts were deep enough, it almost didn't matter where a driver wanted to go—his tires would follow the ruts despite the driver's best efforts to steer out of them. "We called it 'Route 101,' which meant we had a hundred and one different ways to travel," said Stocky, Jr., many years later. The sand along "Route 101" was soft and deep, and there were many stretches where the Midgett's buses could only run about five miles per hour—sometimes not at all.

Russell Twiford of Elizabeth City remembers making trips to Hatteras Island with his father in the '30s and meeting Stocky, Jr., for the first time. The two boys were the same age, and to Twiford, Stocky, Jr., seemed to be a typical kid until he got behind the steering wheel of the bus. "The first time I remember Stocky, he was driving the bus, and he was too small to sit in the seat," Twiford said. "He had to stand up to drive the bus because he couldn't sit in the seat and hit the accelerator. And when you'd hit a soft spot in the sand, everybody got out of the bus and shoveled for a while. Then they got going again."

"I remember there were these wooden bridges over the dunes, and riding in the bus was like a roller coaster ride," said Pat Williams Stevens of Ocracoke Island, who was a young girl when her family rode the bus. "Stocky was usually barefoot when he drove the bus. I had just never seen anyone drive barefoot before."

Most any of the few people living today who can claim to have ridden the Midgett brothers' buses say practically the same thing when asked about it: "You'd ride awhile and push awhile," recalls Mrs. Ormond Fuller. Despite the difficulties, island residents were frequent riders because not many owned their own cars. Almost everyone boarded the bus at its regular stops, but sometimes the boys would find riders waiting in the middle of nowhere. Stevens remembers one such time when a solitary figure waved down the bus in one of the desolate expanses between the villages. "One time they stopped, not in a village, but in a place where there was nothing around," Stevens said. "An elderly woman got on the bus. It was a terribly hot day, and she was wearing black cotton stockings. I watched her with amazement as she spent the next hour pulling sand spurs out of her stockings; they were full of sand spurs. No one knew where she came from."

The brothers figure that up to 90 percent of the population of Hatteras Island used their bus service over the years. And in two-and-a-half decades of operation, fewer than 20 trips were cancelled, those typically because of serious breakdowns and rarely because of weather.

Then there was the time in 1954 when Stocky, Jr., lost the bus in the middle of the new paved highway. It was perhaps the first time that road engineers learned the lesson that pavement wasn't always permanent on the restless barrier island.

Into the teeth of a spring nor'easter, buffeted by wind and engulfed by surging seas, the intrepid bus driver drove northward in about a foot of water along the center of the highway on Pea Island when suddenly the front end of the bus pitched unexpectedly downward and then stopped. Quickly, Stocky, Jr., escorted his passengers out of the rear door of the bus, which was by then tilted sharply into the ever-widening sink hole. Being only two miles south of Oregon Inlet, the lookout in the Coast Guard station tower alerted the men on duty, and a truck was sent out to rescue the stranded passengers. Later that evening at high tide, the bus had sunk so far that only about eight inches of the roof top were visible above the water level. Recovery seemed unlikely. From the Coast Guard station, Stocky, Jr., called his brother and told him he had lost the bus. "What do you mean you lost the bus?" was Anderson's reply. The next day, as the storm subsided and the water retreated, the bus was extricated after about 12 hours of work and was towed back to the garage at Hatteras village where it was almost assuredly diagnosed as "wore out."

Most days over the 26 years of riding the Manteo-Hatteras Bus Line were not so eventful, unless you were a first-time rider unaccustomed to the unnerving occasions when the bus would suddenly swerve in the direction of the pounding surf in order to avoid a soft patch of sand. Life on the Outer Banks similarly followed its own unique rhythm and pace—"island time" some like to describe it—just as the Midgett brothers' bus line adhered loosely to its schedule of stops.

In a 1981 article about the Midgett boys and their bus service, writer Diane Ransom, who rode the bus as a young girl, made note of the fact that the bus stops at Rodanthe were always a little longer than at the other villages because the brothers never failed to visit with their mother, Ersie, who still resided in the family home and managed the fam-

Manteo-Hatteras Bus at Hatteras, NC, post office.

ily's general store at the north end of the island. How could adult passengers complain when their 10-year-old driver delayed their departure in order to visit with his mother?

Pat Stevens didn't mind the longer stops at Rodanthe because the store there featured a special treat eagerly anticipated by young people. "They had this big cooler, and I remember being able to get my favorite soft drink there—Nehigh Grape," Stevens remembered fondly.

Such were the halcyon days when an adolescent was permitted to drive a commercial bus—an age of innocence, days of freedom, and a time of peace and happiness on North Carolina coast. It could be said that the residents of the Outer Banks, and the coast in general, lived an elemental existence—leading simple, unassuming lives shaped by the wind and tides. By the summer of 1941, as America teetered on the brink of war, the Outer Banks seemed to have been bypassed by time, without strategic value and far from the conflict beyond the horizon. Then, one Sunday in early December, when the "Seagoing Bus Line" pulled in at one of its regular stops, a man breathlessly ran out of the general store shouting, "You're not going to believe it. They just reported on the radio: The Japanese bombed our naval base at Pearl Harbor. Our country is at war!"

The age of innocence had come to an end.

CHAPTER 5

Admiral Dönitz greets a returning U-boat to St. Nazaire, France.

A Bang of the Drum

"I will show that the U-boat alone can win the war. Nothing is impossible to us."

Admiral Karl DÖnitz
Befeshlshaber der Unterseeboote

At a few minutes past two o'clock in the morning on Monday, January 19, 1942, a thunderous roar roused 15-year-old Gibb Gray from his bed. Furniture shook, glass and knickknacks rattled, framed pictures unleveled on their hangings, and a low-pitched rumble reverberated through the walls of his family's home in the Outer Banks fishing village of Avon. The cause of the frightening sound was not immediately apparent. A star-filled sky overhead and calm seas offshore meant no storm could have produced a winter thunderbolt. The islands had last felt a tremor 56 years earlier, but an earthquake seemed unlikely. The rumble must have come from an explosion somewhere.

Surprised and concerned, Gibb's father rushed to the windows on the house's east side and looked toward the ocean. "There's a ship on fire out there!" he shouted to his family. As the Gray family crowded around the window, they could clearly see on a heading of east-northeast the residue of a great fireball ebbing against the darkness of the night. Orange flames on the water's surface illuminated an ink-black mushroom cloud towering above, blotting-out the stars in the eastern sky. Then, almost as quickly as the bright flames seemed to appear, they receded, then vanished from the horizon. From such a distance, the phenomena seemed unreal to the observers on shore. How could such an enormous conflagration be extinguished so quickly? There was but one possible answer. Minutes after the ship exploded it slipped beneath the waves and was on its way to the bottom of the sea, most likely with most of its crew members aboard.

A child may have asked his parents, why did the ship explode? Did a boiler explode? Gibb's father had a fairly good notion—as most Outer Bankers expected, German U-boats had likely returned to the coast of North Carolina.

The scene in the Gray house—that of a sleepy family startled by the distant concussion and their faces pressed against the cold windowpanes—was repeated that night in dozens of Hatteras Island homes in Avon, Buxton, and up the beach at Salvo and Rodanthe. Few adults were able to go back to sleep that night, their worst nightmares realized. Boys like Gibb Gray might have climbed back in bed and wondered what it would be like to be on a ship that had been torpedoed by a Nazi submarine. *Were the merchant sailors able to fight back? Did anyone survive? Will they be rescued?* The boy's fathers who spent any time at all on the water were smart enough not to think about it.

As sympathetic as anyone might have felt toward the strangers on the unlucky ship offshore, none could have imagined the horrific suffering of those whose vessel had just violently vanished from the unusually placid winter waters of the Graveyard of the Atlantic.

Seven miles from land and due east of the Little Kinnakeet Coast Guard Station, 22-year-old Robert Fennell, Jr., was sleeping soundly in his bunk aboard the coal-fired steam freighter, *City of Atlanta*. For those lucky sailors who were off duty, it seemed to be a luxurious night for sleeping, especially in the tempestuous Graveyard of the Atlantic, which typically caused sleepless days and nights for those transiting its waters. The air temperature was brisk, and the ship was making nearly 12 knots on gentle swells in light winds. Like constellations, groups of twinkling yellow lights separated by dark gaps off the ship's starboard beam indicated the nearness of the scattered villages of the Outer Banks. Lookouts on the night watch might have gazed at these lights and pondered the precariousness of life for people living at such an exposed and isolated place, as if the inhabitants of the Banks were on a ship permanently anchored far out in the ocean.

The *City of Atlanta* proceeded due south along the longitudinal line 75-20W, a course that would take the freighter a scant three miles east of the deadly shoals off Cape Hatteras, a safe enough distance in good weather. All was normal at the midpoint of the midnight-to-0400 watch, soon to be signaled by the striking of four bells—2 a.m. Eastern Time.

Resonating throughout the interior of the vessel, the rhythmic, heartbeat-like throbbing of the steam-powered crankshafts produced a calming, reassuring white noise for those 33 men who, like Fennell, were off-watch and tucked safely in their bunks. The movement of a ship and the ever-present vibration and rumble of its engines produced a sleep-inducing sensation that has been described by mariners as being rocked like a "baby against their mother's breast." It is one of the unique pleasures of life at sea.

Approaching Cape Hatteras, the venerable 38-year-old freighter was in familiar waters, having been a veteran of the coastal run between her homeport of Savannah and the ports of New York and Boston. The *City of Atlanta* was owned and operated by the Ocean Steamship Company of Savannah, a line founded in 1872 to transport passengers and cargo between ports on the Atlantic seaboard. The "Savannah Line" enjoyed its heyday during the first quarter of the 20th century when the company commissioned the construction of a number of new ships, all named in honor of southern American cities: Chattanooga, Birmingham, Memphis, Savannah, Columbus, and Atlanta.

Almost as a foretoken of darker days ahead, mishap struck the steamship line in 1917

SS *City of Atlanta*

when the *City of Memphis*, a sister ship of the *City of Atlanta* and built at the same yard at Chester, Pennsylvania, was torpedoed and sunk by the German Imperial Navy's UC-66 off the southern coast of Ireland in 1917. Then, accidents began to plague the *City of Atlanta*. Between 1920 and 1930, the steamship was involved in three collisions, sinking in succession a cargo ship, a barge, and a schooner. Despite suffering her own damage requiring major repairs in dry dock, the steamer always managed to survive her calamities. The indomitable *City of Atlanta*'s crew might have thought her lucky, but her underwriters began to wonder if the ship might be cursed.

In 1920, as fewer people traveled between the major cities of the East Coast by sea, the company reconfigured the 337-foot-long *City of Atlanta* to carry fewer passengers and more freight. On the night of January 19, 1942, the ship was returning to Savannah with a mixed lading of foodstuffs both fresh and canned, cake mix, poultry feed, leather products, and a small consignment of Scotch whisky—considered by Naval authorities as an "insignificant cargo" and certainly not war matériel. There were no civilian passengers aboard.

The 47 members of the ship's crew knew the passage between New York and Savannah like the back of their hands. Once they passed the reassuring flash from the lighthouse at Cape Hatteras, they'd round Diamond Shoals and were halfway home—36 hours and 400 miles to go. With luck, Tuesday afternoon they would be in port and by that evening happily back with their families and loved ones seated at the supper table. Young merchant sailors like Robert Fennell, Jr., were naturally excited to return home because there they would be reunited with their wives and girlfriends. In Fennell's case it was Mary, his lovely, auburn-haired bride. She was eight months pregnant with their first child, and Fennell was getting anxious about being away from home as his wife's pregnancy progressed. A framed photograph of Mary hung on the cabin wall above his bunk as he slumbered peacefully— she was his angel with a Mona Lisa smile, watching over for his safety.

On that January night in 1942, as their ship hugged the shoreline on her way southward, Fennell and his shipmates would have welcomed all the divine protection they could get. They just needed to survive the next 36 hours.

The *City of Atlanta*'s captain, Leman C. Urquhart, was not unaware of a new danger to shipping that potentially lurked somewhere off the U.S. East Coast. Before his ship had departed New York harbor on Saturday the 17th, Urquhart had been informed that the Norwegian-owned, Panamanian-flagged tanker had been sunk 60 miles south of Block Island, Rhode Island, reportedly by a rogue German submarine. Even though the U.S. Navy did not perceive the U-boat intrusion to be anything more than an isolated incident, they advised ships departing New York harbor for southern ports on the north-south route to navigate well inside the 10-mile limit, generally in water depths of 60 feet or less, and with navigation lights dimmed, in order to avoid the unlikely possibility that the marauder was still skulking off the American coast. The Navy was confident that a German U-boat would never venture so close to shore or in such relatively shallow water where the submarine could not dive and would be subject to detection and swift American reprisal. "Follow our instructions, and you'll be fine," merchant captains like Urquhart were informed.

Three days earlier, at dusk on Thursday, January 15, 1942, the same "rogue German submarine" that had sunk the tanker *Norness* the night before, rose to the surface a few miles south of Fire Island, near the midpoint of Long Island. None of the German sailors aboard knew what perils might besiege them in what should have been the heavily defended territorial waters of the United States. Before surfacing, the captain of the U-boat ominously commanded his crew to prepare their vessel to be scuttled in the event that they would be attacked or strike a mine and be unable to escape. Recent intelligence received from German Naval High Command, however, assured the U-boat crew that American authorities were unprepared for attack despite the terrible lesson inflicted by Japan at Pearl Harbor in the previous month. That information did little to comfort the "black gang" down in the engine compartments who generally spent their entire time during a 45-day war patrol confined to their claustrophobic machinery spaces. *What is the "old man" up to this time? they might have whispered to one another. Is he intending to run U-123 up the Hudson River?*

The "old man," 28-year-old Kapitänleutnant Reinhard Hardegen, was a daring, audacious, and ambitious commander who, much to the concern of his crew aboard their Type IXB U-boat, was perhaps at times too daring and too ambitious. The unflinching Hardegen was amused but unconcerned by his young crew's childish trepidations. He was soon to achieve something that would have seemed preposterous, even unimaginable to U.S. military authorities. He ordered his U-boat's helmsman to steer toward the opening of Ambrose Channel, where heavily-laden merchant ships could be expected to pass—the grand entrance to America's greatest city, New York, New York.

But would they be poking their nose into a hornet's nest? They would, but the hornets weren't home.

At 10 p.m., five hours after surfacing, U-*123* maneuvered to a point due south of Rockaway Beach, within view of the World War I Army installation, Fort Tilden. The waters were eerily vacant of large merchant ships that typically paraded in and out of the

harbor entrance; only about six fishing trawlers or small pilot vessels could be seen running in various directions, which to Hardegen meant that the approaches to the channel were not mined. More revealing, the absence of armed patrol boats meant that the harbor entrance was not defended at all.

Caught by surprise by America's entry into the war, U.S. military planners had not yet begun to implement orders issued on December 11, 1941, to strengthen the harbor defenses for the entrance to New York's Ambrose Channel. Eventually, Fort Tilden on the New York side, and Fort Hancock at Sandy Hook, New Jersey, would each become fortified as Advanced Harbor Entrance Control Posts or HECPs, equipped with the latest technologies, including harbor surveillance radar systems, underwater listening devices and experimental underwater magnetic indicator loop cables engineered to detect enemy intruders. Lookout towers combined with powerful searchlights and U.S. Army gun batteries capable

Kapitänleutnant Reinhard Hardegen

of firing shells as far as 10 miles were positioned on either side of the entrance. Additional protections included contact mines, anti-submarine nets, booms, and gates. Most of the defenses had been put in place and were operational by the end of 1943, and, after that time, no enemy submarine would have been able to approach Ambrose Channel without being quickly detected and dispatched. Such was not the case in January 1942. On the night of U-123's arrival, the door was left open; there was not a defender in sight.

In the bitter, uninviting winter air atop the conning tower of U-123, Hardegen was stunned by what he was able to see. Above the twinkling lights which delineated the immediate coastline, there was a warm celestial glow emanating from the sprawling city beyond. After having spent 23 pitch-dark nights at sea crossing the North Atlantic, the light produced by New York City seemed otherworldly to the men topside on the conning tower of U-123. Later, Hardegen summarized what he saw in his official Kriegstagebüch (KTB) or war diary.

> "Ahead land in sight. Many lights visible. Seems to be a suburb of New York, whose bright glow is clearly seen on the horizon. Distance from the center of the city about 30 miles. The Ambrose lightship is also not on station. Have 11 meters of water under the keel. It must not get much shallower, because I would not be able to get the conning tower under water. Again many fishing and pilot vessels in the area, assume that mine and net barrages were only brought out in the inner entrance from Sandy Hook to Rockaway Beach. Hoped to find steamers here, but apparently the shipping was stopped for the moment."

```
ausweiche. Etwa 6 Stck. gesehen mit gesetzten Laternen. Da sie
verschiedene Kurse fahren, scheint es hier Linenfrei zu sein.
Stosse weiter vor.
Voraus Land in Sicht. Viele Lichter zu erkennen. Wohl Vorort
von New York, dessen heller Lichtschein wieder deutlich am Hori-
zont zu sehen ist. Abstand von Stadtmitte etwa 30 Meilen."Ambro-
se" Fschff. liegt ebenfalls nicht aus. Habe 11 m Wasser unter
Kiel. Viel flacher darf es nicht werden, da ich sonst den Turm
nicht unter Wasser kriege. Da hier ebenfalls Fischer und Lotsen
```

"Have 11 meters of water under the keel. It must not get much shallower…" Hardegen's KTB.

The luminescent glow stretching across the northern horizon was produced by what Hardegen imagined must have been tens of millions of individual lights of skyscrapers, office buildings, hotels, theaters, restaurants, apartment buildings, homes, automobiles, and trucks—the gleaming glory of America's enormity, potency, wealth, and unity. Did the young U-boat captain consider the symbolic fusion of light produced by the American metropolis and its millions of residents as a metaphor for the nation's oneness and resolve against his Führer's global ambitions? Had Hardegen given any thought to the symbolism he did not record it in his diary.

From their vantage point near the gateway to America and the greatest city in the world, Hardegen and his men could plainly see that the Americans seemed unconcerned and entirely unaffected by their nation's entry into the war. No better example served to prove the Yanks' imperiousness and sense of untouchability than the brilliantly lit streets of Coney Island with its festive Ferris wheel towering above. (Remarkably, the iconic amusement ride known as the Wonder Wheel, built in 1920 by the Eccentric Ferris Wheel Company, is still in use today.)

Without detailed charts and accurate sailing instructions, Hardegen resorted to using shore-based landmarks to navigate the southern shoreline of Long Island. He could hardly believe the vast array of lights that illuminated the night sky. America may have been forced to enter the war, but the nation was hardly operating as if in wartime. For two-and-a-half years, cities and coastal regions of Great Britain, Germany, and German-occupied territories of Europe had been darkened as a defensive measure against the threat of aerial bombardment of cities and to prevent shore lights from illuminating coastal shipping traffic. Britain had instituted national blackouts even before war had been declared in September 1939. Even 81 years earlier, the governors of American southern states had been wise enough to order lighthouses extinguished in advance of the Union Navy's blockading squadron in the first months of the War Between the States. The U.S. government's lapse in extinguishing lights on shore and key aids to navigation like lighthouses was a deadly blunder costing precious lives and treasure.

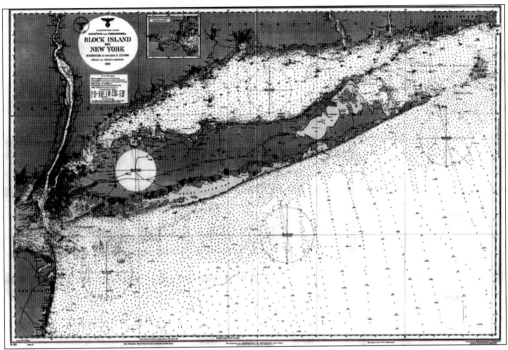

Kriegsmarine charts of the U.S. East Coast were not available to Paukenschläg U-boats.

In a 1992 radio interview at Bremerhaven, Germany, Hardegen recalled his nighttime visit to New York. "I could see on Coney Island houses and lights and motorcars, so it was very easy navigation for me," Hardegen said.

However, he could not see, as was depicted later in Nazi propaganda in Germany, people dancing on the rooftop of the Waldorf-Astoria Hotel. "The newspapers of the United States said I was so near New York, I could see Manhattan and people dancing on the roof of Waldorf-Astoria—that's nonsense because I didn't pass the [Verrazano] Narrows, I wasn't in the upper bay, and even if I had been there, I never could have seen people dancing on the roof of the Waldorf-Astoria!"

Below the conning tower, in the radio cubicle on the starboard side of the U-boat, the ship's radioman scanned the airwaves and listened intently to the AM band and New York's Mutual Broadcasting's flagship station, WOR. He might have heard WOR's popular comedy-panel show *Can You Top This?* and joked that his captain up on the bridge could qualify as a contestant. Who among the millions of people in metropolitan New York at that moment would have believed that a U-boat from Germany was standing at the threshold of their front door!

Like a mountaineer who pioneers the first climb of a summit, Hardegen struggled to express the significance of the moment in his U-boat memoir, *Auf Gefechtsstationen* ("To Battle Stations!"), which was published in 1943: "I cannot describe the feeling with words. We were the first to be here, and for the first time in this war a German soldier looked out upon the coast of the U.S.A."

Admiral Dönitz meets with German sailors.

U-*123* was the sharp thrust of the spear for a hastily organized operation by Admiral Karl Dönitz, Germany's commander-in-chief of its U-boat fleet (Befehlshaber der Unterseeboote or BdU). Dönitz had long been frustrated by America's so-called neutrality. He was angered that America had been able to supply food and war matériel to Great Britain with U.S.-flagged merchant ships that were off-limits to his U-boats. Dönitz also knew that American merchant vessels had been frequently forwarding intelligence of U-boat sightings to the British Admiralty. In the autumn of 1941, as the United States and Germany edged ever closer to mutual declarations of war, Dönitz began to contemplate a radical plan to redeploy a large number of his U-boats to the western Atlantic and the busy shipping lanes off the U.S. East Coast.

Soon after receiving the news of the Japanese surprise and devastating attack on Pearl Harbor, Dönitz was ready to put his own daring plan into action. He was convinced that he could achieve the same shocking, demoralizing impact on the American public. But unlike Japan's naval air forces that hit Pearl Harbor and ran, Dönitz's U-boats could continue to pound away at the Allies' supply lines to Europe, nearer their sources at U.S. and Canadian East Coast ports, rather than chase well-guarded North Atlantic convoys. The primary targets would be the dozens of ships that embarked daily and sailed independently before being consolidated into convoys off the Canadian Maritimes.

Admiral Dönitz was an ardent proponent of the centuries-old military strategy known as "guerre de course," or in World War II terms a "tonnage war," defined as a concentrated effort to disrupt transatlantic supply lines and destroy more ships than the Allies could construct to replace them. Ultimately, Dönitz's goal was to strangle and starve Great Britain into submission as the island nation of 46 million people was only able to function due to the continuous flow of its imports. One hundred percent of Britain's daily consumption of fuel oil and gasoline (four shiploads per day), half of the food and all of the citrus products required by its citizens, and most of the raw materials used for a myriad of vital purposes, were all delivered by merchant tankers, including commodities such as vegetables, sugar, coffee, bauxite for aircraft aluminum, iron, rubber, tin, concrete, phosphate, lumber, and cotton. British authorities estimated that had they been denied their trade, the nation would have been forced to surrender to Germany in fewer than four months. Dönitz estimated that to deny the British their trade, and to knock the legs out from under the Allied war effort, his U-boats would need to sink at least 700,000 gross registered tons of shipping each month, or the destruction of the equivalent of 70 ships at 10,000 tons each. The British computed their own estimate that even 600,000 tons of shipping losses per month would be sufficient to force an end to their participation in the war. Luckily for the Allies, the Germans were only once able to achieve their monthly target figure and never were they able to reach it on a consistent basis.

On December 9, 1941, Hitler revoked all restraints on his navy and allowed U-boats to wage unrestricted warfare against all U.S.-flagged vessels. From his headquarters overlooking the mouth of the Blavet River on the southern coast of Brittany, Dönitz submitted up the chain of command his request to allocate 12 Type IX long-distance U-boats for a special flotilla to cross more than 3,000 miles of ocean and unleash a gut-wrenching blow to the Allied war effort (his preference was to deploy dozens more, but the U-boats were simply not available). The admiral chose for this initial offensive the title Paukenschläg (Drumbeat) to symbolize, much like a startling bang on a drum, the intended result of surprising and embarrassing the American public, their political leaders, and the U.S. Navy. The pièce de résistance of the mission was for each of the U-boats, while patrolling in their assigned areas, to commence their attacks simultaneously on Tuesday, January 13, and to the extent possible at the same hour, to achieve the maximum psychological shock. If Paukenschläg was implemented as Dönitz had planned, ships would unexpectedly explode in flames and sink up and down the coasts of America and Canada in a dazzling display of Germany's military capability and prowess. Much to Dönitz's disappointment, however, Hitler only agreed to release six of the 12 U-boats requested. It is presumed that Hitler, in addition to preferring to marshall his submarine forces around Gibraltar and the Mediterranean, thought that the long transit time crossing the Atlantic and then returning—45 days or more of doing essentially nothing but voyaging—would greatly limit each U-boat's operational time in target areas, thus diminishing potential successes. Hitler's doubts that Dönitz's western-Atlantic campaign would be effective would prove to be wrong, at least for the next few months.

As the date of departure neared, one of the assigned boats was discovered to be experiencing mechanical issues that would preclude its participation. Operation Paukenschläg was reduced to just five U-boats.

On the 18th of December, one of those five boats, U-125, cast her lines and departed

U-*123* returns victoriously to Lorient, France.

her berth inside the colossal Keroman bombproof bunker at the port of Lorient, France. Two days before Christmas, U-*123* would be on her way, then the other three would go—U-*66*, U-*109*, and U-*130*. Dönitz's expectations for his intrepid submariners were as high as his confidence in their skill and daring. He has often been credited by historians for having once declared: "I will demonstrate that the U-boat alone can win this war alone. For us, there is no impossible."

There is probably no greater authority on the story of Dönitz's Paukenschläg and the missions of U-*123* than Michael Gannon, author of *Operation Drumbeat—The Dramatic True Story of Germany's First U-boat Attacks Along the American Coast in World War II.* In an October 2000 interview at Gannon's home in Gainesville, the University of Florida history professor described his impressions of Kapitänleutnant Reinhard Hardegen and his men, with whom Gannon became well-acquainted—even good friends—while conducting research for his book. "They had been given a mission by a man they admired greatly, Admiral Karl Dönitz," Gannon explained. "And Dönitz had developed these men into teams of ship killers. And that's how these officers viewed themselves—as having the single mission of sinking ships. And they went at it with a passion. I found that they were very professional men who pursued their goals with keen enthusiasm and with enormous skill. And I think Reinhard Hardegen was particularly driven by his desire to sink ships."

Twinkling shore lights cast a pale, greasy sheen on Reinhard Hardegen's face as he leaned back against U-*123*'s periscope standard and momentarily savored the achievement of having been the first to "scale the mountain." Ever the professional, however, he did not allow himself much time to be captivated by the imposing radiance of light rising over the vast city beyond the horizon. The disappointing absence of merchant ships either arriving or departing the port of New York tempered the feat of being the first Germans combatants to come within view of the American coast.

The suspension of traffic came as no surprise to the U-boat captain though, as the radioman on U-*123* had a few hours earlier intercepted a news broadcast announcing that the U.S. Navy was reporting the sinking of the tanker *Norness* the night before. Apparently, the authorities had stopped traffic until they could evaluate the seriousness of what was happening offshore. *Such a pity*, he might have thought. What a trophy it would have been to sink a big Yankee ship right in the middle of the busiest channel on the U.S. East Coast, perhaps closing it for months.

Hardegen knew they were wasting precious time and fuel. It was time to move on. After all, they were not tourists but ship killers; they were not there to sightsee but to send Allied tonnage to the bottom of the sea. About five minutes after reaching their nearest point to Ambrose Channel, Hardegen called down the voice tube to the helmsman in the conning tower and engine room below with the order to take them out toward deeper water on a course of east-southeast. As word of their retreat passed through the fore-ends and aft compartments of U-*123*, the crew of 50 men breathed a collective sigh of relief.

"This was a very courageous and daring man, Reinhard Hardegen," historian Gannon said. "And his crew will tell you today—I interviewed them, those who were alive in 1986—that [their captain] took risks that just scared the devil out of everybody on the boat. But they told me, 'We didn't mind the risks because we had the successes.' And the greatest morale you will find in the U-boat fleet is with the crew that has successes."

As U-*123* moved back out toward the eastern end of Long Island, potential success entered the field of view behind them in the form of a lone ship attempting to gain the open sea on a peacetime course, laboring against a northeast wind and heavy waves—*Coimbra*, a 6,700-ton British tanker heavily loaded with up to 80,000 barrels of oil. "Auf Gefechtsstationen," shouted Hardegen as his U-boat maneuvered for a textbook attack. The first torpedo launched by the U-boat tore into the ship aft of the bridge, causing a massive fireball; a second torpedo delivered the fatal coup de grâce. In his war diary, Hardegen recorded his observation of the death of another merchant ship, electing to ignore the gruesome fates of the human souls aboard: "The effect was stunning. A fierce detonation, a column of fire rose over 200 meters high, and the whole sky was as bright as day. For many seconds the sea and horizon around us was clearly visible. These are some pretty buoys we are leaving for the Yankees in the harbor approaches as replacement for the lightships."

As he ordered a course change southward, toward Cape Hatteras, U-*123*'s captain wondered whether or not the pyrotechnics and fiery glow of his latest victim could be seen back in New York City.

At that moment, somewhere in New York City, Robert Fennell, Jr., and his shipmates of the Ocean Steamship Company freighter *City of Atlanta* were likely reveling in a tavern frequented by sailors, enjoying their last night of shore leave. Within 24 hours, Fennell and his buddies would begin their homeward-bound journey to Savannah. Likely, they were unaware of the portentous inferno in the ocean just 60 miles away.

CHAPTER 6

THE BRAVE NEVER DIE

*"Their lifebelts held their bodies
up, and the dead bobbed along,
[following] after the living."*

**George Tavelle
Second Officer, *SS City of Atlanta***

After dispatching the *Coimbra*, Reinhard Hardegen decided to leave the approaches to New York harbor where ship traffic had obviously been alerted to his presence. Southward he would go, along the coast of New Jersey, hoping to spot the darkened shapes of large tankers eclipsing the brightly lit shoreline crowded shoulder-to-shoulder with houses, hotels, and amusement parks. Hardegen knew that his southerly course ought to yield an increased number of opportunities as they would more rapidly encounter fully loaded northbound ships, much as someone would pass a greater number of oncoming cars on the highway rather than when moving with traffic in the same direction.

Upon reaching the Five Fathom Bank near Cape May, Hardegen recorded in his log that the lightship there had been removed from its station and replaced with a lighted buoy. He also noted that the water depth had shoaled to eight meters or slightly more than 26 feet—in other words, the bottom was passing a scant 10 feet below the U-boat's keel, the depth of many swimming pools! For the next two days, U-*123* would reconnoiter the entrance to Delaware Bay where ships loaded with refined gasoline from refineries south of Philadelphia would enter the ocean to begin their solo journeys to join convoys at Halifax, Nova Scotia. Again, Hardegen was disappointed: no tankers appeared, but numerous fishing trawlers were observed, and beyond, more strands of bright lights from the Delaware communities of Rehoboth Beach, Bethany Beach, and Fenwick Island.

Admiral Dönitz's five Paukenschläg U-boats performed an additional function, as critical to his mission as the sinking of the Allies' ships. The initial wave of U-boats were to test American preparedness, defenses, and anti-submarine tactics—to gather and report intelligence to support future missions. Dönitz was already preparing to launch second, third, and fourth waves of submarines.

Each day, as the first muted shades of gray heralding dawn began to rise in the East, U-*123* would reluctantly retire from the hunt and move out to deeper water to settle on the bottom for 12 hours of rest. While it was plainly evident to Hardegen that the U.S. Navy had little or no presence in its home waters at night, it was assumed by the Germans that daylight hours might have been a different story. During the day, aircraft and small coastal gunboats were likely to patrol the skies and seas of the immediate coastline and port entrances, increasing the likelihood that a surfaced U-boat would be spotted and attacked.

U-*123* had six torpedoes remaining and plenty of ammunition for its 10.5 cm deck gun on the foredeck, 3.7-cm gun aft, and twin 2-cm anti-aircraft machine guns on the afterdeck of the conning tower. However, its fuel supply was nearing half of its initial load of 165 metric tons. It had but a few precious days remaining in American waters before it would have to begin the long slog home. But before Hardegen could lay a course for Lorient, he had to unload U-*123*'s torpedoes, and to do that he needed to find ships.

To make the most of the dwindling days of his combat assignment, Hardegen decided to push southward, where he knew north-south coastwise traffic narrowed in order to round the protruding bulge of Cape Hatteras and its hazards of Diamond Shoals. On Saturday, the 17th of January, as U-*123* moved south from the entrance to the Delaware Bay toward the North Carolina coast, the sky was bright and clear, and the ocean was unusually calm. Hardegen decided to take the risk and remain surfaced during the day in order to travel a greater distance. Manually walking a pair of dividers across his chart of the North Atlantic, the U-boat captain figured that if all went well during the next two nights he could be finished with his remaining torpedos and homeward bound by Monday's first light.

About six hours after U-*123* began her daylight dash from Cape Henlopen to Cape Hatteras, the *City of Atlanta* steamed out of New York's Ambrose Channel for her 72-hour run to Savannah. Weather reports and the U.S. naval authorities assured Captain Urquhart of an uneventful winter voyage. With fair skies and smooth seas predicted, and with luck, Urquhart's freighter would reach Cape Hatteras by the early morning hours of Monday, the 19th. Once south of Cape Hatteras, it would be clear sailing to home.

Shortly after midnight on Sunday morning, U-*123* had arrived at the infamous Graveyard of the Atlantic. En route, the U-boat nervously passed beyond the entrance to the busy roadstead of Hampton Roads and its extensive naval facilities. Hardegen's log reflects that sea and air traffic was noticeably more active than what he experienced near New York. Five times it was necessary for the U-boat to crash dive to avoid detection by aircraft, mostly U.S. Navy patrols, and in one instance the lookouts on the bridge sighted a destroyer (possibly the USS *Roe*) farther offshore, which the U-boat was able to evade by turning toward the mainland. At 1:35 a.m., U-*123* was on the surface about 21 miles east of Kill Devil Hills, when a "bright fiery flame" suddenly appeared beyond the horizon on the port side toward the southeast, soon followed by the distinctive echos of two

sharp torpedo detonations. Hardegen guessed correctly that the explosion was likely the victim of his Paukenschläg sister-ship, *U-66*. The victim, the first ship sunk off the coast of North Carolina in World War II, was the Standard Oil tanker, *Allan Jackson*. Not surprisingly, the radio frequency used by merchant vessels became alive with frantic calls that a ship had been attacked and was furiously burning. American sailors were dying and needed help.

Meanwhile, aboard the *City of Atlanta* the family of 47 sailors had settled into their routine schedules of work and watches. Meals and pots of coffee were prepared by cooks Willie Chisholm and Prince Broughton. Engineers Thomas Kenney and John Macher watched over the time-worn machinery. Mates Christian Leppin, George Tavelle, and John Barnett took their turns on the bridge, while Theo Haviland monitored wireless signals in his radio shack forward of the funnel. Deep in the choking, dust-filled air of the coal bunkers and boiler room, coal passers Wallace Harley, Bert Williams, Simon Bruce, and Kewannee Drumwright, and firemen Paul DeBolle, George Hamilton, and Albert Jones labored mightily to keep the steamship fueled and underway. The coal slingers, who had the toughest jobs of all, reminded themselves that—despite their backbreaking work in stifling conditions—every shovel load got them that much closer to home.

So, too, the lookouts on deck had their own, less-arduous method of marking the ship's progress as they checked off the lighthouses they passed—Navesink, Barnegat, Absecon, Cape May, Assateague, Cape Charles, Cape Henry, Currituck. As each distinctive flashing or fixed light faded into the marine haze behind them, they were that much closer to home. Next on the starboard beam were the signature twin flashes of the Bodie Island Lighthouse. Cape Hatteras was dead ahead. The watch officer took a fix off the lighthouse and recorded the ship's time and location at the chart table.

Another 24 hours had passed, and it was now the early morning hours of Monday, January 19. Most of the men were off watch and in their bunks. Captain Urquhart, however, was likely resting fitfully—he had been among the many masters at sea who heard the radio reports the night before when the *Allan Jackson* had been torpedoed without warning. But that attack had occurred far offshore, and the *City of Atlanta* was steaming in shallow water just off the beaches of the Outer Banks. Surely they'd make it through the night unmolested, Urquhart probably thought.

At 2 a.m., the man in the pilot house grasped the lanyard for the ship's bell and rang it four times. Clang, clang, clang, clang. The bell marked the middle of the watch and tolled, for the *City of Atlanta* and nearly all of the souls aboard, a mournful sound—a death knell.

A few miles to the west off the starboard side of the ship were the twinkling lights of the peaceful village of Avon, where most families like Gibb Gray's were soundly sleeping. Only 275 yards to the east, off the port side of the *City of Atlanta*, was the sleek and sinister *U-123*. Shrouded by darkness, surfaced, and perfectly aligned for attack, its electro-mechanical targeting system locked onto the silhouette of the passing freighter, which could be easily seen against the backdrop of shore lights. From behind the wind deflector atop the conning tower, Reinhard Hardegen impassively sized-up his quarry—a relatively small freighter, southbound, probably not transporting anything of military importance. No matter. Her 4,000 tons would still add to his impressively growing total for the Paukenschläg mission. The ship would get one of U-*123*'s last three torpedoes. No consideration was made of the impending fate of the innocent civilian sailors aboard, nor of the future heartbreak of their loved ones, families, and sweethearts at home—all the U-boat captain could see was an Allied ship to kill. The freighter's death sentence was issued with a nod of the head. Hardegen approved the request to launch, and the order was shouted through the voice tube to the torpedo room below, "Los!" With an explosion of compressed air, a 23-foot-long, 3,500-pound G7 electric torpedo jumped through the ink-dark seas at 30 knots, trailing an angry froth of foam on its way toward the unsuspecting freighter. Fifteen seconds later, the torpedo found its mark, aft of the funnel and right into the beating heart of the ship, its engine room, causing an enormous detonation. So close was U-*123* to the blast that the men in the conning tower had to seek shelter as chunks of the stricken steamer came flying overhead and splashed into the sea.

Three men in the engine room were killed instantly. Seconds later, the coal passers in the bunkers were drowned by the rapid rise of seawater.

Thirty-three seconds later, the sound waves rumbled over the narrow strip of Hatteras Island, rattling windows and rousing the sleepy villages of Rodanthe, Waves, Salvo, Avon, and Buxton. Gibb Gray's family ran to their windows in time to see the fading firestorm at sea.

Dazed and disoriented, Robert Fennell must have thought he was having a horrible nightmare. He awoke with a jolt and couldn't understand why an entire wall of his cabin was missing. There had been a deafening blast, what he thought sounded like a pistol going off beside his ear. Oddly, the pounding of the engine crankshafts had stopped, but other terrifying sounds had replaced it—the unmistakable hissing of escaping steam, the screech of steel plates being violently twisted and torn asunder, and a torrent of surging seawater pouring into the sides of the ship. Fennell shoved away debris, rolled out of his bunk, and was struck with an agonizing pain from his right foot, which he suddenly discovered was covered in blood. *What in God's name was happening?* As his mind cleared, the reality became apparent—they must have been torpedoed!

Fennell dressed himself, grabbed his lifebelt, and quickly made his way down the passageway to the outer deck, wincing in pain and hobbling on his left foot. Already the deck of the ship began tilting to port at a noticeable angle. Fennell was nearly outside when he remembered something, something he could not do without. It was the framed photo of his wife, Mary, which had been hanging on the wall of his cabin. Was it still there? Fennell wasn't sure, but he knew he had to go back and retrieve it. It was an impulse that is hard to understand. Why would a person on a sinking ship risk returning to an interior cabin to recover a personal item rather than to run like mad to escape? The pages of history are filled with such stories. Whatever fate held in store for Fennell, he would not face it without his guardian angel. With his ship rapidly sinking, the young seaman limped back to his cabin where he found the picture still on a remaining wall. He removed the photo from its frame, folded it, and carefully slid it into a pocket. He had no reason to believe that the photo might get wet or that he and his shipmates would not be able to board their assigned lifeboats and be rescued within the hour. Before leaving his cabin for the last time, Fennell grabbed his heavy sheepskin coat, intending to stay warm while awaiting rescue.

Second Officer George Tavelle had stepped inside the pilot house after gazing upon the strands of lights punctuating the dark stretches of Outer Banks beach. The bell had rung, and Tavelle decided to oversee the helmsman's course as they closed upon the dangerous Diamond Shoals that were dead ahead. When the torpedo struck the engine room, the concussion blew inward the windows of the pilot house, shredding Tavelle and the other two men with splinters of sharp glass, one cutting Tavelle deeply above his right eye. The force of the blast also jammed the doors leading out to the lifeboat deck, momentarily trapping the men, but Tavelle and the others were able to kick their way out.

As for Captain Urquhart, his worst fears were realized. It was astonishing to think that, as close as they were to shore, a U-boat somehow managed to find them. *And why us*, he might have muttered. Surely there were larger ships in the vicinity with valuable wartime cargos to shoot at. But there was no time for speculating about the senseless tactics of German U-boat captains; within seconds of the explosion, Urquhart was on deck urging his men to get their lifeboats lowered. It was the last place he was seen by those who survived.

Stumbling aft to his assigned lifeboat amid the disarray of debris, Tavelle glanced over his shoulder and noticed that the entire radio shack was missing. He wondered what might have happened to his friend Theo Haviland—obviously, no distress signal had been broadcast. Fires crackled from numerous sources, whipping up a tornadic, heat-induced wind. Injured men shouted above the noise for help, but it was difficult to even to stand up. Even in pitch darkness, they would normally be able to find their way about deck, but "normal" had become chaotic. The starboard deck and hull beneath them were rapidly rising upward as the port side rolled downward into the sea, rendering it impossible to launch the lifeboats. "By the time the davits were swung out, the ship had listed to port so sharply that the boats rested on the [hull]," Tavelle later said. "I [did] not know what was going on on the port side." Seconds later, as he hung over the side attempting to free the jammed lifeboat rigging, a line Tavelle was using to support himself slipped, and he tumbled head first into the frigid ocean.

On the port side, Fennell had arrived at his assigned station and was assisting fellow oiler Earl Dowdy in freeing one of the lifeboats as the gunwale of the ship tipped ever closer to the sea. Suddenly, a belt around Fennell's coat became snagged on the railing just as the *City of Atlanta* rolled over, dragging him underwater. Fennell knew he was finished.

Seven miles away in the Outer Banks village of Avon, Gibb Gray and his family pressed their faces against the chilled window panes of their house and wondered what was happening offshore. It was just as well that they didn't know.

Nearly out of breath but refusing to yield to the call of the abyss, Fennell somehow managed to untangle himself from the plunging wreckage, buoyed perhaps by the photo

of his guardian angel, Mary. He surfaced, gasping for air, and frantically thrashed his way away from the sinking ship, which threatened to drag anything or anyone to the bottom in its vortex. On the opposite side of the overturning freighter, Tavelle had managed to swim a distance away and found a door frame on which to cling. By now, the sea surrounding the stricken vessel was filled with wreckage and the frightened, bewildered sailors from the *City of Atlanta*. As it happened, not a single lifeboat was launched.

From beyond the veil of darkness, the U-boat crept up behind the stern of the ship, within view of its desperate victims as they struggled to survive, eyeing its prey while performing a macabre victory lap. Atop the conning tower, a harshly bright searchlight flicked on, flashing over the burning and broken ship and on the sailors in the water clinging to various pieces of wreckage, some alone and others clustered in small groups, unable to die without a final impudent insult from their voyeuristic enemy. Someone defiantly shook their fist at the German U-boat and shouted, "Wish we could get our hands on you, you goddam Heinies!" Other victims, perhaps more desperate, pleaded for help, calling out to the Germans hiding behind the unsympathetic glare of the searchlight. There was no answer.

The *City of Atlanta* had been attacked many miles west of the warm-water eddies of the Gulf Stream. In fact, the survivors in the water were swimming in the southernmost reaches of the Labrador Current, a significantly colder river of ocean than even what would be experienced south or east of Cape Hatteras, where water temperatures are sometimes 10 degrees warmer. On that January night, the ocean temperature was 47 degrees Fahrenheit. No human can survive for any length of time in water so cold, a fact the merchant sailors knew all too well. Germans were no longer their adversary; time was their enemy.

Ten minutes had passed since the torpedo had struck the ship when the *City of Atlanta* rolled completely over. Her masts, funnel, and other elevated portions of her superstructure became a new hazard to contend with, crashing down on the men who had been unable to swim out of danger fast enough. The ship then slowly settled to the bottom stern first, and eventually the bow succumbed to the seabed. As if they had not already suffered a sufficient ordeal, the men in the water next had to avoid the numerous pieces of buoyant flotsam that broke free of the submerged freighter and rocketed to the surface. Already many of the *City of Atlanta*'s 47 men had perished—three in the initial explosion, a few by drowning when trapped in the lower compartments, some burned to death, and others were crushed by collapsing structures or by the capsizing of the ship. For those who had, so far, clung to life by escaping the ship, they now faced the prospect of slowly freezing to death. In a later interview, George Tavelle said: "I never saw so many die. They tried to cling to bits of wreckage, then they'd slip off one by one." Before long, many men were seen bobbing on the surface face down, their life preservers unable to save them from death by hypothermia. "Their lifebelts held their bodies up, and the dead bobbed along, [following] after the living," Tavelle said.

A few miles to the west, the residents of Hatteras Island who had been awakened by the explosion and who were watching the flickering orange glow on the horizon, suddenly saw it disappear. Whatever had happened out there was swallowed up by darkness and by the sea. They knew they'd hear it eventually, so with nothing more to see and nothing they could do, they went back to bed.

Robert Fennell did his best to hold on to a floating skylight even though his hands were already becoming swollen and numb from the frigid sea water. Every few minutes he'd check his pocket to make sure Mary's photo was still there. Debris was everywhere, often bumping into his back or legs, a sensation which caused an awful fear that he was being brushed by sharks. Eventually, Fennell saw in the gloom a dining room bench floating by, and he abandoned the smaller skylight for more substantial accommodations. Not far away, the industrious Earl Dowdy gathered materials to manufacture a makeshift raft that soon kept him out of the water entirely.

George Tavelle later remembered the misery of "helpless hours spent floating and bobbing at sea." There was a group of about 15 men, including the Chief Engineer Tom Kenney, who tried to stay together. Tavelle looked for his fellow officers, Captain Urquhart and Chief Mate Christian Leppin, but never saw either of them again. The survivors in the water did their best to encourage each other. They joked a little, sang a little, but mostly prayed as they passed the time waiting for their rescuers who they expected to arrive any minute.

As the hours passed interminably, hope evaporated, and the weakest and the injured, one by one, loosened their grips and slipped beneath the waves. Before long, there were no voices, no exhortations to hang on a little while longer, no murmured prayers. When the first blush of mauve painted the eastern sky at dawn, only four men remained alive—Tavelle, Dowdy, Fennell, and a very weak John York, the assistant engineer. With increasing daylight they could see another man perched upon some wreckage in the distance, but he failed to answer their calls.

In one small but important matter, those few *City of Atlanta* survivors were lucky. They were in an area of the Graveyard of the Atlantic where there was little current. Six hours had passed, and the men and the slowly expanding debris field were still within a mile of where their ship went down, still straddling the longitudinal line 75-20w that was being used by most of the north-south traffic. It was the floating wreckage that was first spotted by lookouts aboard the northbound freighter, SS *Seatrain Texas*; then they saw the many floating bodies and, among them, the few frantically waving arms of the living.

The freighter's captain, Albert Dalzell, took a great risk to stop and lower a boat to rescue the survivors. Had he elected to pass them by it would have been forgivable—many ship masters did so under similar circumstances—for Dalzell exposed his own vessel to a U-boat attack, especially when it was dreadfully obvious that one was nearby. The captain's courageous actions affected the destiny of many lives; one example was Fennell's future family, another the future career of Earl Dowdy.

Earl Dowdy was plucked off of his substantial raft, which had been so well-manufactured that Dowdy was said to be entirely dry. In fact, Dowdy was in such good condition that he offered to help row the freighter's rescue boat. You would think that a man like Dowdy who thrived in such harrowing conditions at sea would be well-suited for his profession, and he was. Dowdy was the only one of the *City of Atlanta* survivors who remained in the merchant service, returning to sea within a couple of months. Later in the war he was on a supply ship on the brutal Murmansk run when once again his ship was torpedoed and sunk. Dowdy was rescued by a second ship, which was also soon sunk by a U-boat. Remarkably, Dowdy was rescued by a third ship that eventually succeeded in reaching the Russian port. "Even that hazardous experience did not dampen his love of seafaring," Dowdy's nephew wrote in a letter to the *Sunday Savannah News-Press* in 1992. Dowdy eventually made captain, sailing military supplies to Vietnam in the 1960s. He died of natural causes in 1985.

Tavelle, Fennell, and York were rescued and joined Dowdy in the boat, amazed that their shipmate was able to grip an oar and row. York was in a severely weakened condition and, not long after being hoisted aboard the *Seatrain Texas*, died from hypothermia.

Even as the boat containing the *City of Atlanta* survivors was being hoisted aboard, Captain Dalzell gave the order for the ship to get underway at top speed. The 483-foot-long, 8,000-ton freighter would have made a great prize for Reinhard Hardegen had he not left the area, especially considering the ship's contribution to the war later that same year. In late July 1942, the *Seatrain Texas* had been ordered personally by President Roosevelt to sail from New York harbor for Cape Town and ultimately for the Suez port of Taufiq. The ship's top-secret cargo included 250 Sherman tanks to be delivered to British General Bernard L. Montgomery's command for the looming Second Battle at El Alamein, a battle resulting in a pivotal Allied victory, turning the tide of the North African campaign and denying Nazi access to Middle East oil resources. Historians cite the delivery of the American Sherman tanks by the *Seatrain Texas* as having been an important factor in Montgomery's defeat of Field Marshall Erwin Rommel's Afrika Corps.

With the three sole survivors of the *City of Atlanta* aboard, the *Seatrain Texas* resumed her passage to New York harbor, tying up at Hoboken, New Jersey. The ship had sent a radio message notifying authorities of the disaster, and the news was soon forwarded to the offices of the Ocean Steamship Company of Savannah. Typically, before a home-port ship was due to arrive, families would begin arriving at the company terminal on River Street where there would be a frenzy of activity—a happy occasion allowing for social interaction between wives and children. Instead, on Tuesday afternoon, January 20, 1942, the docks were filled with grieving widows. Joining them were the shocked and angry citizens of the "Hostess City of the South." Who could have imagined that the gracious, modestly sized port city would be, so soon after Pearl Harbor, devastated by the deaths of so many of her citizens by the wrath of a Nazi submarine? It was an unthinkable, rude affront upon the people of the genteel southern city.

"Dastardly" was the word used by Ted Haviland in a 1992 News-Press interview to describe the German's attacks on unarmed civilian merchant ships. "It had a devastating impact on my life," he said. Haviland was 6 years old when he learned that his father, Theo, the radio operator on the *City of Atlanta*, would never be returning home. "It touched me very deeply, and I've never forgotten it." Recalling those fleeting, happy times that never seem to last, Haviland described how he and his mother never failed to stand at a promi-

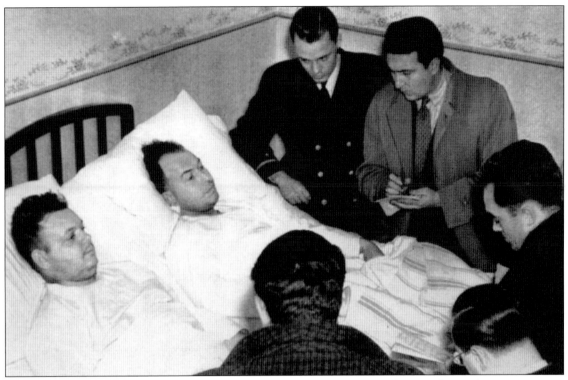

Robert Fennell and George Tavelle meet with press at Hoboken, NJ, hospital.

nent vantage point on the city's riverfront when the *City of Atlanta* would sail, waving as the freighter passed by. Haviland remembers vividly how his father would always be there along the bridge deck railing, waving his hat, remaining on deck as far down the Savannah River as they could see. That vision was the last he had of his father.

There were many such stories of heartbreak, at least as many as there were sailors of the *City of Atlanta* who did not return to Savannah during that bitter January of 1942. Savannahians did not take the loss of their ship to Nazi aggression lightly, and in the coming years they were able to contribute to the war effort in a significant way. Many of the city's residents worked at the Southeastern Shipyard, where they proudly built 88 Liberty ships featuring the names of prominent figures in Georgia state history.

Upon their arrival in Hoboken, Tavelle, Fennell and Dowdy gave their detailed statements to naval authorities. Dowdy was the first to be released to make his way back to Georgia by train. Tavelle and Fennell, both injured, were admitted to a local hospital where they soon became national celebrities, surrounded by the New York reporters who were anxious to publish the sailor's courageous tales of survival. Reporters and photographers from the Associated Press, *New York Times*, the *World-Telegram*, and *Life Magazine*, among others, crowded around their beds asking questions about their ordeal and their observations of the German U-boat. A U.S. Navy lieutenant stood close by, ready to

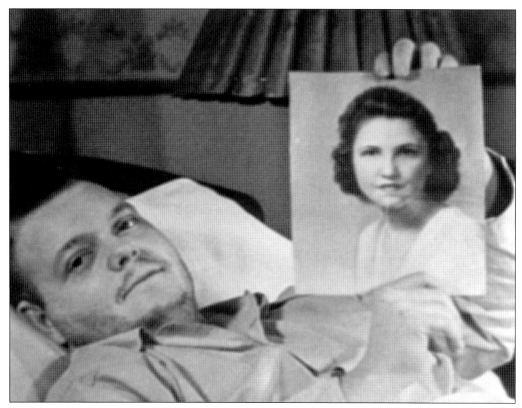

Robert Fennell holding photo of wife Mary at Hoboken, NJ, hospital.

prevent sensitive information from being released. During their time in the hospital, a camera crew from *Paramount News* arrived, keen to capture the miraculous survivors of the U-boat attack on film. The footage was later featured in a movie newsreel titled, "Nazi U-boat Challenge," seen by millions in theaters across the nation.

> Announcer: "Survivors! Hitler's U-boats strike desperately, sinking six ships in one week. Hardest hit was the steamship *City of Atlanta*. These two seaman were wounded. [Forty-four] shipmates lost their lives. The United States Navy announces that some U-boats were sunk and emphasizes the importance of secrecy about counterblows."

The newsreel footage briefly shows Tavelle and Fennell being attended to by nurses and later greeting a pair of uniformed sailors. Perhaps the most remarkable clip was one lasting just three seconds. With an unrevealing glance, Robert Fennell looks into the camera lens as he holds up a slightly creased photograph of a pretty young woman with a Mona Lisa smile. The scene was included without explanation by the narrator leaving viewers to only imagine its significance—millions of American theatergoers who saw the newsreel never knew Robert Fennell's amazing story of boundless love, commitment, and courage.

Shortly before they were released from the hospital, Fennell and Tavelle were visited by Mrs. Christian Leppin, whose husband was the chief mate of the *City of Atlanta*. Leppin's body was never found. She came to the Hoboken hospital to try to get some closure and hopefully to learn about the last moments of her husband's life. Tavelle, the last man to see Leppin alive, told the widow that her husband and Capt. Urquhart were on the starboard side of the ship, struggling to lower one of the lifeboats for the crew. Leppin, he told her, was among the last of the men remaining aboard, courageously urging everyone to get off the ship as it began to capsize. Despite being overcome by grief, Mrs. Leppin responded after a moment of silence with remarkable insight, inspired by the words of the 19th-century Unitarian, Minot J. Savage. She said to Tavelle and Fennell, "Well, the brave never die."

Oftentimes, people who have survived a traumatic event become psychologically distanced from their experience, reporting to others the details of a tragedy matter-of-factly. Such was the case for Fennell, who told his story over and over without really comprehending what he had endured, what he witnessed in the horrible deaths of so many of his friends and colleagues, how extraordinary it was to have survived, and how fortunate he was to be reunited with his loved ones.

As reported in the *Savannah News-Press* in 1992, the three survivors soon returned home to attend a memorial Mass held at St. John the Baptist Cathedral in Savannah—the church many of the *City of Atlanta* crew members had attended. Fennell recalled that it was at that service when he finally understood what it meant to have survived his ordeal. "I really think the whole impact of it never really hit me until the high requiem Mass at the cathedral for the men lost on the ship," Fennell said. Perhaps he was thinking of the unselfish courage of Captain Leman C. Urquhart and First Mate Christian Leppin and how, in memory, they will live forever.

"At the middle of the Mass, it finally struck me, and I broke down and cried," Fennell said. Seated beside him, holding his hand tightly, was Mary. She would soon give birth to a son.

CHAPTER 7

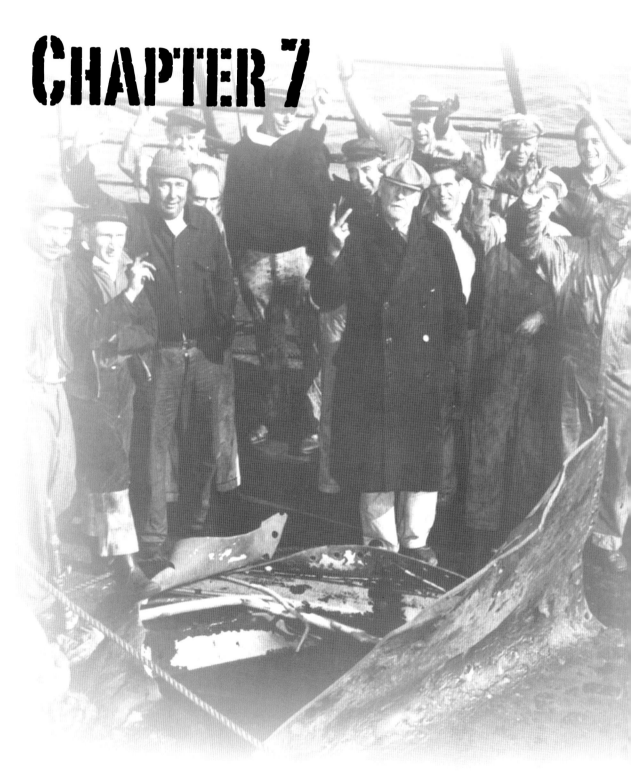

Crew members and captain of SS *Malay* celebrate their survival after being shelled by *U-123*.

DRUMBEAT'S CRESCENDO

"The night of the long knives is over."

Kapitänleutnant Reinhard Hardegen

Some hours after sinking the *City of Atlanta* within view of the villages of Hatteras Island, Reinhard Hardegen recorded the event in his Kriegstagebüch with prose both dispassionate and precise. His entry in U-*123*'s KTB, 2:09 a.m. Eastern War Time:

"Steamer settles fast by the stern, heavy list to port. While I do a victory lap, the steamer capsizes to port with the funnel and masts hitting the water. He lies on the bottom with the stern under water and the bow protruding out of the water. Behind me are several lights, so I head north to get the steamers between me and the well-lit coast, which can be clearly seen. I see five vessels in a long line with their lights on."

There was no mention of the freighter's sailors left to face imminent death, no report of the men flailing in the cold seawater and pleading to be saved as the menacing U-boat's searchlight glared harshly upon them.

In retrospect, Hardegen's apparent lack of sympathy was likely due in equal measure to his U-boat's vulnerability in the unfamiliar inshore waters of the enemy, the shallowness of the sea, and his assumption that numerous shore-based lifesaving facilities would have already initiated a rescue operation for the sailors of the stricken ship. On the latter, Hardegen would have been wrong. Due to the location, 15 miles north of Diamond Shoals and far south of Oregon Inlet, none of the Outer Banks' famed former U.S. Life-Saving Stations, now Coast Guard stations, could have been able to reach the *City of Atlanta* victims in time.

For whichever reason Hardegen ignored the plight of the *City of Atlanta*'s men, he was not the cold, ruthless killer as German U-boat captains have sometimes been portrayed in published history and popular culture. There were at least two notable instances during his two American patrols in 1942 when Hardegen made a diligent effort to aid his victims after sinking the ships SS *Muskogee* and the British freighter *Culebra*. Unfortunately for most of the *City of Atlanta* sailors, they were afforded no such solicitude and were left to drown in the dark.

Perhaps the Germans were also distracted by the parade of ships transiting the waters off the Outer Banks that cold winter night. U-*123* found herself in a situation not unlike an arcade shooting gallery at a county fair—the U-boat was the shooter, and Allied merchant ships were the ducks. In a 1985 interview with historian Michael Gannon, second officer Leutnant zur See Horst von Schroeter described the extraordinary opportunity of having so many potential targets before them. They were able to pass up the smaller steamers in favor of the largest silhouettes, comparing the experience to Prussian deer hunters shooting at the biggest stags as they blithely strolled before the hunter's blind.

The next "quarry" came in the form of the southbound 8,000-ton tanker, SS *Malay*. In the darkness, the Germans could not be see that she was riding high in the water indicating that the ship was steaming in ballast, empty of her normal load of 70,000 barrels of crude oil. (Hardegen might have, however, easily and correctly assumed that any southbound ship was not on her way to Britain with war matériel.)

Being especially buoyant, the SS *Malay* would prove to be a tough one for Hardegen and his team of ship killers to kill. Had they been willing to wait, heavily laden northbound tankers would have soon hove into view. But with daylight in the offing, just a couple of hours away, and their dwindling fuel supply reaching its limit for their successful return to France, the officers of U-*123* were keen to unload their remaining torpedoes and begin their eastward journey home.

Hardegen conceived a tactical plan to follow in the wake of the southbound SS *Malay*, chasing her down and sinking the ship with shells from his 10.5-centimeter deck gun, and then turning about in an arc to torpedo the two ships following behind her. Hardegen considered the possibility that if executed successfully, the mayhem they would cause might be mistaken for the work of multiple U-boats.

Hardegen's plan nearly worked except that, after the SS *Malay* absorbed six devastating shots to her hull and upper decks from the U-boat deck gun, the master and crew were able to heroically keep the ship underway. Little did the Germans know—or perhaps they didn't care—that simply punching holes in the empty cargo holds of the compartmentalized structure of the SS *Malay* would not be enough to sink the ship. Nevertheless, even hitting the darkened vessel just once in the blackness of night from a mildly rocking foredeck of the U-boat at a distance of 650 feet was a fairly remarkable achievement. U-*123*'s gun crew commanded by von Schroeter did better than that, scoring six hits out of 10 shells fired. Their skill pleased Hardegen immensely. "[Hardegen] loved using the gun," Michael Gannon said, recalling details from his 1985 interview. "Horst von Schroeter told me that when Hardegen used the deck gun on the foredeck, he would stand on the bridge and flop his arms up and down with great enthusiasm as the shells blasted out of the barrel."

Crew member of SS *Malay* examines damage from U-*123* deck gun.

With flames erupting from numerous places on the SS *Malay* and her radio trans-mitter broadcasting a distress call that she had been fired upon by a U-boat's artillery, Hardegen implemented phase two of his tactical plan, ordering the helmsman to reverse their course northward in order to intercept the line of ships following the now-disabled tanker. Two vessels, having seen the flashes and hearing the blast of the U-boat's deck gun, not to mention watching the burning SS *Malay* in the distance, sped off before U-*123* could overtake them. Hardegen reluctantly then set his sights on a smallish freighter, upon which he launched his second-to-last torpedo. The ship was the Savannah-bound, Latvian-owned, *Ciltvaira*, which had been too far away to see the burning *Malay* over the horizon and too slow to take evasive action regardless. Two engine room stokers were killed in the explosion, but the remaining 30 men of the ship's roster were rescued after sunup by passing vessels.

The *Ciltvaira*'s cargo of bulk paper headed for Georgia was hardly what could have been considered the "sinews" of war. More important to Hardegen and U-*123*, however, was the addition of the *Ciltvaira*'s tonnage to their tally sheets, putting the total tons destroyed by the U-boat (including ships sunk under the command of its first captain, Karl-Heinz Möhle) at more than 200,000 tons, and for Hardegen personally, 100,000 tons, qualifying him for the prestigious and coveted Knight's Cross commendation. Hardegen proudly made a notation to the fact in his war diary. (So far, however, much of the tonnage sunk by U-*123* during Operation Paukenschläg could not have been considered vital to the Allied war effort. Nevertheless, the German propaganda machine found the American losses resulting from Paukenschläg to be quite useful, regardless of the strategic value of destroyed cargos.)

Hardegen also wrote that he was annoyed by the fact that, based on radio traffic, the SS *Malay*'s crew announced that they had extinguished most of her fires and had her engines running again. The tanker turned northward, gradually increasing her speed. The time was now 5:30 a.m.—the darkest hours of the night. Only a sliver of the waxing crescent moon was visible over the thin strip of the Outer Banks. Hardegen and company could smell the burning SS *Malay*, but they couldn't see it. For 10 minutes or so they resorted to navigating by their noses. Meanwhile, a few miles away, the wounded tanker limped along in the darkness, hoping to sneak past the rogue German U-boat. Suddenly distress flares, known as star shells, rocketed into the air from the crippled *Ciltvaira*. In an instant, night turned into day.

The Germans must have thought, *What a night!* While the brilliant light perfectly illuminated the escaping SS *Malay*, the sky burst also lit up the U-boat and potentially exposed it to the long-overdue (and much-hoped-for) retaliation by U.S. naval defenses. Further south, the few *City of Atlanta* survivors still clinging to life, including Robert Fennell, George Tavelle, and Earl Dowdy, could hear the distant gun blasts and torpedo explosions and could see the flashes, fires, and now the meteor-like star burst to the north. They must have thought that total war had reached the shores of America—the Germans were wreaking widespread havoc. The same thoughts must have also occurred to the inhabitants of the Banks—especially those in the northern Hatteras Island villages of Rodanthe, Waves, and Salvo, who might have been up at that early hour and were on the front row of the drama taking place offshore.

Hardegen was incredulous as he watched the SS *Malay* steaming away at 11 knots under the bright light of the Latvian fireworks display. He was determined to not let the vessel get away; after all, his Knight's Cross was slipping away with the irrepressible tanker. With their last torpedo ready and locked onto its target, the bridge command was shouted into the voice tube: "Los!" The aim was perfect, and 28 seconds later the "eel" ripped into the hull of the *Malay* just forward of the engine room. "Blame yourself for sending a hasty report about being operational," Hardegen later wrote in his war diary, upbraiding the audacity of the SS *Malay*'s captain. Little did Hardegen know that the SS *Malay*'s master, John Dodge, would have the last laugh.

As the SS *Malay* again erupted into flames, Hardegen decided not to press his luck any further. Dawn had come, and U-*123* was fully visible to the numerous merchant ships running the longitudinal line 75-20W. According to the notation in Hardegen's war diary, the water depth was 10 meters, slightly under 33 feet. If this were correct, it would have meant that U-*123* was well within the Wimble Shoals area, placing the U-boat within four miles of the beach. There was no room to dive, no where to hide. Hardegen ordered his helmsman seated at his battle station position inside the conning tower to steer due east for deeper water and ultimately for home. But before U-*123* could put much distance between her stern and the shallows of Wimble Shoals, an enormous, nearly 17,000-ton Norwegian whaling ship suddenly and bravely turned into the direc-

tion of the German raider in an attempt to ram the much smaller U-boat. Like a coyote escaping a henhouse, U-*123* cranked-up her diesels to maximum RPMs, charging away at 19 knots, while the behemoth behind chased them at her maximum of 17 knots. Hardegen's entry in the war diary reads: "The giant turns towards us and tries to ram. This idea had not occurred to me. I thought he would just run away. Distance 400 meters. Diesel engines on emergency speed. Water depth 20 meters. This is too shallow to crash-dive from maximum speed; he will ram us."

The chase lasted two hours until it became obvious to the master of the whaling ship that he was not going to catch the U-boat. As soon as the pursuer turned away, back to her original course, Hardegen turned U-*123* northward, in order to bluff the Norwegian crew. It worked, as the whaler immediately broadcast the U-boat's new heading and bearings for everyone to hear. Once out of sight, Hardegen ordered another course change, this time to the south-southeast, directly opposite of the direction from where Navy patrol aircraft or surface vessels from the Norfolk naval base would be coming. Once the daring U-boat captain was confident that they were out of harm's way, he went below to compose his report of the preceding evening's exciting but harrowing events. Now, far in the distance, distress calls from the SS *Malay* could be heard over the radio receiver aboard U-*123*. "SOS sinking rapidly, next ship please hurry, torpedoed, sinking. Hurry, hurry next ship." Hardegen writes: "We can count [*Malay*] as completely destroyed. The night of the long knives is over. A beat of the drum with eight ships, among them three tankers with 53,060 GRT."

SS *Malay*, however, was not destroyed. A few hours later her crew had restarted her engines once again, and the tanker was hobbling on her way to the safety of Hampton Roads. The next day the tough old tanker, riddled with holes, decks torn open, and a gaping gash beneath her waterline, dropped anchor near the shipyards of Newport News, Virginia.

The Navy issued a statement that they had mounted a "ranging hunt for the submarine pack responsible for the attacks" on the *City of Atlanta*, *Malay*, and *Ciltvaira*, but under the current rules of censorship, they were not allowed to discuss any successes they may have had in sinking the German marauders. Truth be told, the Navy would not lay eyes on the first U-boat inside U.S. territorial waters for another three months despite their numerous claims to the contrary, and by then, dozens of Allied ships would be sunk and many more than 1,000 lives would be lost.

CHAPTER 8

Hatteras Inlet Coast Guard Lifeboat Station.

THE LAST STOP IN CIVILIZATION

"Where'd you think you were, New York City?"

CPO Homer Gray

Following the Japanese attack on Pearl Harbor, America was a nation on the move, like a gigantic, agitated ant colony stirred from its slumber to action by a malevolent threat. It was a time of unprecedented travel as millions of Americans responded to the call for action. By the tens of thousands, cars, trucks, buses, trains, planes, ferries, and troop ships were going this way and that, transporting millions of men and women to military bases, factories, civilian wartime posts like censorship and intelligence offices, and to remote Coast Guard installations along the immense U.S. coastline.

On Monday, January 5, 1942, a lapstrake picket boat with its ensign snapping in the afternoon breeze carefully navigated the serpentine Hatteras Inlet channel. Leaving astern gentle swells rolling in from the sea, the little white boat crept toward the Coast Guard lifeboat station docks at the desolate northeast end of Ocracoke Island. Huddled on the transom with their watch caps pulled down tightly over their ears were two men, both wearing newly issued woolen pea jackets with lapels fully fastened, their hands plunged deeply in pockets and their collars pulled upward to defend against the piercing winter wind. The glum looks on their faces—one more morose than the other—were ones of resignation, like innocent but condemned men on their way to the gallows.

Fresh out of boot camp, the two homesick and disheartened Coast Guard seaman recruits—Theodore Mutro, age 20, of Pennsylvania, and Ulysses Levi (Mac) Womac, age 18, of Tennessee—were on their way to their first wartime assignment. It wasn't quite what they expected, nor was their bus trip down the beach from Manteo, driven by a

cheerfully barefoot 13-year-old boy. They must have felt like they had somehow fallen into a sandy version of Alice's Wonderland.

A few men stood on the dock ready to catch the boat's lines. "Well, boys, welcome to the Bermuda of the U.S.A.!" someone shouted. *Bermuda of the U.S.A.? What sort of wise guy is this?* Mutro muttered to himself as he grabbed an extended arm and pulled himself up on the dock and took a quick look around. Mutro, a gruff native of a rough and tumble shipyard town on the Delaware River, retorted, "Hey, I thought we were at war with Germany; what are we doin' here? Someone's made a terrible mistake." Womac, younger and less self-assured, kept his thoughts to himself.

"You're not there yet, son," a petty officer replied with a thick "hoi-toide" brogue. "And watch that mouth. You boys got another 13 miles to go. Your limousine awaits." The PO pointed to a rusty, weather-beaten International Harvester pickup truck parked nearby. *Oh, brother,* Mutro thought to himself, *more beach driving!*

Mutro and Womac had arrived at the Coast Guard's Hatteras Inlet Lifeboat Station, which wasn't on Hatteras Island at all but located on Ocracoke Island. The station, previously known as Cedar Hammock Life-Saving Station, was not particularly well-situated as the restless inlet it guarded was gradually encroaching southwestward, toward the eroding barrier of sand wrapping around the isolated outpost. The station was easily one of the more remote, austere, wind-swept spots on the U.S. East Coast, and from a vantage point on its landward approaches opposite the inlet, it looked like it sat in the middle of a vast and desolate desert. The installation consisted of four simple buildings, a couple of large cisterns that collected and stored fresh water, and a spindly lookout tower. Leading away from the station toward the distant village of Ocracoke was its tenuous umbilical cord to the outside world, a long line of telegraph poles. There wasn't much

Hatteras Inlet Coast Guard Lifeboat Station at northeast end of Ocracoke Island.

to the place. But what the Hatteras Inlet station had going for it, which especially benefited those unlucky mariners who found themselves in distress on or near Diamond Shoals, was that it had the nearest and quickest motor-lifeboat access to the ocean in that stretch of the Outer Banks. Nevertheless, for new arrivals to the island, it was a forlorn place.

In a 1999 interview, Mutro recounted his first impressions of Ocracoke Island as he rocked back and forth on a swing beside his house. "Last stop in civilization!" he said without hesitation. "This guy comes to pick me and Womac up—Kenneth Smith, I think he was. Me and Womac loaded our sea bags on the back of the truck and climbed inside. [Smith] tells us, 'We've only got one room left—two men to a room,' he says."

An experience not unlike the Midgett Brother's bus ride, the pickup truck's tires spun, the gears ground, the transmission clunked with a sound like it was about to fall out of the back, and off they went along the deeply rutted tracks toward the beach. "Zzzz, zzzz, zzzz," Mutro spits and sputters, attempting to recreate the sound of the stalwart truck bucking its way down the beach. "Shifting and all, he comes on top of the beach, staying in the tracks, zzz, zzz."

Mutro and Womac arrived at Ocracoke village. Mutro: "He comes into the village. Curiosity gets the best of me. I asked him, 'Where's the heart of town?' He says, 'You're right on the main drag now, do you want to get out and look around?' 'No,' I says, 'I've seen everything!'"

Ocracoke village, however, was not without its charms. Mutro and Womac just hadn't discovered them yet.

For nearly 500 years of recorded history—and who knows for how long during prehistoric times—people have been attracted to the island of Ocracoke for a variety of

WAHAB VILLAGE HOTEL AND THEATRE
OCRACOKE, NORTH CAROLINA

reasons, but most of all because it has always been a watering place of sorts, just as it is today. History doesn't recall which European ship was the first to drop anchor near Ocracoke Inlet to collect "sweet" water from a well used by Algonkian Indians frequenting the island during seasonal fishing and hunting excursions. However, there is little doubt that by 1585, Ocracoke had become a reliable resupply point for thirsty seafarers from Europe, including Elizabethan Walter Raleigh's ill-fated Roanoke colonies.

Just as modern drivers, like truckers, regularly drive a stretch of interstate highway and often stop at a favorite exit for fuel, food, or rest, so too did mariners in the old days learn the locations for the easiest access to the best sources of fresh water. During the age of exploration and colonization, there were but a few of these watering places known on the mid-Atlantic coast. The mainland near the mouth of the Cape Fear River (at present-day Southport) had a good source of fresh water, and at Lynnhaven Bay along the south end of the Chesapeake there was another. A third, and possibly more-visited due to its proximity to the Gulf Stream, was Ocracoke, where a fresh-water aquifer was located in the prominent mound of ancient live oak and cedar trees at the place known today as Springer's Point.

Consequently, over the centuries people have come to Ocracoke for fresh water

(mariners), for its reputed seclusion (pirates), for its economic opportunities (harbor piloting and lighterage), or for its alluring attractions as a seaside resort (20th-century real estate speculators, hoteliers, restauranteurs, hunting guides, and charter boat operators). Over time there were many people who were unable to resist the island's captivating charms and decided to make it their home, like the remarkable William Howard, who came within hours of being hanged in Virginia as a pirate in 1718 but received a last-minute reprieve and made the most of it by living to the considerable age of 108. Howard purchased the island in 1759 (perhaps with some of Black Beard's remaining treasure) and was the progenitor of a prolific and well-established line that proudly reigns as one of the island's founding families. That same line led to the sanguine visionary and tireless promoter of Ocracoke, Stanley Wahab. Wahab was the man who conceived the island's tourism slogan, "Bermuda of the U.S.A."

Robert Stanley Wahab was a prodigal son of Ocracoke, and his circuitous course through life was something like the first paved highway on the island, which was at once affectionately and derisively called "the road which started from nowhere and ended at the same place." Wahab's career path took him many places including Norfolk, Virginia; Philadelphia; Atlantic City, New Jersey; and Baltimore, but it was inevitable that he would end up back at his beloved Ocracoke. In fact, even though he frequently found fortune elsewhere, he came back many times. Wahab certainly wouldn't agree that his island home was "nowhere." On the contrary, he was convinced Ocracoke had tremendous potential and could someday become a real tourist destination. It just needed a little help.

In his mid-20s, after having left the island for a few years to get an education, Wahab came home to try teaching at the village's one-room school. During this period of residency, however, he was perhaps better remembered for building and operating in 1914 the first moving picture show—a fairly cosmopolitan venture even for the state's largest cities back in the day. As a young man, Wahab was already exhibiting his faculties for forward thinking. The next two decades led to many other endeavors, all financially successful, and by the early 1930s, Wahab was ready to devote his wealth and experience to develop his beloved Ocracoke into a first-rate tourist destination. The only problems were the island had no harbor, no electricity, no telephones, no paved roads, no access by ferry, and few accommodations. Why would a tourist want to go there?

Undaunted, Wahab got to work. He began by purchasing 1,000 acres of barren land, essentially reacquiring family property previously owned by his ancestor, pirate-quartermaster William Howard. These were the years of the Great Depression, but Wahab knew the economic downturn wouldn't last forever. He initiated the first dredging of the shallow stream and marsh known as Cockle Creek, beginning its transformation into today's Silver Lake. With a little of Wahab's money and a lot of his persistence, the village got an electric generator and an ice plant for fish packing. He bought the old Odd Fellows Hall and former schoolhouse and turned it into an inn. On a tract of land on the outskirts of Ocracoke village, he built a modern hotel called the Wahab Village Hotel and Theatre. Across the street (actually a rutted patch of sand) he built an eye-catching but incongruous adobe hacienda that quickly became a popular watering hole known as the Spanish Casino—a hopping jive-joint featuring live music and dances.

The island between the Wahab Hotel and the beach was a vast sand flat just waiting to be used as a runway for visiting planes so Wahab established the island's first airport, and for a time the island enjoyed air delivery of express mail and packages long before such services were imagined on a national scale. Within a couple of years, on the eve of World War II, the Wahab Village properties were thriving establishments offering rooms, meals, and entertainments for all sorts of guests—from wealthy industrialists visiting the island to hunt waterfowl, to shoe salesmen, and to artists and writers attending summer creative workshops. Now, what the island needed was some positive publicity.

In 1955, when he was recognized as the "Tar Heel of the Week" in a biographical feature published in the Raleigh *News & Observer*, writer Woodrow Price recounted Stanley Wahab's career path: "He has been an oysterman, a sailor, an accountant, a public school teacher, a leader in the business world, and the entrepreneur of an air service. He has been, and still is, a real estate man, a promoter, and hotel owner."

Wahab, too, would have made a good Madison Avenue advertising man because he had a gift for creative marketing schemes, names and slogans, some capitalizing on island lore. It is believed that Wahab came up with the harbor's appealing name of Silver Lake, which is neither silver-colored nor a lake. After the war, Wahab decided that Ammunition Dump Road would sound more enticing if it were named Sunset Road, and sure enough, people were suddenly willing to buy lots along it. Someone on Ocracoke—likely Wahab—keen on boosting tourism during the pre-war years came up with the myth that the notorious pirate Black Beard's headless body swam five laps around his executioner's sloop before the corpse sank into the depths of "Teaches Hole Channel." This even though the water where the fearsome pirate was killed was only a few feet deep (this dubious urban legend has since become firmly ensconced within many respected published historical accounts). Wahab also loved to tell folks how his existence and surname were due to his distant ancestor, an Arabian sailor who was shipwrecked and became a castaway on Ocracoke Island in the early 1700s. It made for fascinating dinner conversation and complemented nicely the legend of wild Arabian horses roaming the beaches, but some contemporary family genealogists take exception to the story, believing the Wahab name is a corruption for Wauchope or Waughob which can be traced to 17th-century settlers of St. Mary's City, Maryland. Stanley Wahab would have none of that, however. As far as he was concerned, he was the descendant of an Arab castaway, and that was a fact.

Likewise, he would not have tolerated anyone contradicting his characterization of Ocracoke as the "Bermuda of the U.S.A.," especially a lowly, one-stripe, freshwater sailor like Theodore Mutro, who disparaged the island as the "last stop in civilization." Maybe "Bermuda of the U.S.A." was a bit of a stretch, but, in time, even the irascible Mutro changed his mind and came to share Stanley Wahab's sentiment. Wahab once described how much he cherished living "along these shores of contentment and happiness, where life is worth living and living is at its best."

There have been many island residents and visitors over the past decades who would heartily agree with Wahab's less-slogan-like endorsement. However, for those hundreds of Coast Guard and Navy sailors who were sent to the island for a couple of years in

the 1940s to defend the nation's shores against the Nazi peril, Ocracoke was, for a few months, a living hell.

When Mutro and Womac's "limousine" lurched to a stop at the new Coast Guard station overlooking Silver Lake, the young men entered the building and climbed the watch tower to have a look around. "Jesus Christ," Mutro exclaimed, "this is an island! And the chief [CPO Homer Gray] said to me, 'Where'd you think you were, New York City?' He said, 'You think this is bad, you ought to go to Portsmouth. We have 12 men over there, no electricity, no nothin.' Got 12 men over there, they come up once per week, get their groceries, kerosene, everything.'"

Mutro and Womac each thought to themselves: *This is going to be some kind of assignment. All we're going to be doing here is lollygagging on a beach waging war against mosquitoes and boredom while our hometown buddies see the world!* Two weeks later, Mutro and Womac found out otherwise.

On a chilly, late-October evening, 58 years after his tour of duty began on the island of Ocracoke, Mac Womac was interviewed at his daughter's modest but attractively decorated home. Wearing a blue-and-white flannel shirt and suspenders, the soft-spoken, kindly great-grandfather of 17 children seemed, at first, hesitant to revisit what he witnessed in 1942, yet he agreed to share his memories. The setting was one that often inhibited the most honest, reflective responses—a large TV camera sat on a tripod in front of him, lights glared, and a microphone was clipped onto his shirt, the cord dangling between his knees. Once, the camera malfunctioned, and an answer had to be restated; during another compelling recollection, the tape ran out. Womac smiled and patiently waited to continue, but there was a risk that important things might not be said.

The second world war had been a long time ago. It would have been understandable if the 77-year-old couldn't remember all that had happened. In the intervening years, Womac had put in two decades with the Coast Guard and 17 more years with the National Park Service. A lot of water had passed under the bridge.

When he was asked: What can you say about a specific wartime activity that you remember the most? "Well, it was walking the beach and standing watch," he replied, describing something to which most seaman recruits in the Coast Guard could relate. They did a lot of walking before, during, and after the war, trudging in the footsteps of the surfmen of the old life-saving service, back and forth, day and night, on the beach in weather fair and foul.

"We were making beach patrols because we thought [the Germans] might try to land somebody here, and we had a few scares that had been reported that they were going to be landing on the beach. We weren't walking then. We just found the highest dune and got on top of it and dug us out a little place to lay where we could look both ways up and down the beach. Stayed there all night."

What could he possibly see on a night when there was no moon?

"All you can do is watch the breakers. You can see them a-breaking and see if there was anything strange in any of the breakers coming in. I know one night I was on patrol, and the guy that was with me said, 'What the hell is that?' I said, 'I didn't know.' I went and hollered. Never got an answer, so I shot one time. Still didn't get and answer, and we kept looking and was getting closer to it and we was ready to shoot, and it was just a life raft been washed up. Wasn't anybody in it."

A lot of empty life rafts and life boats would wash up on the beaches over the next six months. If the rafts or boats ever had anyone in them, the passengers were long gone.

Most days during his first two weeks were spent getting acquainted with procedures, equipment, and boats. There was lots of knot tying and endless rowing and motor life-boat drills. Some of the recruits, like Womac, had never been on a boat in anything more than a farm pond or placid inland lake. Their superiors, the senior ratings at the Silver Lake station, were natives of the Banks, having served in the Life-Saving Service before it was turned into the U.S. Coast Guard. The "old men" at the station had little patience with the "kids" from the mainland—they knew little or nothing about the sea and boat handling. But when the young seaman recruits weren't patrolling the beach, Womac explained, they were usually out in small boats.

Suddenly, Womac's good-natured countenance darkened as he solemnly began to recount another memory, a night spent in a small boat. In the background, a fish tank pump gurgled softly. No one in the room moved or made a sound. The old timer's eyes seemed to focus beyond the walls, beyond the curtain of time, as he transported those listening back through the years, to 1942. The night he remembered was Friday, the 23rd of January, only his third week on the island, the night the British tanker *Empire Gem* was torpedoed about 25 miles due east of Ocracoke Inlet.

"Whenever we got called out, we knew we were going out to a ship that had been tor-pedoed. The guy in charge of the boat knew more about it than we did. He never said more than 'We gotta go, and you all's the ones that are picked so let's haul buggy.' And we did, and it seemed like it took us forever to get there because, like I said, the boat was slow."

The *Empire Gem*, loaded with more than 10,000 tons of refined gasoline, was en route from Port Arthur, Texas, to Halifax, Nova Scotia, to join a convoy headed to England. At 7:40 p.m., the tanker was struck with two torpedoes launched from U-*66*, one of the five Operation Paukenschläg boats operating in concert with Reinhard Hardegen's U-*123*. The British vessel erupted in an immense firestorm, ejecting wreckage and vast quantities of burning gasoline and oil that spread across the black surface of the sea. The great orange glow and towering mushroom cloud could be seen dozens of miles away. A single SOS was transmitted from the ship, and then the radio went dead.

A few minutes later, U-*66* next intercepted the U.S.-flagged iron ore freighter *Venore*, which had been overtaken by the faster *Empire Gem* and was perfectly illuminated by the raging fires nearby. A single torpedo was launched against the *Venore*, inflicting little damage but causing many of the freighter's crew to panic and attempt to abandon ship. Two lifeboats with 20 sailors overturned upon being lowered to the water as the ship was still moving at full speed, drowning all of the men. Less than an hour later, U-*66* fired a second torpedo into the *Venore*, and the ship began to sink. Realizing that their fate was sealed, the captain ordered the remaining men aboard to abandon ship, and then he and the radio operator began to send a steady stream of distress calls. These SOS broad-

casts were also received by the two Coast Guard stations at each end of Ocracoke Island.

Within seconds after the first bright flash appeared over the horizon and the subsequent deep rumble of sound waves rattled the windows of the Coast Guard stations on the Outer Banks, followed by the haunting chirps of the *Empire Gem*'s single SOS transmission, rescuers jumped into action. A 36-foot motor lifeboat (No. 4464) from Hatteras Inlet Station was the first to put to sea in response to the call from the *Empire Gem*. A few minutes later, a similar boat (No. 5426) from the Ocracoke-Silver Lake Station was ordered to head toward the *Venore*. The Hatteras Inlet boat gained the sea quickly; the latter rescue boat had to first navigate the long channel to the sea buoy off Ocracoke Inlet, more than an hour's journey from the station. By the time the lifeboat headed for

British motor tanker *Empire Gem* sinks near Cape Hatteras.

the *Venore* reached the open ocean, she was ordered by radio to change her course and head east-northeast for the more desperate situation at the burning *Empire Gem*. The *Venore*'s captain had by then transmitted a message that his remaining crew had successfully launched a lifeboat. Had there been any survivors of the *Empire Gem*, they were most likely treading water. It took the little lifeboat from Silver Lake more than six hours to reach her destination—an agonizingly long six hours. The four men aboard knew that by the time they arrived, it would almost certainly be too late to find any survivors. Mac Womac was one of four men aboard the Ocracoke Station lifeboat.

"We could see the orange glow in the sky a long time before we got to it," Womac said, almost as if he could still see in his mind the burning *Empire Gem* on the horizon. At 0300 hours, Womac's motor lifeboat finally arrived on the hellish scene, the water ablaze with expanding pools of raging fires, clouds of choking, thick black smoke, and the ocean littered with the tossing flotsam of ship and human remains. The four men from Ocracoke Station couldn't maneuver their lifeboat near the massive hull of the stricken ship. Along the tanker's rail high above, some British sailors, their clothing apparently on fire, could still be seen leaping from the deck to the burning sea below. High seas and scorching

Survivors of *Empire Gem* at Hatteras Inlet Station.

heat from the fires made the rescuers gruesome task nearly impossible. The men from Silver Lake felt helpless. "All we could do is go around and around, hoping to pick up somebody that was alive," Womac said with a huge sigh, his eyes beginning to glisten. "And it's... it's a terrible feeling, especially when you see them jump overboard with flames on to 'em and know that they was going into the fire just as quick as they hit. It had a really bad smell to it. It wasn't all oil burning."

As Womac's boat circled, they spotted three men on the *Empire Gem*'s bow, who had so far been spared from the all-consuming fire between the ship's bridge and stern deck. They seemed to be signaling their desperate desire to be rescued, but high seas and darkness made an approach to the lurching bow by the fragile wooden boat too dangerous. The Ocracoke crew decided to wait for daylight. Meanwhile, the Hatteras Inlet Station lifeboat had been off in the distance searching the dark, pre-dawn waters for lifeboats or life rafts that may have been launched from the British ship. None were found, only bodies.

At 0700, there was finally enough light for the Ocracoke Station crew to position their lifeboat near the ship's bow, and the three British sailors saw their opportunity to jump. One was the *Empire Gem*'s master, Francis Reginald Broad. He was joined by chief radioman Ernest McGraw and McGraw's assistant, Thomas Orrell. All three climbed over the bow's lifelines and leaped, hoping to avoid the flames and the ship's massive anchor chains, which had been cast out with the anchors in an effort to halt the wayward hulk. Their survival was far from guaranteed. The lifeboat maneuvered closer. Large patches of burning fuel surrounded them, pitching and tossing in the turbulent, chaotic seas. In their little boat, Womac and his comrades took their chance and valiantly dashed between the fires to rescue the victims. They successfully pulled Broad aboard, then Orrell. But before they could maneuver and throw a line to McGraw, he was pulled backward into a swirling black cloud of burning fuel and vanished before their eyes. Of the 57 British merchant officers and sailors aboard the *Empire Gem* prior to the attack by the U-66, only Captain Broad and radio assistant Orrell survived. (In a reverse twist of wartime fate, the captain and radioman were also the last two men aboard the *Venore* but both went down with the ship.)

Womac and the Ocracoke station men were soon met by the Hatteras Inlet boat, which took Broad and Orrell aboard in order to land them ashore at the northeast end of the island, which afforded quicker transport to Hampton Roads where the British men would eventually be deposed by U.S. Navy Intelligence. Sometime after landing at the Hatteras Inlet Lifeboat Station, Broad and Orrell posed for a photograph with Chief Petty Officer Homer Gray and two unidentified seaman. In the image, the uniforms of the merchant sailors appear dry, and they are both wearing shoes, which suggests the photo might have been taken a day or two after their ordeal. Both British men exhibit taut smiles, indicating either their gratitude for having been rescued, their sense of guilt for being the only survivors, or their relief to be leaving the deadly war zone off North Carolina's Outer Banks in which were floating or submerged the charred remains of 55 of their shipmates.

Ulysses Levi (Mac) Womac

In the living room of his daughter's home 58 years later, Womac's recollection of the *Empire Gem* rescue began to fade.

The kindly, gentle retiree was asked: How did it make you feel, seeing those British sailors dying such an agonizing death so close to America's shore? "Well, I'll say one thing, if I could'a got close enough to one [of those Germans] I'da killed him. Because those [British sailors] didn't have a Chinaman's chance in Hell! They were just waiting to be shot. And that's a terrible death, burning to death. I've been burnt so I know what it feels like."

Such were the searing memories of boys from the mainland who were once young and innocent and newcomers to Stanley Wahab's "shores of contentment and happiness," a place where they became men in one night.

Shortly after the interview with Mac Womac had concluded, and the TV camera and lights were turned off and the equipment was packed up, Womac's daughter spoke. "That was truly amazing," Debbie Bryan said. "We've never heard my father tell that story before. He's not been willing to discuss those things until now."

What Womac's daughter nor anyone knew at the time was that the kindly, gentle, great-grandfather of 17 children had only a couple more months to live. He had decided it was time to tell his story, as hard as it would be to relive the unspeakable horrors of the *Empire Gem*. Now Ulysses Levi Womac's memories of that winter of 1942 will be preserved forever.

CHAPTER 9

Nags Head Casino

LOCKING THE BARN AFTER THE HORSE IS GONE

"This is objectionable, but... is not at present regarded as creating a problem requiring drastic measures."

Commander, U.S. Navy Eastern Sea Frontier

By the last week of January 1942, U-*123*, U-*66*, and the other three Paukenschläg boats had begun their monotonous three-week cruises back to France. The trip home for the submariners was more commodious but less savory since they had expended not only their supply of torpedos and much of their ammunition, but also all of their preferred provisions. The conquering heroes had no choice but to celebrate by dining on canned food and moldy bread. Hardegen's "night of the long knives" message to Admiral Karl Dönitz was answered a few hours later with hearty congratulations: "An den Paukenschläger Hardegen. Bravo! Gut gepaukt. Dönitz (For the kettledrum-beater Hardegen. Well done! Good drum beating. Dönitz)"

Another kind of drumming was soon heard aboard U-*123*. As the U-boat sped away from the American coast on a heading of 106 degrees east-southeast toward Bermuda, leaving astern the rhythmic flashes of the Cape Hatteras Lighthouse, the tinny-sounding but lively strains of jazz was played throughout each compartment's intercom speakers as the crew celebrated their success. Due to the skywave effect, AM radio stations like Raleigh's WPTF and Charlotte's WBT could be heard during the night at much greater distances than during daylight hours, so German U-boat crews, no longer at battle stations, delighted in listening to their enemy's popular art form. Among the tunes remembered by Hardegen's crew as one of their favorites was Xavier Cugat's 1940 hit, "Perfidia," a Latin-inspired, instrumental arrangement often performed in live broadcasts by Cugat's orchestra at New York's Waldorf-Astoria Hotel. Glenn Miller also performed and recorded his own version of "Perfidia," featuring lyrics sung by Dorothy Claire and the Modernaires:

To you my heart cries out, Perfidia,
For I found you, the love of my life, in somebody else's arms
Your eyes are echoing perfidia,
Forgetful of our promise of love, you're sharing another's charms...
With a sad lament my dreams have faded like a broken melody
While the gods of love look down and laugh at what romantic fools we mortals be...
And now I know my love was not for you
And so I take it back with a sigh, perfidious one,
Goodbye...

As his U-boats bid goodbye to America and returned to their bases in France, Admiral Dönitz noted in his war diary that the operation surpassed his own expectations. Even Hitler, famously unimpressed by his own navy's capabilities, was pleased. To Japan's ambassador in Berlin he said, "I myself have been surprised at the successes we have met along the American coast lately. The United States kept up the tall talk and left her coast unguarded."

Left behind in the wakes of the five Paukenschläg U-boats were the broken and sunken hulks of 25 Allied ships in American and Canadian waters, thousands of gallons of spilled fuel oil and refined gasoline, and tons of valuable cargo destroyed. Five hundred seaman and civilians were killed, and an even greater number of family members and children were suddenly and tragically without husbands, fathers, sons, brothers, and uncles. The disaster represented the largest concentrated loss of merchant mariners' lives in that service's history. One fifth of those killed during Operation Paukenschläg were from the *City of Atlanta* and *Empire Gem*, two ships torpedoed inside the sweeping beam cast by the light of the Cape Hatteras Lighthouse.

Encouraged by his U-boat's impunity against the apparent impotence of the U.S. Navy in defending its home waters, Dönitz unleashed his gray wolves. The second wave of U-boats was already on its way to North American waters. For the Allies and their vital chain of war supplies and troops moving up the eastern seaboard, the coming weeks and months were only going to get worse.

Allied merchant seaman might have imagined themselves the losers in the song, "Perfidia," the chumps who were abandoned by a deceitful and untrustworthy lover—in this instance, their lover being their so-called protectors. Military authorities repeatedly told the press that they would not discuss any specific successes they may have had in sinking the rogue German U-boats at the risk of divulging critical operational secrets (the secret being that the U.S. military had been embarrassed, yet again, by its lack of preparedness five weeks after Pearl Harbor). Instead, the Navy issued a carefully worded but equivocatory communique at the end of January regarding the U.S. counteroffensive against Germany's "excursionists."

> "Some of the recent visitors to our territorial waters will never enjoy the return-trip portion of their voyage. Furthermore, the percentage of two-way traffic is satisfactorily on the decline."

The communique's deceit, however, was that the phrase "recent visitors to our territorial waters [who] will never enjoy the return-trip portion of their voyage" might have just as appropriately applied to merchant vessels of other Allied nations. *Norness* (Panamanian), *Coimbra* (British), *Ciltvaira* (Latvian), *Empire Gem* (British), *Alexander Hough* (Norwegian), *Dayrose* (British), *Lady Hawkins* (Canadian), *Olympic* (Panamanian), and *Varanger* (Norwegian) were just a few of the foreign-flagged vessels lost off the North American coast that decreased the "percentage of two-way traffic" in January 1942.

Furthermore, at the time of the communique's release, there were no verifiable successes of the U.S. counteroffensive, no sinking of U-boats, and no sightings of U-boats, only the grim aftermath of the U-boats' first American patrol.

Meanwhile, a procession of ships each day steamed unescorted off the East Coast of the United States, passing through oil slicks, wreckage, empty lifeboats and rafts, and the protruding bows and sterns of dozens of ships like the many modern roadside memorials placed by families of wreck victims—stark reminders of the recentness and proximity of death.

Francis "Biff" Bowker, a 24-year-old mate on the *Herbert L. Rawding*, one of the few surviving four-masted sailing merchant schooners hauling freight and logwood along the eastern seaboard and in the West Indies, recalled a day in March 1942 when his ship slowly approached the Diamond Shoals Light Buoy off Cape Hatteras. "I saw something up ahead on the port bow, a sort of triangular shape," Bowker said. "I thought maybe they had put a big buoy out there for some reason. The captain got the glasses, and he looked, and he looked, and finally he just handed them to me and went down below without a word. Well, this triangular thing turned out to be the bow of a vessel that had sunk and rolled over, and there was just that triangle sticking up out of the water."

There, but for the grace of God, go I, many a merchant sailor like Bowker might have thought. Men with a pessimistic attitude might have reworded the proverbial phrase differently: *There, in just a matter of time, go I*. As they steamed up the coast, many sailors thought that it was inevitable that they would wind up sunk and for one principal reason—shore lights. For four months or more, the merchant sailor's greatest complaints were the American public's lights emanating from cities and communities along the coast from Miami to Boston, which made darkened ships a perfect target against the horizon's gleam. In certain atmospheric conditions—which occurred frequently—seacoast lights could be seen 30 to 40 miles offshore, diffused and refracted through the marine haze.

"Automobiles going by, down in Florida the hotels wouldn't put their lights out, I tell you, it was the damnedest thing you ever saw," Bowker said. "This country was so unprepared for that war. They just didn't take it seriously, and everybody had their lights on. You'd see cars going down the road, and you'd see houses lit up; and down in Florida, those hotels were lit up beautifully for everybody. Those submarines would just sit out there and knock [us] off!"

Rhodes Chamberlin, in an interview at his home in El Paso, Texas, recalled his experience as a Boatswain's Mate 2nd Class aboard the destroyer, USS *Jesse Roper*, during the days the warship ran anti-submarine patrols off the North Carolina coast. "We could see the coast lights, the glow of the coast lights. Well, if we could see them certainly then

a submarine seaward of us was going to see [our] silhouettes. There was more conversation on the ship about the darn lights on the beach than there was about anything else. Because we realized that they made us stand out also as a target running up and down. So that really was the main topic of conversation—what in hell is going on with the management leaving the lights on?"

It was a good question, and one for which the "management"—namely government authorities in Washington—had difficulty finding a direct and satisfying answer during the winter of 1942. Historians, including Michael Gannon, author of *Operation Drumbeat*, have since offered a few theories as to why the military didn't implement blackout or dim-out regulations sooner: bureaucratic turf-wrangling between the Army and Navy; a misjudgment that the greatest civil defense threat would come, not from the sea, but from Axis aircraft; a reluctance to inconvenience the public or disrupt the economies of coastal communities reliant on tourism; an underestimation of the effect shore lights had dozens of miles out to sea; and the naïve belief that German U-boat skippers were unlikely to operate in shallow water. As for the "shallow water" theory, although the authorities weren't aware of it at the time, Hardegen and U-*123* had already daringly operated in waters just 30-feet-deep. Nevertheless, just two and a half weeks after the British tanker *Empire Gem* was turned into a deadly inferno only 12 miles from Cape Hatteras, Admiral Aldolphus Andrews, commander of the U.S. Navy's Eastern Sea Frontier, issued this statement:

> The lights of beach resorts frequently furnish a background against which vessels running close to the coast may be silhouetted by others further seaward. This is objectionable, but inasmuch as submarines are reluctant to operate in waters less than about 10 fathoms in depth [60 feet], this is not at present regarded as creating a problem requiring drastic measures.

The beach resorts most often cited as having remained callously and indifferently illuminated for the first few months of 1942 were mostly on the New Jersey, Delaware, Maryland, and Florida coasts, although there was at least one instance when a popular North Carolina dance hall may have contributed to the loss of a tanker on Easter weekend. Some historians have gone so far as to suggest that the owners and managers of the casinos and hotels were aware of the effects their bright neon signs and exterior lights had on offshore shipping but blatantly refused to make a change in favor of sustaining their businesses.

Did the owners and managers of these establishments not care that their apparent greed was aiding the enemy and abetting the deaths of hundreds of helpless Allied merchant sailors? Many students of World War II history are taught to think so by scholars such as the esteemed historian Samuel Eliot Morison, who scathingly concluded that the resistance of resort and hotel owners to darkening their establishments was "most reprehensible." In his book, *History of United States Naval Operations in World War II—The Battle of the Atlantic*, Morison wrote: "Ships were sunk and seamen drowned in order that the citizenry might enjoy business and pleasure as usual." Certainly, in some isolated instances this may have been true as the nation's economy was only beginning to revive itself after the long years of the Great Depression and proprietors didn't wish to lose potential business. Also culpable to some degree were the resorts' patrons, who were eager to escape the unrelenting stress and bleak news of the early days of the war by reveling under the bright lights of boardwalk dance halls, albeit some citizens, in all likelihood, were ignorant of the merchant sailor's perilous exposure offshore.

The truth of history, however, may lie in the less-sensational fact that the real "sin" was committed by government, military and business leaders by not acting sooner than they did after Pearl Harbor to implement proactive war-time measures, including blackouts or less-complete dim-outs. "There was extreme reluctance of the Naval and Army authorities, both of whom had responsibility for shore lights, to do anything that would alienate the civilian population," said *Operation Drumbeat* historian Michael Gannon. "And that, of course, would be one of the unforgivable actions of the United States—civilians as well as military, in the first six months of 1942—that they did not practice total blackout as the Germans and British did."

This point of view is especially bolstered by the fact that 80 years earlier southern governors acted much more quickly to extinguish lighthouses and remove lightships and buoys before the Union Navy arrived off their coasts to blockade ports and intercept Confederate trading vessels. North Carolina's governor in 1861, John Ellis, ordered a blackout of navigational aids along the seacoast a month before his state seceded from the Union and entered the war. Ellis proudly informed Confederate President Jefferson

Davis, two weeks after the fall of Fort Sumter, that "all lights have been extinguished on the coast." Why this aspect of military and civil defense history was not remembered or even taught at U.S. military academies prior to World War II is something of a mystery. While some lightships were brought into port in the weeks after Pearl Harbor, they were replaced with lighted buoys, which were thought to be less likely targets of U-boats (in 1918, Diamond Shoals Lightship No. *71* was shelled and sunk by U-*140* during the final months of World War I), but most American lighthouses, despite a few being reduced in candlepower, remained in operation throughout World War II. Even if U.S. military commanders hadn't relied on the tried-and-true lessons of history, they could have at least paid some heed to the reason why blackouts were the norm throughout Europe and Japan since the start of the war in 1939. Again, the false assumption that the greatest threat would come from aircraft blinded many military authorities. Sadly, it took horrifying human suffering and death in U.S. waters before aggressive action was taken on the shores of the western Atlantic. For more than 2,000 merchant mariners, Navy sailors, and civilians, the action came too late.

Only a year on the job, North Carolina's Governor J. Melville Broughton took a trip to the coast in March 1942 to see for himself what was happening off his state's beaches and what was being done about it by the U.S. War Department. Upon his return to Raleigh, the governor hurriedly composed a Western Union telegram, which he sent on March 26 to Frank Knox, secretary of the U.S. Navy. Broughton was appalled by what he saw and by what he had been told, describing his state's military's defenses against U-boat incursions as "wholly inadequate and frequently inept and that there [was] a shocking lack of coordination between Army, Navy, Coast Guard, and air forces." The governor chose not to mention the impotence of his own state civil defense office, which, apparently, was confused as to just what it could accomplish without military approval.

Broughton also wrote of his deep concern that North Carolina's coastal hospitals and medical facilities were being overwhelmed with casualties being brought in from stricken tankers and freighters. Little did the governor know that a vastly greater number of merchant sailors were not surviving the attacks or were not being rescued in the event they successfully escaped in a lifeboat or on a life raft—the hospitals were only seeing a small fraction of the U-boat's victims. In his telegram, Broughton requested an immediate meeting of the region's military commanders between Norfolk, Virginia, and Charleston, South Carolina. Again, Broughton's understanding of the problem missed the mark—only Admiral Ernest King, the U.S. Navy's commander-in-chief, could approve the orders to provide a more robust defense of the Allied merchant fleet, beginning with a national dim-out or blackout along the coasts. As it happened, King was an old dog who could learn new tricks, just not very quickly.

Not long after Governor Broughton sent his letter to Navy Secretary Frank Knox, he issued an appeal to North Carolinians living along the state's 375-mile coastline, asking for their cooperation in reducing the amount of light being cast seaward from their homes and communities. Many coastal residents, including experienced watermen, were equally distressed by the frequent explosions offshore and the daily inundation fouling the beaches and prime fishing waters with oil, empty lifeboats, wreckage, and sometimes,

human remains. Consequently, numerous island families had already begun to take action. The government, however, required more evaluations, more evidence, and time.

After months of meetings, studies, tests, reports, analyses, and debate, during which time Allied ship after Allied ship was sunk by the enemy and thousands of lives were lost, the government finally began to officially order "dim-outs" in April 1942. The darkening of the Atlantic and Gulf coasts began incrementally and varied in timing and completeness according to location. The glittering and gaudy boardwalk communities on Long Island and in New Jersey were an immediate concern because of the high volume of ship traffic entering and leaving New York harbor. As early as March, small, localized steps were being taken to shield lights in coastal New Jersey municipalities.

In Florida, on April 11, 1942, an order was issued by authority of the state's governor and the commanding officer in Key West to darken that state's beach towns. The following was the blackout order posted for residents and businesses at Palm Beach:

> You are hereby requested to take the following steps to comply with the recent blackout order carried in the press.
>
> (1) It is requested that you immediately take steps to have extinguished all street lights on waterfront streets and highways at once, and those actually on the ocean front, not those on the west side.
>
> (2) Screen waterfront sidelights on all streets running down to the waterfront for about four (4) city blocks away.
>
> (3) Screen all advertising lights and lighted windows near beachfront that are facing seaward and are directly visible from off shore.
>
> (4) Screen all bright lights on seawards side, directly visible from the sea, and within two (2) miles from the waterfront, this again does not apply to those low-lying lights on the mainland that maybe already screened by invisible objects.
>
> (5) In case of a brightly lighted installation near beach, have the light so directed and screened so that no direct light can be seen from off shore.

April 18, 1942, is the date often recognized for the implementation of a widespread dim-out along the Atlantic coast, based on an order issued by the U.S. Navy's Eastern Sea Frontier, followed by similar restrictions issued by the Office of Civil Defense (April 25) and the Eastern Defense Command of the U.S. Army (May 16). Dim-out regulations were not imposed on the U.S. mainland's Pacific Coast until August 20, 1942, even though that coast had already been shelled in a couple of isolated incidents by rogue Japanese submarines. The Pacific Coast dim-out extended to 150-miles inland.

On the East Coast, dim-out regulations were in effect for all communities within 16 miles of the sea. By June, the profusion of New York City's lights was marginally reduced with the ban of lighted outdoor advertising, causing a noticeable lowering of attendance at Broadway shows and other nightlife attractions. A caption beneath a Central Press photo appearing in East Coast papers in early May described the unusual scene: "Lights on Broadway are not what they used to be after the Army ordered them dimmed out to eliminate sky glow, which used to silhouette ships at sea and make them easy targets for Axis subs. The gay White Way's spectacular neon and electric bulbs, all lights above the 15th floor, and many below that level, are turned off in the photograph above."

Reinhard Hardegen would have been terribly disappointed.

When government restrictions required the discontinued operation of traffic lights in coastal towns with drivers limited to only using their parking lights to navigate in the dark, there was, understandably, a marked increase in car crashes. For example, the traffic light ban was estimated by civil defense authorities in New Jersey towns to have produced a 100 percent increase in nighttime accidents. Of course, local civil defense officials discouraged nighttime driving except in emergencies. For citizens who chose not to observe the Federal dim-out regulations and who were caught and convicted, the penalties were severe with sentences up to one year in prison and fines of up to $5,000.

For the typical American living on the East Coast, participation in and compliance with the dim-out regulations gave them a patriotic sense of duty. Many individuals who lived on the North Carolina coast during the war have been eager to share their memories of complying with the blackout orders. Using their hands, they would often depict how their car's headlights would be shielded by black tape, or they would describe the heavy blackout curtains that would be hung on eastern-facing windows and how they would carefully peek through the drapes or around window shades in order to see the burning ships offshore. National magazines like *House and Garden* published clever decorating tips for homemakers to make the most of the unattractive wartime look. Most families were proud to prove their allegiance, and theirs' was a noble and heartfelt effort. In fact, millions of Americans on the East Coast, well beyond the 16-mile enforcement area, enthusiastically participated in the dim-out even though it was not required. Unfortunately, by the time these habits had become ingrained in the daily lives of residents throughout the Atlantic and Gulf coasts, the U-boats were gone, and most of the worst damage had been done. Not everyone was so diligent.

On an early spring night at a beach in Dare County, the air was warm, and the sky was hazy from wisps of smoke drifting from a distant forest fire on the mainland. Along the blacktop state road near the slopes of Jockey's Ridge,[2] an enormous rectangular building squatted on the sand. Over the entrance to the building hung a large vertical neon sign with the word "Casino" visible to traffic for miles in either direction, north or south. Along each side of the two-story building were 24 windows with awning-hinged storm shutters propped in the open position, allowing the cool ocean air to enter and the sounds of jazz to drift out. Two sand parking lots on each side of the building were crowded with cars and trucks of all makes, shapes, and sizes—Plymouths, Packards, Fords, Hudsons, Chryslers, Desotos, and a disproportionate number of military jeeps. Late arrivals could hear through the open windows the favorite big band tunes of the time, like Artie Shaw's "Frenesi," Glenn Miller's "In the Mood," and Duke Ellington's "Take the A-Train." It was Saturday night, April 4, 1942—a glorious Easter weekend—and the place was the Nags Head Casino, eastern North Carolina's down-home answer to the more-ostentatious resorts of Atlantic City, New Jersey, Ocean City, Maryland, or Myrtle Beach, South Carolina.

The band on stage was swinging, the dancers on the enormous floor were jitterbugging, and everyone was having a jumping-good time. The casino's owner and impresario, George T. ("Ras") Wescott, Jr., was pleased with the turnout that night despite his worries that the upcoming season would be economically dismal due to the war. Many of his regular patrons were no longer around, having been drafted or volunteered into the service and shipped out to points far afield. The usual girls were still there, and now there were hundreds of sailors on liberty from Navy and Coast Guard installations, as well as a few soldiers with the Army or National Guard who gravitated to the Casino from miles around, like moths to a bright light. It cost men 50 cents to get through the doors; girls got in free. The casino could accommodate between 1,000 and 1,500 guests, and based on the season's start on that all-important holiday weekend, things were going to be okay, Wescott was probably thinking as he watched the building fill.

Wescott was a shrewd entrepreneur who realized that the success of his operation depended on bringing in big-name performers. Despite Nags Head's relative isolation and limited accessibility, Wescott was successful in enticing some of the hottest musicians of the day to play his venue at the Sahara-like setting on the beach, including Duke Ellington, Tommy Dorsey, Glenn Miller, and Artie Shaw, who all came during the summers of 1937 and 1938. By the eve of the war, people were traveling respectable distances, from as far away as Norfolk and Newport News, Virginia, to dance by the sea at Nags Head.

The Casino's ground floor featured 12 duckpin bowling lanes, the latest electrified pinball machines, a soda fountain, and a dining area. At the top of a long staircase was the second-story dance floor—6,000 square feet of hardwood, burnished to a glossy shine with bowling alley wax. Dancers were encouraged to "cut a rug" on the wood floor by doing the Lindy Hop, Jive, or Jitterbug in their bare feet, which is how most Outer Bankers traveled anyway. A counter near the ballroom's entrance welcomed guests to check their shoes, if they were wearing any, when they arrived. Some folks who frequented the Casino remember the busiest nights when so many people were on the dance floor at one time that the floor and the building trembled. They also remember that, during those months that German U-boats stalked their prey off the Outer Banks, "Ras" Wescott diligently darkened the lights and shielded the windows as recommended by state civil defense officials.

But that is not how Rev. Frank B. Dinwiddie remembered the state of affairs at the Casino, at least not on April 4, 1942.

Dinwiddie was a keen and meticulous observer, particularly of weather and atmospheric conditions. For some years after the war he was a Cooperative Weather Observer for the U.S. Weather Bureau and on at least a couple of occasions published highly technical reports of tornado and funnel cloud activity associated with tropical storms and hurricanes that he observed from his house on the southeast side of Jockey's Ridge. Dinwiddie was also a Baptist minister and a pastor for many years at Roanoke Island Baptist Church, and in 1942 he served as the chaplain for Edwards Military Institute in Sampson County. In other words, Dinwiddie was both honest and observant. It was in his role as a military school chaplain, as well as a part-time resident of Nags Head, that Dinwiddie mailed to Governor Broughton a scornful eyewitness account of an offshore explosion that he attributed to a U-boat attack on an Allied vessel about 30 miles north of his home

SS *Byron D. Benson* burns on Easter morning after being torpedoed off Currituck Banks.

at approximately 10:40 p.m. on Saturday, April 4th.

"The initial concussion, presumably the explosion of the torpedo, shook the ground and buildings on the coast and was accompanied immediately by an immediate burst of flame, which lightened the sky for several hours thereafter," Dinwiddie wrote.

The Protestant chaplain had sharp eyes and an astute mind for details. Even at such a considerable distance from the attack (the sound of the initial explosion would have taken nearly two and a half minutes to arrive), Dinwiddie reported seeing "flashes of shellfire" and "rocket flares fired from the sea surface," which accurately corroborated the disaster's survivor testimony that the U-boat blasted as many as 10 artillery shells at the stricken ship while a Navy escort vessel in the vicinity fired star shells overhead in an attempt to locate the enemy U-boat.

The unfortunate target of the attack was the SS *Byron D. Benson*, a 465-foot-long, 8,000-ton oil tanker named for a 19th-century pioneer in the oil pipeline business. The ship was in transit from Port Arthur, Texas, to the oil terminals at Bayonne, New Jersey, and was laden with 100,000 barrels of crude oil, all of which was burned or spilled into the ocean. A torpedo strike on the starboard or seaward side of the tanker caused a catastrophic explosion and furious conflagration of burning oil, which erupted and spilled out of the ship and into the sea like molten lava. Twenty-five crew members were able to escape after crowding into the No. 4 lifeboat while another sailor made it safely away on a raft. The last man aboard, an oiler, watched in horror as the No. 2 lifeboat—containing the captain, three mates, the radio operator, and five seamen—was slowly pulled backwards and consumed by the billowing blackness rising from the burning sea. The oiler barely survived after jumping overboard and somehow escaping by swimming beneath the pools of burning oil. He and 26 others were rescued, but 10, including the Captain John G. MacMillian of Staten Island, New York, perished. A later investigation by Naval authorities found that the entire engine room staff abandoned the ship before shutting down the engines. As a result, the tanker "spewed burning oil over a large area, burning alive the Master and nine men who were attempting to get free in a boat launched forward of the flames."

Even though the *Byron D. Benson*, accompanied by two armed escorts, was steaming northward without navigation lights just 7 1/2 miles off Currituck Banks, the huge ship proved to be an easy target for the U-*552* and its captain, the ruthless Erich Topp. It was four months into the Battle of the Atlantic's war zone along the eastern seaboard, and twinkling shore lights were still backlighting the Allied merchant fleet.

Frank Dinwiddie lived just a few hundred yards away from the Nags Head Casino and was horrified and disgusted by what he observed. To Gov. Broughton he wrote: "At the moment of the attack, a number of bright lights were burning along the ocean front, particularly at the Nags Head Casino where a Saturday night dance was in progress. Numerous cars, coming to and from the Casino, swung their headlights over the ocean in turning around. The lights of Manteo, more than four miles from the sea, produced a brilliant glow in the sky. Any of these light sources seemed sufficient to have brought a ship several miles at sea into clear silhouette as an excellent target for the enemy. Within a few minutes after the attack last Saturday night, the bright lights facing the sea were turned out, and the Casino thereafter showed dim blue lights; but I call that locking the barn after the horse is gone."

Did America's nonchalance toward the predicament of the merchant mariner represent a disgraceful period in American history? Historian Michael Gannon responded to the question: "Yes, it is fair to say—civilians and military leaders alike deserve blame for many of the losses of ships and lives that resulted in the actions of U-boat men silhouetting ships against our shore." Even though it was plainly evident to many, including a Baptist minister, that shore lights were a treacherous betrayal of the unfortunate merchant mariner offshore, some in the government and military decided that it was the merchant mariners themselves who were causing their own demise.

CHAPTER: 10

Survivors of SS *Chenango* wave to rescuers off Currituck Beach, NC.

GROWL YOU GO, BUT GO YOU MUST

"We had strict orders: do not stop to try to pick up any [survivors]."

Francis "Biff" Bowker

As oil tankers nervously paraded past the North Carolina coast on their way to Nova Scotia to join North Atlantic convoys, copies of a simple poster prominently hung in various compartments aboard the vessels. From a distance it seemed to read: "Lights Mean Death." The phrase was surely an ironic one for any civilian sailor or U.S. Navy Armed Guard member who had been out on the night watch, gazing at the twinkling shore lights passing off their vessel's port beam.

Viewed up close, the poster actually read, "Lights may Mean Death whilst in convoy," but the words "may" and "whilst in convoy" were set in small type and were not easily discernible from a distance. The visual deception was deliberate.

The "Lights" the poster referred to were not lights on the beach but the ship's own lights—either interior cabin lights, which, when left burning, would be cast seaward as hatches and doors were opened; and navigation lights, including the commonly recognized red and green running lights indicating port and starboard sides of the ship and the white lights exhibited from atop the masthead and stern. During the first few months of 1942, when ships were being sunk one after another within a few miles of the American coast, merchant captains were said to be contributing to their own demise by neglecting to extinguish their ship's lights, thus exposing themselves to the U-boats' wrath.

"Until we got convoys, we just went straight along," said merchant sailor "Biff" Bowker. "We didn't have any way of doing the zig-zag business, and lots of ships were still shining their lights, especially some of the foreign ships."

"They were very inviting targets for U-boats," Michael Gannon explained. "In the

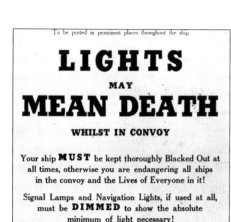

To be posted in prominent places throughout the ship

LIGHTS
MAY
MEAN DEATH
WHILST IN CONVOY

Your ship **MUST** be kept thoroughly Blacked Out at all times, otherwise you are endangering all ships in the convoy and the Lives of Everyone in it!

Signal Lamps and Navigation Lights, if used at all, must be **DIMMED** to show the absolute minimum of light necessary!

Offenders will be dealt with drastically!

You disregard this warning not only at your own Peril but unfortunately at the Peril of Everyone in the Convoy!

early part of 1942, many merchant captains took no evasive action to avoid U-boats, traveled in straight lines from buoy to buoy, and kept all their lights on. They did not practice any kind of discipline, and that's a cause for blame, no doubt. But also, they received very little instruction from the United States Navy on how to conduct themselves in wartime conditions so the blame must be shared with the Navy."

Often in society, when things are going terribly wrong and a solution is not readily apparent or available, it is human nature for authorities to seek someone else to blame. In 1942, Uncle Sam pointed his finger of blame at merchant sailors. The civilian maritime community was accused of exacerbating their losses for two unmerited reasons: disregarding blackout restrictions while operating their vessels at sea and for carelessly speaking about their ship's sailing dates, routes, and destinations in public places.

It was true that some masters of merchant vessels paid no heed to the call for steaming without navigation lights burning. *What difference does it make when we're illuminated by the hotels and resorts on shore?* some captains might have thought. And speeding along without navigation lights exposed merchant ships to another danger—collisions with other vessels, which happened from time to time. Perhaps the worst wartime collision between two ships operating as ordered without lights occurred off Jupiter Inlet, Florida, on October 20, 1943. On that night the tanker *Gulf Bell* crashed into the tanker *Gulfland*, which was filled with refined gasoline. The catastrophic accident killed 88 men, and the fire it produced was reported to have burned for more than six weeks, illuminating the night sky and the blacked-out ships sailing past.

As for civilian sailors giving away particulars about their ship's mission, purportedly the information could be overheard by nefarious Nazi agents, who would then transmit the valuable intelligence so that they could redirect U-boats offshore to intercept the ship on its way and sink it.

The origins of the general notion among U.S. authorities that "loose talk" in taverns and other public places frequented by merchant sailors was somehow aiding U-boats offshore can be traced to a January 22, 1942, Associated Press article appearing in the nation's newspapers with the headline: "How Spy Ring Caused Ship to be Sunk is Told—Farewell of Sailor Gave Tragic Tip." The story quoted Canadian seaman Allan Harvie, who recounted his experiences as a chief steward in the British merchant service and how he had been declared dead after four separate U-boat attacks but somehow miraculously survived each disastrous event.

Harvie speculated to New York reporters while in that port that Germany's successes

during the first 10 days of the January U-boat campaign might be attributed to "loose talk" by U.S. merchant sailors. He based his hypothesis on a gripping tale of espionage that supposedly resulted in one of his four escapes from death.

Allan Harvie: "We on the other side have had to learn the hard way."

An hour before Harvie's ship was due to depart an English port for the Mediterranean, a shipmate sharing a farewell pint with his girlfriend in a local pub mentioned the name of his ship, the particulars about its cargo, and the ship's destination. According to Harvie, a barmaid overheard the conversation and repeated it to the cashier, who in turn repeated it to a man in a nearby movie theater, who then telephoned an agent up the coast, who then signaled the information to a U-boat surfaced off a deserted part of the coast presumably awaiting the information, which then re-positioned itself along the ship's intended course. Consequently, the ship was torpedoed and sunk, the boyfriend was killed, and Harvie lived to champion the cause of wartime secrecy.

Harvie was not at liberty to explain how he knew the information had been transmitted from barmaid to U-boat. "They caught the spies, though," the steward told his gullible American interviewers. None of the reporters apparently made an effort to corroborate Harvie's story, and it served the Navy's propaganda purposes to a T. The press was encouraged by the military to go with it.

"I wouldn't be a bit surprised if some of your present torpedoings so close to your shores were due to fifth-column work," Harvie advised the press. It was just the fable to capture the American public's attention, even if it would disparage the merchant sailor's professional reputation.

And so was born the famous slogan "Loose Lips Sink Ships," no doubt an early product of the newly formed War Advertising Council conceived by a Madison Avenue copywriter. The slogan was succinct, symmetrical, and easy to remember. It also helped to discourage public rumor-mongering and potential panic over the startling number of reports of U-boats marauding within view of East Coast beach communities. Of course, the slogan was also unequivocal. So when the Seagram Distillers Corporation decided to adopt the phrase for production of the well-known poster it sponsored, its agency equivocated and printed the revised slogan, "Loose Lips Might Sink Ships."

For a brief time Harvie, became something of a celebrity. His photo appeared in papers across the country, and he was featured in a widely screened Paramount Studios movie trailer. In the clip, the chief steward is staged—with all seriousness—casually reading a manual titled, "How To Live," which would seem to have been pointless for Harvie to read since he had already proven that he was an expert on that subject. With a heavily furrowed brow, perhaps betraying Harvie's lack of confidence as the spokesman for confidentiality, he recites: "We on the other side have had to learn the hard way. On one occasion, a friend of mine on the ship, in saying goodbye to his girl friend in a bar room, passed on the information regarding the time of sailing, the cargo, and our destination. This was passed up the coast to a deserted place and given to an enemy submarine."

The American public who saw Harvie in the theaters or read his story in the papers, especially those living along the Atlantic coast, were astonished and scandalized that some of their neighbors might somehow be sending surreptitious signals to Nazi U-boats offshore, subsequently producing nightly explosions off their beaches. The "four-times-torpedoed" Canadian steward's role as an instrument of the wartime propaganda machine may have resulted in numerous, ubiquitous urban legends that persist to this day all along the American East Coast.

"When we had all of these shipping losses there was a certain amount of hysteria, some of it created by the United States government," Michael Gannon said. "Namely that there were German espionage agents everywhere listening for sailing dates, and anyone who was alive at that date and going to the local post office remembers posters reading, 'Loose Lips Sink Ships.' But that was never the case. The Germans never needed to know what a sailing date was. There were so many ships out there going north and south in coastwise traffic from Maine to the Florida Keys, more than enough for any U-boat to attack. So, this was a relatively useless campaign carried on by the propaganda organs of the U.S. government. 'Loose Lips Sink Ships' was a famous phrase but a useless one as it happened."

Even so, "Loose Lips Sink Ships" and the deluge of other posters, movie newsreels, and flood of baseless rumors began to wear down the morale of merchant sailors who had to run the U-boat gauntlet as ships burned, their friends drowned, and America looked the other way.

"What were we going to do?" said Biff Bowker, recalling an unhappy time in his life. "They had to run these ships, and we were getting paid to do it, and if we ran off, we were deserters just the same as if we were in the Navy. So, we had to go. 'Growl you go, but go you must,' they used to say. I tell you, it was terrible!"

Neither bright lights nor loose lips had anything to do with the sinking of the 8,000-ton oil tanker, SS *Dixie Arrow*. When the sun rose on the starboard side of the ship as it steamed northward parallel to Core Banks on March 26, 1942, its nervous crew of 33 men collectively breathed a sigh of relief, for they believed that they were out of danger, at least until nightfall. It was commonly believed at the time by military authorities, shipping companies, and merchant crews that German U-boats, like blood-thirsty vampires, would sink to the depths at first light to sleep during the day lest they expose their location and be vulnerable to retaliation by patrolling aircraft or surface vessels. Fifteen miles east of Ocracoke Inlet, U-*71* would prove that notion wrong.

Kapitänleutnant Walter Flachsenberg was on his sixth war patrol as commander of U-*71*, and he was in a desperate need to sink ships. On U-*71*'s five previous sorties from the coast of France, Flachsenberg returned to port with no ship kills, and, no doubt, Admiral Dönitz was losing confidence in his aging, 33-year-old pupil. So when U-*71* arrived

in the target-rich hunting grounds surrounding Cape Hatteras in the spring of 1942, Flachsenberg was ready to take some serious risks in order to prove his worthiness as a U-boat "Kaleun," the crew's nickname for their skipper.

On Thursday morning, March 26, Flachsenberg observed through his attack periscope the triple masts of a large oil tanker rising out of the horizon's early morning gloom, from the direction of Cape Lookout. The ship was blacked-out and zig-zagging on an irregular course close to shore. Obvious to Flachsenberg, the tanker's captain was diligent and was taking no chances. Dawn had arrived with the sea nearly flat calm, dangerously accentuating U-71's "cyclops' eye"—its attack periscope—as it protruded from the sea. The glare from the rising sun, however, would make it difficult for lookouts on the approaching tanker to look in the U-boat's direction and see the periscope, invisible among the sparkles and glimmers of the sun reflected off the water. Flachsenberg was not going to retreat to the ocean floor despite the light of day. He watched and waited. He desperately needed to sink ships.

For 18-year-old Richard Rushton of Kansas, life had become something of a bewildering carnival ride of people, places, and imagery. With the clever confidence of a high school graduate, the teenager decided, better than being drafted, he would plot a safer course and join the U.S. Merchant Marine. Rushton signed-up about as far from the sea as you can get—Nebraska. Next thing he knew, he was shivering in a quonset hut on Hoffman Island in Lower New York Bay, where the merchant service ran one of its training camps. Not long after he arrived, the Japanese bombed Pearl Harbor, but Rushton was too young and naïve to be able to imagine what that meant to him and for his future. Soon enough, he would find out.

After three months of training, they took Rushton and his classmates in the middle of the night out to a tanker in the harbor that was about to set sail for Texas, where it would receive a full load of partially refined crude oil. The tanker had a name which sounded both pleasantly bucolic and reasonably fast: SS *Dixie Arrow*. The teenager was assured that the food would be good, his quarters were commodious, and when they were in port, they would have shore leave more liberal than their Navy counterparts. A tall, handsome young man, Rushton was looking forward to his new job—especially the shore leave, where young women would surely be awaiting.

On their return trip a few weeks later, during the pre-dawn hours of March 26 as the *Dixie Arrow* cautiously rounded Cape Lookout on her return trip to a New Jersey refinery, the crewmen on watch became concerned when they realized they were steaming through seas thick with oil. On the port side of the tanker, off in the distance south of Morehead City, there were numerous fires burning in the ocean and ominous columns of blackness blotting out the night's star-filled sky.

"We knew that there was danger," Rushton said at his home near San Francisco in a 2001 interview. "The captain was very conscious about no lights, so the ship was dark every night—completely dark. [We] hugged the coast as close as we could get. We knew it was dangerous, but that's why we were getting a bonus. It seemed to be a good job."

Rushton recalled that he had just finished his breakfast and was preparing to go on

Oscar Chappell

Oscar Chappell was posthumously awarded the Merchant Marine Distinguished Service Medal, and the Liberty ship hull #1962, *Oscar G. Chappell*, built by the Todd-Houston Shipbuilding Corporation was named in his honor. Chappell's wife, Odelle Barnett Chappell, was present when the ship was launched in late 1943. In 2000, the Navy League of the United States created the Able Seaman Oscar Chappell Award for outstanding maritime stewardship. Annual presentations of the award remember Chappell with these words: "Placing his own safety beyond all considerations, his last thought and act was to assure the survival of his imperiled shipmates. His magnificent courage and selfless disregard of his own life constitute a degree of heroism, which can be an enduring inspiration to seamen of the United States Merchant Marine everywhere."

watch when a torpedo tore into the *Dixie Arrow*'s starboard side at 8:58 a.m. There had been no warning, and none of the men on the bridge, nor the lookouts on the bow, saw the torpedo coming or the U-boat's periscope among the gentle swells of the sea. "When the torpedo struck, there was sort of a rolling motion," Rushton said. "It's not a jarring [motion] because the ship is so big. It sort of rolled the ship, and we came out of breakfast, and we could see the fire and smoke."

Daylight abruptly turned to darkness as oil smoke swirled, undulated and rose. For the men of the *Dixie Arrow*, a "good job" suddenly turned into a living hell. Death beckoned at every turn and sometimes disguised itself as a means of escape.

"One of the older sailors went to a lifeboat, and he panicked," Rushton said. "He took the line off the cleats and dropped the boat, but it was on the starboard side where the fire was. He had [the line] around his arm, and it launched him out into the fire. The boat probably weighed 2,000 pounds or so. Steel, too. Full of supplies. He was one of the older sailors, and he knew better, but he panicked." The sailor vanished into the fire.

Able Seaman Oscar Chappell stared into the eyes of death, and he didn't blink, nor did he panic. Chappell was a 30-year-old Texan from a small town on the rail line between Houston and Dallas. Additional details of Chappell's life before that Thursday morning in March 1942 have eluded history's memory, but what he did on that day ensured that his name will always be remembered.

Chappell was in the wheelhouse when the first torpedo struck almost directly beneath the deck house. He was the only man on the bridge not killed, although he was believed to have been wounded by the first blast. A second torpedo followed and seconds later impacted amidships, fatally breaking the back of the 8,000-ton tanker. Then a third torpedo hit near the same spot. Kapitän-leutnant Flachsenberg was not messing around.

The engine room crew immediately shut down the engines, but the ship continued its

SS *Dixie Arrow* burns off Ocracoke Island.

forward momentum. From his vantage point high above the deck, Chappell could see a group of men running forward who seemed to be cornered by flames spreading across the foredeck. Chappell knew they had only one chance to live. If he turned the decelerating ship into the light breeze, it might momentarily reverse the direction of the flames, although it would also turn the fire upon his own station atop the bridge. Chappell did not hesitate, saving the lives of the seven men huddled near the bow, and sacrificing his own by doing so. Paul Meyers was one of the men Chappell saved. He later reported what he saw: "Fire was shooting up all about [Chappell]. He saw several men trapped by the flames that the wind was blowing around them. He turned the ship's head hard right, which took the flames off the bow but threw them directly upon himself. He lasted only a few minutes after that. He died at the helm."

As the *Dixie Arrow* slowed, cascades of burning oil circled the ship, threatening to engulf the vessel and leave no escape path for those men attempting to get away in a lifeboat or life raft. At the moment of Oscar Chappell's unselfish act of heroism, Richard Rushton was about 400 feet away, near the *Dixie Arrow*'s stern. Explosions both large and small rumbled below, and the crewmen were uncertain whether they were being hit with more torpedoes, gunfire, or the oil tanks were detonating. Even with the best training and coolest heads, a torpedoed tanker crew had to act fast and precisely in an environment of total chaos and confusion.

"The entire starboard side was ablaze, and the oil was pouring out," recalled Rushton. "I got into the [aft port #4] lifeboat and put the plug in the bottom and was getting it ready for launching. It's a tense time, I suppose, but we had practiced this—the lifeboat drill—a time or two. The ship was still underway, and the fire was pouring out and was coming around the back. The fire seemed to be close. We had guys pulling on the big oars, and I remember one guy snapped his, he was pulling so hard. These were probably two-inch-diameter oars."

Rushton was one of eight men in the lifeboat when it was lowered over the side. When the lifeboat splashed into the water, the ship was still moving at a fast enough rate that the lifeboat nearly swamped as it was being dragged along—it was still attached to the falls (ropes and pulleys used to lower heavy objects). The other six men on deck who were tending the falls and who were intending to lower themselves on lines to the lifeboat had to cut the ropes and cast the lifeboat adrift, giving up their own chance for survival. The forward momentum of the ship carried it past the lifeboat, which was then unable to catch up to retrieve the men on deck. The six men on deck were left with no choice but to jump overboard. Now swimming in the burning sea, the six men succeeded in reaching a wooden raft and barely escaped the engulfing surge of burning oil.

Amidst the crackle and roar of the fire could be heard a shrieking wind, although moments before the first torpedo strike there had been reported little or no breeze. The records are filled with similar accounts of burning oil tankers, which often report light or variable winds before the attack. But when the raging inferno of the burning ship heats the air above, which races skyward at an ever increasing speed, cold ocean air rushes in to replace it, creating a nightmarish vortex, a tornadic, 360-degree wind, inexorably drawing everything surrounding the ship back into the fires.

Not far from Rushton's lifeboat was another man, alone on a wooden raft. Flames danced and leapt around him as he frantically tried to escape by paddling. "We tried to get this sailor off the raft because the rafts were no good," Rushton said. "They were made for survival, I guess, but they drifted right into the fire. And they're heavy, and you can't paddle them. So we tried to get this guy to jump in the water." One of the more experienced sailors, an engineer, called out to the man on the raft, but the man responded that he didn't know how to swim. "He wouldn't get off the raft," Rushton recalled. "He went right into the fire." It was a gruesome education for an 18-year-old not long out of high school.

Despite countless lifeboat drills, fire drills, man overboard drills, and years of experience, there quickly came a moment for merchant sailors on a torpedoed tanker when the only chance of survival was to jump. Seven men leaped off the bow of the *Dixie Arrow*, another eight off the stern. Swimmers now had to avoid the flood of black crude oil, regardless of whether it was on fire or not. "The oil is so thick, some people thought you could swim under it," Rushton remembers. "[We had] this training of taking your hands up and splashing, but it was too thick for that. The people who were actually in the water grew like snowballs; they were [completely] black. They floated all right, the oil kept them buoyant, but they could hardly be pulled from the water."

Into the sea jumped the men from the bow, hoping to be able to navigate the circuitous path through the narrowing spaces free of oil. Two men, Fred Spiese and Alex Waszczseyn, got ready to jump together. They were buddies aboard the ship and had said to one another, it's now or never. Spiese looked at his friend and confessed that he didn't know how to swim. But looking behind him, the alternative of burning to death did not look any more appealing than drowning. They jumped. When Waszczseyn surfaced and searched for his friend, Spiese was nowhere to be found—he seemed to have vanished. Waszczseyn assumed that Spiese had been consumed by a pool of burning oil.

Within seconds after the *Dixie Arrow* exploded with a concussion that thundered for

miles around upon the initial torpedo strike, and with the coal-black mushroom cloud that rose to thousands of feet into the air, ships at sea and people for miles along the islands of the Outer Banks knew another ship had been attacked. Motor lifeboats, patrol aircraft, and the destroyer USS *Tarbell* all headed in the direction of the stricken tanker. The first to arrive, about 30 minutes after the attack was the *Tarbell*, which carefully approached the debris field and oil-strewn waters surrounding the foundering tanker, while the destroyer's officers fretted about whether the enemy was still lurking nearby. Rushton's lifeboat was soon spotted, and cargo nets were hung off the gunwales of the warship's stern. "They don't really stop," Rushton said. "They throw these big heavy cargo nets over the side, and they tell you to jump on so they don't stop. Everybody jumped on as they came by our lifeboat. That was an unusual thing I had never done before."

The *Tarbell*'s skipper was extremely edgy. They were taking a great risk by rescuing the oil-soaked merchantmen in the water. Fourteen more men were flailing in the pitching seas or clinging to pieces of wreckage. Before all were fished out of the water, the *Tarbell*'s captain ordered a couple of depth charges to be dropped, simply as a warning should the U-boat still be in the vicinity. The concussion of the exploding charges thumped the few men still in the water so hard that one lost consciousness, but all were rescued alive. Nine men, including Chappell, the captain, and all of the deck officers died aboard the ship. The man on the raft who couldn't swim also perished, as did the older sailor who launched himself into the burning sea. But when the survivors were all gathered on the deck of the USS *Tarbell*, there sat Fred Spiese, nearly unrecognizable under all the oil but alive. On March 26, 1942, Spiese taught himself how to swim.

The Navy destroyer immediately left the scene and delivered the 22 *Dixie Arrow* survivors to Morehead City, where the least-injured were quarantined at the Monticello Hotel. Serious-looking men in dark suits soon arrived and began interviewing the merchant sailors, including Richard Rushton. "We heard it was the FBI who was interviewing us. They kept us confined for two days, quizzing us before they put us on the train and sent us to New York. They wanted to know the particulars, how we happened to take this particular ship and so on. For two days they quizzed us."

Rushton and the other survivors suspected that the FBI believed that there had been a traitor among them, an enemy agent who had shared secret sailing information so that the U-*71* would know where to be in order to sink the tanker. "I don't know," Rushton added, shaking his head. "I can't imagine that anybody would give the secrets out and then get on the ship. It wouldn't be a good way of going."

Not long after Rushton returned to New York City, he sought the nearest Navy recruiter. "My parents probably had something to say about me not going back to merchant ships after [the Germans] fired those torpedoes at us on my first trip. They didn't think it was a very safe occupation so I didn't go back. I decided I wanted to be a pilot so I went into the Navy. It was a pleasant life on the ships, but it didn't appear to [afford] a very good future."

Rushton's change of career paths was not out of the ordinary among those young men serving in the U.S. Merchant Marine in the early months of 1942. Morale was declining as rapidly as ships were sinking. This was a problem that became patently apparent to Naval

Survivors of SS *Dixie Arrow* at Morehead City.

authorities. The March War Diary recorded by the New York offices of the Navy's Eastern Sea Frontier (ESF) commander, Admiral Andrews, quoted a merchant officer who complained that his civilian crewmen often got drunk in port and were hard to handle. To this, the ESF wrote, "As the weeks went by, they were not only hard to handle, they were increasingly hard to find. After a typical trip, one captain stated that it was impossible to keep a good crew on board, that on making his home port he lost 13 of a crew of 30. Another more emotional master gave as his opinion that unless the Navy forced personnel of tankers to sail, shipping would stop, and he himself would wind up in a morgue."

Patriotic propaganda on posters and in movie newsreels attempted to bolster the civilian sailor's resolve to continue their dangerous life at sea. "American merchant seaman know the U-boat's sting, but they sign to sail again," trumpeted one such newsreel. But many merchant seaman didn't sign to sail again. Some rushed to the recruiter's office to join the Army or Marines, opting for foreign foxholes over the risks faced within sight of American beaches. As the losses continued to mount—peaking in U.S. waters in 1942 between mid-March and mid-April—some civilian sailors could no longer be cheered by patriotic propaganda.

"When the losses were still very high, a certain demoralization did enter into the hiring halls of the merchant marine, and some men gave up that life," Michael Gannon said. "They were making more money than people in the Army or the Navy, but that wasn't enough money to continue risking their own lives as they were."

Ironically, for many of those merchant sailors who did sign to sail again, their loyalty was questioned as men who might be sympathetic to the Nazi cause. According to District Intelligence Offices quoted in the ESF War Diary, "That there was, and still is, Axis activity among the crews cannot be doubted." But Professor Gannon believes much of this mistrust was unwarranted: "The principal finger of blame that was pointed at merchant mariners was that they belonged to unions that were allegedly communist dominated," he said. "And they were put down by the people in the military and people in the government at large. But these seaman were taking more hits, facing more danger, than anybody at the time except for our troops engaged in combat in the Pacific. Who was facing the major danger and losing lives by the thousands during the first six months of 1942 in the Atlantic? It was the merchant mariners. And they were not given their due as men of courage, as men of patriotism, as men who, once sunk, went right back and signed on again."

Even if merchant sailors were known to be loyal Americans, the Navy observed, they

were still liable to unwittingly divulge information useful to enemy agents. According to the ESF War Diary, bars in ports like Manhattan's Old Hamburg, the Highway Tavern in Jersey, and Schmidt's in Bayonne, were the German agents' favorite hangouts, where they would often trick the sailors into saying too much. "Various other tricks were resorted to; the most ingenious and least successful being the anonymous telephone call," stated the ESF War Diary. "Wives of men on ships would be called and asked by a feminine voice, 'Has Charlie gotten back yet?' or questions of a similar nature. This ruse rarely worked, and indeed it is hard to determine why so much time was spent trying to obtain such information about coastwise shipping. As the report of one of the District Intelligence Offices said, the submarines could lie off focal points up and down the coast and await the arrival of ships without having any previous knowledge of sailing times."

Richard Rushton

Many young men who were torpedoed off the American coast and chose to give up their better salaries for a less-lucrative enlistment in the military did so for one important reason. As a GI, they and their families back home were eligible for veterans' benefits. Upon returning to shore, the sometimes naked, oil-stained men of the merchant service who survived one or more U-boat attacks and days drifting in lifeboats or on wreckage typically got a handshake and, on some occasions, an advance on their pay so that they could purchase some clean clothes and other necessities. If civilian sailors were to die, their loved ones received little or no financial support. It took more than 35 years for merchant mariners' wartime sacrifices to be rewarded, following a lengthy legal battle and demands by the U.S. Congress. The Defense Department and the Veterans Administration finally recognized their combatant status and awarded veteran benefits in 1988.

Then there were the countless numbers of men—and in some cases, women and children—who may have survived a U-boat attack but were never seen again. Innocent victims of a preventable maritime tragedy, who—huddled in a lifeboat, or raft, or riding atop a piece of wreckage—were swept into the great Atlantic abyss and to their inevitable, lonely deaths. As the months of winter and spring slipped by, the ocean waters off the U.S. East coast were populated with an unknown number of humans hoping and praying to be rescued as invisible currents and eddies of the Gulf Stream or Labrador Current carried them to and fro. After enduring days and nights in frigid seas, suffering pangs of hunger, fending off sharks, and deliriously resisting the powerful urge to drink seawater, there were many instances when survivors were left aghast as vessels, and sometimes amphibious aircraft, would appear from the distant horizon and pass right by without

stopping to rescue them. There were even some instances when passing sailors waved to hapless victims floating on wreckage or on a raft in a macabre sort of encouragement.

"We had strict orders: do not stop to try to pick up any [survivors] because those submarines are probably just waiting for you to stop," Biff Bowker said. "We saw ships sinking; gosh, maybe we didn't see as many as I think we did, but we did see ships sinking and passed right by them."

To be fair, merchant captains had been advised by the military to keep moving no matter what and also that survivors of U-boat sinkings would soon be rescued by Coast Guard patrol boats or the occasional seaplane. Unfortunately, in the first months of the war, patrol boats and seaplanes were few, and the Atlantic Ocean was a great, boundless expanse.

After making one wartime passage aboard the schooner *Herbert L. Rawding*, Biff Bowker was reassigned to a motor vessel transporting the Allies' most precious cargo—troops. "I was third mate on her," Bowker said. "And we saw a lifeboat right ahead. We stopped for just enough time; we came right up to it at full speed and stopped just fast enough to take the men aboard quickly. We had plenty of ropes over the side, and we just got 'em aboard quickly not knowing whether we were going to get torpedoed or not."

Few castaways had the luck of Irishman James Bradley, who, along with Belgian Joseph Dieltiens, withstood the cataclysmic destruction of his Panamanian manganese ore freighter, *Chenango*, 50 miles east of Currituck Beach. It sank so fast (in less than two minutes) that the other 30 crew members went down with the ship. Bradley and Dieltiens had been ejected by the blast into the sea, where they were both able to climb aboard a raft. Twelve days passed, and so did various aircraft, which failed to spot the men on a sea filled with a mind-numbing volume of wreckage. Neither man could speak the other's language so there wasn't much to talk about to pass the hours. With each day, the two men weakened, and their hopes for survival faded, but on the 12th day they were spotted by an army patrol plane and later rescued by a Coast Guard Hall PH-2 flying boat. Bradley and Dieltiens were flown to the Norfolk Navy base where they were rushed to the hospital. Soon after, sadly, Dieltiens succumbed to his injuries and extreme exposure. Bradley, with the luck of the Irish, survived, the only man left from the ill-fated *Chenango*.

Robert Emmet Kelley, 17, of Philadelphia, also had the luck of the Irish. He was a survivor of a tanker torpedoed off of Aruba in late March 1942. For 21 days, Kelley sat with 10 other shipmates in a lifeboat that wandered aimlessly in the Caribbean Sea. As the men died, one by one, the teenager was forced to bury his buddies at sea until he was the only one left. Regrettably, his story was not unique—there are just too many to tell.

One account of survivors adrift that does stand out among the many, and deserves to be told, concerns the victims of the torpedoed American tanker, SS *Muskogee*.

On the 2nd of March, 1942, U-*123*, under the command of Kapitänleutnant Reinhard Hardegen, slipped her lines attached to her tender near the mouth of the Blavet River in France. Hardegen plotted a course that would take the U-boat directly to Cape Hatteras so that they could resume their mission to sever the vital "artery" of war matériel being transported along the southern American coast. Twenty days later, about 975 miles east-northeast of the North Carolina Outer Banks, U-*123* chanced upon the unlucky tanker

Muskogee, steaming alone on its way to Nova Scotia from Venezuela. In his war diary, Hardegen referred to the ship as the U-boat's "Sunday roast."

A single torpedo from U-*123* sent the old *Muskogee* to the bottom, thousands of feet down. Some men were able to escape the sinking ship, but only one wooden raft containing seven men got away successfully. Hardegen maneuvered U-*123* over to the raft to ask his victims the name of their ship, its nationality, and its registered tonnage. The U-boat skipper made

Sailors of SS *Muskogee* greet their executioners aboard U-*123*.

no mention in his log if he offered the frightened men any provisions or directions to the nearest land as he did on some other occasions—perhaps because no land was near enough to which to direct them. It was likely that Hardegen offered them encouragement, assuaging his own conscience that the castaways might somehow survive. The survivors were doomed, however, unless they were to be found by another passing vessel, an improbable occurrence considering their location in that infrequently traveled area of the sea, and far beyond the range of shore-based air patrols.

U-*123*'s German propaganda photographer, Rudolf Meisinger, snapped some pictures of the *Muskogee* sailors who appeared forlorn and helpless as they huddled precariously on their little wooden craft. One man appears to be waving. Another is cupping his hands to his mouth as he shouts to Hardegen who was standing at the railing of the U-boat's anti-aircraft gun platform. In the center of the photo is a sailor who has the grim look of a man who knows his fate—a vacant stare of resignation; the sailor to his right stares at the German camera with an unmistakable enmity.

None of the seven sailors were ever seen again. All hands from the *Muskogee* were lost.

Of the tens of thousands of photographs produced during World War II, none are more haunting, more heart-rending, nor better representative of the plight of the valiant merchant seaman than the Rudolf Meisinger image of the seven *Muskogee* sailors. To date, only three of the men have been identified: Chief Mate Morgan J. Finucane, Third Mate Nathaniel D. Foster, and Able Seaman Anthony G. Sousa.

Thirty minutes before the photo was taken, all seven were safe and contented as they went about their business aboard their ship, unaware that the seconds of their lives were ticking down, that the inescapable pathway to death awaiting us all would soon appear before them. Now, as their fragile wooden raft bobbed up and down alongside the steel hull of the forbidding German leviathan, the American sailors reconciled their fate; they stared into their executioner's eyes and wondered, *Why us?*

CHAPTER 11

CHILDREN IN THE WAR ZONE

"That summer we had to almost give up going swimming in the ocean; it was just full of oil."

Ormond Fuller

By the end of March 1942, an under-publicized but pivotal theater of operations of World War II was centered just 10 miles off the coast of North Carolina, surrounding the approaches to both Diamond Shoals and Cape Lookout Shoals. For centuries, this frequently traversed ocean passage had been feared by seafarers as a graveyard of ships; in the spring of '42, it even seemed foreboding to the mighty U.S. Navy. As north- and southbound shipping routes consolidated off the protruding coastline of North Carolina's Outer Banks, the area became a temporary focal point in the broader Battle of the Atlantic. U.S. military forces, within American territorial waters as a whole, were absorbing a defeat far worse than Pearl Harbor and with far greater consequences.

With the beginning of spring, hardly two months had passed since Operation Paukenschläg's five U-boats returned to France. During that time, as many as 35 more of Admiral Dönitz's U-boats had followed in their wake, sinking or damaging 122 ships along the Atlantic and Gulf coasts of the United States. The loss of ships and war matériel to German U-boats was gradually weakening Great Britain and, if left unchallenged, threatened to delay or jeopardize plans for the Allied invasion of Europe. It may have been the beginning of spring, but offshore black clouds of burning oil towered over burning ships, casting a pall over eastern America.

On the fragile barrier islands off the mainland of North Carolina once forgotten communities were irrevocably changed. Oil from sunken tankers washed ashore in such quantities—in fact, millions of barrels—to make many modern oil spills seem minor. Corpses drifted in the ocean and washed up on the beaches, sometimes to be discovered

by innocent children. Empty lifeboats were found riddled with bullet holes, generating angry claims that the German U-boat crews were shooting survivors. Adults traded rumors with their family members and closest friends about visitors or neighbors who might be German sympathizers, spies, or saboteurs. A centuries-old but diminishing salvage industry was once again active. And thousands of servicemen arrived on the islands to defend America's shores, overwhelming the post offices with mail. It was nothing less than a war zone, and the residents of the North Carolina coast had no choice but to watch as war was waged on their doorsteps.

Gibb Gray of Avon recalls the morning when the *Dixie Arrow* was torpedoed south of the Cape Hatteras Lighthouse. "I was on my way to school, and just before we got to the school house the whole ground shook, a violent explosion," Gray said. "We looked down toward the lighthouse; it was south of the lighthouse where the smoke was coming from. That was the *Dixie Arrow*. We skipped school then; we didn't go to school. We went right over to the beach and started running down and watching the lifeboats."

"You could hear them," said Buxton resident Mary Ormond Fuller, who was in her late teens when the U-boats ravaged the shipping lanes off Cape Hatteras. "You could hear the shots, and you could hear the glass rattle and the things shake when they would go off at night. You could see the fires offshore burning."

"You would see the warfare in the ocean, the ships being sunk and fires at night," recalls Stocky Midgett, Jr. The professional bus driver had reached the ripe old age of 14 by the spring of 1942, and, despite the alarming reality that the murderous tides of World War II had washed-up on the beaches of Hatteras Island, Stocky, Jr. and his brothers continued to make daily trips between Whalebone Junction and the village of Hatteras. The important service the Midgett brothers provided now included transporting Navy and Coast Guard men to their new assignments at various stations on Hatteras and Ocracoke islands.

The boy bus drivers had a new hazard to avoid, in addition to sudden sinkholes and axle-swallowing sand. "Why, during the days a lot of times, you would see a lot of wreckage wash up on the beach," recalled Midgett. Few Coast Guard patrols saw more of the beach on a daily basis than the Midgett brothers, so there were many times when they reported war-related flotsam to the authorities. "We were in contact with [the Coast Guard] from time to time," Midgett said. "Back then, a little bit of everything would wash up on the beach; some of the ships that were wrecked as well as some that were destroyed, different parts had washed up."

Midgett seemed to remember something else, but he was reticent to say more. He was asked if he saw bodies on the beach. "Yeah, I have seen some bodies on the beach," Midgett replied with a look that made it clear that he didn't want to say anything more about the human toll inflicted by the Germans or the lasting impact it may have had on a youngster's psyche.

"We had concerns, but there wasn't a whole lot we could do about it," Midgett added. "We lived here, and we worked here, and it became a natural thing to us. [But] there were deep concerns. I've been upstairs with my mother, and we had to have black-out curtains at our houses. Of course, you would peek through the windows to see the explosions at night."

Ocracoke native Blanche Howard Joliff was in her early 20s when the war was fought

Lifeboats washed up on Outer Banks beach.

off of her island, and she remembered how the war altered life at the once-tranquil harbor village. "We'd hear these explosions almost any time of the day or night, and it would shake the houses," Joliff said. "We got all of our drinking water and most of the water we used from cisterns, and sometimes the explosions cracked the cisterns and damaged the plaster in some of the houses."

The war being fought fewer than a dozen miles from the villages of the North Carolina coast became an ordinary facet of daily life. "We sort of got used to it, you know, hearing it," said Gray. "It would mostly be in the distance, the explosions were. We wasn't too scared. It just become a regular, routine thing of hearing all of this going on, all these explosions."

Manson Meekins of Avon recalled the local sentiment as U-boat attacks peaked in late-March of '42 when he briefly returned home after enlisting in the Coast Guard. His father, CWO-4 George H. Meekins, was the chief of the Coast Guard installation located near the point of Cape Hatteras (in the same buildings on Lighthouse Road used today as a ranger station by the National Park Service).

The younger Meekins doesn't remember his father as being much of a talker. The elder Meekins didn't share with his son much about what was happening offshore; he didn't have to—torpedoed ships were visible for anyone who cared to look. One day, the younger Meekins climbed the lookout tower at his father's station. "By use of binoculars I scanned the area of the ocean, and I counted 13 different wrecks. There were freighters, tankers, mostly tankers, I suppose. And some had their bows sticking out of the water; some had their sterns sticking out of the water; and mostly [there were] masts you could

Oil on the Beaches

In an unofficial accounting of the quantity of petroleum cargoes carried aboard tankers torpedoed and sunk between Cape Lookout and the Virginia border between January and July 1942, it is estimated that more than 150 million gallons of oil was spilled in the ocean or carried to the sea floor in unruptured tanks. (This quantity of unrefined oil would produce approximately 75 million gallons of gasoline and fill the tanks of 3.75 million cars, as well as produce additional petroleum products.) The amount of oil lost in the ocean, a considerable portion of which washed up on the beaches of the Outer Banks, represents 15 times the volume of oil spilled by the *Exxon Valdez* in the Gulf of Alaska in 1989, based on the official estimate of 11 million U.S. gallons by the State of Alaska's *Exxon Valdez* Oil Spill Trustee Council. This unofficial estimate would rank the WWII disaster off North Carolina's coast among the top 10 spills in world history but less than the 184 million gallons spilled during the 2010 BP/Deepwater Horizon Gulf Oil Disaster or the 336 million gallons estimated to have been spilled in the Persian Gulf during the 1991 war to liberate Kuwait.

see." The sea surrounding Diamond Shoals was a ship cemetery, and the hulks of Allied ships served as their own tombstones.

As for the general attitude of the island's residents, a well-earned stoicism prevailed, forged from years of natural disasters and hardship. For Outer Bankers, catastrophe and suffering had always been ever-lurking shadows in their daily endeavors.

"It was a lackluster type of feeling," Meekins said. "People knew what was going on, and they were making statements of sympathy while the merchant seamen out there were being torpedoed and drowned and burned in the oil. But no one seemed to be afraid or worried. It was just something that was happening. They'd go about their business as if nothing was going on. You'd hear an explosion go up, 'rrrooom,' and somebody would say, 'there goes another one.'"

Adult residents would do their best to live their lives as normally as possible. Young people, however, sometimes found themselves knee-deep in the war's remnants.

"That summer we had to almost give up going swimming in the ocean; it was just full of oil—you'd get it all over you," Fuller said. "Most families around had this bucket or can with this brush on it that you kept at the front door that you [used to] clean the oil off every time you came in if you'd been to the beach. Oil was everywhere."

"If any oil had washed up during the night and the wind had blown from the southwest, you couldn't see it, it was covered up by that fine sand," said Gray. "We'd step in it before we knew it, and we'd probably be 5 or 6 inches deep. What we'd have to do then is come right back to the village to my dad's store over here. He sold kerosene, and we'd get rags and clean our feet of that oil. It was hard to get off. Then we'd go back over [to the beach] and continue swimming. You know, those hot summer days."

Gray was a bright, inquisitive, and observant

adolescent during the war years. Every day for him was an adventure and a learning experience. The things Gray and his friends were being taught in school seemed not nearly as interesting and educational as what was happening outside of the classroom. They were living in a war zone for all practical purposes, just as if they were children in Europe or on an island in the South Pacific. It was an exciting time for an adolescent who didn't know better.

Back then, each Outer Banks village had its own school house, and during the war years the teachers were often older adults who came out of retirement to fill-in while the younger teachers were elsewhere serving their country. Gray remembers how easy it was to escape the classroom when more interesting opportunities awaited outside.

"We had older people, right old teachers, and we just went wild then," Gray said. "We didn't have much discipline with them old teachers. You could do anything. When we wanted to get out, [there] was a large blackboard a little to the side of the classroom with a window behind it. It had a pencil sharpener on the end, and when the weather was warmer the window was up. When we wanted to get out, to go out somewhere, we'd go up to sharpen our pencil. [We'd] keep looking at the teacher, and when he turned his head, we would dart behind the blackboard and jump out of the window. Two or three fellows could do it, and [the teacher] never knew what happened." At least, in Gray's mind, the teacher never seemed to know what happened.

There was a lot going on that would interest young boys outside of the classroom in 1942. Every now and then, the youngsters could see in the sky aircraft of various kinds and they prided themselves on being able to identify each one by its profile—Consolidated PBY Catalina flying boats, Lockheed Hudson A-20s and A-29s, Vought OS2U Kingfishers, privately owned Stinson 10As and Fairchild 24s, and K-type non-rigid airships. Likewise, offshore, mirage-like shapes of freighters, colliers, transports, tankers, cutters, and destroyers could be discerned through the wavering haze of the inversion layer above the horizon like shape-shifting ghosts. Every now and then, youngsters—and adults, too—would swear that they had seen the distinctive shape of a submarine; everybody wanted to be able to say that they saw one. And, of course, along the beaches could be found the peculiar and exotic treasures of war.

"When the wind was mostly from the east, we knew something would probably wash up with the east wind," Gray begins as he recalls a favorite memory. "One morning, me and a friend of mine, we went over to the beach early, and the first thing we saw was a lifeboat [that] had washed up during the night. On the side of her was the SS *Alexandria*, and it had shrapnel holes in it, like from a torpedo blast, I guess. And it had compartments around the side. [But] we didn't have no way to get the thing open so we came right back into the village and got a hammer and a screwdriver and went back to go get in her."

Gray was a smart lad—and a hungry kid. He knew something good to eat might be found among the survival supplies hidden inside the lifeboat's watertight provision lockers. National rationing had not yet begun during the first six months of 1942, but many favorite foods, notably sweets, were hard to come by, nowhere more so than on the isolated barrier islands off the coast of North Carolina. Gray knew, despite his young age, that lifeboats often contained chocolate, candy, or chewing gum. And even though his father owned a general store in Avon village, the few sweets they had in stock were for

Maude White

paying customers. Now Gray and his friend had a chance to get for themselves a tasty treat without having to pay for it. Unfortunately, the boys didn't return to the lifeboat quickly enough.

"There was a Coast Guard truck there," Gray said with a smirk and a slight shake of his head portraying his disappointment. "They had gone and took the provisions out. There were chocolates and canned water and something called [pemmican].[3] It was a mixture of some healthy food or some other."

The boys, unintimidated by the military patrol, informed the Coast Guard men that the contents of the lifeboat were theirs on the basis that they had found it first only a short while before. Their pleas fell on deaf ears.

"We thought they'd give us some candy, but they didn't offer us nothing!"

The Coasties must have been hungry, too.

The populations of small beach communities along the coast of North Carolina more than doubled in the spring of 1942 with the arrival of thousands of servicemen assigned to new Navy and Coast Guard bases, hospitals, harbor control installations, artillery emplacements, and lifeboat stations. Adding to the numbers, a flurry of civilian contractors and laborers joined Navy Seebees and the Civil Engineer Corps, building dozens of barracks, ammunition dumps, radio and watch towers, heavily reinforced gun mounts, and aircraft hangers. Unlike the black gooey morass of oil which befouled the beaches of the state and the legs of her young people, the arrival of men in uniform was mostly welcomed by island residents. To some extent, the many servicemen made the islanders feel a little safer, in the unlikely but widely feared possibility that the enemy would launch a full-scale assault of their sparsely populated and lightly defended part of the coast. The outsiders also spent money at the local grocer's or at the nearest entertainment establishment, producing an appreciated uptick in the islands' post-Depression economy. They also frequented the post offices, which soon became burdened with incoming and outgoing mail. "We had a lot of people here during the war, a lot of people," said Blanche Joliff of Ocracoke, who worked for Postmaster Elizabeth O'Neal Howard at the village post office in her early-20s and remembers all of the extra work. "We worked hard. We really did. There was a lot of mail coming in."

Like many small, rural communities in America, residents of coastal villages in North Carolina were close knit and suspicious of newcomers, but during the first months of the

war they quickly became overwhelmed with strangers, many of
whom were men in their late-teens
or early-20s and carrying guns.
"They were from everywhere,"
Gray remembered. "They each carried a 38-caliber pistol with them."

The remote islands of the coast
of North Carolina have always
been cherished as outposts of liberty, where people could go about
their business unrestrained by the
arbitrary edicts of government
or their fellow man. A spirit of
freedom existed since the earliest
days of the Colonial era when the
islands were initially populated
by shipwreck survivors, runaway

Mary Ormond (White) Fuller

servants, subsistence fishermen, stockmen, and wreckers. Outer Bankers, especially,
believed they had been endowed with a birthright to freely roam their sandy islands and
fish the seas without limitations. But in 1942 all that changed. Much of the islands, and
some of the offshore waters, were restricted for civilian travel at night, primarily for the
safety of the local inhabitants. The children of the islands and of the sea, however—especially the curious and inquisitive—found it hard to follow orders. Sometimes, even the
adults had difficulty minding their own business.

Mary Ormond (White) Fuller had come home to Buxton for the summer of '42 after
attending college in Raleigh. Fuller's parents were like many adults on the economically
disadvantaged Outer Banks—they toiled tirelessly at numerous jobs to keep their families
fed, housed, and clothed. In some instances, the parents saved enough money to send their
children, like Fuller, away to college. Her mother, Maude Leigh (Miller) White, was postmaster for the village, a teacher, and ran a boarding home. Fuller's father, Estus Preston White,
had worked on survey boats and helped manage a Civilian Conservation Corps camp at Cape
Hatteras before the war; he also helped run the boarding house during the war. Both were
active in politics. They also enjoyed a nightly game of cards with their closest friends.

Fuller, whose given name and ancestry are believed by her family to have originated
from the purported 14th wife of Black Beard the pirate, recalled a night in 1942 when
curiosity got the best of both her and her mother.

"The gentleman who was in charge of the Cape Hatteras Coast Guard Station [the afore-
mentioned CWO George H. Meekins] came to our house quite often—my mother loved to
play cards, and so did my daddy," Fuller said. "They played cards nearly every night, and
when something would happen [and Chief Meekins] was needed at the station, the Coast
Guard boys would come after him. When that happened, we knew something was going on."

On one such night, something had happened that required Meekin's attention. Fuller

continued the story: "My mother said, 'Something's going on, or they wouldn't pull him out like that. Let's go see.'"

So, in a flagrant violation of wartime restrictions, mother and daughter drove the family car in the dark of night, with headlights and taillights turned off, out to the Cape Hatteras Lighthouse and parked near the former keeper's quarters.[4] It was a flagrant violation, particularly on the part of Maude White, because at the time she was serving as a volunteer for the U.S. Navy's Coast Watcher program, and looking over the Coast Guard's shoulder was not part of her watching responsibilities.

"We left the car and crawled up the sand dunes, and out in the distance we could see this lifeboat floating in the water. We laid there in the grass on top of that dune for one hour, I reckon. It was getting real late so my mother said, 'Let's go home, it's nothing.'

"The next day, Mr. Meekins came over, and not being warned to keep my mouth shut, I asked, 'Was there anything in that lifeboat last night?' And he looked at me real funny, and he said, 'What did you say?' And I said, 'Was there anything in that lifeboat last night or any bodies or anything?'

"He said, 'Girl, how did you know there was a lifeboat out there? How'd you find that out? How'd you know?' Then I knew I said something wrong." Fuller's mother apparently made no effort to come to her daughter's defense.

"I hated to tell on my mother so I said, 'Well, after you left last night, we went out and crawled up on the dunes and watched.' He put his finger in my face, and he said, 'Let me tell you something. You are going to be the only casualties in this war!' He said, 'Don't you know that those boys patrolling those beaches are from out West somewhere, and they've shot up everything on the beach. Everything that moves, they shoot it.' He said, 'Don't you know you're lucky you wasn't killed! If you had moved and they had seen you, they'd have shot you.' He said, 'Don't you ever do anything like that!'

"But I never did tell on my mother. I just said, 'we,' and I didn't tell him it was my mother," Fuller said with a grin. The astute first-year college student, no doubt, was well acquainted with the slogan, "Loose lips might sink ships."

The White family of Buxton included a fourth member—Fuller's younger sister, 13-year-old Carol, a self-styled tomboy. Since the 1950s, tens of thousands of North Carolina young people have become enthralled with a novelized character loosely based on the wartime adventures of Carol, her real-life Ocracoke pony, Ivy, and her hound dog, Boozie. Carol White Dillon's fictional name was Taffy—Taffy of Torpedo Junction—made famous by a children's novel of the same name written by retired school teacher and journalist, Nell Wise Wechter. Wechter's novel follows the rambunctious exploits of a 13-year-old Cape Hatteras girl as she and her pony discover a small ring of German spies and saboteurs operating in an old and mysterious house secluded on a sand hill in Buxton Woods. The true story, which also involved Carol's older sister, Ormond, and their postmaster mother, was equally enthralling and involved real German spies who were part of a much larger espionage network that has since been well-documented by the Federal Bureau of Investigation.

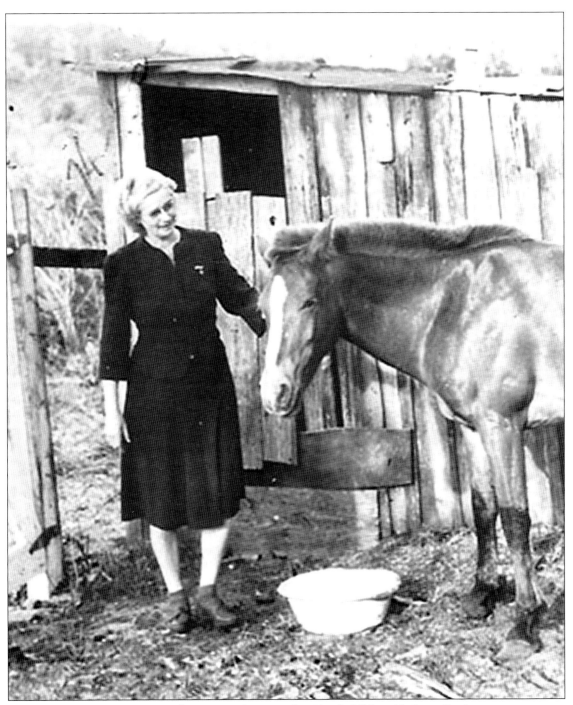

Buxton postmaster and U.S. Navy Coastwatcher Maude White with Outer Banks pony.

CHAPTER 12

SPYING ON THE SPIES

*"We kept asking mother several times,
'Do you reckon they're spies?'"*

Ormond Fuller

On a hot summer's day in the summer of 1942, the Midgett Brother's "Sea-going Bus Line" was on its daily southerly run from Whalebone Junction to Cape Hatteras with stops at the villages of Avon, Buxton, Frisco, and Hatteras. Bouncing on their seats and clinging to handholds as the bus zigged and zagged its way down the sand road known as "Route 101" were the usual mixture of locals, traveling salesmen, servicemen, and strangers from the mainland.

Among those strangers and seated apart from the rest, most likely in the rear of the bus, were a man and woman who appeared unremarkable except for their large dog, which lay quietly in the center aisle. They spoke as little as possible, usually just nodding with a friendly smile in response to the other passengers, who might have commented on the roller-coaster-ride, the passing scenery, or the young boy driving the bus. Had the well-dressed, heavyset man uttered more than a few, single-syllable words, the others on the bus might have become suspicious. Had the others on the bus been able to look over their shoulders, they might also have found it odd how the couple seemed to be unusually watchful of the ocean and how they whispered to one another and jotted down notes when military jeeps passed by on the beach.

After a brief stop at the Avon post office, the bus began to traverse the narrow isthmus known to Hatterasers as "The Haulover," which crossed the long-extinct Chacandepeco Inlet. It was there that the distinctive black-and-white barber-pole stripes of the Cape Hatteras Lighthouse finally hove into view, and first-time visitors would know that they would soon arrive at the famous Cape.

As the road approached the north side of the government-owned lighthouse com-pound, it made a sharp bend to the west, then to the northwest, as it skirted creeks and climbed high sand ridges in the maritime forest on its way to Buxton Landing and the post office on the soundside of the island. About a half mile before reaching the post office, at a sharp bend to the left, the boy driver shifted the bus into neutral to allow the soft sand to ease the vehicle to a stop. He stood up and announced with an island brogue, "Miz White's boardin' how-se."

Among those disembarking the bus were the quiet couple with the dog, for they were going to be guests at the boarding house for the coming days. It turned out not to be the best choice of lodging, for the strangers are believed to have been German espionage agents, and Maude White was a civilian coastal observer for U.S. Navy Intelligence.

"This German couple—I won't ever forget them," recalled Ormond Fuller, White's daughter. "They brought with them the biggest dog I've ever seen in my life—the paws on that thing were that big," she added, indicating with both hands what would have been an exceptionally large paw.

From time to time, Outer Banks boarding houses accommodated eccentric or myste-rious individuals, but most guests typically stayed for weeks or months at a time. Con-spicuously, the German-accented strangers who showed up at the White boarding house in the summer of 1942 only stayed a few days before they packed up and headed back north. That fact alone raised some initial suspicions. "We kept asking mother several times, 'Do you reckon they're spies? Do you reckon they're down here gathering up infor-mation?' And all she'd say is, 'Could be—I don't know.'"

Without the benefit of knowing what the White family knew at the time of recent news and developments in Germany's effort to gather intelligence on the United States before and after the nation entered the war, one might be inclined to think that the White family seemed to rush to judgement about their newly arrived, German-accented house guests. But the entire nation had been for several years gripped by sensational news reports of Nazi spy rings operating within the United States.

Since 1936, Germany's military intelligence branch, Abwehr,[5] had begun recruiting and training, both in Europe and the United States, volunteer espionage operatives who were bilingual German-born but naturalized U.S. citizens and who were able to freely travel between the two countries aboard German ships. These initial agents, sometimes referred to as the "First Ring," were members of the Nazi-American support organiza-tion, Friends of New Germany (later known as the German American Bund). The first ring was primarily based in the New York area. These agents were tasked with the re-sponsibility of collecting information on general economic, political, and military issues that could be gleaned, clipped, or copied from national newspapers and magazines. Over time, more specific intelligence items appeared on the Abwehr's shopping list: data on ship sailings and cargoes being sent to Britain; U.S. manufacturing potential; advance-ments in aircraft construction; and information regarding transportation routes, anti-submarine techniques, and maritime navigational matters.

Thanks to an unlikely discovery by a Scottish postal deliveryman of a large volume

of mail originating in the United States that was being sent to a woman's address on his route—which turned out to be an Abwehr mail drop—the New York office of the Federal Bureau of Investigation was able to identify and monitor the spy ring in 1938. Eighteen New York-area residents were accused of spying, but only four were brought to trial after the others were able to escape, possibly with the help of other German agents. The investigation was led by FBI Special Agent Leon G. Torrou, who became historically noteworthy for pioneering the first FBI polygraph administered in an espionage case in the United States. While Torrou's polygraph equipment seemed to function as expected, his faith in the results fell somewhat short of perfection. The testimony of the prime suspect of the spy ring, Bavarian physician Ignatz Theodor Griebl, encouraged Torrou that he was cooperating—Griebl willingly implicated his co-conspirators in the case. Griebl's answers in the polygraph test "made us relax all vigilance, all watchfulness over him," Torrou said. Five days later, before he could be taken into custody, Griebl slipped out of the FBI's grasp and was on his way back to Germany aboard the steamship *Bremen*. A number of Griebl's other accomplices fled as well, causing an enormous embarrassment for FBI officials. Torrou did manage to recognize an opportunity to cash in on the case and resigned from the FBI to write a series of articles published in the nation's newspapers and a book published later that year titled, *Nazi Spies in America*. When Torrou's letter of resignation reached the desk of FBI Director J. Edgar Hoover, Hoover refused to accept it and instead fired Torrou for allowing so many of the spies to escape. Torrou's byline in the newspapers, nevertheless, described him as "America's Foremost Spy Investigator."

The news coverage associated with the German spy trials of 1938 was considerable and widely known. On June 20, 1938, when three indictments naming 18 suspected spies were issued by a New York federal grand jury, the Associated Press headline appearing in thousands of American newspapers read: "18 Caught in Spy Net—Germans Among Group Named by Grand Jury."

The New York spy ring also inspired a movie released in the United States on May 6, 1939, just four months before the outbreak of the war in Europe. The film, produced by Warner Brothers Studios, was titled, "Confessions of a Nazi Spy." Featuring Edward G. Robinson in the starring role of the principal FBI agent, the film was considered to be the first anti-Nazi production made by Hollywood, and its producers intended it to be a clarion call to Americans who were inclined to favor isolationism. The popular film, one in a series of Warner Brothers films based on recent news headlines, had a wide distribution and was seen in theaters in coastal North Carolina towns like Wilmington and Morehead City, as well as theaters frequented by visiting Outer Bankers in Norfolk, Virginia.

Even while "Confessions of a Nazi Spy" was being seen on the silver screen, a subsequent and more effective German spy ring was in the process of being exposed by the FBI following two years of surveillance. That spy case likewise became well-publicized in the national press. The "Duquesne spy network" attempted to obtain intelligence on American military and industrial preparations. William Sebold, a naturalized U.S. citizen of German ancestry, had been equipped with a short-wave radio and a list of contacts in America who worked at key factories and strategic installations, including the ring's leader, Frederick "Fritz" Joubert Duquesne. Even before returning to the United States to begin his mission,

Sebold had notified American authorities that he wished to work as a counterespionage agent. Consequently, the FBI was able to monitor Sebold's incoming short-wave messages from Germany and also control the information that was being sent in return. Once the FBI's investigation was deemed complete, 33 spies and their accomplices were captured and convicted of espionage. The verdicts were handed down in Federal District Court in Brooklyn, New York, just six days following the bombing of Pearl Harbor. FBI Director J. Edgar Hoover called the case "the greatest spy roundup in U.S. history."

There can be little doubt that press and radio reports of the Griebl and Duquesne spy cases were on the minds of coastal residents of North Carolina even before the outbreak of U-boat attacks off their islands. Adults read the papers and listened to the news on the radio as their children hovered nearby, absorbing the latest spellbinding developments in wartime espionage. The closer a family lived near the ocean where Nazis might first set foot on U.S. soil or where agents were expected to collect intelligence, the more likelihood that fascination with spies turned into hysteria. "People were frightened to death. And if we saw anything strange, any strange people, we would think they were Germans," said Ocracoke resident Blanche Styron.

For the first time in memory, Ocracoke residents began locking their doors at night. Styron's brother, Calvin O'Neal, recalled Blanche's increasing concern for their safety. "My sister, Blanche, would come around here after dark, and the first thing she'd do is go make sure Mama had fastened the door. And Mama would say, 'Blanche, why did you do that?' And Blanche answered, 'Because you don't know when those Germans are coming ashore!'"

Whether from the news or from films like "Confessions of a Nazi Spy," young people on North Carolina's coast became intrigued with what has since become known as "spycraft"—invisible inks, clandestine meetings, letter drops, secret short-wave radio messages, ciphers and codes, and double agents. It was enough to cause some island youths to want to become spies, or counterspies, which is exactly what happened on Ocracoke Island.

They arrived at Ocracoke around the 1st of July, 1940, a large number of strangers who were perhaps the most eclectic and peculiar group of visitors the island had, to date, ever seen—a statement which is especially noteworthy, considering that the avant-garde list of Ocracoke passersby has included Elizabethan privateers, pirates, and centuries of sodden shipwreck survivors.

The group of strangers in 1940 was comprised of instructors, students, and organizers of the "Island Workshop for Artists and Writers," a two-month-long retreat offering courses in painting, sculpture, art history, creative writing, radio script writing, history of literature, Indian crafts, and physical education. Remembered by islanders as "the artist's colony," the conference was headquartered at Stanley Wahab's hotel and casino in Wahab Village. Those same islanders—many of whom were teenagers at the time—recall that at least some of the strangers were almost assuredly Nazi spies.

For years, the details of the Ocracoke artist colony remained murky until the fall of 2008, when island historian and business owner Philip Howard uncovered a treasure trove of information after months of diligent and persistent research. Other facts of the case, which are based on some island memories previously gathered, complete the story.

The "Island Workshop for Artists and Writers" was conceived by the manager of Wahab's Spanish Casino, Vernon Ward, a recent graduate of the University of North Carolina with a degree in English and interests in creative writing and poetry. Ward was able to entice a coterie of accomplished artists, writers, educators, psychologists, and intellectuals to travel to Ocracoke and lead the workshop's classes. As it happened, the number of teachers may have exceeded the number of students, leaving one to think that the workshop was as much for the faculty as it was for the pupils. Lecturers included an early founder of Montessori schools in the United States, a sculptress, a Cherokee Indian chief, and a Beethoven historian. But the participant of the artist colony Ocracokers remember best was the traditionally dressed and heavily accented Austrian national, Madame Helene Scheu-Riesz.

"She dressed in an Austrian style," recalled Blanche Joliff of Ocracoke. "She said she was from Austria. She wore those bodices, you know, that have eyelets, and they string up and tie in a bow. She wore full skirts, and she had a very strong accent. Very friendly. Very, very talkative." And naturally, as a result of her accent, her conspicuous dress, and her inquisitiveness, the 60-year-old Austrian woman was assumed by the Ocracokers to be the ringleader of the Nazi spy ring.

Scheu-Riesz was a relative newcomer to America, having emigrated in 1937 following the death of her husband. Her sudden appearance on Ocracoke three years later happened to coincide with the nation's preoccupation with Nazi spies. Years later, residents of Ocracoke would say that they had no idea how Scheu-Riesz and the others got to the island. They just "showed up," according to one islander (spy clue #1). It was the first piece of the espionage puzzle that lead to the foregone conclusion—they had to be spies!

The artist colony is remembered for having spent much of their time going out to the beach, which should have been understandable on the hot summer days of July and August—after all, that is what most visitors to Ocracoke do. But they never seemed interested in getting in the water (spy clue #2). "They were very... you might say, sneaky, in the way they did things," said Calvin O'Neal, an employee at the Wahab Hotel at the time. "It wasn't like they were going to the beach to sunbathe; they never wore beachwear, bathing suits, or shorts or anything like that."

Scheu-Riesz was remembered to have an unusual curiosity about the nearby navigational aids—buoys, markers, and the island's lighthouse (spy clue #3). "They asked a lot of questions, especially the older lady," Joliff remembered.

Wahab arranged for a local taxi driver with a flat bed truck to drive the workshop participants out to the beach. Once there, Scheu-Riesz peppered him with what seemed like unusual questions. "She questioned them about the buoys and the tides," Joliff added. And when they returned to the hotel, some members of the group acted suspiciously, covering their books or writing materials when other guests or hotel staff approached (spy clue #4).

Calvin O'Neal and his best friend, Laney Boyette, the daughter of the Wahab Hotel's manager, decided to take matters into their own hands. They would expose the Nazi spies! They just needed a little hard evidence.

"I remember [Mme. Scheu-Riesz] was in the north apartment; there were two women in there, I think," said O'Neal. "And the hotel manager's daughter and I were counter-spies. We tried our best. Every chance we'd get, we would go into their apartment [to search for evidence]. And, of course, when the father [manager Clenon Boyette] caught us, we got reprimanded. We never found anything, but the rumors were there."

The islanders' memories about the outcome of the Madame Scheu-Riesz spy case are not entirely consistent. "We had thought they were a bit far out in the beginning so we weren't too surprised when we heard they were picked up by the Coast Guard," Joliff recalled. O'Neal, however, remembered it a little differently: "They just left. I never heard any more about them." And for many years, that was the spy story told on Ocracoke.

It wasn't until Philip Howard decided to finally get to the bottom of things that the real story came to light. The Ocracoke spies were not spies at all. They really were there for a legitimate summer workshop for writers and artists, although, according to Howard, the participants may have been progressives who discussed and shared socialist or communist ideologies, hence their furtiveness. In fact, the workshop was held for a second summer season in 1941. Then, the war intervened, and the colorful and creative crowd no longer returned to the island. According to Howard's research, many of the participants continued to lead fairly successful careers. And so concluded Ocracoke's counterfeit Nazi spy case.

At Cape Hatteras, however, the German-accented man and woman who checked in at Maude White's boarding house in 1942, might have been another matter entirely. They were likely engaged in legitimate espionage, with connections leading to spy rings in New York or larger networks in Mexico or even Brazil. If so, their efforts were, at best, a last-ditch effort to collect useful intelligence because by the time they arrived at Buxton, most of Germany's spy networks in the United States and Latin America had already been dismantled.

On March 13, 1942, approximately three months before Maude White's suspicious guests had arrived at her home at Cape Hatteras, newspapers in North Carolina ran a small A.P. news story, sandwiched among the dominant front page stories of the war's latest developments in Europe and the Pacific. The story's headline read: "Sentences Total 117 Years in Spy Conspiracy Trial." The story announced the convictions in New York's U.S. District Court of the "Joe K" spy ring led by U.S.-born Kurt Frederick Ludwig, a successor to the Griebl and Duquesne groups. The capture of Ludwig and his accomplices was the culmination of two years of painstaking investigation by the FBI, British Imperial censors in Bermuda, and a bizarre but fortuitous car-pedestrian collision in New York's Times Square.

During the 27 months between the outbreak of World War II in Europe and the Japanese attack on Pearl Harbor, Germany's Abwehr expanded its efforts to establish and maintain numerous spy networks in the United States, South America, and Mexico, despite the misadventures of the Griebl and Duquesne spy rings. According to U.S. Department of Navy documents declassified in 2002, "These [new] groups must be credited with accomplishments which were probably of considerable value to Germany. Not only did they forward a quantity of basic economic data useful to Nazi analysis, but the ship-

ping information supplied resulted in the loss to submarines of British and Allied ships."

The most successful of the spy rings were two groups based in Brazil, which additionally served as relays for information of a more general nature, including intelligence originating in the United States, forwarded by such agents as Georg Nicolaus in Mexico. The Brazil group also had its own contacts on ships between the United States and Brazil. Through use of channels along the west coast of South America, connections with Europe via clandestine radio, and the Italian national airline, LATI, these scattered but interrelated groups were able to escape British censorship and maintain contact with Abwehr stations in Hamburg, Cologne, and Berlin.

According to Navy documents, "the activities of these espionage groups in Latin America had not gone unnoticed by counter-intelligence agencies, but prior to the United States' entry into the war, there was little that could be done about them."

It wasn't until March 18, 1941, when a taxi in Times Square accidentally struck and killed Spanish Consulate courier, Don Julio Lopez Lido, that the Nazi spy networks began to unravel. Lido was discovered by investigators to be an Abwehr agent whose real name was Captain Ulrich von der Osten. This revelation set in motion a chain of events that eventually exposed the Joe K spy ring, resulting in the trial and convictions of Kurt Frederick Ludwig and his associates, as well as taking down the Georg Nicolaus ring in Mexico City and much of the Brazilian network. In their post-war analysis, U.S. Navy intelligence authorities determined that prior to their liquidation, the Brazilian spy network had made strenuous efforts to obtain military information from the United States.

The successful spy interventions by Allied intelligence services virtually decapitated the German espionage "hydra," even though the Abwehr's tentacles—its minor, far-flung U.S. field agents—continued to twitch and seek useful intelligence, possibly in places as remote as Cape Hatteras, a productive operational area for U-boats. Likely to be among the Abwehr's twitching tentacles in the United States, grasping for useful intelligence were the German-accented man and woman snooping around Cape Hatteras in the summer of 1942.

Maude White was an inconspicuous but ideal volunteer counter-espionage agent, being the proprietor of the boarding house and postmaster at Cape Hatteras. With all of the recent news regarding the arrests of spies in New York, Mexico, and Brazil, White kept a watchful eye on her new guests. "She became suspicious because they would go out and move around the island and come back, and she would note them sketching things and mailing them," said White's daughter, Fuller. "And from the amount of mail they were mailing, she became suspicious of them.

"One day [the man] wanted to ask questions about the lighthouse, and he wanted to visit the area and see if there was anyone he could get to take them out there," Fuller recalled. (The Cape Hatteras Lighthouse was about one and a half miles from the White boarding house.) Maude White suggested that her daughter could drive them out there. "I became the first one in her mind, I guess. So, this girlfriend of mine, who was spending the summer with me, [we] agreed to take them out to the lighthouse."

The college-age girls and the suspected German spies were in the car as it slowly approached the massive lighthouse when the man noticed the adjacent brick oil house

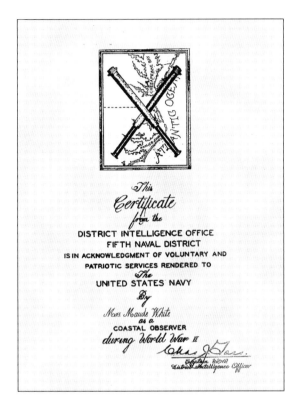

This Certificate from the
DISTRICT INTELLIGENCE OFFICE
FIFTH NAVAL DISTRICT
IS IN ACKNOWLEDGMENT OF VOLUNTARY AND
PATRIOTIC SERVICES RENDERED TO
The
UNITED STATES NAVY
By
Mrs Maude White
as a
COASTAL OBSERVER
during World War II

partially buried beneath a large sand dune, making it look like it may have been purposely hidden. "He said, 'Vhut that? Vhut that?' in that brogue of his, and I didn't say a word," Fuller said with a bit of drama. "Then, this girlfriend of mine said, 'Oh, that's where we hide the guns and ammunition.' I whirled around and looked at her. I was dumbfounded to think she would come up with something like that. But that was just like her, full of fun and full of mischief. I was anxious to get home so we circled around and left. I wanted to tell mother what she had done."

The suspected German agent must have been disgusted, thinking that he might have deserved a little more respect from the impertinent American girls.

As the days passed, the man and woman, along with their dog, were observed going to various places on the Cape, and then each evening they returned to record their activities on paper. "He was sketching and drawing maps and things," Fuller said. "At night, on mother's front porch, he had this board he leaned against, and he would be sketching I don't know what. We didn't see, but he would roll them up and mail them." Of course, being the postmaster, Maude White's suspicions were further piqued by the amount of mail that the German-accented couple was sending.

In a few days, the work of the visitors was complete, their mail was sent, and they checked out of the boarding house, catching the northbound "Sea-going Bus Line" to their next destination, driven by the barefoot bus driver. No one at Cape Hatteras confidently remembers their names, their code names, or their aliases. No one really knows what they were up to or if they really were Nazi spies. Fuller says that the family had heard that the man and woman were picked-up by the authorities before they got to Norfolk, somewhere after they crossed Oregon Inlet. Attempts to verify the suspected Cape Hatteras spies in the Navy's records have been fruitless.

However, there may be one small piece of evidence that lends some credence to the story. As a volunteer U.S. Navy coastal observer, Maude White was sworn to secrecy; she never said much more about the suspected German spies to her children. But today, her descendants possess a simple but official-looking certificate, which was presented to White a few years later, thanking her for providing a valuable service to her nation in time of war.

CHAPTER 13
MYTHS: FACT VS. FICTION

"Throughout the war, they got these warnings that spies may be coming ashore at night."

Billy Brown

A writer in search of a good story, Nell Carolyn Wise was intrigued by the notion that German spies had infiltrated Hatteras Island.

Wise was a 29-year-old teacher from the mainland who boarded at Maude and Estus White's home at Buxton during the school season when she was teaching at Cape Hatteras School. While Wise may not have been present during the few days in the summer when the German-accented, suspected spies were residents at the White's boarding house, she certainly heard plenty about it well after they were gone. One of her students was the White's 13-year-old daughter, Carol, a spirited and independent red-haired girl who roamed Cape Hatteras riding bareback on her Ocracoke pony, Ivy, and was chased by her hound dog, Boozie. It was Carol's wartime adventures and her mother's story of spies visiting the island that gave Wise an idea that blossomed into a children's novel published 15 years later.

The novel, *Taffy of Torpedo Junction*, follows the exploits of a rambunctious 13-year-old Cape Hatteras girl as she, her pony named Sailor, and her hound dog, Brandy, discover a small ring of German spies and saboteurs operating out of the old Snyder house secluded in thickets on a sand hill in Buxton Woods.

The fictional Taffy is a spirited and independent red-haired girl much like Carol White was in 1942. Taffy and her "Gramp" live in a ramshackle house on the Cape, which provides them with a front row seat to the mayhem being caused by German U-boats shortly after Pearl Harbor. Taffy's curiosity and fearlessness repeatedly lead her into danger. She and her dog help the Coast Guard capture a German saboteur, who came ashore in a rubber raft loaded with dynamite. Later, when Taffy and Sailor pass the suspicious-looking Snyder house after dark, she, in turn, is captured by Germans who have been assisting U-boats offshore for months by sending secret radio messages with information about merchant ship locations, routes, and cargoes. With Taffy bound and gagged, the Nazi spies douse the house and its radio equipment with gasoline, preparing to burn it all down with the teenage girl inside as they ready their escape from the island.

As a teacher, Wise had been profoundly affected by haunting thoughts of merchant seaman being burned and drowned when window-shattering explosions offshore occasionally interrupted her classes at Cape Hatteras School during the first few months of 1942. "She had a great thirst for knowledge," Marcia Kass said of her mother in a 1996 interview with journalist and newspaper editor Irene Nolan of Hatteras Island. "She took history very personally. She lived through some interesting times."

The war influenced Wise's life more than just providing literary inspiration. She met a Coast Guardsman stationed on the Outer Banks, Robert Wechter, whom she married in 1943. Wechter was raised in Wisconsin but had been born in Germany. He is depicted in *Taffy of Torpedo Junction* as "Big Jens," the chief warrant officer at the Cape Hatteras Coast Guard station.

The school teacher and novelist would one day become well-known as Nell Wise Wechter, a name beloved by tens of thousands of schoolchildren. Since 1957, generations of young people—and teachers, as well—have read Wechter's spell-binding book and have, in the process, been taught how World War II had an impact on the coast of North Carolina, how German U-boats ravaged the shipping lanes, and how spies and saboteurs aided the sleek and sinister submarines offshore.

Many adults who read *Taffy* as children today possess a conception of World War II history off the North Carolina coast based primarily on the book. For example, a Charlotte newspaper editor wrote in 2007 that "the stories of saboteurs landing at Nags Head or Kitty Hawk are true, but no one told it better than Nell Wise Wechter." Another newspaper journalist who wrote a recent book about Hatteras Island claims that the real spy who inspired the Taffy story, named Hans Haas, was actually arrested by the FBI in New York. No such name is listed in FBI records.[6]

"Partly based on a true story" is a cautionary phrase often used by the book's publishers, reviewers, and journalists. It is an unfortunately misleading statement. Most everyone who reads the book believes that its major plot points actually happened.

While *Taffy of Torpedo Junction* has, no doubt, provided an important and irreplaceable source of inspiration for school children, the book's adult fans who sing its praises don't point out that its deviations from history have done a disservice to those same youths. There are scenes in the book that were only loosely inspired by historical facts; at other times the author time-shifted events to accommodate the storyline. If history's lessons will ever be useful to future generations, history must be known accurately. Consequently, it is essential to distinguish Taffy's fictions and facts, especially since the book has sometimes been listed as required reading for North Carolina students; otherwise, historical errors will forever be repeated.

In the book, Taffy's Gramps is ordered by the commander of the nearby Coast Guard

station to hang blackout curtains over the windows so that light could not been seen beyond the beach, but in the book this occurs prior to Pearl Harbor. Later, the book describes "a strict blackout." In reality, the U.S. government did not begin to enforce lighting restrictions until late-April 1942, and from that time until the end of the war the restrictions only required a dim-out along the coast, not a total blackout. While it is true that diligent residents and business owners hung "blackout curtains" on their windows, interior lights and some exterior lights were allowed to remain burning. In Great Britain and on the European continent, an enforced blackout meant that all lights were extinguished at night.

Likewise, in *Taffy of Torpedo Junction*, Wechter's pre-Pearl Harbor Coast Guard facility at Cape Hatteras is described as a "DF" (radio high-frequency direction finding, commonly called Huff-Duff or HF/DF) station with a newly installed radar system, which Taffy believes may be the intended target of the German saboteurs. In fact, the nearest HF/DF and radar facility was located at Ocracoke, and it was months after Pearl Harbor before it became operational.

Other deviations from historical fact found in the book include references to the sinking of a U-boat within view of Taffy's classmates as they stood on the beach at Cape Hatteras, U-boats operating in packs of two or more off the North Carolina coast, and a U-boat mother ship supplying several baby subs offshore. None of these literary inventions ever occurred.

Perhaps the most commonly believed and often-repeated myth spawned by Wechter's *Taffy of Torpedo Junction* involves German saboteurs who land on Hatteras Island with the intent of blowing things up.

Hatteras Island residents have been heard to say that everyone knew the Germans were coming ashore, but no one was especially worried since there was little on the island that would have made a strategic target for the saboteurs. "We didn't at the time realize we were in any danger," the real-life "Taffy," Carol Dillon, said in an interview. Dillon remembers that the islanders surmised that Germans landing on the beach were only attempting to infiltrate. "And," she said, "I don't think many infiltrated from here because you couldn't get off the island then. Kids back then weren't afraid because there really wasn't anything to be afraid of. This was a very safe place. The only things I remember being stolen were watermelons and chickens."

If watermelons and chickens were being stolen on Hatteras Island during the war, there must have been someone other than German saboteurs who were doing it. According to U.S. Department of Navy and FBI records, there were only three documented cases of German agents or saboteurs landing on U.S. soil during the war and one occurrence in Canada. The best-known case, Operation Pastorius, involved two sets of four men who were landed at Amagansett, Long Island, New York, on June 13, 1942, and at Ponte Vedra Beach, Florida, four nights later. On November 29, 1944, two more agents were landed in Frenchman Bay near Bar Harbor, Maine. In each case, all of the saboteurs involved were captured by the FBI—either as a result of voluntary surrenders on the part of the German agents or as a result of incompetence and carelessness.

When four saboteurs were landed at Amagansett's Atlantic Avenue Beach from *U-202*, they were chanced upon by John C. Cullen, an unarmed, 21-year-old Coast

Operation Pastorious saboteurs seated on deck of U-202.

Guard seaman on patrol shortly after midnight.[7] There was no moon, and dense fog drifted toward the island from the sea. According to FBI files, the saboteurs were initially dressed in military uniforms so that they would be treated as POWs in the event that they were captured immediately upon landing. The Germans brought ashore in a rubber raft "enough explosives, primers, and incendiaries to support an expected two-year career in the sabotage of American defense-related production."

Prior to departing Germany, the men were trained in "chemistry, incendiaries, explosives, timing devices, secret writing, and concealment of identity by blending into an American background." The saboteur-trainees were "taken to aluminum and magnesium plants, railroad shops, canals, locks, and other facilities to familiarize them with the vital points and vulnerabilities of the types of targets they were to attack. Maps were used to locate those American targets: spots where railroads could be most effectively disabled; the principal aluminum and magnesium plants; and important canals, waterways, and locks. All instructions had to be memorized."

Despite their extensive training, the Germans' first few minutes on American soil did not go well. Seaman Cullen had barely begun his patrol when he stumbled upon the Germans. One of the saboteurs had already changed into civilian clothes, but the others were still wearing undershorts as they struggled to pull their raft ashore. The following transcript of the encounter, which reads like a radio comedy sketch of the time, is from Coast Guard records:

> "Cullen called out, 'What's the trouble?'
>
> "Nobody answered. The man on shore started toward Cullen.
>
> "Cullen called again, 'Who are you?'
>
> "There was no answer. The man kept advancing.
>
> "Cullen reached to his hip pocket for a flashlight. The foremost man saw the motion and, apparently thinking the Coast Guardsman was reaching for a gun, cried out, 'Wait a minute. Are you the Coast Guard?'
>
> "Cullen answered, 'Yes. Who are you?'
>
> "'A couple of fishermen from Southampton who have run aground.'

"'Come up to the station and wait for daybreak.'

"Cullen recalled later that the weather seemed to get worse, and the fog closed in.

"The spokesman snapped, 'Wait a minute--you don't know what's going on. How old are you? Have you a father and mother? I wouldn't want to have to kill you.'

"A fourth man in a bathing suit came up through the fog, dragging a bag. He started to speak in German.

"Cullen spoke up, 'What's in the bag?'

"'Clams.'

"Cullen knew there were no clams for miles around.

"The man in civilian clothes said, 'Yes, that's right.'

"Cullen's pretended gullibility appeared to influence him. In a friendly voice he said, 'Why don't you forget the whole thing? Here is some money. One hundred dollars.'

"Cullen said, 'I don't want it.'

"The man took some more bills out of his wallet. 'Then take $300.'

"Cullen thought fast. He answered, 'Okay.'

"The stranger gave him the money, saying, 'Now look me in the eyes.'

"As Cullen explained to his superiors later, he said he was afraid he might be hypnotized. The stranger insisted. Cullen braced himself and looked directly at the man. Nothing happened to Cullen's relief. As he looked at him, the stranger kept repeating, 'Would you recognize me if you saw me again?'

"When Cullen finally said 'No,' the man appeared satisfied."

The man wearing civilian clothes was George John Dasch, a former dishwasher and waiter who had been made the operations's leader. Dasch had grave doubts about his team's capabilities and the likelihood that they would avoid detection before they could succeed in their mission—especially after his encounter with Cullen. Within 24 hours of landing on the beach, Dasch was on the phone with the New York office of the FBI. Nervous that the German Gestapo had infiltrated the FBI, Dasch told the FBI agent on the phone that he would only deliver his information in person to J. Edgar Hoover in Washington, D.C. Five days later, Dasch convinced FBI agents at Justice Department headquarters that his story was legitimate by dumping his entire budget for his two-year mission on a senior investigator's desk—$84,000 in cash. Within days, all of Dasch's accomplices and the four Ponte Vedra saboteurs were captured in New York and Chicago.

For the next three months, news of Operation Pastorius and the seizure of its operatives and many of their associates and family members in the United States made the front pages of the nation's newspapers. Arrests, convictions, and the spy trial all occurred quickly. By late June 1942, the story became public; by July 8, the saboteurs stood trial before a seven-member military tribunal; on July 13, the FBI announced the further arrests of 14 alleged associates and "immediate contacts" of the Pastorius saboteurs; and by

August 4, convictions were handed down, and the case was closed.

One of two defense attorneys appointed by President Roosevelt to represent the Pastorius agents was Goldsboro, North Carolina, attorney and Army colonel, Kenneth C. Royall. Royall argued that the secret military tribunal was illegal and that the Germans should be tried in a civilian court. Royall's argument was rejected by the U.S. Supreme Court in "Ex parte Quirin, 317 U.S. 1 (1942)," which established a precedent that was cited again in 2001 as the legal justification for holding military commissions to judge suspected terrorists held at Guantanamo, Cuba. All eight Pastorius agents were convicted and sentenced to death. Roosevelt, however, commuted the sentences of Dasch and Ernest Peter Burger, who both provided information that led to the arrests of the others. The other six men were executed at the District of Columbia Jail on August 8, 1942. Justice was swift in World War II—only seven weeks had passed since Dasch turned himself in.[8] Thus ended Germany's most serious effort to sabotage U.S. facilities.

Saboteurs and sympathizers supplanted spies in the suspicious minds of Americans in 1942. Almost every unexplained act of vandalism, fishy behavior, or destructive result of nature was, at first, attributed to Nazi saboteurs or sympathizers.

There was a report that someone on Ocracoke Island was sending secret Morse code signals to a surfaced U-boat offshore by flashing the taillights of his automobile parked at a secluded spot in the dunes, but he had yet to be apprehended. Manteo's Billy Brown tells the story of the time his father, Aycock Brown, a civilian investigator for U.S. Navy Intelligence, was called in the middle of the night to look into claims that the suspicious activity was occurring yet again.

"Throughout the war, they got these warnings that spies may be coming ashore at night," Billy Brown said, repeating a story his father told him. Aycock Brown roused a Navy sailor to accompany him on his dangerous mission. "And they got into an argument over who was gonna walk up and investigate what this was. They only had one .45 caliber pistol [between the two of them]. My father said he didn't know much about shooting a .45 pistol, and the other guy said it was [my dad's] job because he was the officer. So they argued about that."

Once the elder Brown and his unarmed subordinate settled their dispute they made their way out to the place where the vehicle was flashing its lights toward the U-boat lurking unseen in the darkness offshore. "He said they looked and saw these lights blinking, these red lights blinking," Brown said. "And my dad, he said he didn't know Morse code, and the guy with him didn't know Morse code so they couldn't read the message." (Of course, even if the two men could read Morse code, presumably the message would have been sent in German.)

"Finally, my dad started up this sandy path where this car was parked and the tail lights blinking every once and awhile. He crept up, and he snuck around, and he looked inside. He had the greatest relief he ever had in the world. He said there was a young couple in there makin' out. No German spies! [The young man's] foot was hitting on the break pedal, I guess, every once in awhile."

On the north end of Hatteras Island a large brush fire once lit-up the night sky, caus-

ing many residents to suspect that it was purposely ignited by saboteurs to silhouette merchant ships for waiting U-boats offshore, but no written documentation validates the claim. Similarly, in April 1942, a railroad trestle over Bear Creek on the Atlantic and Eastern Carolina Railway west of LaGrange in Lenoir County was destroyed by a suspicious fire, temporarily severing a vital supply line to Marine bases at Cherry Point and Camp Lejeune as well as the state port at Morehead City. The incident was investigated by the FBI and naval intelligence officers and determined to be of domestic origins.

According to Department of the Navy records, there was "no enemy inspired act of sabotage within the United States during the war. And while Germany did from time to time obtain information relating to war production, shipping, and technical advances, the intel was almost always too late, too inaccurate, or too generalized to be of direct military value."

Numerous allegations of sabotage were investigated by the FBI during World War II. Every suspect act traced to its source was the result of vandalism, a desire for relief from boredom, the curiosity of children "to see what would happen," or other personal motives.

During the summer of 1942, stories describing the "startling case" of the Amagansett and Ponte Vedra landings appeared nearly every day in the papers. For example, *The Robesonian*, a newspaper published in Lumberton, North Carolina, featured on its June 30th front page a photograph taken in Florida of the German saboteurs' buried cache of dynamite and other sabotage materials, including electric blasting caps, pen- and pencil-delay mechanisms, detonators, ampoules of acid, and other time-delay devices. During and after the war, these "Nazi saboteur" stories, no doubt, left a lasting impression on the minds of Americans who lived along the U.S. East Coast, including those in North Carolina. Consequently, for the past 70 years, far-fetched urban legends were invented by coastal residents, from Maine to Florida, wishing for their communities to share in the intrigue. The theft of watermelons and chickens by German agents on Hatteras Island is among the least diabolical. Some myths are ubiquitous; others stretch the bounds of credulity to new limits.

Perhaps the most pervasive is the story of U-boat sailors—either dead or alive—who were found with recently purchased tickets to an American movie theater in their pockets, suggesting that German's were coming ashore for entertainment during lulls in the action. Along the Cape Fear River in North Carolina folks repeat the story of a corpse washed ashore from a sunken U-boat on which was found a ticket to—depending on who you talk to—the Amuzu Theater in Southport or the Bailey Theater in Wilmington. The same story is told about theaters around Virginia's Hampton Roads area, in New Jersey and New England, at Halifax, Nova Scotia, and most vociferously in Florida.

The Palm Beach, Florida, region is particularly fertile ground for World War II folklore, partly due to its large population and to the fact that the landmass protrudes eastward, well into the shipping lanes in the Straits of Florida, much like Cape Hatteras, which put its residents close to the U-boat action. They tell the story of the theater tickets, too, as well as one about a U-boat crew that came ashore to drink at Palm Beach bars or dine at one of the area's posh restaurants.

An adaptation of the theater ticket myth involves German U-boat crews coming ashore in rafts or even "midget submarines" to stock-up on supplies at the local general store. The story, regardless of where it is told, often includes the mention of Holsum or Wonder Bread wrappers discovered in the galley of a nearby sunken U-boat by sport divers, thus proving the Germans were getting their provisions from U.S. stores. A woman once whispered one such story—she had been sworn to secrecy—about a time when she was a child on Ocean Isle Beach during the war. She recalled her parents frantically calling all of the children into the house one evening after an alert had been issued that two German midget submarines had landed on the beach and the Nazi crews had broken into the nearby general store to get food for the mother ship offshore. (Perhaps the woman's parents were simply using an effective means to get their children to come in after dark.)

A similar tale has been told on Harkers Island, North Carolina. In this case, the event happened late in the war, and the U-boat crew was starving and desperate, having depleted their provisions. As the story goes, they somehow eluded the considerable coastal defenses and patrols established by that time and purchased a prodigious amount of bread and other supplies, which somehow were transported back to the sub in an inflatable raft. The emaciated landing party paid for the provisions with gold bars stamped with Nazi swastikas—they didn't ask for change. Naturally, the store's proprietor asked no questions and did not contact the authorities. Even to this day, islanders "in possession" of the Nazi gold are unwilling to reveal the bars with swastikas, lest they be arrested for aiding the enemy.

The landing of midget submarines at various points along the U.S. East Coast is also a popular story. Historian and retired Naval officer Wilbur D. Jones, Jr., author of a book about Wilmington, North Carolina, during World War II, relates the story of four Germans who landed at Federal Point in a midget submarine and whose mission it was to sabotage the shipping channel in the Cape Fear River. Germany did build hundreds of one- and two-man miniature submarines of the classes Seehund, Hecht, Biber and Molch but not until late in the war and exclusively for harbor defenses in the European theatre of war, and not particularly effectively. Midget submarines could only be deployed from large surface vessels and never worked in tandem with the larger, long-range U-boats.

Most people don't understand just how large a German Type VII or Type IX U-boat actually is, hence stories like the following have survived the years. A wealthy Palm Beach woman who sympathized with the National Socialist Party of Germany and her Nazi butler hid a German U-boat in a secluded cove behind her estate. According to the legend, she had been using a short-wave radio to communicate with U-boats offshore, and then she had to kill an FBI agent who had been snooping around. Eventually, the FBI caught the woman and her butler, and the hidden U-boat was destroyed by an aerial strike.

Similarly, on the Outer Banks of North Carolina, there are often repeated stories about local fishing trawlers which had been detained by a U-boat to offload the trawlers' diesel fuel. There are even rumors that some trawlers aided the Germans willingly. In an interview published in an October 1943 issue of *American Magazine*, FBI Director J. Edgar Hoover stated that "his office investigated, between January 1942 and May 1943, more than 500 reports of refueling enemy subs on our shores, signaling to them, and the like; but 'every report...was a false alarm.'"

In spite of diligent FBI investigations and reams of archived documents proving that such things never happened, myths persist and are repeated by the faithful, including academic historians. Such was the case when a German U-boat purportedly surfaced off Kure Beach in July 1943 and proceeded to fire shells at the Ethyl-Dow Chemical plant. The plant had been instrumental in producing an ingredient for the production of aviation fuel and somehow the German U-boat crew had been provided this intelligence, they knew precisely where the plant was located, and were capable of targeting it in the dark. Suspiciously, the source for the story was the same individual who provided the facts about the midget submarine landing at nearby Federal Point. The legend's underpinnings crumble under the weight of the facts. According to a thorough analysis of declassified British Admiralty submarine tracking records and the daily war diary and standing orders of Admiral Dönitz, no German U-boats were anywhere near Kure Beach in July 1943.[9] Furthermore, the Ubootwaffe had by then removed deck guns from most of its operational boats in the Atlantic. Nevertheless, the legend continues to be sustained by the town and the state historic site of nearby Fort Fisher, which claims that while the legend is difficult to prove, it has yet to be proven wrong.

Sometimes even authors of World War II historical non-fiction get in on the act of disseminating outlandish mythical tales. In a 2003 interview broadcast on a North Carolina public radio station, a popular American writer recounted, with all seriousness, a story told to him by a woman who lived on Hatteras Island during the war. As the story goes, it was laundry day, and the woman was hanging her clothes on the line to dry in the afternoon breeze. Coincidentally, the German crew aboard a passing U-boat near to shore was also hanging their laundry out on the jumping wire that ran between the conning tower and the boat's bow and stern. The Hatteras woman and the U-boat crew spotted each other and waved, all laughing at the serendipitous moment. Unfortunately for radio listeners, they can't see when someone is winking as he is telling a story. In this case, many North Carolinians were left believing that the story was true. The reasons why the story could not be true are many, but the most convincing explanations are that a U-boat would have never called attention to itself in such a way in enemy waters nor would the relatively shallow depths off Hatteras Island's beaches allow a U-boat to come in close enough for its crew to see or wave at the residents on shore.

Whether there were saboteurs landing at Carolina Beach, midget submarines raiding the local pantry, or groups of U-boat sailors munching on popcorn and enjoying *Yankee Doodle Dandy* at the Bijou, not one of these occurrences was ever covered in the nation's papers that had been assiduously reporting the nearly daily events about the legitimate spy cases or the few landings of saboteurs during the war.

"There is no substance to the stories that U-boats stopped fishing boats at sea to obtain their diesel oil—a fishing boat would not have nearly enough diesel oil in the first place to take care of the needs of a U-boat," said Michael Gannon, author of *Operation Drumbeat*. "And there is no truth to the story that U-boat crews went ashore to buy fresh vegetables, eggs, or even to the movies as some urban legends have it. None of these things occurred, and I'll tell you how we know. I interviewed the chief of U-boat communications, and I asked him about each one of those cases, and he laughed at each one. He said, 'No, we never stopped other vessels to get oil from them. No, we never put ashore to get provisions. I was in charge of all communications, I would have known.'"

But there was an even greater reason why U-boat crews remained aboard their vessels—Admiral Dönitz had issued strict orders that his men were to never leave their U-boats for any reason other than to exchange equipment or information with other U-boats. "Such a man going against those orders would have been executed upon returning to their French base," Gannon said.

Despite speaking emphatically about the impossibility of most U-boat urban legends in public lectures, Gannon is still told stories by believers. "There is almost always someone who comes up to me and sometimes whispers to me—'You know, U-boat men came ashore here, and I can show you the restaurant where they went into to eat.' And I tell them, 'I'm sorry, that story could not possibly be true. Think of what these men would have looked like going into this elegant restaurant. They would have been in their coveralls covered with grease, their hair and beards matted with grease, smelling of all the foul odors that permeated the interior of a U-boat. If a group like that had walked into a restaurant, someone would have grabbed the phone and called the police!'"

There is one North Carolina urban legend Dr. Gannon has probably not heard and it should win the prize for most outrageously inventive and absurd, even more absurd than the "U-boat laundry day" story.

Few small American cities value their history more than New Bern, North Carolina, a place noted for its colonial and antebellum architecture, Civil War battles, and for being the birthplace of Pepsi-Cola. But who would have guessed that New Bern celebrates its purported brush with German U-boat legend as well. Someone attending the New Bern Historical Society's annual ghost-walk, might hear the following story performed with utmost sincerity and panache. John Leys, historian for the Historical Society, unabashedly summarizes the basic "facts" for readers:

> "According to 'Shoot' Hall, who was the head of the [New Bern] bus station—they called him early one morning, say 3 o'clock, and said that a German U-boat off the coast had caught fire and sunk. And the survivors, the Germans, they had taken prisoner. And they said, 'We're gonna put them on a school bus and send them up to you. And since you're the head of the bus station, you can then put them on a bus to Charleston, South Carolina, where there was a POW camp.' So, 'Shoot' said the bus arrived at 5 a.m., and lo and behold, the U-boat had burned, in the process, all the sailor's clothes. So it was a busload of naked German sailors. 'Shoot' said he had to wait until J.C. Penney's opened, and he went in and talked to Ruby, who was the head of the men's department. And Ruby said, 'Do you just want regular clothes?' He said, 'No, I want the cheapest thing you got because I'm gonna have to pay for it.' So, he bought pajamas. They put pajamas on the German POWs, put them on the bus to Charleston, and sent them to the POW camp."

American folklore doesn't get much better than that.

CHAPTER: 14
MARCH OF TERROR

"Every time I'd come up,
I'd come up on fire."

Herbert Gardner

Kapitänleutnant Erwin Rostin would pay for dearly for his deeds. He would die, as would his entire U-boat crew of 53 men, in a frightful fashion feared by all submariners. On June 30, 1942, U-*158* was surprised on the surface and attacked with depth charges dropped by a U.S. Navy Martin PBM bomber-flying boat, 445 miles east-southeast of Cape Hatteras. Rostin and his men were crushed, then drowned inside their crippled U-boat as it plunged 16,000 feet to its eternal grave on the ocean floor.

It was a just reprisal, Ocracoke residents would someday say, for Rostin had earned the hatred of the entire population of their island. They despised the German U-boat captain because Rostin had killed one of their own.

On March 14, 1942, Chris Gaskill was walking the beach on the south end of Ocracoke Island when he spotted a rectangular object washing up with the surf. He decided to investigate and discovered it was a large frame that held an official-looking certificate. To Gaskill, it looked like other documents may have once been inside the frame, but now there was only one. He examined it more closely. The document was a license issued by the U.S. Department of Commerce to certify the qualifications of a third mate aboard an ocean or coastwise steam vessel.

When Gaskill read the name of the person to whom the license was issued, he was at first puzzled then gravely worried. How did this end up here, he might have wondered. The license belonged to his cousin, Ocracoke native son Jim Baughm Gaskill, third mate on the SS *Caribsea*, a 250-foot-long steam freighter, which was operated by a New York

Jim Baughm Gaskill

shipping company. Chris Gaskill hadn't known of his cousin's whereabouts since the war began, but finding the license washed-up on the beach was an ominous sign. Gaskill promptly returned to the village, notified the family and then the Coast Guard.

Jim's father, the late William D. "Cap'n Bill" Gaskill, had for many years owned and managed the Pamlico Inn, a popular hotel located on the edge of the Pamlico Sound and Teaches Hole Channel south of Silver Lake. Cap'n Bill was lost at sea while fishing in 1935 but the family continued to operate the inn. It was there, the day after Chris Gaskill found Jim's mate certificate, that someone at the inn noticed a floating piece of wreckage that appeared to be a spar or an oar banging against the pilings of the inn's pier. The timber was retrieved, and a ship's name was discovered etched on one side—SS *Caribsea*. By then, Jim Baughm Gaskill's family and friends knew of his tragic fate.

Four days earlier, the SS *Caribsea* had been steaming past Cape Lookout on her way to Norfolk from Santiago, Cuba, with 3,600 tons of highly combustable manganese ore in her cargo holds. Believing that the greatest threat from U-boats lay 60 miles ahead, the Navy asked the *Caribsea*'s master to reduce speed to four knots so that the freighter would not approach Cape Hatteras until after daylight. Third mate Jim Baughm Gaskill's watch had ended, and he was asked by the officer relieving him if he was going to remain in the wheelhouse until they raised the Ocracoke Lighthouse off the freighter's port bow. Gaskill replied that he had seen the lighthouse often enough—his father's hotel was practically next door—and that he needed some sleep. Gaskill retired to his berth. A short time later, two torpedoes struck the ship—the first hitting #2 hold; the second exploding the ship's boilers. Only the seven men on deck or in the wheelhouse survived. Twenty-one men were killed instantly, including Gaskill, as the ship went down bow first in less than three minutes. Had Gaskill waited to see his beloved Ocracoke lighthouse one more time, he might have lived. His body was never found.

Among the pieces of wreckage floating in the sea after the ship violently blew apart were Gaskill's third mate license and the oar marked *Caribsea*. It took three days, but these two artifacts somehow floated to Ocracoke Island more than 43 miles away against great odds, heavy seas, and a contrary current. The license and the oar were the only artifacts of the *Caribsea* to be found. The oar's travels were particularly remarkable, having miraculously navigated the serpentine channel through Ocracoke Inlet and against the daily tidal outflow of Teaches Hole Channel, avoiding sandbars and shallow bays to land at Jim Baughm Gaskill's birthplace, his father's Pamlico Inn.

"It was unusual for a thing like that to happen," said 82-year-old Owen Gaskill, Jim's cousin, in a 1997 interview. "The many people who comb the beach, it happened to be his first cousin that found his license. My brother found the big frame and all the licenses

Cap'n Bill Gaskill's Pamlico Inn at Ocracoke.

were gone but Jim Baughm's. His was the only license left in the big frame, and that wasn't storm damaged at all from the water."

Ten hours after drifting on pieces of the ship's wreckage, two officers and five crewmen were rescued by a passing ship and were taken to Norfolk. Gaskill's sisters—Mary, Lillian and Nellie—traveled to Norfolk to visit the *Caribsea*'s survivors in order to learn more about their brother's final hours. "They went up and talked to the captain, and he told them that Jim Baughm had just been relieved from his watch, and he had just about had time to get to bed and get to sleep when the torpedo struck about directly through his berth," Owen Gaskill said solemnly. His cousin was thought to have been killed instantly.

Ocracoke resident Homer Howard was given the oar so that a cross could be fashioned out of it. Ever since, the cross has stood upon the altar of Ocracoke's Methodist Church. For the typical visitor, and from a distance, the plain wooden cross appears unremarkable. Not until one looks closely at the base can he see two small plates with the inscriptions: "In memory of Captain James B. Gaskill, July 2, 1919 - March 11, 1942. This cross constructed from salvage of the ship upon which Capt. Gaskill lost his life."

Soon after unleashing his torpedoes on the unlucky *Caribsea*, Kapitänleutnant Rostin ordered his helmsman to steer U-*158* into Onslow Bay, the broad body of water between Cape Lookout and Cape Fear. Two days later and 13 miles southeast of Carolina Beach, Rostin found what he was searching for—a large, heavily-laden tanker, the 523-foot-long SS *John D. Gill*.

The ship, loaded with almost 142,000 barrels of crude oil, was on its way to Philadelphia from Texas and had been ordered to wait off Charleston due to potential danger from U-boats in the sea lanes to the north, but the ship resumed her voyage on March 12. Nine hours later, the tanker was struck in her #7 tank with a single torpedo from U-*158*.

A huge hole was torn below the ship's waterline, and a torrent of crude oil began to pour into the sea; yet the initial explosion failed to ignite the fuel. However, in the rush to abandon the ship, a crew member tossed overboard a life ring with a self-igniting carbide light, which set fire to the massive amount of oil encircling the ship. Within seconds, the tanker's crew were surrounded by a murderous firestorm. One lifeboat loaded with 15 men was launched safely. A raft with eight sailors and three members of the U.S. Navy Armed-Guard managed to frantically paddle away from the all-consuming fire. But when the #4 lifeboat was lowered, it jammed on the falls, tossing its occupants into the terrifying maelstrom of fiery waves where at least two of the men were sucked into the still-turning propeller. Two other men desperately clung to the lines dangling above the voracious vortex of water produced by the gigantic rotating screw. One of them, Herbert Gardner, did his best to help the other man to hold on. He urged him to climb upward, but then suddenly Gardner was alone. The other man lost his grip and vanished into the unspeakable horrors below. "That's bothered me all my life," Gardner later said in an interview.

Once the propeller finally stopped turning, Gardner let go, and began to swim away from the enormous tanker, which was soon completely ablaze as one oil bunker after another detonated in a violent, apocalyptic display of destructive power. Despite having strapped around him a cork lifebelt, Gardner repeatedly dived and swam beneath the waves in a desperate effort to escape. "When you're scared, you can do anything," Gardner said. "Every time I'd come up, I'd come up on fire. My head and my hands would be on fire." After an enormous effort, Gardner finally swam clear of the flames and was pulled aboard the raft. From a safe distance, the survivors were awestruck by what they could see of the ship that minutes before had been their home. "It kept burning and burning and blowing up and blowing up, until it finally just literally blew itself to pieces," crew member Floyd Ready later said.

Twenty-three men from the *John D. Gill* perished: six officers, 13 crewmen, and four members of the U.S. Navy Armed Guard. The survivors in the lifeboat were rescued by a passing tanker and taken to Charleston. The 11 survivors on the raft were picked up by the Coast Guard cutter *Agassiz*, which had responded to the attack, and were taken into Southport where they were admitted to Dosher Memorial Hospital. The staff at the small community hospital was suddenly overwhelmed with critically injured men.

"We didn't think even half of them hardly could live," said Josephine Hickman, a Red Cross volunteer nurse who had only recently received her training. "They were so burned, almost to a crisp, and covered with oil. Some of them were burned so bad that the bandages were all over their heads. Only their mouths were open. You just fed them in between the bandages."

Hickman and the doctors and nurses at the hospital worked courageously to save the *John D. Gill* sailors for more than 20 hours straight. "We'd barely gotten our training when this tanker was torpedoed offshore, and here we were faced with this terrible tragedy, but we managed to save every one of them," she said.

Kapitänleutnant Rostin and the crew of U-*158* were not finished with their march of terror off the North Carolina coast. They retraced their course back to the Cape Lookout area where they found the unarmed tanker SS *Ario*, steaming to Texas in ballast.

The Germans launched a single torpedo that fatally holed the tanker and then began indiscriminately firing their deck gun at the ship. The *Ario*'s captain ordered his crew to man the lifeboats and abandon the ship, but as it was being lowered, the #3 lifeboat was struck by one of the U-boat's shells, killing five of its occupants. Three other *Ario* sailors later died who are believed to have been in the #3 lifeboat; there were 28 survivors.

The shooting or shelling of merchant sailors escaping their torpedoed vessels has long been a disputed and highly controversial subject of U-boat operations in U.S. territorial waters. Throughout 1942, numerous lifeboats were found washed-up on East Coast beaches, including many in North Carolina, that were riddled with bullet holes, causing widespread rumors that German U-boat crews were shooting survivors. Manteo native Arnold Tolson was a 19-year-old chief petty officer in the U.S. Coast Guard in command of an 83-foot patrol boat, and he remembered hearing the stories. "There were some lifeboats that washed ashore that had bullet holes in 'em where they'd shoot the lifeboats after they got in 'em and stuff," Tolson told the author. "I don't know, and I didn't see it; that's hearsay, but I saw the boats."

"German U-boat crews did not machine gun survivors," said Michael Gannon, author of *Operation Drumbeat*. "This is an urban legend, one that continues to be told today by people who live along the eastern seaboard. No, they never shot up survivors, and I'll tell you the reasons why. There was a camaraderie among men who went to sea, and no seaman, even in conditions of war, would shoot an innocent, helpless person in the water. A second reason for this was a directive that went out from Admiral Dönitz to all his U-boat fleets. They were not to harm survivors in the water or in lifeboats. First, because it would be inhumane. And second, because then the U-boat crews would think that the same might happen to them someday, and that would cause a loss of morale."

Professor Gannon's defense of Dönitz's Ubootwaffe notwithstanding, there were a few isolated but well-documented instances when Allied merchant sailors, while attempting to escape their torpedoed ships, were killed by German bullets or shells, striking the victims either errantly or intentionally. In addition to Kapitänleutnant Rostin's shelling of the *Ario*'s men off Cape Lookout, on April 2, 1942, 23 crew members of the collier SS *David H. Atwater* were killed as they attempted to launch their lifeboats by machine gun fire from Kapitänleutnant Erich Topp's U-552. This incident, 10 miles east of Chincoteague Inlet, Virginia, was observed from a distance by a Coast Guard patrol boat. Overall, however, there are few such documented cases of the shooting of survivors. The vast majority of lifeboats found on beaches riddled with bullet holes were the result of U.S. and British patrol vessels that may have found the lifeboats empty and drifting offshore and would attempt to sink the boats so that others patrolling the ocean would not continually find them.

Kapitänleutnant Rostin and U-158 departed the U.S. coast after the attack on the *Ario* and returned to France by the end of March. Following a two-month refit, the U-boat and its crew returned to the western Atlantic, this time patrolling the Yucatan Channel west of Cuba and U.S. ports along the Gulf of Mexico, sinking 12 ships and more than 62,000-tons, making it the 5th most successful U-boat patrol of the war. Fifty-six days into her patrol and on her way back to France, U-158 intercepted the Latvian steam freighter *Everalda*, 360-miles southeast of Cape Hatteras. The U-boat was out of torpedoes and nearly out of ammunition. The Germans expended their last rounds firing at the freighter but had to board the vessel in order to sink it by opening its sea valves. Rostin then ordered the capture of the freighter's master, Janis Martinson, and a Spanish crew member. Unfortunately for U-*158*'s two hostages, they were aboard the U-boat the next day when it was sunk by an American aircraft.

The deaths of Rostin and his men could hardly be considered an equitable atonement for the 187 Allied merchant sailors who died by their hands during the three previous months, including Ocracoke's Jim Baughm Gaskill.

With much anticipation and relief, the audience hushed as the curtains parted. Shafts of light flickered and pierced the haze of cigarette smoke as the projector sputtered, gaining speed. Then, a movie newsreel suddenly burst upon the silver screen. The theater might have been the Carolina in Elizabeth City, the Bailey in Wilmington, the Turnage in Washington, or dozens of others throughout the coastal region of North Carolina. The patrons in the movie house were there for a brief respite, to laugh at Bud Abbott and Lou Costello in their latest madcap misadventures and to forget the war with its thunderous explosions and sobering reminders of sailors suffering, burning, drowning, or disappearing into the sea. But before the main attraction began, the audience was expected to watch the latest patriotic newsreel from the U.S. Office of War Information (OWI).

As the film began, swirling seawater filled the screen, and a U-boat conning tower broke the ocean surface. His white skipper's cap tilted high on his head as he pressed his eye against the optics of the attack periscope, a U-boat captain turned to his crew and shouted, "Auf gefechtsstationen (to battle stations)!" In the distance, a violent explosion erupted, and superheated fragments of molten steel streaked across the sky like a thousand meteorites. The narrator's voice was strident:

> "The U-boat was beaten in the last war. It can be beaten again. But every Nazi sub surfaced for the night kill postpones our victory over Hitler. American action now will keep the Atlantic convoys sailing. Every ship worker, every civilian everywhere on the job—America's all-out production guarantees triumph over the U-boat. American merchant seaman know the U-boat's sting, but they sign to sail again. Army and Navy air patrols guard the convoys. The Navy hunts the U-boats. Teamwork America, teamwork now, and in the Fuherer's face!"

Meanwhile, even as the Office of War Information's patriotic newsreels played in theaters across North Carolina, U-*123* surfaced for the night kill, driving through heavy swells as she approached the North Carolina coast for her second American war patrol. The date was March 30, 1942. For seven weeks since their triumphant return to Lorient, France, and the conclusion of Operation Paukenschläg, Reinhard Hardegen couldn't wait to return to Cape Hatteras, to add to the Graveyard of the Atlantic's list of sunken ships. He now proudly possessed a Ritterkreuz des Eisernen Kreuzes—Knight's Cross of the Iron Cross—awarded by Admiral Dönitz after Hardegen's first American patrol in recog-

nition of supreme bravery and leadership in wartime. The honor, highly coveted among the members of the German armed forces, was presented immediately upon their return on February 9 before his admiring crew, a cheering crowd, and a military band. Then, following a three-week refit, U-*123* untethered her lines again and rode the tide out of the Blavet River for her second long voyage westward to the United States.

His quartermaster's dead reckoning was spot on. Just as expected, a loom of light flickered once over the horizon; then again seven and a half seconds later; then again and again. Hardegen later wrote these words in his Kriegstagebüch—his war diary: "Cape Hatteras Lighthouse is in sight, our old friend from the last patrol."[10] Remarkably, the lighthouse was still in operation, faithfully flashing its light and guiding both friend and foe.

During the week preceding their sighting of the Cape Hatteras Lighthouse, Hardegen and his men of U-*123* attacked and sank the American ships SS *Muskogee* and USS *Atik* (disguised as the merchant freighter *Carolyn*) and the British tanker *Empire Steel*. They were nearly late to Germany's march of terror.

The last 16 days of March were the most devastating and deadly days of the war for Allied vessels in the western Atlantic. With U-*124* leading the charge of 11 of Dönitz's ship-killing U-boats, captains Johann Mohr, Walter Flachsenberg, Georg Lassen, Helmut Möhlmann, Erich Topp, Johannes Oestermann, Erwin Rostin, Otto von Bulow, Heinrich Schuch, Johannes Liebe, and Reinhard Hardegen ruled the waters of the American eastern sea frontier, sinking or damaging with impunity 31 ships and sending an appalling number of men, women, and children to their watery grave. Six-hundred-eighty-three people perished during those 16 days. The period was the bleakest, most-desperate, and most heart-rending for the U.S. government and military authorities.

In stark contrast, the men of Germany's Ubootwaffe began to refer to the period as "Zweite Die Glückliche Zeit" or the "second happy time."[11] During U-*124*'s patrol off the North Carolina coast in March, Korvettenkapitän (lieutenant-commander) Johann Mohr had so much success that he was inspired to sum up his accomplishments by composing his radio report to Dönitz in verse. After sinking or damaging nine ships in seven days, Mohr wrote:

> "The new-moon night is black as ink
> Off Hatteras the tankers sink
> While sadly Roosevelt counts the score—
> Some fifty thousand tons—by Mohr."

As March passed into the record books, the U.S. Navy's Eastern Sea Frontier command staff reluctantly published not poetry, but the following forthright prose: "The Eastern Sea Frontier was the most dangerous area for merchant shipping in the entire world."

Such were the conditions when Reinhard Hardegen gazed upon his old friend from the last patrol, the Cape Hatteras Lighthouse. At the same moment, somewhere in the ocean to the northeast, probably fewer than 30 miles away, lifeboat #4 from the passenger-freighter *City of New York*, pitched and wallowed in heavy seas and darkness, crowded with despondent and seasick survivors and the ever-hopeful Desanka Mohorovicic clutching her newborn child.

Although World War II has long since ended, a contentious battle of a different sort has been waged for many years over the veteran status of merchant sailors and due recognition for their service.

President Franklin D. Roosevelt purportedly promised that mariners of the U.S. Merchant

Marine and Army Transport Service would be given veteran status and a Seaman's Bill of Rights for their wartime service. In a letter of congratulations to apprentice seamen in training, Roosevelt acknowledged the vital role performed by civilian sailors: "The entire country joins me in wishing you every success and in paying tribute to you men of the Merchant Marine who are so gallantly working and fighting side by side with our Army and Navy to defend the way of life which is so dear to us all."

According to the organization "American Merchant Marine at War" (usmm.org), Roosevelt's promises died with him. Following the war, numerous applications were made over the years on behalf of merchant seamen to be afforded the well-deserved benefits enjoyed by military veterans including health care, compensation for service-related disabilities, educational assistance, and burial and memorial services. The requests were repeatedly denied by the Office of Veterans Affairs. *American History* magazine in 1993 called the post-war treatment of mariners by Washington bureaucrats "reprehensible."

It was not until 1987 when three mariners took their case to United States District Court, Washington, D.C., that a motion to require the Civilian/Military Service Review Board to reconsider applications for benefits was granted. The Department of Defense finally relented and granted veteran status under Public Law 95-202 to the men of the U.S. Merchant Marine. Unfortunately, by then, many wartime mariners and their spouses were no longer around to receive the government's thanks.

Another controversy arose when a bill was introduced in Congress titled, "Belated Thank You to the Merchant Mariners of World War II Act of 2007," to provide a monthly cash benefit and burial option to eligible merchant seamen and their spouses. During the vigorous lobbying process, a claim was made which became accepted as historical fact and disseminated to the public in such sources as Wikipedia, that merchant mariners died at a rate of one in 24, which, if true, would represent the highest rate of casualties of any U.S. military service. According to historian Charles Dana Gibson, the ratio was based on an erroneous number of 250,00 for the total number of civilian sailors serving during World War II. Research by Gibson and others concluded that the total mariner force numbered closer to 450,000, resulting in a casualty ratio of one in 67, which is less than the U.S. Marines (one in 34) but more than the U.S. Navy (one in 113). The total number of merchant mariners who died in the war was 6,185.

What no one can argue is that the war could not have been won without the men of the U.S. Merchant Marine.

From a U-boat off the North Carolina coast, a German telegraphist rapidly tapped out a morse code message. The enciphered signal was sent in digits and dozens of groups of five letters, "H6R 3TLE 224 DKRKI CUZAF AWXVJ DVZNH…"

In a building next door to Admiral Dönitz's chateau at Lorient, 3,700miles away, a radio operator received the U-boat's "gibberish" and decoded it into a readable dispatch detailing its location and operational intel. The device that encrypted and decrypted the message in both the U-boat and at BdU was known as a Funkschlüssel-Machine, or by its manufacturer, Enigma. The Enigma was an immensely complex electromechanical cipher machine that had been developed in the 1920s for German bank transactions but was adopted by the intelligence and communications services of the Wehrmacht prior to the war. The coded messages the Enigma produced—identified in different forms as "Hydra" and "Triton"—were trusted by Third Reich commanders to be unbreakable. However, at various stages throughout the war, the British were reading the messages.

H6R	5RH	DE	C	1346	= 3TLE	= 2TL	224	= HUW	XNG	=
DKRKI	CUZAF	MNSDC	AWXVJ	DVZNH	DMOZN	NWRJC	KKJQO			
ELWIK	XDUUF	ECEGN	OUNNQ	CIIZX	FUTKF	BTNWI	GOECK			
CMYUC	KTTYB	ZMDTU	WCNWH	OXOFX	ERVQW	JUCVY	PQACQ			
EBMXE	NOQKF	LWRWR	LGKXZ	BPYWR	GQVYG	WJDGA	QXKVC			
MQQJJ	PVSLG	WFZJZ	HHWQG	YFCQQ	RMVRR	QQIDQ	QVVIW			
LJLBH	LHHDI	OFWUY	JJQGX	BWPZ						
CCT	2/3	RCGGN								

At the same instant that the U-boat's message was received in France, in any one of 32 sites known as Y-stations across Britain—at places like the village of Chicksands in Bedfordshire or the windswept chalk cliffs of Beachy Head in Sussex—diligent listeners intercepted the German coded signals over shortwave receivers and frantically copied the nonsensical letters and numbers onto a piece of paper. Y-station operators recall that when something big was happening, the wires were "alive" with morse code. Sheets of intercepts were handed to a motorcycle courier who then raced across miles of hedgerow-lined country roads to Station-X, otherwise known as Bletchley Park, a Buckinghamshire manor house and estate smartly located between Oxford and Cambridge. Station-X was the headquarters of Britain's Government Code and Cipher School where hundreds of brilliant cryptanalysts, engineers, translators, and clerical workers toiled day and night to break, and read, the German Enigma codes.

"For intercepts of U-boat signals to be useful the decryption had to done quickly," said Patrick Beesly, Deputy Chief for the Admiralty's Submarine Plotting Room. "Intelligence more than forty-eight hours old was liable to have been overtaken by events and to be of use only as background information."

The world's first computers were invented and built to speed the process because the complexity of the Enigma machines was staggering. By multiplying a machine's variations of rotors, rotor sequences and positions, and wire and plug connections, the theoretical number of cipher combinations totaled 160 trillion. The achievements of the code breakers and the daring capture of secret documents and Enigma machines aboard U-boats at sea by Allied naval forces changed the course of history. Sir Harry Hinsley, the official historian of British Intelligence in World War II, said that breaking the Enigma code shortened the war "by not less than two years and probably by four years; moreover, had the code not been broken, it is uncertain how the war would have ended." Also uncertain is how many hundreds of thousands—even millions—of lives were saved as a result.

CHAPTER: 15

USS *Jesse Roper* (DD-147)

HUNTING HORNETS
ALL OVER THE FARM

"On more than one occasion I would lay there thinking how there was three-eighths-of-an-inch of steel between me and a torpedo or a shell."

Rhodes Chamberlin

On Wednesday, March 4, 1942, Americans living along the eastern seaboard awakened as usual and went about their normal morning routines. Coffee was percolated, toast was buttered, and the morning papers were unfolded revealing the latest war news. Front page headlines cheered the U.S. Navy's recent downing of 16 Japanese heavy bombers while repelling an aerial attack on a carrier task force near the Gilbert Islands in the western Pacific. In Europe, Royal Air Force bombers pummeled French factories near Paris that had been "a vast source of supplies for Hitler's war machine." Mid-Atlantic states, including Pennsylvania, West Virginia, and Ohio, were recovering from a record-setting late-winter snow storm that forced tens of thousands of people to take a day off from work.

Almost lost among the less-important news on page two was a small Associated Press story, not much more than four column-inches, with the headline: "Closer and Closer—U.S. Destroyer Sunk Off New Jersey; 100 Lost—Only 11 Saved Out of Some 145 in Crew in Loss Close to Cape May." The story briefly summarized a "tersely worded" Navy communique issued the day before, which described the sinking by a German U-boat of the World War I-era, *Wickes*-class flush-deck destroyer, USS *Jacob Jones* (DD 130). According to the AP, the *Jacob Jones* was "the first United States warship ever torpedoed and sunk by an enemy submarine in home waters." The devastating attack and humiliating loss to the Navy occurred five days earlier on February 28, 35 miles due east of Rehoboth Beach, Delaware.

The tragic loss of the destroyer and her men was not only terribly painful for the 138 families who were suddenly without a father, a son, a brother, or an uncle, but also for the Navy, which had very few of its warships in U.S. territorial waters capable of hunting and destroying German U-boats. In fact, the *Jacob Jones* was the first—and for some weeks, the only—U.S. destroyer assigned full-time anti-submarine patrol duty in the Atlantic off East Coast beaches.

The U.S. Navy destroyer, "with its speed, maneuverability, superior sound gear, and ability to keep the sea in conditions that drive smaller craft into port, is the deadly and traditional enemy of the submarine," stated the ESF War Diary for March 1942. Unfortunately for Admiral Andrews and his staff who were responsible for defending the ocean waters of the home front—and protecting the Allied merchant fleet—there were few, if any, destroyers available under his command. For weeks, Andrews repeatedly sent requests to Admiral Ernest King, Commander-in-Chief, United States Fleet,[12] for more destroyers to be assigned to anti-submarine patrol in U.S. coastal waters, but King rejected the requests. King needed the destroyers for convoy duty in the North Atlantic.

Worldwide during the month of March, 79 Allied and neutral vessels were sunk by Axis forces, yet 50 percent of those losses occurred within the Eastern Sea Frontier and its boundary 500 miles out from the U.S. littoral. Only 6 percent of sinkings during that month occurred along the convoy routes between Nova Scotia, Iceland, and Britain in the northern waters of the Atlantic. Yet despite the obvious disproportion of losses between the waters of the home front and the North Atlantic, the latter was assigned 41 percent of the Navy's destroyers in the Atlantic, while the former—the place where U-boats were sinking the greater number of ships—had temporary access to only 5 percent of the warships that the Navy said was the "traditional enemy of the submarine."

The ESF staff complained bitterly up the chain of command. The March War Diary stated: "From the beginning, it has been understood that the dangers from the submarine can be eliminated only through the action of superior forces. Such forces have not been available in the last three months. There was a shortage of every kind of ship and plane that could be used effectively against the U-boat, but especially there has been an insufficient number of destroyers."

In Washington, D.C., Admiral King was not oblivious nor insensitive to the plight of unescorted merchant vessels making the dangerous dash around the North Carolina coast in March 1942. He issued orders permitting destroyers not assigned impending convoy sailings, and also those that were being redeployed to other ports and others that were en route to maintenance yards and refueling docks, to spend a little time "hunting" for U-boats off the Atlantic states. The more-accurate characterization might have been "chasing" U-boats.

During the deadly month of March, when Admiral Dönitz had concentrated his U-boat forces to the waters of the mid-Atlantic coast, Admiral Andrews had at his disposal an average of two destroyers per day to counter the German offensive. At various times during the month, USS *Herbert*, USS *Dahlgren*, USS *Dickerson*, USS *Jesse Roper*, USS *Cole*, and USS *Dupont* had more than 400,000 square miles of ocean in which to search for U-boats. The *Herbert* spent the most number of days, 18 in March, patrolling U.S. waters; the *Dickerson* and the *Roper* each were allowed 8 days of the month under

Andrews' command. The remaining destroyers were out for only a couple of days. While on patrol, the destroyers mostly spent their time speeding to the coordinates of a torpedoed and sinking merchant ship only to find smoldering wreckage, oil slicks, and empty lifeboats. It was the only way the Navy could narrow down the U-boats' locations—albeit, where the U-boats had been, not where they were at the moment. Not a single destroyer had yet seen a U-boat, heard a U-boat's screw turning on their hydrophones, or bounced a sonar ping off a U-boat's hull. The U-boats were phantoms!

It was said by a president: "Somebody has got to think out the way to not only fight the [German] submarine, but to do something different from what we are doing." The President was Woodrow Wilson, and he made that brazen, unvarnished statement during World War I in an address to the officers of the United States Atlantic Fleet in August 1917. President Roosevelt, 25 years later, could have dusted off Wilson's speech and presented it to his current naval staff because Wilson had gone on to say something that proves that life's lessons are often forgotten and that history repeats itself. "We are hunting hornets all over the farm and letting the nest alone," Wilson said. "None of us know how to go to the nest and crush it and yet I despair of hunting for hornets all over the sea when I know where the nest is and know that the nest is breeding hornets as fast as I can find them."

In the late winter and early spring of 1942, Admiral Andrew's part-time sub-chasing destroyers were doing little but chasing the hornets all over the sea. It was a nerve-racking time for all, but none more than for merchant captains and their crews, who all shared an extreme allergy to the sting of the German "hornet."

Captain Albin Johnson was one who had good reason to be anxious. His cargo ship, SS *Liberator*, was uncomfortably close to the hornets. As his ship was passing Cape Lookout on its way north on March 18, Johnson and his crew witnessed the attacks and blazing fires of the tankers *Papoose* and *W.E. Hutton* about 15 miles behind their stern in the sector of the sea through which they had just passed. As twilight yielded to inky darkness, ahead of the *Liberator* lay Cape Hatteras and Diamond Shoals, the epicenter of U-boat activity within the entire Eastern Sea Frontier.

The *Liberator*'s crew was already weary from a day of unceasing worry and watchfulness as SOS and SSSS signals jammed the airwaves, but Johnson exhorted everyone on watch to maintain a sharp lookout—their very survival depended on their eyesight and concentration. Four men of the U.S. Navy Armed Guard stood by their four-inch gun, which was loaded and ready to fire. The men were twitchy, anxious, and fatigued.

As they steamed north of Cape Lookout, the gun crew's commander, Coxswain Frank Camillo, peered through his spyglass off the starboard beam into the concealing shroud of night and saw what looked like a U-boat: long, low, dark, and suddenly turning toward the *Liberator* at a rapid rate of speed. Camillo instantly ordered his men to open fire, which they expertly did, firing a deadly artillery shell into the "conning tower" of the suspected U-boat. Unfortunately, the U-boat was, in fact, the USS *Dickerson*, which was attempting to identify the *Liberator*. The destroyer took a direct hit on the starboard side of her chart house, which inflicted mortal wounds upon the destroyer's skipper, Lt. Cmdr. J. K. Reybold, the sonar operator, the radar operator, and killing a seaman

outright. The *Dickerson*'s executive officer, who had been off-duty, took command and ordered the disabled warship to set a course for Norfolk with great haste, hoping to arrive in time to save the badly wounded Reybold and the other casualties. The next day, 10 minutes before the destroyer arrived at the Navy pier at Norfolk, Reybold died.

At a few minutes past 10 a.m. the next morning, the *Liberator* suffered the very fate her men so feared and was torpedoed and sunk just a couple of miles south from the seaward end of Diamond Shoals, in less than 90 feet of water. Five of the freighter's engine room watch were killed; 31 men survived, including the ship's gun crew and its master, Albin Johnson.

The friendly fire incident upon the USS *Dickerson* stunned Naval authorities and left Admiral Andrews, at least for a few weeks, with one fewer destroyer with which to chase U-boats at a time when Dönitz was dispatching a new wave of his forces. (The *Dickerson* was quickly repaired and was back on duty in April.) The Navy, in its home waters, was on its heels, and its senior officers knew it. The March War Diary acknowledged their predicament: "For those on the defensive, this is a constant disadvantage. With them lies the necessity to adjust to changing conditions, to improvise answers to new techniques, to follow after an enemy shifting into new territories. Success in anti-submarine warfare depends greatly on the rapidity with which those on the defensive can act to close the gap of this time lag."

Admiral Andrews and his staff knew the solution to the mounting losses of merchant ships in the Eastern Sea Frontier. Admiral King and his staff knew the solution, too. Winston Churchill and the British Royal Navy, better than anybody, knew what was needed to defeat U-boats in U.S. waters. Even Admiral Dönitz had anticipated how the U.S. Navy was going to put a stop to his U-boats' successes. But achieving solution for the Allies was going to take time, and more time meant more needless sinkings and deaths. Everyone hoped for a miracle.

USS *Jesse Roper* (DD-147)

The tragic loss of the USS *Jacob Jones*, followed by the deadly mishap involving the USS *Dickerson*, were not only tough on the Navy brass, but also had the potential to weaken the morale of those men serving on the scant few other destroyers patrolling the waters off East Coast beaches. Rhodes Chamberlin was a 19-year-old Boatswain's Mate 2nd Class radioman aboard the USS *Jesse Roper* during the time when the destroyer was on anti-submarine patrol off the North Carolina coast. "My bunk was down below, next to the hull, and on more than one occasion I would lay there thinking how there was three-eighths-of-an-inch of steel between me and a torpedo or a shell," Chamberlin said.

Whether they affectionately called their ships, "tin cans," "four pipers," "flush deckers," or "World War I antiques," the *Wickes*-class destroyer men had a love-hate relationship with their ships. The men who sailed on the destroyers often complained that even in moderate seas the forward topsides, including the bridge deck and gun positions, were constantly wet, and in the heaviest sea conditions the vessels could roll at frightening angles. The 314-foot-long destroyers had a poor turning radius and a limited range without refueling. But the "four pipers" were fast, up to 35 knots at maximum power, and most bristled with weaponry. The *Roper*, for example, carried six 21-inch torpedoes, depth charges with K- and Y-guns, six-3"/50 caliber guns,[13] and four .50-caliber machine guns.

Regardless of the name of the ship on which they sailed, the men of the destroyers shared a common bond. The *Roper*'s men had been friends with the crew of the *Jacob Jones*. They had trained together, went to sea together, tied up together in port, and when the opportunity presented itself, they raised hell together in the bawdy bars on Norfolk's Main Street or other East Coast ports.

When the *Jacob Jones* went down, the men on the *Roper* were badly shaken. "That had a reasonably strong impact [on us], because we knew many of those guys who were on the 'Jakie,'" Chamberlin said. "I had two friends that had gone to radio school [with me] that were on the 'Jakie.' All four ships that were in the division—the *Jacob Jones*, the *Roper*, the *Herbert*, and the *Dickerson*—we would see each other tied-up against each other. There was a lot of transferring of men between the old four pipers. When a ship needed a particular rating [a Navy enlisted man's occupation or skill], the bureau would often pick one from another four piper and move him to that other ship."

Perhaps, for men on destroyers like the *Roper*, even more demoralizing than the loss of their friends on the *Jacob Jones* were the endless, futile days and nights of chasing phantom U-boats and being called to General Quarters to drop depth charges on submerged hulks of ships the U-boats had already sunk off the North Carolina coast.

"We were on this 'finding a needle in a haystack' situation, looking for submarines by ourselves, and, considering the number of square miles that are out there in the ocean, [the U-boats] really were a needle in the haystack," Chamberlin said. "We would see partial wrecks, the debris floating everywhere, the oil slicks, which would bring to mind what caused them. On those Cape Hatteras patrols, it was GQ, GQ, GQ quite frequently, and we got a little tired of that. It got to the point that we got [sonar] contacts so frequently that we'd drop a pattern of depth charges without sounding General Quarters— not that [the sonar contacts] were submarines, but there were so many wrecks. We'd drop a pattern of depth charges just to be on the safe side."

Because the *Roper* was shorthanded, watch schedules had been set for four hours on, four hours off. For the destroyer's men who were off watch and trying to fall asleep—even when they weren't being called to their action stations on deck—the round-the-clock detonations added to the strain and their exhaustion. At random times during the day and night, they might be awakened by a shuddering sound—boom-boom-boom—and then they'd often lie awake waiting for their next watch to begin.

The destroyer men were assigned an impossible task. Their warship had been designed and built, and their training had been conducted, for the sole purpose of seeking, engaging, and destroying the enemy. In March 1942, the four pipers assigned to the Eastern Sea Frontier had seemingly become powerless, reduced to conducting search and rescue of torpedoed survivors.

The Navy sailors relied on their professionalism to carry them on. "We got to a point a little detached," Chamberlin said. "We went through the motions and tried to do just what was necessary without getting [emotionally involved]. When we brought survivors on board, there would be empathy for them, but we tended to be more empathetic than sympathetic. You almost had to, because there was so much going on. You still had your job to keep the ship running. I don't know that anyone sat around and moped about it because there was so much [devastation around], there was no point in getting personally involved. Hatteras being what it is, we were often hanging on to the ship because the sea would get rough."

"Now hear this: Set material condition 'Affirm,'" announced the voice from the bridge over the ship's intercom, ordering that the destroyer should be made water tight for potential action. All bulkheads dogged tight; hatches battened; ventilators shut down;

pre-assigned ready guns manned; everyone prepared, at a moment's notice to rush to their battle stations; and repair parties were at the ready. On Palm Sunday morning, March 29, the USS *Jesse Roper* was on patrol east of Cape Hatteras in the most dangerous waters in the world. Within the previous few hours, U-boats had been observed and reported by numerous merchant vessels to be at various locations in the patrol sector. The evidence of the U-boats' presence was starkly evident—to the north of the *Roper*'s position was the smoldering wreckage and floating corpses of the Panamanian freighter, *Equipoise*; to the south of Cape Hatteras, stars were eclipsed by the towering column of black smoke marking the grave of the tanker, *Dixie Arrow*.

Like prey being chased in a forest, the destroyer changed course every five minutes in the zigzagging pattern dictated by division headquarters. All available eyes peered into the darkness, but all that they could see were ghosts. Despite each man's efforts to block his thoughts of their dead friends, visions of the *Jacob Jones* and the *Dickerson* filled everyone's minds.

At 5:05 a.m., from a position about 23 miles due east of Little Kinnakeet Coast Guard Lifeboat Station, the *Roper*'s watch sighted the loom of the Cape Hatteras Lighthouse, over the horizon to the southwest, refracted by the marine haze.

The destroyer crept across the ocean's surface at a reduced speed so that the sound of its sonar pings would not be drowned out by the loud rumble of her engines. "Ping... Ping... Ping...," bleated the sonar transmitter, unceasingly searching for solid underwater objects and the reflected sound or echo as it would be bounced back to the ship's sonar receiver, much like a lonely songbird calling for companionship.

Suddenly the sonar operator heard a response: "Ping-ping, Ping-ping, Ping-ping!"

At 10:20 a.m., the *Roper* located a good sound contact, and the ship's speed was increased from 15 knots to 20 knots in order to conform to a depth charge attack. The klaxon wailed, "ah-wooga, ah-wooga," calling General Quarters. The ship's intercom barked commands, men flew into action, and a pattern of 16 depth charges were dropped. The *Roper* whipped hard to starboard, then to port, the ship's rudder carving great arcs of froth on the ocean's surface. Twenty minutes later, seven more depth charges were launched; an hour later, five more were dropped. Nothing appeared on the surface, no oil nor debris were observed which would have indicated that the *Roper* had successfully sunk a U-boat. The sonar echoes fell silent. The contact was lost. At noon, conditions were set to normal. Lunch was served. The log entry for the next four hours was entered: "Steaming as before."

Later that afternoon, another sound contact was made, the destroyer dropped five more depth charges, and a school of fish floated to the surface. Zigzagging continued, speed and course were continually altered and the *Roper* went to-and-fro, hour after hour, crisscrossing the waters that had become known as "Torpedo Junction." So far, they had not done much but kill some fish.

CHAPTER 16

Red Cross nurse holds baby at Norfolk.

A Son of Neptune

His cry sounded "like an echo of the howling wind."

Desanka Mohorovicic

Beyond the barrier islands of North Carolina, the Atlantic Ocean's vast expanse, the dark of night, and the perpetual motion of the sea disguised the chaos and danger present in every square mile. German hornets had left the nest and were swarming the "farm" surrounding Cape Hatteras, but the "farm" was a very big place.

On March 29, at the same pre-dawn moment when lookouts aboard the USS *Jesse Roper* spotted the flash of the Cape Hatteras Lighthouse, U-*123* was 75 miles east of the destroyer's position and headed their way. In just under 24 hours, Reinhard Hardegen would also gaze upon the light of the Cape's lighthouse, the "old friend" from his previous visit.

A few hours later, between the locations of the *Roper* and U-*123*, the life-altering Palm Sunday drama at 35.16N 74.25W soon unfolded. Oberleutnant zur See Georg Lassen of U-*160* heard the accidental distress call sent from the *City of New York*, and he patiently waited for the American passenger-freighter to appear from over the horizon. When it did, Lassen commenced his attack and sank the Farrell Lines flagship. Located only 25 miles west—an hour's distance at cruising speed—the USS *Jesse Roper* was once again in the wrong place at the wrong time.

Steaming as before, the *Roper* continued her futile and frustrating patrol east of Diamond Shoals, even as lifeboats, life rafts, and solitary victims clinging to pieces of wreckage from the *City of New York* were inexorably swept to the northeast by the currents of the Gulf Stream. Despite the destroyer's best efforts to find it, the U-boat that had sunk the *City of New York* seemed to have vanished. The *Roper*'s radar, sonar, hydrophones, and human eyes were unable to locate Lassen's U-*160*.

Steaming as before, the USS *Jesse Roper* patrols the ocean off Cape Hatteras.

Ironically, the next day at 5:45 p.m., almost immediately after U-*123* rose from the seafloor after a day's rest, lookouts in the conning tower observed a periscope protruding above the ocean surface about two miles away, in the direction of Cape Hatteras. Even though the U.S. Navy had been unable to locate U-*160*, Reinhard Hardegen was able to find it, simply by being in the right place at the right time.

Meanwhile, after chasing another phantom U-boat reported to be near Cape Lookout, the *Roper* came upon a "large wooden section of deck and cargo hatch" floating off Core Banks. There was no way to know from which ship the wreckage had come, but there were lots of possibilities. Wreckage was everywhere, and wreckage was not what the *Roper* was looking for. The destroyer reversed course and headed back to the northeast where they might do some good. A patrol aircraft had recently sighted and reported numerous lifeboats rapidly being carried out to sea somewhere east of Wimble Shoals.

By midnight Monday, the *Roper* was steaming in water 11,000 feet deep east-northeast of Cape Hatteras, near the axis of the Gulf Stream, and it was zigzagging on a base course of 70 degrees true. The wind had temporarily eased during the preceding hours, and the waves had diminished to five to eight feet. Visibility was 20 miles, although, as was typical, a shallow, intermittent cloud of fog hovered over the warm Gulf Stream waters. The waxing gibbous moon occasionally shone brightly above, illuminating billows and tatters of stratus clouds streaming in from the west. Occasional flashes of lightening appeared from the direction of the mainland. It seemed an idyllic night to be at sea, unless you were in a lifeboat.

A red flare rocketed into the sky off the *Roper*'s starboard bow. The bridge was alerted, and the destroyer's heading was altered toward the area from where the flare was fired. The officer of the deck, 23-year-old Ensign Kenneth M. Tebo, briefly considered the possibility that the flare was a U-boat ruse designed to draw the destroyer into a trap, and under the circumstances it would have been a good one. Tebo, however, had little choice but to respond to the distress signal. It had been reported that survivors of the torpedoed *City of New York* might be in the area, but up until that moment nobody knew exactly where. Then, five minutes later, a faint flashing light from approximately eight miles ahead seemed to confirm the likelihood that the survivors may have been found. Three short flashes, three long flashes, three short flashes—an SOS!

Tebo ordered the destroyer's speed reduced to 15 knots, then 10 knots, then to five knots, as the 314-foot-long ship began delicate but risky maneuvers to bring alongside a comparatively small lifeboat crowded with people. Most every man aboard the *Roper* held his breath and prayed—they were now a sitting duck for any U-boat potentially lurking nearby.

At 12:47 a.m., the *Roper's* engines were stopped, and the crew commenced taking aboard 27 survivors from the torpedoed *City of New York*. It took an anxious 17 minutes to get the weary survivors up the cargo nets draped over the port side gunwale of the stern. The men, women, and children who gained the deck of the *Roper* were shivering, soaked to the bone, and eternally grateful to have been found by the U.S. Navy warship. Most of the survivors were crewmen of the passenger-freighter, but there were a few civilians, two parents and their son, and two members of the Navy's Armed Guard. The *Roper's* sickbay was suddenly crowded with the infirm. One man, Peter D'Addio, the ship's barber, was in shock when he was lifted aboard the *Roper*. He died within the hour.

While the *Roper* got underway and resumed the search for other survivors, the ship's sonar operator continued to transmit sonar pings, at the same time hoping the pings would not be returned—finding a U-boat now would increase the risks to the remaining survivors nearby should an engagement occur and depth charges or torpedoes were launched in the area.

Back and forth the *Roper* went, steering west, then north, then east, as they searched the darkened peaks and valleys of the restless sea for more survivors. At 2:40 a.m., another flare shot skyward, and a life raft was found with nine desperate survivors shouting and waving frantically. At the moment these men were being lifted aboard the *Roper*, the sonar operator reported a sound contact bearing 45 degrees, and everyone's worst nightmare seemed possible—a U-boat might yet be nearby. *Roper* sailors on the stern yelled as the survivors were being hoisted up the cargo nets, "Hurry, hurry, hurry, go, go, go!" The destroyer immediately sped off toward the source of the sonar contact. At 3:10 a.m., a single depth charge was dropped, but no U-boat was found.

Five minutes later, another flare appeared in the sky, and another raft was found to which were clinging 12 crewmen of the *City of New York*. The morale of the U.S. Navy sailors aboard the *Roper* was, so far, only marginally boosted by the rescue of the survivors—had the destroyer been sinking U-boats instead of chasing them, rescue missions would have been unnecessary.

As of 4:00 a.m., Tuesday, 48 survivors of the *City of New York* had been rescued by the *Roper*; 97 people were still unaccounted for. Neither of the two life rafts nor the lifeboat recovered had included among the survivors a 26-hour-old infant. Lifeboat #4 had not yet been found. As a result of the variability of the currents and eddies of the Gulf Stream, Desanka Mohorovicic's lifeboat had drifted faster, farther, and nearly 15 miles to the northwest of the first lifeboat found by the *Roper*. There was a good chance it would not be found.

Dr. Leonard Conly had successfully completed the most unusual medical procedure of his career—he had delivered a baby without complications in pitch darkness, 15-foot seas, and in a crowded lifeboat. His job done and with the baby cradled to his mother's breast, Conly awkwardly shuffled to the stern of the lifeboat. He sat next to Sarah King, who observed the doctor wincing in pain from his two broken ribs and having been bent over on his knees for the past few hours. Someone passed King a raincoat, which she wanted to give to her friend, Robert Gates, who was only dressed in a thin cotton shirt. Before she could give the coat away, Conly said, "I would like to have that coat to put around me." Conly and King then huddled together and shared the raincoat.

Desanka Mohorovicic's two-year-old daughter, Vesna, sat on King's lap at various times. Except for when she would be intrigued by the flying fish that occasionally flew over the lifeboat, King recalled that the little girl was not happy, and it was difficult for King and the girl to get comfortable. Vesna was cold, so King tried to keep the child bundled in her skirt, all the while the lifeboat pitched up and down on the rolling seas. Every now and then, piercing the roar of wind and waves, could be heard the cries and whimpers of the baby.

Charles Van Gorden, captain of the lifeboat, wanted to get out of the Gulf Stream as soon as possible. Guided by the stars, he did his best to steer the lifeboat westward, perpendicular to the flow of the current. All of the men in the boat—whether civilians or merchant sailors, injured or not—took their turns on the oars, including Dr. Conly, the *City of New York*'s bartender, and a man Sarah King called Robinson Crusoe because of his bushy red beard (probably this was Francis Nangle). Those who were not rowing bailed water. "We would get a little warmer, then shipped water, and we would all be wet and cold again," said King. When the wind picked up, Van Gorden had the men raise the boat's sail. For awhile, King recalled, "We sailed along nicely." Van Gorden knew they were being carried rapidly eastward into the farthest reaches of the Eastern Sea Frontier, which was well beyond the patrol areas of aircraft and where they would encounter con-siderably fewer ships. Their chances of being found diminished with every mile traveled, became less likely with the passing of every hour.

In a June 1942 article for "The Methodist Woman," Sarah King described what hap-pened next aboard the crowded lifeboat: "[On Monday night] there was a storm com-ing up. There was thunder, lightning, and rain in the distance. We had our sail up but couldn't use it because the wind was too strong, but we couldn't get it down without taking the mast down. They were afraid to try to get the mast down for fear it would hit somebody. They were afraid to leave it up for fear the boat would go over or that it would attract the lightning. We didn't know what to do! That was the only time I felt desperate. Here the rain was coming and nothing but a soggy blanket over this mother and child, and if we got the rain we were just about done for."

It had been more than an hour since the USS *Jesse Roper* last found survivors from the *City of New York*. To the officers on the bridge, it was beginning to seem like they had found all the survivors that were going to be found. The destroyer began working its way to the left of the search area, toward shallower water and the more-traveled sector of the ocean. The warship was due east of Kitty Hawk, 100 miles from land. The sea was vacant from horizon to horizon.

Then, at 4:28 a.m., a brilliant light shot into the night sky, about eight miles due north of the *Roper*'s position. Lieutenant (junior grade) M.M Sanford had relieved Ensign Tebo as officer of the deck, and he ordered the destroyer to rush to the signal flare's source. There they found a lifeboat with 21 survivors from the *City of New York*, plus one additional person who had joined the others in the lifeboat 26 hours earlier, Desanka Mohorovicic's newborn son.

The sea had become rougher with strengthening winds from an approaching cold front. A sailor shouted from the deck of the destroyer to the lifeboat rising and falling on 10-foot-seas that they might have to wait until after daybreak to attempt to transfer the survivors to the ship. Not willing to risk their one chance to be rescued, Van Gorden and his crew maneuvered the lifeboat to the leeward side of the destroyer where they could more safely pull alongside. A cargo net was draped over the gunwale of the *Roper*, and men began to leap out of the lifeboat, timing their jumps as the lifeboat was lifted on the waves.

"We need a stretcher for Mrs. Dahlberg," someone yelled from the lifeboat, and a stretcher was quickly passed down. In the confusion and haste of the moment, the men in the lifeboat forgot to strap Dahlberg to the stretcher. As the stretcher was lifted toward the deck of the destroyer, the elderly woman who had successfully escaped the Nazi's in Europe and survived a German torpedo at sea slid from the stretcher and was nearly crushed between the tossing lifeboat and the hull of the destroyer. The men quickly pulled her back into the lifeboat, safely secured her, and back up she went.

"Send the baby up next," someone in the lifeboat shouted. The sailors on the deck of the ship weren't sure they heard correctly over the sloshing of the waves and the whistling of the wind—send the baby up? The mother, however, was not so eager to hand her newborn to strangers on a strange ship in total darkness—after all, she had held the baby closely for more than 24 hours and had survived the German U-boat attack and nights drifting in the notorious Graveyard of the Atlantic. Making matters more worrisome, the lifeboat pitched and yawed, and the gap to the destroyer's hull rapidly widened, then narrowed. *What if they drop him?* she must have thought. But her moment of indecision was brief.

"Then they took the baby up—it had no clothes, and I was afraid they would drop it," said Sarah King. The records have not recorded the man's name, but a sailor on the *Roper*'s crew who must have had very good hands reached down and clutched a wet and slippery 8-pound, 27-hour-old infant. Many years later, when she told her amazing story, Desanka Mohorovicic's most vivid memory was the look on the young sailor's face when he realized he had been handed a newborn. The baby was immediately rushed to the *Roper*'s sickbay. Even before he arrived there, word of his rescue began to quickly make its way through the ship. "It was a big deal," remembered Rhodes Chamberlin. "Just talking about the fact that it was a newborn baby—everybody wanted to see it."

Meanwhile, at the stern of the destroyer, the rescue operation continued. One by one, the survivors were lifted aboard the *Roper*. Understandably, Desanka Mohorovicic had some difficulty jumping over to the cargo net, but she was anxious to gain the more stable deck of the ship and to be reunited with her child. Two young sailors reached down and quickly pulled her up by the arms. She "then walked the full length of the vessel to take a shower before going to bed," according to a report in the *New York World-Telegram*.

Sarah King was next. "My legs would not work," she said. "I had been able to stand in the boat, but I had the side to cling to." The sailors lifted her up, too. In time, all 22 passengers were out of the lifeboat and aboard the *Roper*. As was fitting for a captain of his vessel, no matter its size, Charles Van Gorden was the last to leave the lifeboat before it was cast away.

At 5:26 a.m., the *Roper* sped away in search of more survivors; 75 people were still missing. The survivors aboard the *Roper* had seen two more of the *City of New York*'s lifeboats escape the sinking ship, but neither lifeboat had been seen since late Sunday afternoon.

Shortly after 6 a.m., another flare was spotted to the south, but after heading in that direction the destroyer could find no trace of survivors. A few hours later, an empty lifeboat was found, but there were no markings indicating that it had come from the *City of New York*. The *Roper*'s gun crews were ordered to sink the lifeboat but after firing rounds from the #2 machine gun and two shells from the #2-3"/50 caliber gun, the lifeboat continued to float and the destroyer, having more important business to attend to, left it behind. Later that day, the *Roper* passed another empty lifeboat and three empty life rafts. It seemed that the seas off the North Carolina coast hosted a forlorn procession of unoccupied lifeboats and life rafts.

Where had the other victims gone?

The *Roper*'s crew didn't dwell much on the depressing scene in the water. The entire atmosphere aboard the ship had suddenly and dramatically changed. On a ship designed for war, 70 men, women, and children needed to be clothed, fed, and berthed. The women, like Mohorovicic, King, and Dahlberg, were provided the better accommodations in the officer's quarters, which were far from luxurious—they were each offered a bunk bed. "My clothes were so stiff and wet I could hardly take them off," said King. "I managed to undress myself and get into bed where I stayed all day. They brought us breakfast and were wonderfully good to us in every way."

Sailors who previously had been sullen and fatigued from fruitless hours of patrolling "Torpedo Junction," from the incessant wailing of the klaxon punctuated by exploding depth charges, from days of feeling helplessness, and vulnerability, and from their sense of grief for their fallen comrades were suddenly inspired by all of the activity aboard their ship and the unmistakable looks of gratitude on the faces of the survivors. "Well, of course, [we] appreciated the looks on the survivor's faces and [that] we were able to make them comfortable in our bunks," Chamberlin said. "It was like having a big play pen aft with the kids running around. The crew enjoyed it because we had saved them. The kids put some happiness into the ship, certainly."

One "kid" especially gave the *Roper*'s crew reason to celebrate. "The sailors on the ship were thrilled with the baby," King recalled. "He was made a boatswain's mate and I don't know what all. They said he must come up to the bridge and asked to have him named for the destroyer." However, there is some disagreement in the records as to how the baby's name was decided. According to the *New York World-Telegram*, Mohorovicic had already made that decision even before she had departed her lifeboat. After learning of the name of the ship that had rescued her young family, she announced that the baby would be called Jesse Roper Mohorovicic. At least, that is what Desanka told reporters a few days later.

If the sailors on the *Roper* had not already been enlivened by rescuing the baby, the news that the newborn would be named for their destroyer enthralled the men immensely.[14] "We thought that was great, that the baby was going to be named Jesse Roper," Chamberlin recalled with a big grin. "That was a real shot in the arm. The fact that we were able to stop and save these people and the fact that one of them was this baby, it really made a difference." A positive difference, or a real contribution to the war effort, was something the USS *Jesse Roper* needed very badly, and it was something the *Roper* would soon get.

Even as the *Roper* continued to search the seas for more survivors of the *City of New York*, the crewmen decided to take up a collection for young Jesse Roper Mohorovicic. Some of the passengers of the *City of New York* also contributed to the fund, bringing the total raised to $210 in honor of the newborn. Desanka Mohorovicic was overcome with gratitude when she was given the money. When Jesse grew old enough to comprehend the incredible story of his birth, his mother would often proudly tell him that the young U.S. Navy sailors of the *Roper* and the courageous merchant sailors of the *City of New York* were the boy's true godfathers.

By 3:00 p.m., Tuesday, Lieutenant Commander Hamilton W. Howe, commanding officer of the USS *Jesse Roper*, discontinued the search for more survivors and ordered the destroyer's course be set for Norfolk Naval Operating Base. At 10:55 p.m. that evening, the *Roper* tied up to the south side of pier #5. The gangway was lowered to the pier, and *Roper* crewmen accompanied *City of New York* merchant sailors and civilians down to the pier. Two sailors solemnly carried the canvas-wrapped body of Peter D'Addio.

A large crowd had been awaiting the arrival of the destroyer, and Naval officers, reservists, Red Cross nurses, and military photographers cheerily greeted the disembarking passengers. Flash bulbs popped one after another. A blue-eyed nurse was photographed holding baby Jesse Roper Mohorovicic, warmly swaddled in a blanket, his head barely visible in the photo. Another photograph shows a naval officer carrying Richard Wrigley's daughter June, sound asleep and also bundled warmly.

Ambulances, buses, and cars transported the 70 survivors first to the Norfolk Naval Hospital, and then the next day most were transferred to a city hotel where they were confined until they could be deposed and discharged by U.S. Navy Intelligence. Desanka Mohorovicic, Vesna, and baby Jesse were moved to St. Vincent's Hospital in downtown Norfolk, along with Dr. Leonard Conly and others who were still recuperating from various injuries.

Hours before the *Roper* had returned to port, Lt. Cmdr. Howe had sent a message to his superiors informing them of his special passengers, the Mohorovicic family. Word of the rescue quickly worked its way through the military and government bureaucracies, and Naval authorities and the Office of War Information soon saw a tremendous public relations and morale-boosting national story in the making—"the baby born in a life-

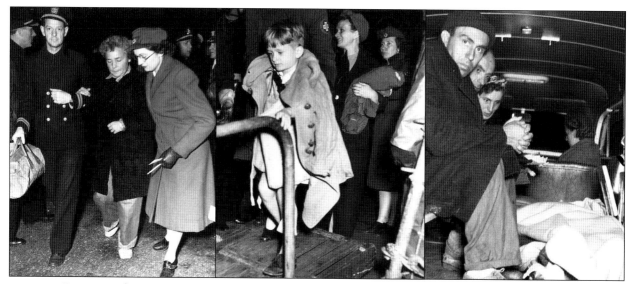

Passengers from MS *City of New York* disembarking at Norfolk (at right is body of Peter D'Addio).

boat." The initial published report was a brief bulletin that appeared in major papers on Wednesday, April 1. The story summarized the basic details of the story framed around the sensational fact that a baby had been born in a lifeboat after its mother's ship had been torpedoed off the East Coast of the United States.

In New York, the attache for the Yugoslav consulate in the United States Joseph Mohorovicic unfolded the morning paper as he prepared to eat his breakfast. Mohorovicic had been anxious as he awaited news of his wife's ship, which was overdue for its arrival at the Farrell Lines pier in New York harbor from Cape Town. They had intended to make the voyage together, but at the last minute, South African immigration officials prohibited Desanka from departing. There was no explanation, but the Mohorovicics suspected that it had something to do with Desanka's condition or perhaps because the departing vessel had no qualified physician aboard. Either way, Joseph was grateful for the unexpected change of plans because his ship was torpedoed by an Axis submarine on February 17. He was injured in the attack and had to spend a few days in a hospital before resuming his journey.

Joseph Mohorovicic's world had been in turmoil since Germany invaded and conquered the Kingdom of Yugoslavia in April 1941. Loyal to the royal family and the king's prime minister, Dušan Simović, Mohorovicic escaped the chaos and bloodshed at home and went into exile with his government. He yearned to provide his young family with the stability, freedom, and opportunities that American democracy offered, so he was thrilled with the prospect to serve with his Royal Government's diplomatic mission in New York. It was a decision that did not come easily—moving to America likely meant that Joseph and Desanka would never see their Yugoslav families again. It was also a terribly risky decision, as the sea lanes in both the South Atlantic and North Atlantic had become dangerous and deadly places to travel. As he prepared to read the morning paper, Mohorovicic reminded himself that all would be well, just as soon as his pregnant wife and daughter arrived in America safe and sound.

Mohorovicic looked down and read a small, late-breaking bulletin: A baby had recently been born in a lifeboat off the U.S. East Coast. Despite the fact that the names of the people and the ship involved were omitted in the article, the instant he read the story Mohorovicic knew the woman was his wife, Desanka. "You can imagine how I felt," he

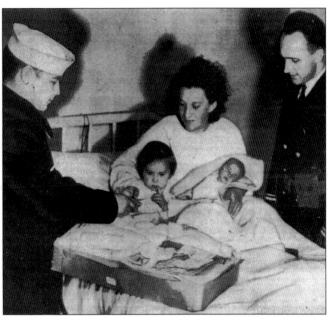
Desanka Mohorovicic is presented with layette by U.S. Navy.

later told a reporter. Hours later, Mohorovicic was officially notified that his 28-year-old wife, the baby, and daughter Vesna, were among the survivors of the torpedoed *City of New York*, and all three had been rescued and taken to Norfolk. He quickly packed a bag, rushed to Penn Station, and purchased a ticket on the next train to Norfolk.

When Joseph Mohorovicic arrived at St. Vincent's Hospital, he encountered a frenzy of activity in his wife's room. The press had been there most of the day, having discovered what they considered to be journalistic gold. The "lifeboat baby" story was just the news the nation needed at a time when the future of the war could not look any bleaker. Sailors from the USS *Jesse Roper* had previously visited their ship's namesake in the hospital and delivered the cash gift and a box of cigars. Charles Van Gorden and Francis Nangle, from the *City of New York* crew dropped in to see how the boy was doing. The two mariners were photographed smoking a cigar in Jesse's honor. Reserve Naval officers from the Office of Navy Relief presented Desanka with a layette of linens and toiletries for the newborn. Red Cross volunteers arrived with a manicurist and hairdresser should Desanka want their assistance. All of the attention made the shy Yugoslavian woman a little uncomfortable.

Reporters jostled and competed to ask questions. "Were you surprised to give birth in a lifeboat?" someone asked. Desanka, a well-educated woman who could speak several languages and was fluent in French, only had a rudimentary command of English. She did her best to reply: "I thought he'd be here in New York, in free America. But it wasn't so bad. We're here; we're well. Grace de Dieu."

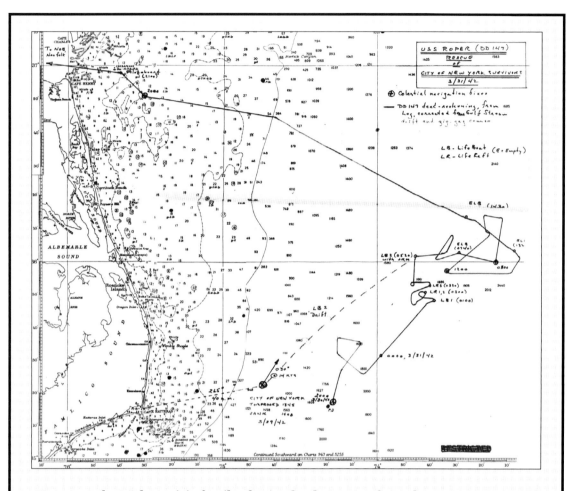

In 1944, the Mohorovicic family obtained a document from the U.S. Coast Guard that officially verified the circumstances of his birth, recorded in the Official Log Book of the M/V *City of New York*. The log entry, dated March 30, 1942, stated that "upon arrival at [the] Hospital, Norfolk, Va., the mother of the child named him Jesse Roper Mohorovicic." But the log did not include a reference to the location of his birth. Over the years, the question of exactly where he was born became an increasingly annoying riddle for Jesse. In 1979, the question was partially answered by an acquaintance, Commander Daniel Seacord, USNR (Ret.). Seacord acquired a copy of the USS *Jesse Roper*'s log and statements from the *City of New York* survivors, from the Naval Historical Center. Seacord painstakingly retraced the route of Jesse's drifting lifeboat based on the speed of the Gulf Stream and the *Roper*'s celestial navigation fixes at various times. Using Seacord's plot, and with a moderate degree of certainty, this writer has approximated Jesse's place of birth as 35-36N 74-27W, which is roughly 50 miles due east of Rodanthe village.

"What were the conditions like in the ocean?" a reporter asked. "The sea, she very, what you call it, rough," Desanka answered, waving a hand up and down to simulate the motion of the waves. "I was in the cabin with her," as she gestured to Vesna. "The torpedo strike. I take up her, and blankets, and start up the stairs. The second torpedo, she strike us; I falled [sic] down the stairs. See, marks on me," she said, pointing to the bruises on her leg.

Before her arduous and remarkable ordeal, Desanka, as a child growing up in Yugoslavia, had always been an avid swimmer. After her experience in the lifeboat, tossed topsy-turvy on the turbulent seas off Cape Hatteras, she was never truly comfortable sitting on a beach or being near the water for the remainder of her life, according to family members.

Dr. Leonard Conly, too, became an overnight celebrity. He was described in one newspaper as "the latest hero of submarine attacks on shipping along the Atlantic coast." In another paper he appears in a large photograph with a big grin, and the caption reads: "A doctor laughs at life—and well he might, for he delivered an eight-pound baby to Mrs. Desanka Mohorovicic in an open lifeboat as it tossed in the wild waves of the Atlantic." Conly told reporters that the mother's labor and delivery were unexpectedly easy. "The child was born in two and a half or three hours after labor began," he said. "After that first night, when [the mother] was too weak to move, she sat up and stayed there the rest of the time holding the almost naked baby against her chest. She is a remarkable woman."

There was so much excitement and activity in the halls of the hospital that Conly almost forgot about his own wife and family. It wasn't until Wednesday night that Conly was able to call home and let his wife know he was okay and would be coming home by train instead of by ship. Earlier that day, some of his family members in Brooklyn had heard the news of the sinking of the *City of New York*, but no one knew the fate of Conly. "The first news was bad," Mrs. Conly told reporters. "They heard only that one boatload of survivors had been saved and no officers were included. The first I knew was when my husband called me last night to tell me he was safe." By Thursday, Conly had his broken ribs taped, and he was on a train back to New York and Herkimer Street in Brooklyn. It isn't known if he ever went to sea again.

"Joseph Mohorovicic is one of the happiest men in the world today," read the caption beneath a newspaper photograph of the joyous reunion of his family at St. Vincent's Hospital, where he met for the first time his four-day-old son. He beamed as he told reporters in the room that "he was very happy" and that the family looked forward to starting "a new life together in America where everybody and everything is superlatively splendid." The Yugoslavian diplomat had no quarrels with not having a say in choosing his son's name.

Ten days later, the Mohorovicic family departed Norfolk by train for New York—Dasanka had insisted that she never travel by water again. Late that same day they arrived at their new home—a sparsely furnished apartment in the upper westside of Manhattan. As a member of the press spoke with Joseph about their future plans, "the dark haired, plump, and healthy Jesse Roper interrupted with a lusty squall." Desanka laughed and told the reporter that his cry sounded "like an echo of the howling wind [that] whipped up 15-foot waves on the night that she gave birth to him."

The couple hoped to establish citizenship for their son. However, the form they were expected to fill out presented a bit of a problem. They were not sure how to complete the

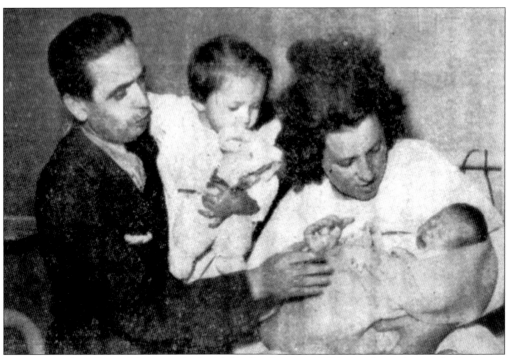

Joseph Mohorovicic is reunited with his family at Norfolk's St. Vincent's Hospital.

blank for "place of birth." The national papers had referred to the lifeboat baby as "a son of Neptune," but that was hardly going to satisfy U.S. immigration officials. For the time being, Joseph filled in the blank for place of birth with, "somewhere in the Atlantic." He told a United Press reporter that day that unless the issue were settled by a court of law, he would wait until his son was old enough to determine his citizenship for himself. As it happened, Jesse didn't have to. By virtue of having been born in a lifeboat belonging to a ship of United States registry, and because he landed first on U.S. soil, Jesse Roper Mohorovicic had already become a citizen of the United States.

The national press often referred to Jesse as "the lifeboat baby." The family's Jewish neighbors in Washington Heights coined the more potent phrase, "The Baby Hitler Couldn't Get." The press couldn't capitalize enough on his remarkable story. A major newspaper ran an update with the headline, "Lifeboat Baby Gains Two Pounds."

The Mohorovicics were bemused by their unlikely fame but gracious in accepting their celebrity role. Letters from mothers across America were sent to Desanka, telling her how her courage and determination provided them with inspiration. The president of the Farrell Lines shipping company made sure the family was well cared for. The exiled Yugoslavian government of King Peter II also kept a close eye on the newborn's progress. On the occasion of his first birthday, Jesse was baptized at St. Patrick's Cathedral in

New York, and the story made national headlines. Yugoslavian Prime Minister Dušan Simović traveled to New York from London to become Jesse's "official" godfather.

Over the years, the New York media kept the public informed of Jesse's health and well being. In 1953, the Daily News ran an update with the headline: "Lifeboat Baby, Now 11, Loves the Ocean and the Dodgers." At the CBS Television Studios in New York, a celebrity panel tried to guess Jesse's unusual secret on a 1959 episode of the popular TV game show, "I've Got a Secret," but Jesse's coy responses left them without the correct answer. Jesse was also a contestant on CBS' "To Tell the Truth," along with two "Jesse" impostors, but on that occasion he was unable to fool the show's panel.

Jesse Mohorovicic eventually dropped the "ic" at the end of his surname to make it easier to pronounce. In his adult years, he was somewhat demure when he was asked to talk about his famous birth. "I compare my participation in the story akin to being the football in the Rose Bowl," he often told those who asked about it.

Jesse Roper Mohorovic

In January 2001, Mohorovic was asked to participate in an interview for the documentary film, *War Zone—World War II Off North Carolina's Outer Banks*. Initially, Jesse declined, saying that there wasn't much he could say since he obviously didn't remember the circumstances of his birth in the lifeboat. His company headquarters was in the process of being relocated from Richmond, Virginia, to Jacksonville, Florida, and his availability was severely limited. "Well, I had really hoped to learn a little bit more about your mother, what was she like?" he was asked, just before Mohorovic was about to say goodbye. "Okay," he said, "Come to my office, and I'll chat with you."

It was agreed that he would give his answers during the interview in the third person, as someone who knew Desanka Mohorovicic, but he did not want to necessarily identify himself as her son—"the lifeboat baby," "the son of Neptune," or "the baby Hitler couldn't get." There were more important things, other than himself, that he wished to discuss.

"She was a woman of very strong faith, very, very strong faith," Mohorovic said, after describing the events leading up to the baby's birth. "And a courageous woman, obviously. And a woman who had great trust that her daughter, her newborn son, would

"[Theirs'] was a very quiet kind of courage, and I would say the purest kind of courage."

somehow come out of it. She really put her trust in God—maybe not so commonly heard today, but that was her view. And also, she told many people how, in that situation, you're pretty preoccupied. So, you're wanting to make sure that the child is warm, that the child is nursing. That the sister, Vesna, is finally getting more comfortable and not alarmed at every flying fish that came over [the boat]."

Mohorovic took a deep breath and sighed. He seemed to want to say something more. He seemed momentarily uncomfortable telling the story in the third person, unwilling to be disassociated from the remarkable woman, Desanka Mohorovicic. Then, he looked directly into the lens of the TV camera and said, "Well, Mrs. Mohorovicic was my mother. And she passed on in 1993, and I loved her like every son loves their mother." In the documentary film, a title graphic appears at this moment and for the first time identifies the speaker as Jesse Roper Mohorovic.

"You asked what kind of woman she was—she was a grateful woman," Mohorovic continued. "She was truly, truly, truly, grateful, as [my father] was. So grateful [for those] quiet young boys as she called them, so grateful to the sailors of the *Jesse Roper*, all of the merchant mariners who she often called, 'the true godfathers to the child.' She knew she owed her life and her children's lives to the protection and courage of these fine people."

Mohorovic was out of time, but he wanted to conclude the interview with an important point about the valor of the merchant sailor. "[Theirs'] was a very quiet kind of courage, and I would say the purest kind of courage," he added. "Courage for courage's sake rather than seeking accolades or honor. The people who did this job had to be very motivated—by not [just] a sense of duty. You don't do this easily. When the guy next door, who [a merchant mariner] grew up with and went to high school with, comes back with Marine ribbons, or the fellow from the Navy or Army comes home to [a celebration]. And then these merchant mariners are out there, just putting everything on the line, unprotected, knowing the odds, knowing the casualties, knowing the amount of victims. These guys just did their jobs with great, great, quiet courage."

In 2003, Jesse Roper Mohorovic retired after a successful career in the shipping business. Two years later, "the son of Neptune" passed away of cancer at the age of 63.

At the same time that the USS *Jesse Roper* was conducting its recovery operation of the *City of New York* survivors, occupants of the third launched lifeboat and a couple of rafts were found elsewhere by the USS *Acushnet*, a 34-year-old fleet tug that had been pressed into service as a anti-submarine patrol vessel. According to Navy records, the *Acushnet* picked up as many as 37 survivors, including the *City of New York*'s captain, George T. Sullivan, and delivered them to Norfolk Operating Base on April 1. At that time, the *City of New York*'s fourth lifeboat had still not been located.

Eleven days later, a military aircraft spotted a lifeboat drifting 90 miles east of Cape May, New Jersey, containing 13 people. It was determined to be the fourth lifeboat from the *City of New York*, which had been adrift for 14 days, traveling 216 miles from the point where the ship had sunk. The lifeboat had escaped the sinking ship with 20 occupants including the ship's first officer, but as the days and nights passed for the passengers without food or water and with exposure to unrelenting cold, seven perished, and their bodies were cast into the sea. Two more passengers tragically succumbed to extreme exposure and dehydration just a few hours before the lifeboat was finally reached by a U.S. Coast Guard patrol boat from Lewes, Delaware. One of the deceased found in the lifeboat was Mrs. Sora Etter, the mother of a three-year-old girl, Miriam, who was seated beside her and who miraculously survived the ordeal. Also discovered in the lifeboat were personal belongings of Yugoslavian General Milo Djuknovic who was on his way to Washington, D.C., for an official visit. The general and the ship's first officer were among those who died and were unceremoniously buried at sea.

CHAPTER 17

Ensign Donald Mason with (L-R) Betty Grable, Carole Landis, Claudette Colbert, and Ruth Hussey.

SIGHTED SUB
SANK SAME

"Well, it's really quite elementary."

Ensign Donald Francis Mason

During the brief time that the USS *Jesse Roper* remained in port, bundles of the Thursday, April 2, 1942, edition of the *Norfolk Virginian-Pilot* were delivered to the destroyer. Appearing on the front page beneath a title, "Boychild Born in Crowded Lifeboat," was a large photograph taken at St. Vincent's Hospital of a smiling Desanka Mohorovicic holding a sleeping Jesse and greeting a young U.S. Navy sailor. No doubt, officers and sailors aboard the *Roper* took great pride in seeing the photo and knowing their role in making it possible. However, the Associated Press story adjacent to the photo must have, at the same time, caused the *Roper*'s men some measure of chagrin. "Navy Sinks Three More Axis U-boats—Two in Atlantic" read the banner headline.

Beneath the headline and a subtitle reading "Hero of 'Sighted Sub, Sank Same,' Does It Again," was a report that heralded the Navy's latest victories over Hitler's U-boats. The "hero" the story referred to was a Navy pilot, Aviation Machinist's Mate First Class (AMM1c) Donald Francis Mason, who was reported to have recently sunk his second U-boat of the war on March 15, southeast of St. John's, Newfoundland. The article quoted the Navy's claim that the total number of Axis submarines sunk since America entered the war had increased to 28, and, although "there [was] evidence of additional sinkings, no claims would be made to these until they [were] absolutely certain." The preceding statement from the Navy caused most everyone to believe that all previous U-boat sinkings had already been confirmed and were absolutely certain. Many had not been confirmed and were not certain.

AMM1c Mason's purported first U-boat sinking occurred on the afternoon of January 28, also southeast of Newfoundland. After patrolling the boundless and vacant waters of the

Atlantic for two hours, Mason's crew suddenly spotted an unusual object protruding from the surface—a periscope, trailed by the froth of a vessel's wake. Mason sharply banked his PBO-1 Hudson bomber (#82-P-9), dropped altitude, and swooped down for the kill. The commander of the U-boat took no evasive maneuvers to avoid the attack and probably was unaware of the bomber's approach from astern. Mason released two depth charges from an altitude of 25 feet as the plane traveled at 165 knots. He later reported to his superiors that "plumes of the explosions were seen to spread, one on either side of periscope, estimated distance 10 feet from wake line and nearly abreast the periscope. The submarine was lifted bodily in the water until most of the conning tower could be seen. Headway of submarine seemed to be killed at once, and she was observed to sink from sight vertically. Five minutes later, oil began to bubble to the surface and continued for 10 minutes."

Ten minutes later, in order to make it back to their landing field at Argentia, Newfoundland, before dark, Mason left the scene satisfied that the U-boat had been destroyed. According to Mason's testimony and an official Navy communiqué, while returning to base Mason consulted his codebook for a simple message to convey his accomplishment. As the story goes, Navy brass had been insistent that radio traffic be expressed as succinctly as possible. He chose his words and then transmitted the radio message to Argentia Air Traffic Control: "82-P-9 calling; Sighted sub, sank same."

Mason could not have been more succinct. Mason's message, in fact, became almost as militarily significant as his presumed U-boat kill. The PR people at Navy headquarters in Washington were charmed by the morale-lifting potential of Mason's accomplishment and by his message's pithy prose. The four sibilant words were destined to become as well-known a wartime slogan as "Loose Lips Sink Ships." Just five days after the military had instituted a policy of strict secrecy about anti-submarine efforts within the Eastern Sea Frontier in the wake of the Paukenschläg disaster, the policy was temporarily suspended in order to publicize Mason's historic U-boat sinking. On January 29, the Associated Press reported the Navy pilot's remarkable story.

> Washington, Jan. 29—Associated Press:
>
> "Sighted sub sank same."
>
> "Thus did a United States Navy petty officer, piloting a war plane somewhere on the vast ocean spaces, report to his superiors, and those superiors were so impressed by the classic brevity of the message, that they gleefully relaxed their rule of secrecy on anti-submarine warfare and give it to the world tonight. While all detail was lacking, there was speculation the submarine was one of those preying on coastal shipping along the Atlantic seaboard."

Upon sinking a second U-boat on March 15, Mason was awarded his second Distinguished Flying Cross, was promoted to ensign, and became an overnight national celebrity. Even though the 28-year-old ace seemed to be one of America's few, lethal threats to Hitler's U-boats, the Navy decided that he would be more valuable to the nation waving to the public on boulevards and main streets from coast-to-coast. On June 8, 1942, Mason joined 14 other American and British war heroes on a national tour of major cities,

starting at New York. The heroes were feted in parades, at lavish dinners, and at other well-orchestrated press events. They arrived in Hollywood on June 28 where the men were swarmed by adoring actresses. *Life Magazine* reported: "At the sight of real heroes in a land of make-believe heroes, Hollywood went wholeheartedly wild with delight."

Mason was photographed with Claudette Colbert, Carole Landis, and Betty Grable, using his left hand to depict the diving angle of his aircraft when he became, purportedly, the first U.S. serviceman to sink a German U-boat. Grable seemed especially captivated by Mason. The high-flying pilot was in rarified air. (The following year, Grable would become the most-famous pinup girl in history when 5 million copies of her alluring over-the-shoulder poster were printed and distributed to GIs around the world.) In a whirlwind of four months, Mason had gone from the dreary, storm-swept isolation of Argentia, Newfoundland, to a glittering dinner-dance at the Cocoanut Grove at Los Angeles' famous Ambassador Hotel.

Mason's fame did not fade with the end of World War II. He appeared on "I've Got a Secret" on May 16, 1956, during a special broadcast in celebration of Armed Forces Week. His secret, whispered to Gary Moore and superimposed on the screen: "I said: 'Sighted sub, sank same.'" Panelist Bill Cullen quickly figured out Mason's secret after two deliberately incorrect guesses. Moore then asked Mason how he managed to compose a phrase only a advertising writer could conceive.

> Moore: "How did you happen to pick out those words, 'Sighted sub, sank same?'"
>
> Mason: "Well, it's really quite elementary."
>
> (laughter) Moore: "To you. Not to me, it isn't."
>
> Mason: "We had a codebook, that all messages had to be enciphered. And, you opened it up, and there was everything on S."
>
> Moore: "All the words that you wanted to use happened to start with S."
>
> Mason: "Yes."
>
> Moore: "So, it's that simple, you see. The great thing about it is, this happened in January, and the war had started the month previous, and this was among the first subs that our side had ever sunk, and it was a tremendous morale boost to the entire country." (Applause)

The unfortunate fact about Mason's so-called morale boosting U-boat sinking in January was that he did not sink the U-boat, and Navy PR people are suspected by some historians to have conceived the famous phrase.

While Mason was being groomed to be a national celebrity in early-April 1942, back at Hampton Roads there was little time for the lifeboat baby's Navy godfathers to celebrate their small, moral victory at sea. As copies of the April 2 edition of the *Norfolk Virginian-Pilot* lay about the *Roper*, the destroyer cast off from pier #5 at Norfolk Naval Operating Base and returned to duty off the North Carolina coast. Five fruitless days later, the *Roper* came limping back to Norfolk in need of urgent repairs—dropping depth charges on phan-

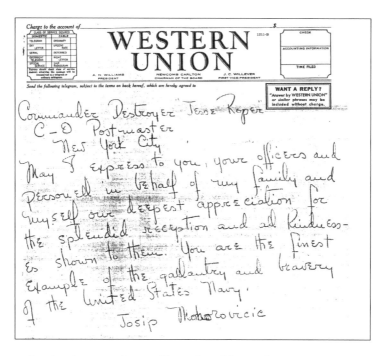

tom U-boats was beginning to take a toll on the old warship. The crew's euphoria from rescuing the survivors of the *City of New York* also had not lasted long. They were once again frustrated, tired, and feeling just a little impotent. When they got beck to Norfolk, however, a telegram awaited them that might have refortified their resolve.

Joseph Mohorovicic sent, soon after his family had arrived at New York in early April, a Western Union telegram to Lt. Cmdr. Howe of the USS *Jesse Roper*, reaffirming his profound gratitude for the rescue of his family:

> To: Commander Destroyer "Jesse Roper"
> May I express to you, your officers, and personnel in behalf of my family and myself our deepest appreciation for the splendid reception and all kindnesses shown to them. You are the finest example of the gallantry and bravery of the United States Navy.
>
> (signed) Josip Mohorovicic

The telegram was delivered to Lt. Cmdr. Howe on the 10th of April and was read to the men aboard the destroyer. At the same time, a package arrived from the New York offices of Farrell Lines; it contained a silver loving cup from the shipping company and the passengers and crew of the *City of New York*, inscribed with a statement of gratitude to their heroes aboard the destroyer. Four days later, while on patrol off of Nags Head, the men of the *Roper* would find what they had been so desperately seeking, recompense for their extraordinary tenacity and valor.

On April 5, 1942, a 220-foot, Type VIIb U-boat basked in "magnificent sunshine" off

the East Coast of the United States. The peaceful weather caused the U-boat's crew, on watch atop the conning tower, to be occupied with thoughts of home at springtime—of verdant pastures, of budding flowers, of picnics with family and friends. They had been at sea for nearly three weeks, and they had no idea when they might see their home port again. The U-boat's commander, Oberleutnant zur See Eberhard Greger, instead had visions of achieving fame in the target-rich waters off the capes of North Carolina's Outer Banks.

U-85 returns to port.

What the handsome 26-year-old Greger did not know was that he and his U-85 were already famous. His was the U-boat that AMM1c Donald Francis Mason, and America, had assumed had been destroyed off the Newfoundland coast on January 28, 1942. Unbeknownst to Mason and America, U-85 was undamaged by the attack. The pilot's eyes had been deceived. The observation of a depth charge's point of impact while flying at 165 knots and 25 feet above the ocean can be misleading. Despite Mason's claim of seeing the U-boat sink vertically with oil bubbling to the surface, an hour and a half later the U-85 rose from the dead and sailed on to fight another day. On February 23, the U-boat was back at St. Nazaire, France, to refit and refuel for her next Atlantic patrol. The U-boat had become yet another German poltergeist—a phoenix resurrected from the sea.

In his 10 months as commander of U-85, Greger had achieved little success, apart from escaping from Mason's depth charges. On his previous war patrol of 47 days, his U-boat had sunk just one ship. The 43-day patrol before that yielded no results. Since receiving his command during the summer of 1941, Greger had sunk only two ships totaling less than 10,000 tons. His career in the Ubootwaffe was in jeopardy. Admiral Dönitz's patience would not last long.

Greger knew that one or two successful nights off Cape Hatteras could reverse his fortunes. That's where the Knight's Cross heroes of the Ubootwaffe—men like Reinhard Hardegen, Johann Mohr, Erich Topp, and Georg Lassen—had hunted with impunity, like lions among helpless wildebeest. Greger knew that in the waters surrounding Cape Hatteras his destiny called; there, his future as a U-boat commander would hang in the balance, as would his own Knight's Cross.

The U-85 departed St. Nazaire, France, on the 21st of March and was ordered by Dönitz to head directly for American waters. Perhaps the admiral had hoped that Greger might turn his dismal career around on his next patrol. En route across the Atlantic, the

U-boat commander was handed a sheaf of papers from his "puster," or radioman, which included the latest wireless dispatches from BdU near Lorient, France.

"*Männer! Hört gut zu*," (*Now, men, listen carefully*), Greger announced over the U-boat's intercom to the 45 men aboard. The U-*85*'s skipper then read a communiqué transmitted on March 24, which saluted the recent success of U-*124* in the waters off North Carolina's Cape Lookout. According to the dispatch, Kapitänleutnant Mohr had claimed to have sunk 13 ships, including seven tankers, totaling more than 80,000 tons. Mohr may also have sunk a vessel of 11,000 tons, but he had been unable to confirm its destruction. "This is where we shall commence our operations," Greger may have told his crew.

Eighteen days later, Dönitz's office transmitted to its U-boats, including U-*85*, another communiqué, extolling the exploits of Kapitänleutnant Topp, who had recently "distinguished himself in U-boat operations off the American coast, having sunk a total of 31 ships of 208,000 tons." These messages, which were read over the U-*85*'s intercom, both challenged and inspired Greger, who knew he would have to muster uncommon audacity and nerve among his men in order for him to join the pantheon of U-boat legends. His men would be satisfied with just getting home alive.

Erich Degenkolb, for one, was one of those crew members who was anxious to return to France. He was typical among those young sailors who served in the Kriegsmarine's most elite branch, the Ubootwaffe. When on land, these men were looked upon as German "Poseidons," veritable gods of the sea. Whether returning from the unimaginable winter weather of the North Atlantic or the frenzied bloodlust of a wolf pack assault on an Allied convoy, U-boat crews conducted themselves back home as fearless, invincible warriors. It made them quite appealing to women. Every man aboard a U-boat had at least one woman, the mental image of whom could divert his concentration while on watch and dominate his dreams while off watch. For Degenkolb, that woman was 18-year-old Lieselotte Lang. Degenkolb resolved, were Providence to smile upon him, he would be with Lieselotte for her birthday back home in Germany in July. The hazardous-duty bonus he would earn for his current assignment on a "Frontboot" (combat vessel) would purchase lavish gifts for his girlfriend. Degenkolb made a notation in his diary of Lieselotte's shoe and glove size. Just maybe, he would ask her to marry him.

The U-boat's intercom suddenly hummed to life, snapping the men, like Degenkolb, out of their reverie: "*Now, men, hear this. The boat is now only 300 miles from America; Washington is just 660 miles away. We must all be vigilant. That's all. 'Click.'*"

Oberleutnant zur See Greger might have imagined that an attack directly on Washington, D.C., would make his U-*85* the most famous of all U-boats, but he quickly dismissed such silly thoughts and traced his finger along a line on the nautical chart, indicating their course to North Carolina's Outer Banks—just a few days more.

Three days later, somewhere between Nantucket Island and Cape Hatteras, the U-*85* chanced upon the Norwegian motor vessel, *Chr. Knudsen*, which was steaming unescorted out of New York bound for Cape Town. Greger launched two torpedoes into the freighter, sinking it instantly and killing all 33 men aboard. As the sun shined brightly upon the glistening U-*85*, Greger's prospects were already beginning to improve.

A U-boat crew in the early days of an Atlantic patrol.

CHAPTER 18

Hampton National Cemetery

BUT TIME AND CHANCE
HAPPENS TO THEM ALL.

*"All hands man your battle
stations. This is not a drill."*

On Monday morning, April 13, the crew of the USS *Jesse Roper* fired-up her boilers and made preparations to get underway for another patrol off Cape Hatteras. At 6:28 p.m., they cast her lines and maneuvered the ship into the channel leading out of Chesapeake Bay. Two and a half hours later, the destroyer passed False Cape, Virginia, and then entered the waters traditionally known as the Graveyard of the Atlantic.

The warship was darkened and zigzagged along a base course to the south-southeast, parallel to the barrier islands. As usual, the bridge set the ship to material condition "Affirm," and the first watch followed their well-practiced routines of manning guns, dogging bulkhead doors shut, and positioning lookouts to scan the horizon. The state-of-the-art radar antenna, looking like a revolving spring mattress at the top of the mast, scanned the seas in all directions, while sonar pings plumbed the depths with their plaintive calls. Seated in a tiny cubicle aft of the bridge with headphones clutched tightly to his ears, the sound operator listened intently for the tell-tale sounds of a turning screw in the offing. The night sky was clear and strewn with stars, the sea nearly perfectly calm, and the ocean teemed with marine bioluminescence. Off to the west-southwest, the double flashes of the Bodie Island Lighthouse reassured the navigator of his ship's location. At midnight, the *Roper*'s middle watch reported for duty, commanded by Ensign Tebo.

Six minutes later, as the watch had barely wiped sleep from their eyes and wearily assumed their respective tasks, the sailor watching the flickering green radar screen and mesmerizing sweep of its beam suddenly saw a faint glow signifying a solid object about a mile and a half ahead off the starboard bow of the destroyer. The indistinguishable blob on the screen could have been practically anything—a small patrol boat, a fishing trawler, or a submarine. *Could it be a U-boat?* the operator might have wondered. No destroyer in U.S. waters had yet to track a U-boat on their newly installed radars.

Regardless, the contact was reported to Tebo who, by routine, ordered the helm to change course to investigate the unknown vessel. Almost immediately, the sound operator reported hearing a rapidly turning propeller ahead emanating from the same direction. Nine minutes after acquiring the initial radar contact, lookouts on the *Roper* spotted the mysterious vessel's wake, glowing on the darkened ocean surface like a trail of stardust. Lt. Cmdr. Howe and his executive officer, Lt. William Vanous, were summoned to the bridge. Tebo ordered another course change so that the destroyer would continue to follow the vessel ahead but slightly off its starboard quarter. The *Roper* seemed to leap forward as its speed was increased to 20 knots.

Suspiciously, the vessel ahead began to turn incrementally to the east, its wake clearly revealing a wide arc to the left. There was deeper water that way; so far, the vessel's tactical behavior was consistent with that of an enemy submarine. Still, the *Roper*'s watch officers were uncertain as to what they were following and believed that it might be a small Coast Guard craft. After all, they had had dozens of similar run-ins with their Coastie colleagues over the past many weeks. The helmsman continued to skillfully steer the destroyer to remain slightly to the right of the evading vessel.

At 12:34 a.m., the men of the *Roper* got their answer—an Axis greeting card. A torpedo, trailing its own luminescent comet tail of agitated marine organisms, came streaking out of the gloom directly toward the American warship. Visions of their dead comrades on the USS *Jacob Jones* momentarily flashed before everyone's eyes—would the *Roper* suffer a similar fate? Not this time—50 yards off the port side of the *Roper*, the torpedo passed by harmlessly and then crossed astern of the destroyer's wake. It was a very close call.

"Ah-wooga, ah-wooga," wailed the destroyer's klaxon. A voice over the loudspeakers exclaimed, "This is not a drill; this is not a drill. General quarters; general quarters. All hands man your battle stations. This is not a drill."

Sailors rushed to the deck of the destroyer, groping their way in the darkness to reach their respective stations. They could hardly believe what was happening. Word quickly spread aboard the ship: We nearly caught a torpedo! The USS *Jesse Roper* had finally found one of Germany's phantom U-boats and it was frantically attempting to escape.

The range between the *Roper* and the U-boat gradually decreased as the minutes ticked by—1,000 yards, 500 yards—then, when the distance between the two dropped to 300 yards, the U-boat made a sudden, sharp turn to starboard. The U-boat captain seemed to be trying to align his bow toward his pursuer, in order to launch another torpedo.

Eleven minutes after avoiding the lethal torpedo, at 12:45 a.m., the *Roper*'s 24-inch searchlight powered on, illuminating the sleek, menacing shape of a German U-boat and the unmistakeable movements of men rushing from the conning tower to the 88-mm "bootskanone," or deck gun, on the fore-casing of the U-boat. Even if the Germans were unable to launch a torpedo, the U-boat was capable of sinking the *Roper* with just a single shell from its "88."[15]

"Auf Gefechtsstationen!" screamed Oberleutnant zur See Greger. The ambitious U-boat commander was in a terrible fix. His U-85 was being pursued by a fast American warship. "It's an American destroyer," confirmed the hydrophone operator from below, who had just heard the unmistakeable sound signature of the chasing vessel as that of a U-boat's most lethal enemy.

Greger had made a poor choice to approach Cape Hatteras so close to shore to begin his nighttime operations. The seafloor was less than 100 feet beneath his keel. The continental shelf and deep water, where his U-boat had room to evade the enemy's depth charges, lay far to the east, nearly an hour's cruising distance away. His U-boat was moving too fast to crash dive, and the water was too shallow to dive, regardless. Diving in such shallow water would be like being pinned to a dart board as depths charges rained down upon them.

Greger shouted to his helmsman to turn to port, "steer for deeper water;" it was one of only a few cards he held in his hand. But the destroyer kept coming, the glowing froth of her bow wave plainly visible in the distance, rising as the warship's speed increased faster and faster. From his conning tower, Greger hastily ordered his one remaining stern torpedo fired at his pursuer. He knew it would be a desperate attempt to sink the destroyer—on the same relative course as the U-boat, the ship presented an awfully small target. Within seconds, Greger knew the tactic had failed; the torpedo missed its mark. His options were decreasing as rapidly as his distance from the enemy. A successful surface engagement was their only hope—there was still a chance that they might turn more sharply than the destroyer in order to launch a bow torpedo. "Gun crews to stations!" yelled Greger, "Schnell, schnell, schnell!" To his helmsman he growled, "Hard to starboard; get us pointed at that schwein, now!"

BM2c Chamberlin's watch ended at midnight, and the young radioman was eagerly making his way to his bunk to get some shut-eye in the aft compartment of the *Roper* when the klaxon sounded. He and his fellow watch members must have grumbled, *What now?* Chamberlin dutifully scrambled back up the ladder leading to the hatch adjacent to the #5 gun, which, he observed, was not yet fully manned by its six-man crew.

Climbing the ladder behind Chamberlin, "Pappy" Felts, the *Roper*'s first class cook, was the next to emerge topside. The powerful beam of the destroyer's 24-inch searchlight probed the darkness and then flashed on a deceivingly small, low-slung shape of a vessel about 300 yards off the *Roper*'s starboard beam. "Aw, that's just an E-boat," Felts told Chamberlin, referring to the World War I-era Eagle Boat. A few of the 25-year-old patrol craft were among the ragtag fleet of surplus or dilapidated vessels used by the Navy to chase U-boats off the American East Coast. The Eagle Boat's deck sloped slightly downward, fore and aft, with a small superstructure amidships, which, from a distance, could sometimes look like a U-boat's conning tower. Chamberlin knew Felts was mistaken: "'Pappy' Felts needed his glasses because there was not a doubt that it was a submarine."

Little did anyone aboard the destroyer know that the U-boat they were looking at was the same phantom U-boat of AMM1c Mason's "Sighted Sub, Sank Same" fame.

Even though the men of the *Roper* had finally found what they had been searching for

BM2c Rhodes Chamberlin

over the past many weeks, many of them could still not believe their eyes. "It surprised everybody because we had always felt that finding one in that space of sea was going to be all but impossible," Chamberlin said. "It didn't surprise us when we were convoying to make contact with submarines because that's what they're after, but to be able to find one just running up and down the coast, that was a surprise."

The *Roper* had indeed found a U-boat, but now it had to sink it, and that was an outcome that was far from guaranteed. A German Type VII U-boat had a much sharper turning radius than a *Wickes*-class four piper, and the enemy vessel was clearly attempting to align its bow torpedo tubes at the American destroyer. On paper, however, the odds were greatly in favor of the *Roper*, which had 115 officers and men aboard against the U-boat's 46 men. The destroyer carried a total of 10 deck guns (six artillery and four machine guns) against the U-boat's four guns (one artillery and two multipurpose machine/anti-aircraft guns). The *Roper* had the capability to launch six torpedoes against the U-boat's four torpedoes loaded in its bow tubes. And last but not least, the *Roper* had dozens of depth charges, the diabolical weapon most hated by World War II submariners.

As the U-boat initiated its turn to starboard, so did the the destroyer. The *Roper* was not able to turn as tightly as the U-boat, but the ship was moving faster, so she was quickly able to be broadsides to the enemy vessel. Lt. Vanous, from his station on the flying bridge, communicated to the conning officer beneath him in the pilot house details about the U-boat's movements. Seven hundred yards apart, the two vessels began to circle one another, like two fighters about to lunge into one another in mortal combat—a violent waltz to the death.

As soon as the searchlight revealed the enemy, Lt. Cmdr. Howe ordered all of his gun batteries to commence immediate action against the German submarine. During the preceding weeks, the *Roper*'s gunners had proven their proficiency at shooting empty lifeboats at sea, but would they be able to do the same against a German U-boat?

The #3 3"/.50-caliber gun atop the galley deck house was the *Roper*'s ready gun and was the first to open fire. "Click"—the gun misfired. Its ammunition failed; the projectile remained in the gun's breach. Frantically, the men had to manually clear the gun, but minutes would pass before it would again be operational. One of the *Roper*'s other 3"/.50-caliber guns on the starboard side of the ship was loaded, aimed at the U-boat, and its trigger pulled. "Click"—that gun, too, misfired. Also atop the galley deck house was one of the .50-caliber machine gun, and it also misfired five times due to primer failures.

Time momentarily seemed to freeze. Fractions of seconds suddenly passed like

hours. For one observer on the deck of the *Roper*, this pivotal moment in history seemed to pass before his eyes like a movie in slow motion. "I would say it was like slow motion," said Chamberlin, whose action station was the emergency radio forward of the well deck. "I've thought about it many times afterwards. It was really interesting that I stood there and watched the whole affair without giving, really, a thought to the danger we were actually in."

The danger to the *Roper* was becoming increasingly acute. Up to a dozen German sailors were attending to the U-boat's 88-millimeter deck gun, preparing it to fire by hurriedly hand-cranking the gears of the gun's pivot in order to aim it at the destroyer and passing forward by hand the gun's ammunition. The large muzzle of the German gun swiveled, ever closer to being pointed directly at the Navy warship. The *Roper*'s officers could do nothing but watch in horror and curse like respectable sailors as seconds ticked by. They shouted to their gun batteries, interspersed with expletives, "Fire, fire, fire!" Nothing happened.

Oberleutnant zur See Eberhard Greger

On the U-*85*, Greger exhorted his men to quickly aim and load the 88-mm gun. The American destroyer had been clever to initiate a turn to starboard on a wider arc than his U-boat. As long as the two vessels rotated together on concentric circles, the U-*85* would not be able to launch a torpedo at the enemy warship. Greger was down to just two options: Sink the enemy with his deck gun, or scuttle his U-boat and hope for the best as POWs. From his vantage point atop the conning tower, Greger's vision was partially blinded by the harsh glare of the destroyer's searchlight. Why have they not shot at us? he likely wondered. It was inexplicable but fortuitous. But Greger didn't need an explanation—his deck gun was nearly ready to fire, and the Yankee searchlight was helping his gunners with their aim. One shot beneath the bright light into the waterline of the destroyer, and it would be over. The Oberleutnant zur See would surely get a promotion for sinking an American destroyer!

What happened next was a small but consequential moment in history. As Winston Churchill wrote of the Second Battle of El Alamein in North Africa, the unfolding drama 18 miles east of Nags Head was a "hinge of fate" upon which the future of the war zone in American waters, and perhaps the broader Battle of the Atlantic, depended. The fortunes of men—German submariners, U.S. Navy sailors, and their commanders and political leaders on shore—turned with a flash out of a gun's muzzle.

A 3"/.50-caliber gun on the foredeck of USS *Jesse Roper*.

Chief Boatswain's Mate Jack Edwin Wright's responsibility on the *Roper* was to make sure the "kids" under his command were properly trained and squared away, not to do their job for them. One such "kid" was manning the #1 .50-caliber machine gun aft of the ship's bridge. The young sailor could not get his gun to fire; the ammunition kept jamming as a result of having been partially loaded for days and subjected to the corrosive effects of salt spray and wide fluctuations of temperatures. The "kid" didn't know what to do, and the expletive-laced encouragements from the officers on the bridge wing were of little help. Chief Wright had seen enough and jumped into action. Wright shoved the young sailor out of the way and cleared the gun. He then began firing with precision at the Germans working the 88-mm deck gun, brightly illuminated by the *Roper*'s searchlight. Some of the U-boat men were hit; others scrambled across the deck to seek cover behind the conning tower. Wright's heroic efforts purchased the *Roper* some time, but a .50-caliber machine gun alone was not going to sink the enemy U-boat.

On the U-*85*, Greger's visions of promotions and Knight's Crosses vanished with the muzzle flash of the American machine gun. Some of his men lay wounded or dead; others had fallen or jumped overboard. The rest withdrew from the U-boat's deck gun. His options were down to one: scuttle the boat. Amidst the screams of his men, the U-boat skipper shouted into the open hatch leading down into the control room: "*Alle Mann aus dem Boot Raus! Raus! Alle Mann raus! Schnell! Versenken dem...*" (*All men from the boat out! Get out! All hands out! Quick! Scuttle the...*)

Coxswain Harry Heyman had never been in charge of a gun during a live firing. Just two days earlier, Heyman had been made gun captain of the #5 3"/.50-caliber gun when the previous gun captain was detached from the ship at Norfolk. He wasn't sure why none of the other ship's guns were firing, but the orders to engage had been issued. The #5 gun was located near the stern of the destroyer, half a football field aft of Chief Wright's position. The gun was loaded and ready. The junior gun captain's inexperience

didn't matter—his shipmates lives were at stake. Heyman skillfully spotted his target and shouted, "Fire!" An armor-piercing projectile left the gun at 2,700 feet per second. The *Roper* shuddered. In the destroyer's wardroom, the *City of New York* loving cup, dedicated to the bravery of the *Roper*'s men, shook slightly on the mess table but remained upright. It took less than a second for the shell to strike the hull of the German U-boat near the waterline below the base of the conning tower. The submarine immediately began to sink by the stern.

Before Greger had been able to complete his command to scuttle the boat, an enormous and violent explosion erupted below the base of the conning tower, throwing Greger

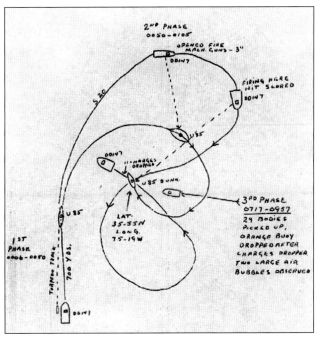

Reconstruction plot from analysis of Action Report of USS *Jesse Roper* by U.S Navy Anti-Submarine Warfare Unit.

and the others near him into the sea, their bodies ripped apart by a hailstorm of deadly shrapnel. Some members of the gun crew who were protected behind the conning tower's port side leaped overboard. A torrent of seawater poured down from the sky. Down below, within the shattered and darkened confines of the U-*85*'s control room, panicked shipmates fought each other as they struggled to escape the sinking U-boat up the conning tower ladder. Some were wounded; others were stunned and disoriented from the impact of the shell that slammed the men against steel bulkheads, valves, and each other. Men nervously fumbled with the clasps to their life vests or inserted into their mouths the breathing tubes of their underwater breathing apparatus. No amount of training had prepared them for their ordeal. Seawater poured into the starboard aft corner of the control room. As the deck tilted steeply toward the bow, water rushed toward the stern, causing the men from the engineering compartments to have to scramble like they were climbing a waterfall. Cold sea water quickly rose above the deck plates. Not all of the Germans would make it out of the U-boat alive.

From the perspective of the *Roper*, the U-boat was stopped dead in the water and was beginning to submerge. For a second or two, there was uncertainty among the *Roper*'s officers as to whether the hit actually caused the U-boat to sink. Consequently, Lt. Cmdr. Howe ordered that one of the destroyer's torpedoes be launched at the enemy vessel, but before the order could be executed, the U-boat disappeared from the ocean surface. BM2c Chamberlin witnessed the explosion when the shell struck the U-boat followed by a large geyser of water. "By the time the [geyser of] water settled down, the U-boat started going down stern first," Chamberlin recalled. In Howe's official report on the destruction of the submarine, he speculated that, because it went down slowly and stern first, the vessel may have been purposely scuttled.

According to the *Roper*'s log, the destroyer maintained a speed of 20 knots as it continued in a starboard turn after firing the shell into the U-boat. As a result, it took two minutes for the Navy warship to cover the 1,413 yards in order to reach the point where the U-boat had disappeared. During that time, the sonar operator reported that he had received a solid underwater contact bearing 110 degrees and 900 yards from the destroyer. Was it a second U-boat? Was the U-boat presumed sunk by the *Roper* undamaged and attempting to escape, or worse, about to launch one of its own torpedoes at the destroyer? Tactical evaluations had to be made by Howe quickly and decisively.

Meanwhile, as the *Roper* charged forward through the dissipating wake of the U-boat, it began to pass German sailors in the water. "There were men in the water; I could see a few of them," Chamberlin said. The life or death fight between Axis and Allied warships had suddenly become a rescue operation. "[Our officers] called down from the bridge to let go the life raft on the well deck. We had a large life raft on each side, about 10 to 12 feet in length. I reached up to pull the lanyard to release the life raft, and it snagged on the ways. I got my knife out and was in the process of cutting it loose. While I was cutting the line on the life raft to release it, I could hear screaming, calling from the Germans in the water." Some published historical accounts describe the U-boat men in the water pleading for help in both German and English. Chamberlin, who watched as the destroyer swept past the Germans, doesn't remember it that way: "I can't really say that I remember any distinct words. It seemed like they were yelling to each other."

In Howe's official report, it was estimated that before the U-boat sank there were about 40 Germans on its deck; after the U-boat sank, about the same number of men were sighted in the water. Chamberlin—who was not an officer of the destroyer but who had a unique opportunity to observe the event—distinctly recalls seeing fewer men on the U-boat's deck: "I think the captain's report says there were 40 men topside at that point. But that's definitely not true. There were about 15 men on top when she started going down. There were maybe more coming up as she was going down. A number of the survivors had mouth pieces in their mouths where they had obviously used an [escape apparatus] to get up from the sub."

The *Roper* stormed through clusters of German survivors in the water. Howe had a difficult decision to make. His training, and the lessons learned by the British Navy, reminded him that there had been occasions when desperate U-boat skipper's faked their own sinking, even abandoning some of their crew, in order to temporarily retreat and then remount the attack. Howe could take no chances. Because his sonar man reported a solid contact, and because there was uncertainty as to whether the U-boat was destroyed, the destroyer's commander had no choice as to what to do next. He ordered a pattern of 11 depth charges from the destroyers racks, Y-guns, and K-guns, to be dropped over the estimated point of the U-boat's sinking. Two hundred yards away, the U-boat crew in the water observed the "wasserbombes" hit the surface of the ocean and then sink. They

knew they had just seconds to live before the charges detonated.

When Chamberlin had finally gotten the life raft untangled, the destroyer was too far away from the survivors in the water for them to have reached the raft had it been launched. Someone on the bridge called down and told Chamberlin to wait until the next time around. That was just seconds before Howe issued the order to drop the depth charges. After the depth charges were dropped, there was no longer any reason to launch the raft. "It was tough, really tough, when we dropped the pattern of charges, knowing that there were survivors in the water, and they were watching depth charges go off our fantail," Chamberlin said somberly. "We knew their chances of survival were small. Unfortunately, it killed all of them."

Forty-six minutes after first detecting it on its radar, the USS *Jesse Roper* had engaged and defeated the first German U-boat in United States territorial waters since the nation declared war against Axis forces in December. In more than 400 years of recorded maritime history along the coast of North Carolina, and throughout five major wars fought off the beaches of the state, the naval engagement between the *Roper* and the U-85 was among the most decisive and had the most far-reaching effect on the future of innumerable lives. Even though the *Roper* found the U-85 mostly by chance, the destroyer had finally exacted its retribution for the sinking of the USS *Jacob Jones*, had gotten a small measure of revenge on behalf of the crew and passengers of the *City of New York*, and atoned for the deaths of thousands of merchant sailors and innocent civilians. Paraphrasing the words of Churchill, it wasn't the end for U-boats operating in United States waters, but it was the beginning of the end.

At 1 a.m., the *Roper* secured from general quarters, and sailors off watch began to return to their quarters, except for the ship's officers and gun crews who began to investigate why some of the guns had malfunctioned. Hardly anyone slept for the remainder of the night. Thirty minutes later, the 5th Naval District communications office at Norfolk received a garbled transmission from the *Roper*, composed somewhat inelegantly compared to Mason's "Sighted sub, sank same:"

> "We hit sub with gunfire, and sub went down. Also dropped one DC. There were about 25 men in water about 10 minutes ago. I don't think sub will surface again, but she might be able to."

Then at 3:45 a.m., another message was received:

> "*Roper* (DD) reports she sighted sub on surface in 35-55 N., 75-13 W. Engaged with gunfire. Sub crew abandoned ship, and sub apparently sank. Made two runs dropping DCs. Will stand by until daylight and endeavor to pick up survivors."

The destroyer remained in the general area for the rest of the night, zigzagging and sending out sonar pings. Lt. Cmdr. Howe's report stated that "wreckage could not be de-

The dead crew members of U-85 on the deck of USS *Jesse Roper*.

tected because of darkness. On two occasions this ship passed near the survivors, but the fact that German submarines frequently work in pairs made the conduct of any rescue work before daylight far too dangerous to risk." There were no pleas coming from the Germans in the water to be rescued. The "survivors" by then were almost assuredly dead.

At 7 a.m., after being directed to the appropriate location by two Navy aircraft that had arrived on the scene, the destroyer began efforts to recover bodies from the water. A detail of sailors was mustered, and the *Roper*'s motor whale boat and captain's gig, each in charge of an officer, were launched. Over the next two and a half hours, the destroyer's men recovered the bodies of 29 German sailors and returned them to the ship. Two additional bodies were found but were allowed to sink after the clothing had been searched for personal effects that might aid the forthcoming investigation by U.S. Naval Intelligence.

The men of the *Roper* had spent weeks chasing U-boat phantoms off the U.S. eastern seaboard to no avail. During that time, their mental image of the enemy was that of a malevolent, sinister "Nautilus" with a protruding Cyclops eye—a nefarious Nazi machine comprised of hardened steel and diabolical torpedoes, hiding beneath the waves, ruthlessly sinking merchant ships, and killing innocent civilians. The image of the German U-boat monster was every U.S. destroyer sailor's nightmare. Now, the *Roper* sailors could see, firsthand, the evil killers who operated the German leviathan. The U-boat men looked just like themselves.

They shared a common bond. Except for their beards, any one of the enemy sailors would have looked right at home aboard the *Roper*. The Germans were young men, sailors, men of the sea, just like the Americans. Like U.S. sailors on any given day, the U-boat men praised God for good weather and for not being seasick, they appreciated a delicious meal, and they dreamed of their wives and girlfriends when they were off watch. They had a job to do, which many would have preferred not to do. They were proudly serving their country just like the Americans. As the bodies of the U-boat men were individually hoisted up to the deck of the *Roper*, the U.S. sailors shared a broad range of emotions. BM2c Chamberlin felt sympathy.

"Looking at the bodies was more like viewing an acquaintance in the funeral home," Chamberlin remembered. "There were no feelings against them; there were feelings of sorrow, because we had killed them. We would have felt much better about the whole operation if we had picked up live survivors."

Of course, the ensuing 59 years after the sinking of the U-boat had given the *Roper* men like Chamberlin time to reflect on the event and reappraise their attitude toward their enemy. But during his interview, Chamberlin's memory was fairly certain that the prevailing attitudes in 1942 toward the bodies being brought to the deck of the *Roper* was solemn and respectful. "We understood that this was part of our job, part of what transpires in any conflict," Chamberlin said. "People are going to die, but we aren't out there to kill people. The men on the destroyers and the men on the submarines—we were all sailors. Even with the loss of the USS *Jacob Jones*—which was basically our sister ship—I can't say that I heard any man on our ship say that it was good that we killed [the Germans] or that he hated them."

The passage of time has also caused others to reflect on the destruction of the U-boat and the deaths of its men east of Nags Head with a very different and provocative perspective. German historian and former commander of U-*802*, Helmut Schmoeckel, suggested in a 2002 interview for the book, *Kriegsverbrechen in Europa und im Nahen Osten im 20. Jahrhundert* (*War Crimes in Europe and the Middle East in the 20th Century*), that the *Roper*'s launching of depth charges 200 yards away from the survivors in the water constituted a war crime that was not properly investigated by judicial inquiry. Schmoeckel's point of view, no doubt, disappointed and angered those few *Roper* sailors who were still alive in 2002.

There may be some people today who, without a direct, personal connection to those who served in World War II, would believe that Schmoeckel is correct.[16] However, a compelling argument can be made on behalf of many who were unjustly killed by U-boats—and their families—that the Germans killed by the *Roper*'s depth charges got what they deserved. One only has to be reminded of the 23 men of the collier, SS *David*

H. Atwater, who were machine gunned to death by Kapitänleutnant Erich Topp's U-*552*, or the five men of the SS *Ario* shot to death by the crew of U-*158*. Those victims of U-boats not to be forgotten include Oscar Chappell, who engulfed himself in flames to save his shipmates on the *Dixie Arrow*; Mrs. Sora Etter's daughter, Miriam, who watched her mother die just hours before being rescued; or the civilian sailors who burned to death in oil or were torn asunder by their ship's propellers. Savannah's Ted Haviland, who used the term "dastardly" to describe Germany's attacks on unarmed civilian merchant ships, probably represents the attitude of countless family members who lost a loved one within the territorial limits of the United States and who would say the *Roper*'s actions were more than justified. Furthermore, it could be said that even the seemingly humanitarian acts of U-boat captains providing their civilian victims in lifeboats or rafts directions to the nearest point of land and then leaving them at the mercy of the sea were committing war crimes. In the words of Major General William T. Sherman: "War is cruelty, and you cannot refine it; and those who brought war into our country deserve all the curses and maledictions a people can pour out."

Lastly, on the question of whether Lt. Cmdr. Howe acted appropriately when ordering depth charges dropped while helpless survivors were nearby, a similar event occurred just 19 days earlier when the commander of the USS *Tarbell* ordered a pattern of depth charges dropped in the vicinity of Allied survivors of the torpedoed SS *Dixie Arrow* east of Ocracoke. Following a thorough review, Howe's superiors commended him for his actions, and as a result, he received the Navy Cross for "extreme gallantry and risk of life in actual combat with an armed enemy force and going beyond the call of duty." The crew of the *Roper* got to paint the silhouette of a German U-boat on one the destroyer's smoke stacks.

During the *Roper*'s search for bodies, an airship from Elizabeth City Air Station flew overhead and was joined by as many as seven planes. All served as spotters for floating debris and corpses. When it was decided that all of the bodies that could be found had been recovered, the *Roper* discontinued the search and recovery. Just before noon, the destroyer set a course for Hampton Roads.

Despite sailors' memories of feeling sympathy for, or a brotherhood with, the dead U-boat sailors, a photograph taken of the corpses stacked in a heap on the *Roper*'s well deck surrounded by the ship's crew depicts a different sentiment. Amidst a tangle of arms and legs can be seen men wearing their breathing apparatus, others with life vests, and some who were barefoot. Lt. Cmdr. Howe had the bodies guarded, and no one was permitted to search the German's clothing or remove any of their personal effects.

The *Roper* stood into Lynnhaven Roads, an anchorage on the southern end of the Chesapeake Bay, where it was met by the U.S. Navy tug, *Sciota*. The bodies were then transferred down the *Roper*'s gangway to the *Sciota*, which then ferried the German bodies on to Norfolk Naval Operating Base. More photographs were taken, and again, the Germans can be seen stacked like cordwood on the stern of the tug that was covered by a large, oil-stain tarpaulin.

In a small aircraft hanger at the Naval Air Station adjacent to Norfolk NOB, the 29 bodies were laid out in rows on the floor, and one by one, they were photographed, ex-

amined by Navy physicians and searched by officers of U.S. Naval Intelligence. All 29 bodies were identified using various items of evidence including identification tags. Oberleutnant zur See Hans Sanger, the U-85's "Leitender Ingenieur" or "LI" (Chief Engineering Officer), was the only officer among the men. Greger's body was never found. The whereabouts of the remaining 15 German sailors have never been determined (two bodies were discarded during the Roper's recovery efforts). The most reasonable explanation for the fates of the missing 15 men is that they were all killed when they had been exposed to the machine

Personal photos recovered from bodies of U-85 crew members.

gun and artillery fire from the Roper prior to the U-boat sinking.[17]

The shipboard occupations of 10 men were determined, and it was revealed that most of them worked in the engine rooms and machinery spaces aft of the control room. Six bodies were wearing escape apparatus, and two still had the mouthpiece in their mouths. Some of the men had coins in their pockets; others had various items of jewelry or personal photographs they may have retrieved from their lockers before escaping from the sinking U-boat. One man, perhaps anticipating he would need something to read while spending the remainder of the war in a POW camp, had tucked his hometown newspaper, the *Offenburger Tageblatt*, in his pocket, (no doubt he had read the paper many times in the previous three weeks since leaving home). It can be safely concluded that those sailors having money, photographs, or a newspaper in their pockets or wearing escape apparatus were not among the initial 15 men seen on deck prior to the shooting. The personal photographs, which were removed and are now preserved at the National Archives in Washington, D.C., depict happier times for various members of the U-boat crew—while at sea, at home, and at their favorite drinking establishments.

Two men had in their possession personal diaries, something that was strictly forbidden by U-boat command to have aboard a U-boat. Erich Degenkolb was one who broke regulations and kept a diary; Stabsobermaschinist (Senior Chief Petty Officer) Eugen Ungethüm was the other. It was not until April 15, when Naval Intelligence officers scrutinized the possessions of the German sailors that they were able to determine that the U-boat sunk by the Roper was the U-85. It was not until Naval Intelligence officers read the diaries of Degenkolb and Ungethüm that they discovered another startling revelation.

Burial of U-*85* crew members at Hampton National Cemetery.

The entry in Ungethüm's diary for Wednesday, January 28, was written as follows: "Off Newfoundland. 2048 [1:48 local time] Alarm (airplane). One bomb near hit. No damage. 2200 Surfaced. Made off at 3/5 speed."

In his diary, Degenkolb wrote, "Baptism of fire. Aircraft Attack." Degenkolb, however, thought the date was January 27th. Because Ungethüm's entry is the more detailed of the two, it should be considered to be the more accurate. The time Ungethüm listed for the aircraft attack is within three minutes of the time Mason reported to U.S. military authorities of his attack on the enemy U-boat. There are no other reports in either U.S. Navy or German Kriegsmarine records that indicate other U-boat/aircraft encounters in the waters off Newfoundland at that time. There can be no other conclusion but that the U-*85* was the U-boat thought to have been depth charged and sunk by AMM1c Donald Francis Mason on January 28, 1942—the U-boat sunk by the *Roper* was none other than the famous sub of "Sighted Sub Sank Same" fame!

When the examinations of the corpses from the U-*85* were completed by U.S. Naval

Intelligence, the bodies were placed in standard Veterans Administration specification caskets and shipping boxes and loaded into the back of a military transport vehicle. In the meantime, 52 prisoners from Fort Monroe near Hampton, Virginia, were taken late in the afternoon of April 15 to the Hampton National Cemetery to dig 29 graves. Even though there had been no public statement by military authorities of the sinking of the U-85 and the recovery of the bodies of 29 German sailors, a large crowd of spectators from the surrounding neighborhood gathered on the other side of the cemetery's perimeter wall. Clearly, word had somehow spread—history was in the making.

By 8:00 p.m., the caskets had arrived, the crowd of spectators had increased, and a large detail of U.S. Army soldiers were on hand to serve as pall bearers. Military police stood by to maintain order. The U-85 sailors were accorded a proper military burial service with prayers for the dead read by Catholic and Protestant chaplains. An honor guard of 24 sailors fired three volleys over the graves followed by a playing of taps.

At his headquarters near Lorient, France, Admiral Dönitz's communications officer repeatedly transmitted longwave and shortwave radio messages to the U-85, requesting that the U-boat respond immediately with its position. Days passed, and no response was received. Finally, on April 20, Dönitz dictated to his clerk an entry into his Kriegstagebüch or war diary: "U-85 has not replied to repeated calls to report position. Her loss must be taken into account. This is the first boat that has probably been lost immediately under the American coast. There are no clues as to place and circumstances of sinking."

For the USS *Jesse Roper*, the job was not done. When the Navy tug, *Sciota*, left the side of the destroyer, the *Roper* unceremoniously hoisted its anchor and set a course for the waters off the North Carolina coast to resume its anti-submarine patrols. For the gallant and brave men of the *Roper*, there would be no ticker-tape parades, no star-studded gala dinner-dances at the Cocoanut Grove, nor, much to their disappointment, did they get to tell their story to Betty Grable. The last entry in the ship's log for that fateful day of April 14, 1942, when the *Roper* became the first American warship to sink a German U-boat in United States waters, reads: "Steaming as before."

At sea, Providence awaited.

> "I returned, and saw under the sun, that the race is not to the swift, nor the battle to the strong, neither yet bread to the wise, nor yet riches to men of understanding, nor yet favor to men of skill; but time and chance happens to them all."
>
> Ecclesiates 9:11

CHAPTER 19

U.S. Coast Guard photo

STOUT HEARTS

"We are dropping rapidly and are going to crash!"

Frank Cook, pilot

Despite newspaper reports and movie newsreels crafted by Navy PR offices claiming the sinking of 28 U-boats within U.S. waters, the Navy had so far sunk only one— the U-*85*. So when the USS *Jesse Roper* rode the tide out of Chesapeake Bay under the new moon of April 15, its men were understandably proud of their freshly painted victory tally on the ship's #2 stack. For them, the solitary silhouette of a U-boat symbolized an outstanding accomplishment.

For the Allied war effort overall, it was scarcely significant—hardly a drop of rain in the ocean. Beyond the slender bow of the *Roper* as it knifed its way into the vast ocean, there were 100 more German U-boats on operational patrols in the North Atlantic, and 200 other U-boats either preparing to go to sea or returning to their ports to refit and resupply—a military force with the potential to sink thousands of Allied merchant ships. It had taken the U.S. Navy four months to sink its first U-boat in its home waters—those were odds and a casualty rate that Admiral Dönitz and his Nazi superiors were happy to live with.

If Dönitz was undaunted by the sinking of the U-*85*, the British were unimpressed. America's ally was well aware that at Bremen, Hamburg, and Kiel shipyards Germany was building new U-boats at a furious rate: 237 were scheduled for completion in 1942; 284 more were on the books for 1943. In addition, a new class of U-boat had recently been added to the fleet: the large but lightly-armed Type XIV boat nicknamed Milchkühe (milk cow) was capable of rendezvousing in mid-ocean with the Atlantic combat boats to resupply it with fuel, torpedoes, and food. Ten Type XIVs were commissioned between late 1941

U.S. Coast Guard photo

and early 1943, and consequently, Dönitz was able to extend the range of his U-boat attacks to distant strategic ports at Aruba, Panama, and along the Texas and Louisiana coasts.

Radar-equipped destroyers and destroyer escorts proved to have a distinct advantage over surfaced U-boats, but the tactical lessons learned from sinking the U-85 would have little or no effect on the future of the war. On the water, luck continued to be an essential aspect of anti-submarine warfare—four and a half months into the war, the U.S. Navy was still doing little but hunting hornets all over the farm.

On paper, however, at the headquarters of the commander of the Eastern Sea Frontier and at the Washington, D.C., offices of Admiral Ernest J. King, commander-in-chief of the Navy, plans were finally being prepared to establish interlocking north-south coastal convoy routes stretching from the Gulf of Mexico to the Canadian Maritimes and Newfoundland, that would ultimately discourage the German invaders from American waters. Those plans, unfortunately for merchant mariners, were going to take time to implement.

In the meantime—in the indomitable American way with stout-hearted spirit, ingenuity, and energy—U.S. sailors, soldiers, Coast Guardsmen, and civilians defended the home front on foot, on horseback, in small wooden boats, and in small planes—remarkably modest measures against the strengthening German colossus of the Ubootwaffe.

When hundreds of Coast Guard recruits like Ocracoke's Theodore Mutro and Mac Womac arrived on the coast of North Carolina, they were ordered to patrol the beaches—all 375 linear miles of sand—day and night. Their primary objectives were to observe (but not interdict) potential enemy landings; to recover flotsam (lifeboats, rafts, and bodies) that might be of intelligence value; and to apprehend anyone who might be attempting to signal enemy vessels at sea (but not young lovers parked in a sandy hideaway). At various locations like Oak Island, Topsail Island, Ocean Isle, or Bogue Banks during the first few months of the war, the Coast Guardsmen simply made an observation post out of a high sand dune; in other places the "sand pounders" trudged in the footsteps of Life-saving Service surfmen of years gone by. It was tough duty. Winter winds from the ocean made the temperature unbearably cold, and blowing sand blasted the men's faces and eyes. Frequent rain squalls or pleasant, windless days beset by tempests of voracious mosquitos or biting flies made the Coasties wish they had chosen a different branch of service. The soft sand made it nearly impossible for a man to walk more than a couple of miles during a patrol, but the mosquitos and flies made the same man able to run great distances for cover.

A military planner came up with a brilliant alternative—mounted horseback patrols. It wasn't such a radical idea. On certain barrier islands along the North Carolina coast—places like Core Banks, Shackleford Banks, Portsmouth Island, Ocracoke Island, and Currituck Banks—roamed large populations of native horses believed to be the descendants of shipwrecked Spanish mustangs. These horses were well suited to their surroundings and could feed and water themselves. Children on the Outer Banks, like Buxton's Carol White, had proven how easily the horses could be trained. But instead, the military insisted that horses from the U.S. Army Quartermaster Remount Service be used. The Army had found itself with a surplus of horses in World War II due to the widespread mechanization of its forces. As a result, more than 3,000 horses from the mainland were sent to the coasts of America to serve the Coast Guard's beach patrols. At the outset, the military assumed that the horses needed experienced riders. Along the Pacific Coast, for example, help-wanted ads recruited volunteers. According to Coast Guard records, "a mixed bag of people responded, including polo players, cowboys, former sheriffs, horse trainers, Army Reserve cavalrymen, jockeys, farm boys, rodeo riders and stunt men."

U.S. Coast Guard photo

On the shores of North Carolina, polo players, rodeo riders, and stunt men were hard to come by, so the newly arrived station recruits were assigned the task of training the horses. The men assigned to Ocracoke Coast Guard Station would never forget how that worked.

"We had to walk the horses up and down the beach—about two or three weeks—to get them familiarized with the surf and everything," remembered Mutro, a city boy from the Philadelphia area. "And then when we thought we had 'em broke in, we'd put a saddle on 'em, he'd jump, and down you'd go. There goes the horse! Then, the Navy guys [who worked at an installation on the outskirts of Ocracoke village] would call and say, 'Hey, we just seen a riderless horse go by here.' Oh, Jesus! I'd get a jeep and go run the horse down and bring him back to the stable. They were from grazing lands, you know. And they weren't used to the surf. You'd march him along the surf, and they'd hear a wave crash; they'd throw the rider and off he'd go. Oh, brother!"

The Coast Guard horse patrols, which were not officially authorized until September 1942, were ultimately considered a success, even if, by then, the German U-boats were long gone. Men patrolling the beaches on horseback covered more ground, could be better armed, and were also able to carry radios, which were too heavy and cumbersome to carry on foot. Nevertheless, official Coast Guard photographs taken of sailors on horseback evoke humorous thoughts of Wild West cowboys waiting to ambush and corral German saboteurs landing on the beach.

Man's best friend also joined the U.S. Coast Guard in the fight against potential enemy landing parties, saboteurs, and secret agents. The first dog-assisted patrols were implemented near Atlantic City, New Jersey, in August 1942. Within a year, dogs and their handlers, who had been trained at installations in Pennsylvania or South Carolina, were assigned to 10 Coast Guard districts on the Atlantic, Gulf, and Pacific coasts. A dog's keen sense of smell and protective nature made it an ideal partner during nighttime beach patrols when Germans were expected to sneak ashore. Many official Coast Guard photographs taken of dog patrols during World War II reveal that the preferred breeds were ironically German Shepherds, Rottweilers, and Doberman Pinschers (it isn't known if these breeds were intentionally chosen to track villainous agents of the Third Reich). Just as with mounted horse patrols, the introduction of dogs to the nation's coastal defenses came far too late to be of any consequence.

One modest defensive measure that proved to be surprisingly effective was the use of small private craft for anti-submarine patrols, which became known officially as the U.S. Coast Guard Corsair Fleet, but known unofficially by the personnel assigned to it as the Hooligan Navy. Before it was finally implemented, the concept had been proposed numerous times to naval authorities, including to Admiral King, and numerous times it was dismissed by the Navy as impractical. King strongly asserted that small vessels were only useful for the rescue of survivors.

Months before the Japanese attack on Pearl Harbor, but at a time when many Americans expected the country to enter the war, an owner of a Rhode Island-based swordfishing fleet proposed to the Navy that it install radio telephone equipment on his boats so that they might be used for observation purposes as picket boats. The Chief of Naval Operations politely declined the offer on the basis that it would be in violation of the Hague Convention of 1907, which protected civilian commercial watercraft from capture by enemy vessels as long as the civilian vessels were used exclusively for fishing and trade, not for military purposes.

At the same time, the Cruising Club of America and its commodore, Alfred Stanford, also made a proposal to the Navy that privately owned powerboats and sailing yachts could supplement the few small patrol craft the military had available to guard the nation's coastal waters. The brilliant idea, like so many during the war, was borrowed from the British. It was, in fact, inspired by the well-publicized 1940 British evacuation and sealift from Dunkirk, France, which employed 700 "little ships" or civilian small craft to transport 331,226 British and French soldiers across the English Channel to avoid capture by the advancing German army.

Stanford and his organization presented an excellent justification for the use of sailing yachts equipped with auxiliary engines, which, once at sea, would patrol noiselessly by the power of the wind. U-boat hydrophones would not be able to detect their presence. Sailing vessels of lengths between 50- and 90-feet were capable of withstanding heavy seas and winds; they could cruise for weeks without the need for fuel or re-provisioning; and they could hold a static position at sea for extended periods by heaving-to (a

U.S. Coast Guard Corsair Fleet at Ocracoke's Silver Lake

maneuver where the boat's headsail and rudder are set in opposition). A hove-to vessel with a tall mast provided a good observation platform, although one likely to produce instant seasickness for most observers unless on the calmest of seas.

By April 1942, the Cruising Club of America had organized and volunteered 70 sailing yachts and 100 other small craft for the Navy's use—primarily for observation and rescue. Admiral King curtly turned the offer down on the basis of "operational difficulties." A month later, following withering criticism from the public, the admiral reversed his course and ordered that the Coast Guard Reserve assume responsibilities for organizing the coastal picket patrols. Apparently, the Navy was in such a fix that the Hague Convention of 1907 no longer mattered.

With much élan, American boaters adopted the "Dunkirk spirit" and put to sea in their little boats to search for German submarines. At first, according the the Coast Guard's history of the Corsair Fleet, the Temporary Reserves who formed the crews were made up of "college boys, adventurous lads of shore villages, Boy Scouts, beachcombers, ex-bootleggers, and rum-runners. Almost everyone who declared he could reef and steer, and many who couldn't, were accepted." It was the diverse nature of the crews which inspired the name, Hooligan Navy. Some of the vessels' names were no less dubious. One motor yacht employed to find U-boats was named *Poodle Pub*. Others were sleek and elegant, like the Sparkman & Stephens-designed racing yawl, *Edlu II*. By July 1942, 143 boats were participating in the Coast Guard's picket patrols, although the Navy's PR offices, ever prone to embellishment, had proudly informed the public that 1,200 civilian craft had joined the anti-submarine effort.

When it was decided that the Corsair Fleet could use a morale-lifting mascot and emblem, Walt Disney Studios offered the mercurial Donald Duck dressed as a swashbuckling pirate replete with eyepatch, cutlass, brace of pistols, and a knife clenched in his bill—something like a feathered, web-footed Black Beard. Surely more than one Hooligan sailor laughed at the likelihood that German U-boats were going to be chastened by sub chasers named *Poodle Pub* emblazoned with this fearsome pirate-duck.

Gradually, active-duty Coast Guardsmen began to replace the Temporary Reserves crews. One such regular was Mac Womac. "We were on a wooden sailboat that was 70-feet-long," Womac said. "It was equipped with a sonar that we dropped over the side. It was a big, brown, wide thing, and we dropped it over, and the guy listened on ear phones to see if he could pick up a ping or anything. We never used our main motor except for coming in and out of the harbor—had a six-cylinder diesel engine in it. All we had on board were six rifles and one pistol. We couldn't do much, but they had us out there; we had to go." A photograph taken from the observation tower at the former Ocracoke Coast Guard Station (it was under U.S. Navy control at the time) at the entrance to Silver Lake, shows three vessels of the Corsair Fleet at the docks—a schooner, a sloop, and a ketch.

Before leaving the dock for the first time, Navy ordnance technicians appeared and told Womac and his fellow Hooligans that they needed to load some depth charges onto a 90-foot Alden schooner. There were two depth-charge racks on the port and starboard sides near the stern, each holding up to two, 325-pound charges (total weight). The Navy issued instructions to the young sailors to never set the depth to any shallower than 50 feet for the charge to detonate and to make sure the sailboat was making at least 10 knots of speed, regardless of the depth—15 knots would be even better. The men scratched their heads and rolled their eyes. They knew that a 90-foot wooden sailing vessel's maximum speed under sail was, at best, no more than eight knots.

"We didn't have a gunner's mate so the First Class Bosuns Mate that was in charge of the boat, he set the charge to whatever he thought the depth was," Womac recalled. "We were lucky. We never found a U-boat. It would have probably done more damage to us than it would the submarine because we were wood—wood busted easier than steel does."

A few Corsair Fleet boats did find U-boats. In one instance off the coast of Florida reported in a 1944 story in the *Saturday Evening Post*, the 40-foot yacht *Jay-Tee* responded to a distress call following an engagement between a U-boat and a merchant ship. When the *Jay-Tee* arrived, the merchant ship was gone, but a U-boat surfaced, then submerged, nearby. The *Jay-Tee* remained in the area to observe further developments. Abruptly, the small craft was suddenly struck and then lifted out of the water by the surfacing U-boat. The U-boat then quickly submerged again—its commander had apparently intended to teach the impertinent yacht a lesson. The *Jay-Tee* was badly damaged but was able to return to port with an amazing story to tell.

The crew of another picket boat off the Florida coast was stunned when a U-boat unexpectedly surfaced next to them. As the seawater cascaded off the conning tower, the hatch opened, the captain climbed out and, with excellent English, said to the dumbfounded Hooligans: "Get the hell out of here, you guys! Do you want to get hurt? Now, scram!"

All of the Corsair Fleet boats had something aboard more effective against U-boats than depth charges or firearms, and that was a ship-to-shore radio. While none of the Hooligan vessels ever sank a U-boat, their presence harassed the German submariners, and they were frequently able to radio sighting reports that are believed to have contributed to a few attacks.

The "Dunkirk spirit" also fueled the passions of America's civilian pilots, who were anxious to do their part to repel the German invaders. Much like the birth of the Corsair Fleet, the genesis of the nation's Civil Air Patrol developed in the pre-war years when concerned general aviation pilots observed that the flights of their counterparts in Britain and German-occupied Europe were banned or strictly curtailed. While not anticipating that they would soon be chasing German U-boats, civilian aviators proposed an auxiliary organization that would keep them flying, assisting the domestic needs of the Navy and Army Air Corps and serving as an early warning system for aerial incursions. Admiral Andrews saw the potential and sent up the chain of command a proposal for the Navy to utilize the civilian pilots and planes as a "Scarecrow Patrol," with the intention that the presence of aircraft in the sky, regardless of their small size or lack of ordinance, would inhibit U-boat activity. Admiral King thought about it and rejected the idea on the familiar grounds of "operational difficulties." Army leaders were more open-minded and appreciative than their Navy counterparts.

The idea took off, first becoming a reality with the New Jersey Division of Aeronautics. National Civil Defense chief Fiorello LaGuardia (the former New York City mayor and WWI pilot) took the New Jersey plan and expanded it into a national civil air patrol operation, formalizing the creation of the Civil Air Patrol (CAP) on December 1, 1941.

In North Carolina, civilian pilots who were cognizant of the developments in other states like New Jersey formulated their own plan, and the state's civil air wing soon became a division of the national organization. By the spring of 1942, the Old North State's division included more than 500 pilots and hundreds of small planes.

Governor Broughton tasked the North Carolina Office of Civil Defense with the job of choosing a location for a patrol base ideally situated near the greatest need—the epicenter of U-boat attacks off Cape Hatteras. Consequently, a previously established private airfield at the small settlement known as Skyco, south of Manteo on Roanoke Island, was selected and became Base 16 of 21 similar bases along the East and Gulf coasts. This location offered easier delivery of fuel supplies than other potential sites on Ocracoke or Hatteras islands. From Skyco, single-engine Stinson Voyagers and Fairchild 24s could be over Diamond Shoals in 30 minutes or less. A year later, a new airfield was built near the north end of Roanoke Island to serve as a Navy Auxiliary Air Station, and the CAP's Coastal Patrol Base 16 moved to the new facility (today's Dare County Regional Airport). A second North Carolina CAP base was also opened near Beaufort in Carteret County in 1943.

Pilots volunteered their own planes and services for one to two weeks at a time. Each

Sikorsky S-39 amphibian aircraft

aircraft was manned by a pilot and an observer, who was typically a pilot, too. The observer also served as radioman. When U-boats or lifeboats with survivors were sighted, radio transmissions were made in the clear without using pre-arranged coded signals in order to initiate immediate action. Two planes flew together for added safety, although on rare occasions solo flights were permitted. At the outset, the coastal air patrols were intended to be for observation purposes only—the planes were only "armed" with radios. After an un-armed CAP plane off the Florida coast in May 1942 missed a golden opportunity to destroy a U-boat stranded in shallow water for 45 minutes near Jupiter Inlet, military authori-ties authorized the civilian pilots to carry one 325-pound depth charge or two 100-pound bombs. Single-engine planes were authorized to patrol up to 50 miles offshore, while multi-engine amphibian aircraft could go out as far as 200 miles. The intrepid CAP pilots flew everyday from dawn to dusk, sometimes in weather conditions that grounded military flights. They considered themselves America's "flying minutemen."

Living conditions at some of the CAP bases were spartan. At a base on Virginia's Eastern Shore, the pilot's flight operations office and barracks occupied a rundown farm-house and chicken coop. At the Skyco base, the mosquitos were so unrelenting that the pilots and ground personnel had to wear nets over their heads just to access the aircraft. It is no wonder that the pilots couldn't wait to get airborne.

CAP pilots were paid $8 for each day that they flew, although payments sometimes arrived months late (the observers on a patrol were paid $5 per day, regardless if they were also pilots). They had to pay for some of their own expenses—except for fuel—and after the war it was estimated that the 40,000 members of the Civil Air Patrol spent $1 million of their own money to help defend their country. Sun Oil Company, which had founded the Tanker Protection Fund, raised $25,000 from oil industry members to help support the vital coast patrols.

Women were recruited to serve for ground support roles and as pilots for inland mis-sions—many of which were dangerous, like towing anti-aircraft targets for gunnery train-ing. Eventually, women constituted 20 percent of the Civil Air Patrol. One female pilot, Margaret Bartholomew, was one of many CAP pilots who lost their lives; her plane crashed into the Allegheny Mountains of western Pennsylvania on a courier flight to Cincinnati.

National advertisers like R.J. Reynolds Tobacco Company and Borg-Warner were quick to capitalize on the patriotism of civilian aviatrices with magazine ads inviting them to smoke a Camel or launder their family's clothes with Norge Appliances once they got back on the ground. "Flying sentries guarding our coastlines—they've got what it takes!" read one ad, and so they had.

Literature published by Civil Air Patrol historians states that, during its 18-month period of service, CAP planes flew 24 million over-water miles, logged more than 244,600 flying hours, spotted 173 U-boats, bombed 57,[18] damaged 17, and sank two. Perhaps least appreciated is the fact that CAP coastal patrols summoned help for 91 ships in distress and for 363 survivors of U-boat attacks.

In recent years, however, the often-quoted, unequivocal claim that CAP planes sank two U-boats has quietly been in dispute, primarily by U-boat researchers. No numerically identified U-boat has ever been confirmed to have been destroyed by one of the civilian patrols, nor has any other corroborating evidence been offered other than the description of oil rising to the ocean surface to prove the kills. Until such evidence is provided, the sinkings of U-boats by CAP planes must be considered as being unproven, especially considering the long-suspected truth of AMM1c Donald Mason's purported sinking of a U-boat on January 28, 1942.

CAP Cadet Sgt. Mary Ellen DeDominicis Chestnut, High School Civil Air Patrol, worked in flight operations during WWII. Her older brother was killed in April 1942 when his merchant ship was torpedoed by U-*754*.

Nevertheless, the extraordinary courage and sacrifice of Civil Air Patrol pilots during the second world war is indisputable and beyond measure. During its 18 months of wartime service, 59 pilots lost their lives, and 26 were lost during coastal patrols. Ninety aircraft were lost at sea, sometimes forced to ditch after the aircraft ran out of fuel or because of engine failure. It was similar circumstances that two North Carolina pilots found themselves in extreme peril over the ocean near Pea Island in Dare County on Monday, December 21, 1942.

At 4:30 p.m., shortly before dusk, the radio receiver at Coastal Patrol Base 16 at Skyco suddenly crackled to life. The panic-stricken voice coming out of the speaker belonged to Frank Cook, a Concord, North Carolina, pilot who had taken off from the airfield just 30 minutes earlier to fly a sector of ocean off Hatteras Island for what was supposed to be a routine submarine patrol.

"We are dropping rapidly," the pilot shouted, "We are dropping rapidly and are going to crash!" Cook's companion in the aircraft was Julian Cooper of Nashville, North Carolina. According to news reports, the pilot's radio transmitter was still on when the plane ditched into the sea, and the impact was clearly heard by appalled listeners back at the base. A second CAP aircraft circled overhead and observed both Cook and Cooper struggle to escape their sinking plane. The sea was frigid, the water was rough, and it was getting dark fast. The men in the second aircraft tossed out a couple of rubber jackets to Cook and Cooper and then had to return to Roanoke Island due to low fuel and approaching darkness.

The story of the crash was reported in Elizabeth City's newspaper, *The Daily Advance*, on the day after Christmas:

> "The evening was bitter cold. No human could withstand the cold for long. The spray that flew over the heads, shoulders, and arms of the two men froze almost as soon as it struck them, making them helpless to fight for life. It is reported that one of the men apparently was numb before the companion plane left, as his head was dropped over his shoulder, while the life jacket still kept him afloat. The other waved to the companion plane as its pilot left and headed back to the base."

Rescue attempts were launched by the nearby Coast Guard stations at Oregon Inlet, Chicamacomico, and Pea Island. The all African-American crew at the Pea Island station, the nearest to the scene of the crash, repeatedly attempted to launch their surfboat into the pounding surf. The *Daily Advance* reported that "Each time they would thrust their boat into the breakers, it would be thrown back at them overturned. Reports have it that it was an almost impossible task to put a surfboat off the back of the Pea Island beach that evening."

The bodies of Cook and Cooper were never found. Both North Carolinians were posthumously awarded the Air Medal for "meritorious achievement while participating in aerial flight."

One of the singular examples of the intrepidity of the Civil Air Patrol—or of any the defenders of the American homeland, civilian as well as military, in 1942—involved the rescue of a Civil Air Patrol pilot by other CAP pilots on July 21.

Maj. Hugh Sharp and Lt. "Eddie" Edwards responded to a faint distress call, which had been received at 4:40 p.m. at their airfield, Control Base No. 2, at Rehoboth Beach, Delaware. One of the base's planes had gone down 20 miles offshore. The two pilots scrambled their single-engine Sikorsky S-39 amphibian aircraft and flew to the crash site, where they soon located one of the two downed aviators in the water. Without hesitation, Sharp performed a skillful emergency landing in order to rescue their comrade. But in the rough seas (possibly exaggerated in the reports as reaching eight- to 10-feet high), the Sikorsky's left pontoon became so battered that it could provide no floatation for the aircraft. Without the pontoon, Sharp and Edwards would be unable to takeoff.

Edwards succeeded in rescuing CAP Lt. Henry Cross, but Cross's observer and radioman, Charles Shelfus, had disappeared. At 6:20 p.m., Cross was safely aboard the aircraft, which slumped precariously to the left on its crippled pontoon.

With no other choice and unflinching temerity, Sharp began to taxi the aircraft toward shore—20 miles away. Soon thereafter, the left pontoon sank beneath the waves. Edwards did the only thing he could do and clamored out onto the right pontoon, hanging on the bomb rack and using his weight to level the aircraft. Over the next two and a half hours, Edwards held his position and was constantly immersed in the cold seawater.

At 8:50 p.m., the Sikorsky was met by a Coast Guard picket boat from Chincoteague, Virginia, which then towed the aircraft and its weary passengers back to its station. Upon their arrival, Edwards was suffering from mild hypothermia and severe muscle cramps. Months later, Sharp and Edwards were summoned to the White House after President Franklin D. Roosevelt heard their amazing story. The President awarded the two pilots the Air Medal, making them the first civilian recipients of the commendation.

A long-time friend of Edwards, Roger Thiel, said on the occasion of Edwards' death in 2009 at the age of 96: "Eddie never considered himself special for the high-profile personal recognition by President Roosevelt, often saying of the rescue for which his Air Medal was awarded, 'Anyone could have done it.'" Thiel could not have expressed a better tribute: "[Edwards'] accomplishments and humility indicate the heroic capabilities of regular U.S. citizens, especially in Civil Air Patrol."

It is worth noting that even though Admiral King's less-than-enthusiastic willingness to entertain the proposals of the Cruising Club of America and civilian aviators in 1942 was well-documented, the passage of time may have fogged his recollections. In his "First Report to the Secretary of the Navy Covering our Peacetime Navy and our Wartime Navy and Including Combat Operations Up to 1 March 1944," issued on April 23, 1944, King touted the Navy's preparedness in organizing privately owned boats and planes. There was no hint of "operational difficulties."

> "We had prepared for this by gathering on our eastern seaboard our scant resources in coastal anti-submarine vessels and aircraft consisting chiefly of a number of yachts and miscellaneous small craft taken over by the Navy in 1940 and 1941. To reinforce this group, the Navy accelerated its program of acquiring such fishing boats and pleasure craft as could be used and supplied them with such armaments as they could carry. For patrol purposes we employed all available aircraft—Army as well as Navy. The help of the Civil Air Patrol was gratefully accepted. This heterogeneous force was useful in keeping lookout and in rescuing survivors of sunken ships. It may have interfered, too, to some extent with the freedom of U-boat movement, but the heavy losses we suffered in coastal waters during the early months of 1942 gave abundant proof of the already well-known fact that stout hearts in little boats can not handle an opponent as tough as the submarine."

Despite having "gratefully accepted" the assistance of the Civil Air Patrol, King discontinued CAP's coastal patrols with a bluntly worded directive issued in the spring of 1943, nearly nine months after Germany recalled most of its U-boats from the waters of the western Atlantic, Gulf of Mexico, and Caribbean Sea.

Americans should never forget that, regardless of their effectiveness against the incursions of U-boats or German saboteurs, those intrepid men and women with stout hearts in little boats, on horseback, and in small planes, will forever be a source of inspiration for those who know their story.

THE "SUICIDE OUTFIT"
U.S. NAVY ARMED GUARD

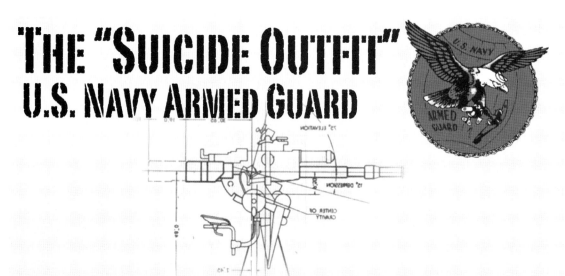

One of the nation's principal defensive measures against U-boats during World War II was among the most dangerous and least recognized—the U.S. Navy Armed Guard. The arming of civilian ships by U.S. Navy gun crews had been tried and tested in World War I when German U-boats and aircraft, for the first time in history, waged unrestricted warfare against the merchant vessels of Great Britain the United States. During the first world war, 384 merchant ships carried Navy guns and crews; by the end of the second war, 6,236 civilian ships were armed.

Wallace Beckham of Avon wanted to be a Navy aircraft mechanic, but once he got out of boot camp, he was told that all of the aircraft mechanic ratings had been filled. The personnel officer suggested that Beckham might like an assignment with the Navy's Armed Guard.

"I asked them, what's the Armed Guard like? They said, 'Well, in the Armed Guard you got a waiter to wait on your table; you get your eggs cooked any way you like in the mornings; you get a choice of two different meats for lunch.' You know, it sounded like an ideal outfit, so I said, 'I'll take that.' So, when I got back to the barracks, my friends asked me, 'What outfit did you get?' I said, 'I'm going in the Armed Guard.' They said, 'Oh my God, that's a suicide outfit.' So, I didn't know what to think being a young boy."

The 17-year-old Beckham was assigned to a gasoline tanker transiting the close inshore shipping lanes between New York and petroleum terminals in the Gulf of Mexico and the Caribbean Sea. Six times his ship ran the gauntlet off Cape Hatteras. On each trip, he got his eggs made to order. "They didn't lie to me when they told me I would eat good and I'd have a man wait on my table," he said. The only problem for Beckham and his Armed Guard buddies was they never knew when a meal might be their last. By virtue of serving with the merchant fleet off the U.S. East Coast during the first six months of 1942, the chances of an Armed Guard member being killed were greater than in any other job in the U.S. Navy.

Beckham's saving grace was that he was on a fast tanker, capable of speeds of more than 15 knots when fully loaded. The disadvantage was—because it was fast—Beckham's ship always traveled alone, making it inviting prey for U-boats.

According to the Office of Naval Administration, "Armed Guards had only one main mission—to defend merchant ships and transports from enemy air, surface, and submarine attacks. Their primary duties, therefore, were watch standing, manning guns, and

maintaining guns and defensive equipments."
A full complement for an Armed Guard crew
assigned to a merchant ship typically numbered
24 gunners led by an officer and three petty
officers. Eight men stood watch for eight hours
each day while at sea—two men at the stern gun,
two men at the forward gun, and a petty officer
and three men stationed near the bridge of the
ship. Lookouts were relieved after two tedious
hours of watching for U-boats. When their vessel was passing through a sector where U-boats
were known to be operating, half of the gun crew
aboard stood watch.

Wallace Beckham

One night, with starlight casting a faint gloom
on the sea, Beckham was on watch at the bow of
his tanker. "We were southbound and we were
traveling alone; all of a sudden I saw something
that looked like a cigar shape," he said. "And there
was another man on the bow—he saw it. We both
hollered to each other, 'Did you see that?' Actually, I saw men standing on the deck of a submarine, and it wasn't one of ours because we didn't
have submarines out there. "

Apparently, the crew of the U-boat was just as surprised by the appearance of the
tanker as were Beckham and his watch mates. "It was probably less than 200 feet, maybe
150 feet away—we almost rammed it," he said. "It happened so fast that we really didn't
have time to do anything. We weren't near the guns. The first thing I did was hit the general
alarm button that was right by me, and I'm sure the U-boat heard it, because it woke everybody up on the ship."

On an earlier trip, Beckham had earned a reputation for overreacting when he misiden-
tified a nearby vessel. "I woke everybody up, and one of them asked, 'Who was on duty?'
Someone said, 'Beckham,' and they said, 'Well, I think I'll go back to sleep.'"

Despite Beckham's lighthearted memories, being in the U.S. Navy Armed Guard was
not such funny business, at least in the early months of the war or on North Atlantic convoys, but as overall U-boat defenses improved, life in the service got better. By late 1944,
the Armed Guard was considered one of the best assignments in the Navy. The good food
served to the enlisted men by stewards—typical on merchant ships but not aboard Navy
vessels—probably had something to do with the Armed Guards being considered a good job,
along with being off watch 16 hours a day.

Still, the post-war tallies of casualties were significant. Of the 6,236 Allied merchant
ships armed by the Navy, 710 were lost by enemy action or other marine casualties; 1,810
officers and enlisted men were killed or listed as missing in action. A few vessels manned by
the Armed Guard successfully engaged U-boats and sank them, mostly on the North Atlantic routes to the Russian port of Murmansk. Off the coast of North Carolina on July 5, 1942,
the guns of the U.S. Navy Armed Guard crew of the freighter SS *Unicoi*, contributed to the
sinking of the U-*576*.

CHAPTER: 20

A U.S. Navy shore-based Spaced Loop "DAB" high-frequency direction finding antenna.

The Mothers of Invention

"You learned the lesson two years ago. We still have to learn it."

Franklin Roosevelt

The Eastern Sea Frontier war diary regarding the U-boat situation at the end of April 1942 concluded: "The outlook for May is still almost as disturbing as it was at the beginning of April, though pessimism should be tempered somewhat by the recognition that ships and planes are gradually accumulating along this coast, and a protective system of considerable strength has been devised for the merchant vessels in our coastal waters." Slowly but surely, American leaders were finding ways to stanch the hemorrhaging of the lifeblood of the Allied war effort.

Each day, an average of 35 tankers and freighters departed ports in the Gulf of Mexico or the Caribbean Sea for destinations in the U.S. industrial northeast or to join North Atlantic convoys departing from anchorages in the Canadian provinces. At any given time, there were as many as 140 ships headed northward between the Florida Keys and New York; an equal number of vessels were, at the same time, headed in the opposite direction. It has been estimated that, daily, there were 60 or more ships making their way north or south in the waters immediately off the North Carolina coast. The protection of so many merchant ships from the onslaughts of German U-boats was a daunting and seemingly impossible task. But the inability of each ship's cargo to reach its destination had far-reaching consequences on the future of the war, not the least of which were the prospects for an Allied invasion of Europe and the ability of the Russians to halt the German invasion on the eastern front. The war against the Nazi tyranny could be won or lost off the beaches of the United States.

Coastal convoys escorted by a sufficient number of fast, well-armed warships were the solution that had been vigorously proposed by the Royal Navy, begrudgingly accepted by Admiral King, and desperately desired by shipping companies and their underwriters. The problem the Navy had with implementing the convoys was that it simply did not have enough escort vessels. A late-March conference of naval officers charged with developing a plan to institute coastal convoys in U.S. waters determined that it would require 31 destroyers and 47 smaller patrol craft. On the day that their report was submitted to King, there were but three destroyers on duty in the Eastern Sea Frontier and only eight other patrol craft. Furthermore, King's staff maintained that assigning any number of the few available destroyers like the USS *Jesse Roper* to shepherd civilian vessels would deprive the warships of their primary mission to hunt and kill the U-boats.

Old habits were hard to change. Up until that time, the conventional wisdom among America's senior naval officers was that instituting coastal convoys was likely going to attract U-boats. British leaders advised, from their hard-earned experience, that this was just what the Americans should want so that they weren't hunting the hornets all over the farm. In a letter to Prime Minister Winston Churchill written in March, President Roosevelt famously lamented: "My Navy has been definitely slack in preparing for this submarine war off our coast. You learned the lesson two years ago. We still have to learn it."[19]

The British were worried that it would take too long for the Americans to learn their lesson; so in order to supplement the availability of escort and patrol craft, the Royal Navy dispatched to New York 24 armed trawlers, which had been previously converted from North Sea fishing vessels into anti-submarine patrol boats for the purpose of defending the coastal waters of Britain. In mid-February, the 170-foot trawlers sailed from England for their newly assigned ports at Boston, New York, Norfolk, and Charleston. By the end of March, most of the vessels had arrived, and 14 were quickly overhauled and prepared for service. The remainder joined the coastal patrols in the coming weeks. Warships with distinctly sounding British names soon appeared alongside their American comrades-in-arms in the patrol log for the Eastern Sea Frontier: *Lady Elsa*, *Lady Rosemary*, *Stella Polaris*, *Kingston Ceylonite*, *Northern Duke*, *Norwich City*, *Northern Isles*, *Hertfordshire*, *Bedfordshire*, *Senateur Duhamel*, and *St. Zeno*. Perhaps inspired by the British example of using fishing boats to fish for German U-boats, the commander of the Fifth Naval District commandeered 35 menhaden fishing boats (also known as "pogey boats") to assist in patrols.

As the ESF war diary for April noted, sufficient numbers of ships and planes were gradually being accumulated. America's shipyards and aircraft factories were ramping up production at an unprecedented rate, and new classes of destroyers and destroyer escorts, short-range bombers, and lighter-than-air blimps were on the way. But pending the first coastal convoy that was scheduled to depart in mid-May, Admiral Andrews had another tactical trick up his sleeve—Bucket Brigades—a name borrowed from firefighters who would pass buckets of water to extinguish a fire.

During the first few months of the war zone in U.S. waters, it had been assumed by naval authorities—albeit, incorrectly—that U-boat skippers were reluctant to conduct their attacks during daylight hours. So a plan was devised by military planners for merchant ships to be shuttled through the most dangerous waters south of Virginia's Cape

Henry between sunrise and sunset, putting in at pre-designated, well-protected ports and anchorages along the way.

Depending on weather conditions, the average merchant ship could travel about 250 nautical miles over a 24-hour period. Consequently, Andrews's staff determined that northbound ships traveling independently through the Florida Straits could safely stop overnight at anchorages at Jacksonville, Charleston, the west side of Cape Fear, and the west side of Cape Lookout, before continuing onward to the entrance to Chesapeake Bay.[20] For the 225-mile overnight passage between the anchorage at Cape Lookout and the entrance to Chesapeake Bay, plans called for 12 to 20 merchant ships to be formed into abbreviated, escorted convoys. Slower merchant ships unable to keep up with the convoys were to stop for the night in an anchorage that would be created on the west side of Cape Hatteras.

The unique geography of North Carolina's three capes—Cape Hatteras, Cape Lookout, and Cape Fear—had long presented mariners with a treacherous navigational challenge. In 1942, the capes theoretically presented the U.S. Navy with a life- and cargo-saving advantage. Each cape and its attendant shoals formed a bay—alternatively known as a bight—on its western side that could be made into a temporary, safe anchorage for ships, provided that some means of defense—either guard ships, shore-mounted gun batteries, minefields, or a combination of all three—were in place to protect the merchant ships occupying the anchorage. Establishing a protected anchorage for the purpose of conducting coastal convoys or harboring fleets was, naturally, another naval tactic borrowed from the manuals of the Royal Navy. A protected anchorage was a naval precept dating back to the days of the Roman occupation of the British Isles.

Prior to the outbreak of the war between Germany and the United Kingdom, the British Admiralty had developed comprehensive plans to establish minefields to protect strategic estuaries, bays, and ports—such as the River Thames and the Royal Navy's principal base at Scapa Flow in the Orkney Islands, but also at imperial bases at Malta, Singapore, Hong Kong, and Alexandria, Egypt. The British also pioneered numerous other defensive measures to protect anchorages from marauding U-boats and surface-running motor torpedo boats, including gate-like anti-submarine nets and booms, underwater listening and magnetic detection devices, gun batteries with base-end stations for targeting enemy vessels, radio direction finders, radar, and high-powered searchlights.

Long before the United States entered the war, the U.S. Navy also contemplated various passive harbor and coastal defense measures, basing many ideas on British practices. In February 1942, the Navy proposed establishing a minefield, much like the British minefield guarding the Thames estuary, across the 43 miles of open water between Cape Cod and Cape Ann in Massachussetts, effectively creating an enormous protected anchorage off Boston for ships gathering for North Atlantic convoys. After careful consideration, Admiral Andrews strongly recommended against proceeding with the minefield due to insufficient numbers of support vessels for patrol and minesweeping duties; because the cost and effort would diminish potential offensive actions that he believed would be more successful at deterring U-boat activity; and, for the all-important reason that mines didn't know the difference between an enemy U-boat or an Allied vessel. The idea of a Cape Cod-Cape Ann minefield was shelved.

In spite of Andrews's sound reasoning to discourage the Cape Cod-Cape Ann project, two months later he approved plans to establish a smaller minefield at the Cape Hatteras anchorage.[21] The plan was intended to accommodate those unlucky merchant captains whose slower, independently steaming ships wound up halfway between Cape Lookout and Chesapeake Bay at sunset with no where to hide. Unfortunately, the plan failed to take into account the recent daylight attacks on ships like the SS *Dixie Arrow* and the SS *City of New York*, which proved that U-boat skippers were growing bolder and had no qualms about torpedoing ships in daylight hours. Even so, the Cape Hatteras minefield was expected by the Navy to reduce the number of ships being sunk. It had, in fact, the opposite effect and fulfilled Andrews's concern that mines would sink ships indiscriminately.

By the first of May, work began. By the end of the month, 2,635 Mark-6 Naval Contact Mines were anchored in place along a 35-mile-long semi-circle extending from Diamond Shoals to a point off the beach about four miles east of Ocracoke village. Each mine was chained to ride a few feet below the ocean surface. The Mark-6 contained an explosive charge of 300 pounds of TNT that would be triggered by a contact pistol when the mine was bumped by a vessel, regardless of whether it was a German U-boat or an American ship.

On the western perimeter of the minefield, a few miles southeast of Ocracoke village, an opening wide enough for tankers to pass in and out of the protected anchorage led to the designated area where the ships were to drop anchor for the night—a 36-square-mile box directly south and east of Hatteras Inlet. When ships steaming independently appeared from the south in the mid- to late-afternoon, a U.S. Coast Guard pilot boat would signal the inbound ship, ordering its captain to follow the pilot boat through the minefield opening and to the anchorage below Hatteras Inlet. At dawn on the following day, the routine would be repeated in reverse with the pilot boat guiding the departing ship to a buoy well south of the minefield and then directing the ship's master to steer a course due east until the merchant vessel was east of longitude 75.20W, where the ship could safely clear the minefield and resume its northward journey. On paper, the operation seemed simple enough, but plans on paper often don't take into account bad weather.

 Seventeen days after the Cape Hatteras protected anchorage opened for business, the Standard Oil tanker *F.W. Abrams* arrived for the night. By the next morning when it was time to leave, the weather had turned foul, visibility was poor, and the ship's captain was having a hard time keeping the pilot boat in view as it guided the big tanker past the gauntlet of mines that framed the pathway out. Suddenly, according to its crew, the *F.W. Abrams* seemed to have been struck by a torpedo on its starboard side. (Had the civilian sailors been thinking clearly, they would have realized that it would have been highly unlikely that a U-boat would have fired a torpedo from that direction because, off the starboard side of the ship the island of Ocracoke was but a few miles away.)

The *F.W. Abrams* began taking on water but not enough to cause it to sink, so the captain ordered the crew to drop anchor. The anchor cable jammed, and the ship began to drift in the heavy rain and fog. In less than an hour, two more explosions rocked the ship, finally sinking it. The captain and crew abandoned the vessel and made it safely to shore at Ocracoke Island. They were certain that they had been relentlessly attacked by a German U-boat. Instead, they had run into three, American-made, Mark-6 contact

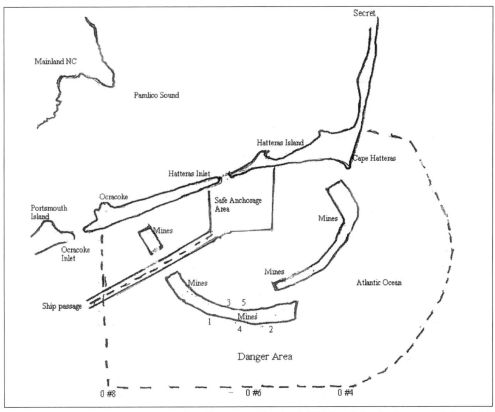

Diagram of Cape Hatteras protected anchorage and minefield (sketch by Carlton Ward Garrish).

mines. The Cape Hatteras minefield had claimed its first victim.

Two months later, two ships that had been part of a convoy, which had been torpe-doed but not sunk, attempted to run toward shallow water off Ocracoke Island. Both struck mines in the Cape Hatteras protected anchorage, and one was sunk. The next day two tugboats were sent from Norfolk to aid the stricken ships, and one of the tugs struck a mine and was sunk. Soon after, an embarrassed and angry Admiral Andrews ordered that the Cape Hatteras protected anchorage be closed indefinitely. Plans for establishing mined anchorages at Cape Fear and Cape Lookout were quickly forgotten.

A year later, the Cape Hatteras minefield was swept by the Navy to remove the Mark-6 mines. Fewer than half of the mines moored in 1942 were recovered. Overall, it has been estimated that the U.S. Navy placed 20,000 mines in United States waters for defensive purposes during the war. Not a single German U-boat or Axis vessel was ever sunk by the mines, but three Allied vessels were destroyed by the Cape Hatteras minefield.[22]

Stationing lookouts around a harbor entrance or protected anchorage was the most ba-sic of submarine detection methods, but distance, darkness, fog, high seas, and submerged U-boats deterred successful detection. During World War I and in the years following the

U.S. Navy "Loop Receiving Station" at Ocracoke Island including surface and fire control radars.

war, Great Britain devised, tested, and installed numerous technologies for anti-submarine detection at many of its strategic ports, harbors, and outlying anchorages. It might be fair to say that Great Britain was the mother of invention with regard to the war against German U-boats. One of the more intriguing, little-known, and highly secret British technologies proved its effectiveness in 1918—an underwater magnetic indicator loop.

British naval scientists discovered that a submarine, even when its magnetic field had been neutralized by degaussing, continued to emit a small electric current that could be detected by electromagnetic induction via an underwater stationary loop of cable connected to sensing equipment on shore. By such a method in 1918, the British Navy detected the incursion of a German U-boat, UB-*116*, into the mined anchorage of the naval base at Scapa Flow, and it was able to destroy the U-boat by remotely detonating nearby mines.

In 1938, when war with Germany seemed imminent, magnetic indicator loops were improved and systematically deployed at the most important Royal Navy harbors in Great Britain as well as its dominions and territories around the world. At the same time, the technology was shared with the U.S. Navy, which developed and tested its own system prior to America's entry in the war. The first installation of an underwater magnetic indicator loop in the United States was completed at Fort Story near Cape Henry, Virginia, during the summer of 1941. Before the war's end in 1945, the Navy placed about 50 indicator loops along the American coasts and at other operational harbors in the Pacific and European theaters of the war. In the spring of 1942, one of those indicator loops was installed at the Cape Hatteras Protected Anchorage with its control station located on Ocracoke Island. It became one of the most top-secret military installations in North Carolina during the war, and it was the only such facility in the state.

In the United States, an underwater magnetic indicator loop and its control station were generally part of a larger military installation known as a Harbor Entrance Control Post or HECP. HECP facilities were most notably located at places like Fort Story, which overlooked the entrance of the channel leading to the largest naval port in the United States. There were dual HECPs surrounding Ambrose Channel leading to New York Harbor with facilities located at Fort Tilden at Rockaway, New York, and Fort Hancock at Sandy Hook, New Jersey. One of the earliest Harbor Entrance Control Posts to become operational—three days before the Japanese bombed Pearl Harbor—was Fort Miles on the Cape Henlopen side of the entrance to the Delaware Bay, which featured gun batteries, indicator loops, and underwater listening devices. While the Cape Hatteras Protected Anchorage and its indicator loop installation on Ocracoke Island did not qualify as a HECP, it did contain numerous advanced technologies that were being installed at other major port entrances along the East Coast.

Typical control station with three fluxmeters.

The Navy selected a site for the Ocracoke station atop an ancient sand ridge, about halfway between the village and the beach. The ridge, which in places rose to 30 feet above sea level, overlooked the barren tidal flat that separated the island's beach and the village.[23] The natural dunes provided a relatively high vantage point for the buildings and towers that would be built there; the setting also made the secret station plainly visible to the nearby village residents. As a point of comparison, the British went to great lengths to locate similar facilities in settings that would shield them from prying eyes.

The well-guarded complex at Ocracoke was surrounded by a barbed wire fence and comprised an area of about 11 acres. As many as eight structures linked by wooden walkways and sandy paths were eventually built at the site, including odd-looking towers and peculiar rotating antennas. The Navy referred to the installation as a "loop receiving station." The residents of the village of Ocracoke called it "Loop Shack Hill."[24] No one but the Navy men assigned to the station were allowed to go near it; even the Coast Guard men stationed at Ocracoke were ordered to keep away. Most people had no idea what was going on at the mysterious new Navy facility about a half mile east of the Wahab Hotel; however they had an inkling that it had something to do with German U-boats.

The station was designed to serve many high-technology defensive measures in support of the Cape Hatteras Protected Anchorage by the time the Navy completed it, but the installation's first and foremost function was the operation of its underwater magnetic indicator loops. In late May and early June 1942, a Navy net tender from Norfolk, USS *Rosewood*, laid at least two indicator loop arrays on the ocean bottom beneath the approaches to the entrance of the mined anchorage. The loop arrays were anchored to the bottom at a sufficient distance from the minefield to allow advance warning that a sub-

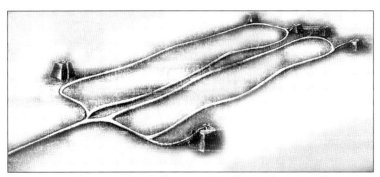

U.S. Navy drawing of typical magnetic indicator loop installation.

merged U-boat was approaching the area. Each array consisted of a 1.3-inch-diameter, lead-sheathed, single-core cable that was configured in two rectangular-shaped loops. The two loops were positioned adjacent to one another so that there was an outer leg, a center leg, and an inner leg. In U.S. Navy indicator loop installations, the average length of a single loop field was two to three miles; the longest could be up to six miles long. The spacing between the legs was specified at 200 yards. The cables forming the two loops were spliced to a tail cable, which connected the array to the receiving station on shore. Tail cables could be many miles long depending on the distance from the receiving station to the location of the indicator loops offshore.

When a vessel, either on the surface or submerged, crossed over the indicator loop array, an induced voltage was produced that was detected on an instrument called a flux-meter at the receiving station, and the result was recorded on a paper chart. The watch-keepers on duty would interpret the electronic signatures on the chart and then use a telescope to determine if a surface vessel was crossing the loop field. If no surface vessel could be seen, it would be assumed that a submarine was approaching, and appropriate action would be taken by patrolling vessels.

At the loop receiving station on Ocracoke, a concrete casemate housed the operations building that contained all of the facility's detection equipment including fluxmeters, chart recorders, communications gear, telescopes, and furniture for four men. The Oc-racoke station also was equipped with an early version of a microwave surface-search ra-dar system, which was erected on top of the operations building. In addition, underwater activity surrounding the Cape Hatteras Protected Anchorage was monitored by the use of radio sonobuoys or cable-connected hydrophone listening devices, which were placed near the loops in order to indicate what part of the loop has been crossed and to provide additional information as to the direction, speed, and type of vessel. Many of the Navy's other receiving stations and HECPs included a third line of defense known as a Harbor Echo-Ranging And Listening Device, or HERALD, which emitted sonar pulses to allow a shore-based operator to be able to establish a range and bearing to an intruding vessel. (It is not known if the Ocracoke station had been equipped with HERALDs.)

Beyond the need to defend the protected anchorage south of Cape Hatteras, the Oc-racoke station also included a building dedicated to locating German U-boats anywhere in the Eastern Sea Frontier and beyond through the use of high-frequency radio direction finding, also known as HF/DF or "Huff-Duff." HF/DF was yet another anti-submarine technology pioneered by the British.

Prior to the war, the British Radio Security Service (MI8) successfully experimented with the use of two or more radio receivers for the purpose of locating the source of a radio transmission. Once the war began, dozens of wooden huts known as Y-stations were established on the desolate and craggy coasts of Britain, for the purpose of receiving the high-frequency signals being sent by the vessels of Germany's Kriegsmarine.

Admiral Dönitz's headquarters was in constant communication with his U-boats; with an almost obsessive need to know where they were, he ordered his commanders to transmit their locations on a frequent basis. Dönitz assumed the U-boat radiotelegraphy transmissions might be intercepted by the enemy, but he believed that if his radiomen limited their transmissions to 30 seconds or less, the British would be unable to locate its source. However, ever-vigilant and skilled British HF/DF operators, bravely huddled in tiny shacks on the heathlands, were able to pinpoint the compass bearing to the source of the signal in 10 seconds or less. As a result, by combining multiple bearings from various stations, the U-boat's estimated location could be triangulated. On a plotting table in the Admiralty's Submarine Tracking Room in the basement of a concrete building in London, the locations of U-boats and other German naval vessels were marked by pins on an enormous chart of the Atlantic Ocean. The accuracy of a U-boat's location derived by HF/DF was far from precise—the positions, on average, were within a 30- to 50-mile radius. Nonetheless, the importance of this critical capability was paramount. HF/DF made it possible for Allied vessels to be alerted to the presence of U-boats or even reroute convoys away from known U-boat positions.

For the same purpose, the U.S. Navy Office for Communications Security oversaw the installation of HF/DF stations along the East Coast. In addition to the "Huff-Duff" hut at Ocracoke's loop receiving station, similar HF/DF receiving stations were located at Coast Guard Lifeboat Stations at Cape Lookout and Poyners Hill, which was south of the Currituck Beach Lighthouse.[25] From these stations, radio intercepts of U-boat transmissions were immediately forwarded to the Navy's Intelligence Center on Constitution Avenue in Washington, D.C., and to the Enemy Submarine Tracking Section at the Joint Operations Office at the headquarters of the Eastern Sea Frontier in the Federal Building in lower Manhattan. At the latter, the information was analyzed, and, if it was deemed accurate, the suspected location of the U-boat would be plotted on a 12-foot-high wall chart. HF/DF was proven to be one of the truly effective defensive measures during the war.

During the frenetic months of devastating merchant ship losses and defensive reactions on the part of the U.S. Navy, it was decided that the Cape Hatteras Protected Anchorage should also be defended with shore-mounted gun batteries. To this end, a newly developed fire-control radar system was added to the Ocracoke station in a building at the northeast end of the property. Plans called for the U.S. Army to place two 155-millimeter artillery pieces further down the beach, but difficulties in finding a suitable location protected from frequent ocean overwash eventually eliminated the installation. Were a U-boat spotted on the surface, the 155-millimeter guns would have been capable

Remains of Ocracoke's top-secret Loop Shack.

of firing an explosive projectile to the approaches to the mined anchorage, which was about 12 miles to the south of the island.

By the time the Navy got done building, equipping, and manning Ocracoke's top-secret loop receiving station, it was one of the more expensive, state-of-the-art defensive installations on the East Coast—but that is about all it was. Because the Cape Hatteras minefield caused the embarrassing sinking of four Allied vessels that resulted in its removal in 1943, it can be concluded that Ocracoke's Loop Shack made no contribution whatsoever to the effort to defeat German U-boats in the war zone off North Carolina's coast. Not once at Loop Shack Hill did the fluxmeter's paper plotter record the signature of an enemy U-boat, nor did the Navy's surface search radar system register a U-boat's blip, nor were other useful results produced for the future development of anti-submarine warfare.[26] Even so, there can be no question that Ocracoke's top-secret Loop Shack was an interesting technological adjunct to North Carolina's World War II history.

The defensive measures protecting the entrances to North Carolina's two major ports at Wilmington and Morehead City varied significantly. Neither port entrance was designated as a Harbor Entrance Control Post like those found at the larger East Coast HECP installations near Boston, New York, Cape Henlopen, Norfolk, Charleston, and Key West.

Beaufort Inlet and the anchorage within Cape Lookout Bight were considered to be of key strategic value to the Navy. The anchorage, which was also mined, was substantially more active than the one at Cape Hatteras, and it was used for a few months as a staging area for northbound Bucket Brigades and as a harbor of refuge for slow, independently traveling ships. The inlet provided convenient deep-water access for medium-sized anti-submarine patrol vessels such as the 165-foot *Thetis*-Class Coast Guard cutters or the 170-foot British armed trawlers, which patrolled one of the U-boat's favorite hunting grounds on the approaches to Cape Lookout. The port at Morehead City, which was much closer to the sea lanes than its sister port at Wilmington, became an indispensable coaling station for these steam-powered warships, and coal was supplied by the Atlantic and Eastern Carolina Railway.

In December 1941, the U.S. Army took possession of Fort Macon from the state's division of parks in order to construct the harbor defenses of Beaufort Inlet. Armaments included the emplacement of four 155-millimeter guns in fortified revetments—two guns located in the dunes immediately south of the fort and two guns positioned west of Atlantic Beach. Six months later, the initial gun emplacements were

Remains of gun battery at Cape Lookout ca. 1974 (courtesy of Leon Reed).

removed and replaced with two 6-inch Naval guns mounted on fixed concrete pads at the fort. Concrete base-end stations were built on both sides of the inlet—one on Bogue Banks and the other on Shackleford Banks—for the purpose of sighting enemy surface vessels (not U-boats) and controlling the accuracy of the shore-based guns. By using surveying-like instruments including a M-19 azimuth telescope for spotting and a depression position finder, men in the base-end stations would simultaneously acquire a range and bearing to the target that would be communicated to a plotting room at the fort. The plotting room would compute the targeting data and then forward it on to the guns. Later in 1942, a wooden combat information center was built on top of the parapet of the fort. Two additional 155-millimeter guns mounted at Cape Lookout were subsequently replaced with two 5-inch Naval guns mounted on concrete pads. The Cape Lookout guns were controlled by a Fixed Coast Artillery medium wave radar placed atop a nearby tower. Between Atlantic Beach and Cape Lookout numerous watchtowers and seven high-powered portable searchlights were erected.

Even though the Cape Fear River led to North Carolina's largest port at Wilmington and Admiral Andrews's staff at ESF Headquarters often referred to Cape Fear as a theoretical anchorage for Bucket Brigades and independently steaming northbound ships, the defenses protecting the river entrance were less robust than those at Beaufort Inlet or Cape Hatteras. The U.S. Army, U.S. Navy, and U.S. Coast Guard all had a presence at Fort Caswell, a 19th-century masonry fort at the eastern end of Oak Island. The fort hosted a depot for the Army, a section base for the Navy's inshore patrol, and a harbor for Coast Guard rescue craft. Once coastal convoys were initiated, an anchorage on the west side of Cape Fear became nonessential.

CHAPTER 21

Ocracoke's Spanish Casino.

THE UNCONDITIONAL SURRENDER

"What is it about this place that you don't like?"

Ollie Styron

There was a lot of work to be done to turn Ocracoke into a useful anti-submarine patrol base. In addition to the construction of the loop receiving station, the Navy made plans to establish a Section Base at the island, due in large measure to its proximity to the sea lanes off Cape Hatteras, but also because of the potential for a well-protected harbor to be built inside the tidal estuary and marshy area surrounding Cockle Creek. The creek was the historic anchorage for the island's small fishing, oystering, and clamming boats, around which the village of Ocracoke grew during the preceding three centuries. Under the supervision of the U.S. Army Corps of Engineers, two large dredges arrived at Ocracoke to extend the deepening of the harbor that had begun in 1933. Thousands of cubic yards of mud, sand, and marsh grass were scoured out of the creek, increasing its depth to 14 feet so that the new harbor could accommodate the deeper drafts of 83-foot Coast Guard patrol boats, Navy tugs, freight and supply vessels, and the yachts of the Corsair Fleet.

The long-cherished solitude and tranquility of Ocracoke had come to an end in 1942. Construction at the Navy base on the north side of what was to become Silver Lake proceeded on a mammoth scale by the traditional standards of the tiny fishing village. Every day villagers heard a cacophony of nails being hammered, boards being sawn, and pilings being driven into the soft sand of the harbor. In time, a large administration building and 30-bed hospital were erected, barracks and a mess hall were built, a machine shop and storage facility appeared along the docks, and radio and water towers rose from the sands. Flimsy temporary quarters for oil-stained and sodden survivors of U-boat attacks were hastily built behind the Coast Guard station and supplied with cots, spare clothing, and other necessities sent by the Red Cross.

The war brought a welcome economic boom to the island. It also brought a lot of strangers. During the Great Depression, many of Ocracoke's men—especially the younger ones—had to leave the island to find work elsewhere. When war broke out, many were at East Coast ports, like Baltimore, Philadelphia, and Norfolk working on tugboats and dredges and serving in the Merchant Marine. Consequently, labor was in short supply. As Ocracoke's Navy Section Base began to take shape, boats with construction workers and materials arrived with regularity.

While all of this activity was occurring, merchant ships were still being attacked and sunk by U-boats offshore. Week after week, the men of the Coast Guard like Ted Mutro and Mac Womac continued their depressingly futile work of patrolling the beaches, mucking horse stalls, responding to SOS calls offshore, and investigating reports of wayward lifeboats, wreckage, and bodies. To make matters worse, when ashore, the quality of life the men were afforded was getting poorer, not better. As more and more Navy men arrived at the village, the Coasties were displaced from their more-modern and spacious quarters at the recently constructed Coast Guard station near the harbor entrance and sent to reside at the worn and cramped rooms at the Ocracoke Lighthouse keeper's house on the south side of the creek.

During the first five months of the war, the Coast Guard men on Ocracoke were commanded by a non-commissioned officer, Chief Petty Officer Homer Gray. Once the Cape Hatteras Protected Anchorage was completed in early June, five 83-foot wooden-hulled boats were transferred to Ocracoke to patrol the minefield. Along with the 70 men who crewed the boats, there were dozens more—officers and rates—who were sent to Ocracoke to support the mission as radiomen, mechanics, fuelers, and supervisors. This greatly expanded Coast Guard contingent required a senior officer to manage them, and the man sent for the job was Capt. Henry Coyle. Coyle had previously become known across America as the commander of the Coast Guard cutter *Mendota*, after it rescued survivors of a sinking Greek freighter off Cape Hatteras in 1937. The story, touting the heroic capabilities of the U.S. Coast Guard and Capt. Coyle, was featured in a *Paramount News* newsreel seen in theaters across the nation.

After experiencing his brief brush with Hollywood fame, Coyle's new assignment on Ocracoke must have felt like a demotion. But to the young Coasties on the remote island who had been up until then largely self-supervised, the captain's presence among them caused no small amount of trepidation, especially to those unaccustomed to seeing gold braid on the sleeves of a uniform.

"Yeah, this Captain Coyle, he was a four striper!" Mutro reminisced sarcastically. "He came ashore here with four ensigns." Coyle might have intimidated the youngsters, but he soon proved to be their hero.

"We ran out of water," Mutro said. "[Capt. Coyle] asked the chief, 'What do you do when you run out of water?' And Homer Gray said, 'We just do without.' "[Capt. Coyle] asked, 'Did you ever call the District [headquarters]?' And Gray said, 'Yeah. They told us to pray for rain.'"

Coyle could hardly believe what he was hearing. Pray for rain? The 53-year-old veteran got on the station's phone and rang up Norfolk. In Mutro's words: "'District office, this is Captain Coyle down here at Ocracoke lifeboat station. What do you think we are, a bunch of camels? Send us some water!' Next day, a buoy tender comes in. Captain Coyle says, 'How much water you got on board?' The buoy tender says, 'I got 9,000 gallons, sir. I've got orders to deliver four and a half thousand gallons to the Diamond Shoals Lightship and four and a half thousand gallons to Ocracoke.' And [Capt. Coyle] said, 'You say you've got 9,000 gallons on board? I want every drop of it. Now go get Diamond Shoals a load!'"

Some of the Coast Guardsmen stationed at Ocracoke were holdovers from the old days when it was a Life-Saving Service Station. They were natives of the village

Capt. Henry Coyle, USCG

who had lived there all of their lives and who had homes and families in the village. The younger Coasties often resented the local men who, at the end of the day, could go to their homes and eat a meal with their wives and families. The younger men, instead, were homesick and cramped. Thirty men, including Mutro, were squeezed in a 100-year-old keeper's house designed to accommodate 12 people.

Being assigned to the island of Ocracoke for the young Coast Guardsmen was like being aboard a ship without ever getting liberty. Until Capt. Coyle arrived, the ratings' pleas to go off the island fell on deaf ears. One day, Coyle mustered his men at the docks where his station's boats were tied up. "How long you been here?" Coyle asked his men. Someone answered, "Four or five months." Coyle asked another man, "Have you seen the mainland yet?" "No, sir," was the reply.

Mutro recalled that Coyle went down the line and kept asking each man how long they had been on the island. Mutro continues the story: "Finally, he turns to Homer Gray and he says, 'What are you doing, keeping these men in a concentration camp? It's bad enough being stationed on an island. Turn 'em loose once in awhile!'"

According to Mutro, the next day two men at a time took turns enjoying 72 hours of liberty by taking the mail boat to the village of Atlantic in Carteret County and then hitching a ride to Morehead City.

On one occasion, Coyle saw one of his men who was supposed to have left for shore leave returning to the station with his bag in his hand and a dejected look on his face. The captain shouted to the enlisted man, "What happened to you?" The disappointed sailor said, "I missed the mail boat." "Missed the mail boat, huh?" Coyle replied. He then

Coast Guardsmen on dock at Willis pier on Silver Lake.

turned to some of the other men loitering nearby and said, "Well, what do you think we've got that picket boat for? Get in that picket boat and run the mail boat down, and if you can't catch the mail boat, carry this man to Atlantic."

"Yeah, that Captain Coyle, he looked after us," Mutro said proudly.

The men stationed at the Hatteras Inlet station, at the northeast end of Ocracoke Island, would often go over to Hatteras village for their R&R. There wasn't much to do, but they could buy beer at places like the Burrus General Store. If they wanted to find a local girl to date, they had to strike a deal with the Midgett Brothers. Stocky Midgett, Jr., recalled a service they patriotically provided all of the local branches of the Armed Forces. "The Army used to send a patrol in here every evening to patrol up and down the coast," Midgett recalled. "And this friend of mine and I [had this arrangement with them]. If we got them a date with one of the local girls, they would let us use their jeeps."

So, what would a 14-year-old boy want with a jeep after he had been driving a bus all day from one end of Hatteras Island to the other? Something he couldn't do with a bus. "We'd run the hell out of them," Midgett said, laughing. "Driving on the beach and driving all over the dunes and what have you. It was a lot of fun, as a kid, to experience it. That was a highlight."

After endless hours of mind-numbing boredom punctuated with occasional confrontations with the frightful horrors of war, sailors assigned to the Outer Banks had few diversions to help them forget. Stores on Ocracoke were not allowed to sell alcohol, although there were always times when men returning from liberty were able to sneak some back onto the island. In March 1942, three Navy sailors, including Ocracoke native Wilbur Gaskill, were looking for something to get them drunk. They decided to break open a ship's compass and drain its contents, which everyone knew contained alcohol. What not everyone knew or remembered was that the contents consisted of 45% denatured alcohol. For two of the men, it was a fatal mistake that had been made many unfortunate times during Prohibition—denatured alcohol was deadly. Gaskill somehow survived. "It killed the Navy guys and never even bothered the Gaskill boy," Womack remembered. "They said he didn't even have a hangover the next morning—he must have had a cast-iron stomach."

Some Coast Guardsmen stationed on the Outer Banks resorted to desperate measures to get reassigned elsewhere. At the isolated Little Kinnakeet Life-Saving Station north of Avon, a young rating shot himself in the hand just to get a pass off the island. "The officer in charge came to our store to use the telephone to call the doctor down at Cape Hatteras," Gibb Gray recalled. "This boy had shot himself in his hand with a .38 caliber pistol, right between the fingers. He said he knew he had to shoot himself to get stationed away from here. It was too isolated for him."

The men on Ocracoke thought their assignment was so isolated that they began referring to it as the "Siberia of the 5th Naval District." The appellation stood in stark contrast to promoter Stanley Wahab's "shores of contentment and happiness, where life is worth living and living is at its best." Later, an officer in the Coast Guard Reserves, Cmdr. Thomas Sheridan, succeeded Capt. Coyle[27] as Ocracoke

Coastie at Hatteras barbershop.

base commander. In a memorandum to his superiors at the 5th Naval District, Sheridan famously characterized the bleak conditions at Ocracoke. "It is realized that much of the melancholy moaning about duty off this base comes from a deep distaste for Ocracoke in the minds of the men of the ships that call here. This sentiment seems to be universal and is due to the isolated position of the base, the poverty of entertainment of any kind, no liquor, and a lack of supply of the ladies of negotiable affections sought by sailors."

No one seemed to hate Ocracoke more than Mutro. His first problem with the place was all the sand. There were no paved roads. If you walked anywhere, in no time your shoes would be filled with sand. Of course, military men were expected to be in uniform when they were on duty, and that included shoes. The locals knew better. They didn't bother with shoes. It was a reality that Mutro had a hard time accepting. He also had little tolerance for the civilian population in general, especially when they refused to follow regulations.

"You weren't allowed to have lights showing on the ocean side—no kind," he said, describing a night when he was heading out to the beach for a patrol and passed the Spanish Casino. "I heard music in there, and I stopped, and I said, 'I want that juke box shut off at 11 o'clock when I come back by here.' So, I went out on patrol and punched the clock (a recorder mounted on a post on the beach that verifies the completion of a patrol). When I

Mutro & Ollie Styron

get back at 11, I hear 'Just Remember Pearl Harbor' playing on the juke box."

Inside the southwestern-styled cantina, the patriotic song performed by Sammy Kaye's band played loudly, while a mixture of locals and servicemen danced:

His-tor-y in ev'ry cen-tur-y records an act that lives forevermore.
We'll recall, as into line we fall, the thing that happened on Hawaii's shore.
Let's remember Pearl Harbor, as we go to meet the foe.

Mutro was furious and about to confront his foe. "I head inside and pulled my pistol out and, bang, bang, bang." (During the interview, Mutro makes a gesture that indicates he shot three times into the ceiling of the little building.) "They all looked at me, and I said, 'I told you. The next shot is going in that juke box!' They all said, 'Oh my God, don't do that! You'd ruin the only recreation we got.'"

Every romantic relationship begins with a fateful moment—a first encounter. Sometimes it's magical; other times it is not. But regardless of whether it is love at first sight or, to all appearances, an inconsequential introduction, there is a pivotal moment in time when two lives intersect and their futures are irrevocably altered. Such a phenomenon occurred for the fractious Ted Mutro in Ocracoke's Spanish Casino.

As Mutro threatened to shoot the juke box, a feisty 21-year-old island girl named Ollie confronted him. "What is it about this place that you don't like?" For a moment, Mutro was stunned that the petite woman with a noticeable island brogue would challenge him. "The whole damned place," he said. "It's the last stop in civilization!"

"Well, if you don't like it, why don't you get out of here?" Ollie snapped.

Mutro looked her in the eye and said, "Look, I didn't come here because I wanted to come here. I came here because the government sent me here to look after you people." Many years later, Mutro was able to laugh about it. "Boy, her face got red, and she blessed me out."

When it comes to the many ways for a woman to find her way into a man's heart—each to his own. For Ollie Styron to capture Mutro's heart practically all it took were deliveries of clean laundry and bushels of steamed oysters.

When the cisterns ran dry at the Ocracoke Lighthouse keeper's quarters, the Coast Guardsmen billeted there were unable to wash their own clothes. Word got around the village, and some enterprising young women found a way to make some extra money, Styron included. There must have been something about the gruff-talking Coastie from Pennsylvania that Styron liked—she offered to do his laundry for him. "She used to come over in the row boat to pick up my laundry," Mutro remembered. "I said, 'What do I owe you?' She said, 'Fifty cents.' I said, 'Fifty cents! Jesus Christ!' Well, I was only making 36 dollars a month."

Styron decided that Mutro didn't like Ocracoke because he didn't understand it and he couldn't recognize its charms. She decided to change his opinion of the island. "Well, she starts showing me around. She showed me around Black Beard's old house—there was still a place where they claimed Black Beard had a tower. There was an old round cistern there. She took me around and showed me different places there. Kind of took up my spare time."

It took awhile, but Mutro's opinion slowly changed. "I start getting it, I mean, liking it, you know. Before, I was like, Jesus Christ, they didn't wear no shoes, most of them. Me, here, all dressed up in my uniform and shoes. Can't keep the sand out while we're walking. After a while you have to stop and get all the sand out. You finally get tired of that and go barefooted. We'd go to the dance hall barefooted—no shoes."

Womac & Marie Spencer

"She'd take me over to her mother's," Mutro continued. "We'd have steamed oysters. I never ate oysters in my life until I came to Ocracoke. They'd get a bushel of oysters, and we'd steam 'em there in the yard."

Most everyone on the island knew how to fish, and when it came to fishing for a husband, Ollie Styron knew just what she was doing. Before long, Mutro was hooked. Even so, he still tried to wriggle loose before it was too late.

One day in February 1943, with a tie around his neck and his shoes in his hand, Mutro and his fiancee went searching for Preacher Dixon. "Yeah, it was [her], and her mother, and me, and another witness, Jerry Midgett. We walked around to Preacher Dixon's house, and we knocked on the door. And his wife said, 'He's at the Boy Scout meeting.' I said, 'Ah, we'll come back some other time.'"

Mutro's fiancee and her mother would have none of that. "The women didn't want to walk around no more, so we went in to wait for Preacher Dixon," he recalled. "The preacher comes in. He said, 'Well, I see you finally got him, Ollie. Let's get it over with before he changes his mind.'"

Thus was concluded Boatswain's Mate 2nd Class Theodore Mutro's unconditional surrender on Ocracoke.

Mutro was not the only serviceman who was captured by the charms of the island and its women. It is one of the more memorable wartime ironies that some of the men who often called Ocracoke the "Siberia of the 5th Naval District" or "the last stop in civilization" lived much of the remainder of their lives there and produced new generations of island families. There's an old adage among mainlanders who long ago visited the island and had a hard time leaving—once you get Ocracoke sand between your toes, you can never get it out.

In his scrapbook of wartime photos, Mutro documented a number of the island romances. There are photos of couples embracing: Oakie and Isabella, Ed and Dicie, and the lovely Marie Spencer with Mutro's good friend, Mac Womac. "Yeah, Ulysses L. Womac, he married Marie," said the curmudgeonly Mutro with just a hint of wistfulness.

CHAPTER 22

USCGC *Icarus* arrives at Charleston NOB.

THE *ICARUS* ASCENDANCY

"They heard a hail of depth charges, some of them extremely close."

Office of Naval Intelligence

Providence once more favored a warship of the United States when, by chance, it encountered a U-boat off the coast of North Carolina on May 9, 1942.

On the mild Saturday afternoon about 29 miles south-southeast of Beaufort Inlet, the USCGC *Icarus*, a *Thetis*-Class cutter, was en route to Key West, Florida, from New York. A mantle of leaden clouds draped over the glassy sea as gentle swells rolled toward the south. Cruising at 14 knots on a southwest heading, the Coast Guard patrol vessel had just cleared the bell buoy marking the southern extremity of Cape Lookout Shoals.

"Ping... ping... ping..." pulsed the cutter's sonar as it trawled the depths for solid objects. A positive sonar return typically produced a sharp, clear pitch. At 4:20 p.m., Sound-man 3rd Class Bill Rabich heard what was commonly termed a "mushy" contact— "Ping... pom"—a dull-sounding echo about a mile off the port bow that could have been a whale, a rock, or a submarine beneath a thermocline layer. Rabich reported the contact to the pilot house.

The officer of the deck and executive officer of the *Icarus*, Lt. (j.g.) Ed Howard scanned the horizon. Visibility was nine miles—no other vessel could be seen on the surface. Howard wanted to be certain, and he decided to hold off before taking action. *No need to disturb the men until we know for sure what we're dealing with*, Howard might have thought.

Five minutes passed as the cutter maintained its course. The echoes continued to sound indistinct. Meanwhile, Rabich observed that, whatever the submerged object was, it was moving slower than the *Icarus* but on a parallel course—*maybe it was a whale.*

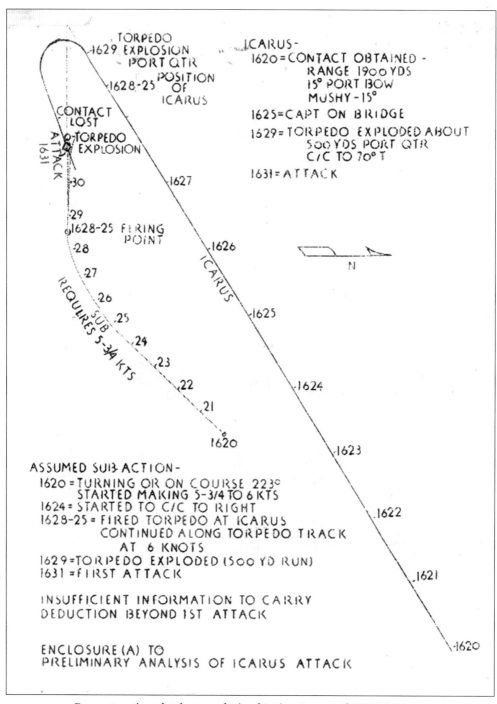

Reconstruction plot from analysis of Action Report of USCGC *Icarus*
by U.S Navy Anti-Submarine Warfare Unit.

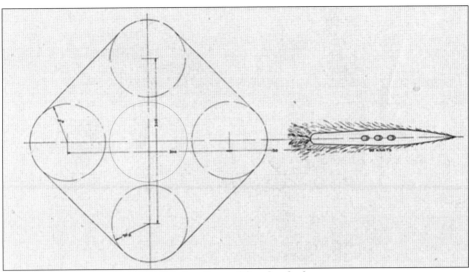

A diamond pattern of five depth charges.

The cutter began to overtake the object off its port beam. It was still a mile away.

"Ping-ping!" Suddenly, the contact sharpened; all signs suggested that it was a submarine. Howard called the skipper, Lt. Maurice Jester to the bridge.

Jester, 52, of Chincoteague, Virginia, was an old lieutenant by Coast Guard standards. He joined the service in 1917 as a surfman and rose in enlisted rates over the next 20 years to Chief Boatswain's Mate. In December 1941, Jester was commissioned as a lieutenant and offered command of the *Icarus*, which was assigned to the Third Naval District based in New York. In a few short months, Jester and the *Icarus* had become seasoned veterans of the war against U-boats, having conducted numerous patrols off the New Jersey and New York coasts since January. On one of those patrols in February, *Icarus* dropped 13 depth charges on what was believed to be a U-boat near the entrance to Ambrose Channel. In the spirit of Donald Francis Mason, Jester reported to his superiors at district headquarters that the suspected submarine had been sunk. Ten days later, the cutter assisted the ill-fated destroyer USS *Jacob Jones* in the pursuit and purported sinking of another U-boat northeast of Asbury Park, New Jersey. Jester and his men on the *Icarus* were hardly amateurs. They may not have actually sunk any submarines, but they knew the drill.

Even so, on that Saturday afternoon, Jester and his executive officer took their time to act. The officers were considering what to do next, when, at 4:29 p.m., the ocean 500 yards off the vessel's port quarter suddenly erupted with an explosion and geyser of water. General Quarters was sounded; and Jester took over command of the ship. By then, there was no doubt on anyone's mind that the sonar contact was a U-boat and that it had fired a torpedo at them, but fortunately for the cutter, the torpedo's guidance system malfunctioned, sending it into the ocean floor where it exploded. The *Icarus* very nearly shared the fate of the *Jacob Jones*, but unlike its Greek mythology namesake, the

Icarus survived its brush with death. The USS *Jesse Roper* had been similarly lucky. For the second time in a month, a United States warship was favored by the fickleness of fate.

"Hard-a-port!" shouted Jester, ordering his helmsman to make a 180-degree turn and head directly toward the sonar contact and the spot where the torpedo had exploded. Crewmen at their action stations held on tightly as the 165-foot-long ship heeled sharply toward its starboard side to make its turn. Two minutes later, when the *Icarus* was only about 180 yards away from the swirl of water where the torpedo had exploded, Rabich abruptly lost the sound contact. There was but one possibility—the U-boat was momentarily cloaked from the cutter's sonar pulses beneath an area of agitated seawater. Instinctively, Jester took no chances and ordered an attack on the invisible enemy by unleashing a "diamond" pattern of five depth charges—one at each corner and one in the middle. In targeting the U-boat, Jester used what the after-action report called the "seaman's eye." In other words, it was not "by the book."

For a split second, in five different places aft of the speeding cutter, the placid ocean surface shuddered violently with a spreading dome of white froth, followed instantly by a volcanic eruption of water shooting skyward. The machinists mates in the cutter's diesel room felt five heavy punches in their chests—what the Germans felt inside their U-boat down below was anybody's guess.

As the geyser of water rained back down, large pockets of air were observed billowing to the surface. Jester ordered another 180-degree turn. The men manning the cutter's 3"/.23-caliber gun and six .50-caliber machine guns held on tightly and waited for the U-boat to come to the surface.

"Ping-ping, ping-ping, ping-ping." Fourteen minutes later—seeming like an eternity to both Americans and Germans—the cutter was back over the target, indicated by sonar to still be creeping toward the west. Three more depth charges were dropped. The ocean quaked. More air bubbles broke the surface.

The sandy bottom was a mere 120 feet down—the U-boat had no where to hide, but where was it? Jester ordered another reverse in course, and on the third pass the *Icarus* dropped a single charge on the spot where the bubbles were seen. When the water set-tled, what the Coast Guardsmen had hoped to see still did not appear—no oil, no debris, no U-boat. Thirty-seven minutes after the first depth charges were dropped, a fourth attack was made; and one more depth charge was launched, this time to the right side of the air bubbles. A minute later, at 5:09 p.m., the severely damaged U-boat lurched to the surface, forced upward by the blast.[28]

The *Icarus* swung around and charged toward the U-boat, which, for a moment, wal-lowed on the surface like a crippled whale, its scarred bow tilted skyward to reveal a hull covered in barnacles. A 1,000 yards from the U-boat and closing rapidly, the cutter's six machine guns began blazing furiously. Then the 3" gun fired. Its first projectile hit short of the target but skipped off the ocean surface and ricochetted into the conning tower. The next shell was long and went whistling over the U-boat's deck. The third shell was a direct hit, as were five of the next 11.

Two minutes after the U-boat came to the surface, men could be seen "tumbling from the conning tower in clock-like precision and swimming rapidly away from the boat." Three hundred yards away on the *Icarus*, the officers on the bridge saw the Germans abandoning their vessel and ordered all guns to withhold firing, but due to the deafening noise and the gunner's bloodlust, it took three full minutes for the guns to cease.[29]

Meanwhile, the frantic Germans emerging on the U-boat's bridge did their best to shield themselves from the incessant fire coming from the American warship before they jumped into the sea. One after another, they continued clambering out of the con-ning tower until the U-boat suddenly began sinking. On the ladder leading up from the control room, some men hesitated, not eager to join their screaming shipmates on deck who were exposed to the torrent of bullets and shells pelting the steel hull of the U-boat. Others, no longer waiting patiently to ascend the ladder in an orderly fashion, began to panic—those above them had to take their chances being shot, because if they didn't escape soon enough, they would all surely drown.

Five minutes after the U-boat surfaced, it suddenly slipped beneath the surface and sank. As it did, a flood of water poured down through the conning tower hatch, and the queue of men climbing up the ladder were torn from their perches and hammered to the control room deck. Twelve Germans failed to escape the U-boat as it plummeted to the ocean floor.

For the next half hour, the *Icarus* circled the spot where the U-boat had vanished. When it appeared from rising pockets of air that the U-boat might again be headed to the surface, the cutter dropped another depth charge. Finally, the air rising from below stopped, a large amount of diesel oil appeared on the surface with a strong kerosene-like odor, and the sonar echoes indicated that the sunken U-boat was no longer moving. Jester was satisfied that it had been destroyed.

Unlike the inadvertent incident when the U-*85* survivors were killed by depth charges from the USS *Jesse Roper*, the *Icarus*'s U-boat survivors were hundreds of yards away from the area when its last depth charge exploded. Their life vests were keeping the 33 German survivors afloat, but they were being carried away by a steady current moving toward the northeast. Four men had been badly wounded by gunfire or shrapnel; two were critical with severed limbs.

As the Germans floated away, the *Icarus*'s commander was unsure as to what he should do next—his orders and Coast Guard regulations were not specific when it came to rescuing enemy combatants. Should they resume their course for Key West or rescue the Germans in the water? Lt. Jester knew his cutter was ill-equipped to accommodate so many prisoners of war. Would the Navy dispatch a rescue vessel? He needed some answers quickly. Jester ordered his communications officer to send out a signal in the clear: "Have sunk submarine. 30 to 40 men in water. Shall *Icarus* pick up any of the men?" The message was first transmitted on a frequency directed to 5th Naval District Headquarters at Norfolk. A dozen minutes passed, and no response was received. The Germans drifted farther away.

"What now? asked the radioman.

"Send the message to 6th District Headquarters—see if they're listening," came the order. The message was sent, minutes passed, and still no reply. The cluster of U-boat men became harder to spot. What must have the Germans been thinking as the American warship seemed to circle aimlessly? Do the Yanks intend for us to be eaten by sharks?

The radio on the *Icarus* remained silent as Jester paced back and forth across the pilot house. Then, at 5:50 p.m., the receiver sputtered to life: "*Icarus*, NOB Charleston. Pick up survivors. Bring to Charleston." Historians have since found no explanation as to why it took so long for the Navy to make a decision regarding the U-boat survivors. The *Icarus* had clearly accomplished something for which the authorities were unprepared. Perhaps the delay involved Naval Intelligence, which had to be consulted. A report filed after the incident by Naval intelligence officers stated that "second only to the U/B itself, survivors are considered valuable booty. Aside from the humanitarian point of view, their rescue is desirable." As far as the Germans were concerned, they were just grateful that a decision had finally been made, and the cutter was headed their way.

The *Icarus* put its two lifeboats over the side and proceeded to rescue the men in the water. They were brought aboard the cutter over the starboard gangway and searched. Their life vests and escape apparatus were removed along with other personal possessions. Remarkably, with typical German precision, the prisoners filed onto the cutter in order of their rank after the wounded had been taken aboard first. At 6:05 p.m., the *Icarus* set a course for Charleston, South Carolina.

Upon stepping on the deck of the Coast Guard cutter, the U-boat commander introduced himself as Kapitänleutnant Hellmut Rathke of U-*352*, a 500-ton ship. Rathke appeared to be a spirited, well-disciplined, politically motivated officer who was hardly cowed by the American sailors who had just sunk his U-boat. His captors found him to be professionally courteous but at the same time arrogant, cooperative with facts of a personal nature, but reticent on military matters. Later, during lengthy interrogations, the 32-year-old Rathke professed "unqualified admiration for Hitler and National Socialism." He described Hitler as a "genius" who [had] unified all the German peoples of Europe. Rathke was not the only fervent Nazi aboard the U-*352*. His midshipman, Ernst Kammerer, was described as a "characteristically truculent product of the Hitler Youth movement." The politicized crew members of the U-*352* were atypical among the majority of Dönitz's men of the Ubootwaffe—most fought for the Fatherland but were not so admiring of the Führer.

The prisoners were described as "small, healthy, loyal German subjects, well-disciplined in security and noticeably military in bearing and appearance." The submariners' average age was 22; 13 were under 21.

The sailors of the *Icarus* may have been somewhat awed by the defeated but redoubtable military spirit of the German sailors whom they had just plucked from the sea. An intelligence investigation suggested that there had been "some fraternizing between captors and prisoners." At some point, someone had asked the Germans if they had been close enough to glimpse the American coast. The answer was no, but they did confess to being quite fond of jazz from American radio stations, which they were allowed to listen to over the boat's intercom when it rested on the ocean bottom.

In spite of the deadly gunfire from the *Icarus*, only four men rescued from the water were wounded. One German, Machinist-Gefreiter Gerhard Keussel, had lost a leg; another man had lost an arm. The other injuries were considered minor—a broken wrist, a graze from a bullet. Keussel was kept on a litter on deck due to the severity of his condition. He died at 10:50 p.m.

Naïvely, Lt. Jester permitted all of the Germans be confined together—officers and enlisted men—in the forward crew compartment of the *Icarus*, which allowed Rathke to maintain his iron-fisted authority over his men, reminding them to not speak of anything that might benefit the enemy. According to Naval documents, even while they were floating in the water, Rathke had "harangued" his men of the necessity of refusing to divulge information.

The *Icarus* arrived at the Charleston Naval yard at 11:30 the next morning where the prisoners disembarked, again in order of their seniority. They assembled and stood at attention before a large gathering of Naval officers, military police, and curious onlookers. Rathke shook hands with Lt. Jester and thanked him for the good treatment his crew received.[30] The U-*352* crewmen were then marched to a temporary detainment building as a fascinated group of sailors lined the road and watched, curious to learn firsthand that their fiendish, phantom U-boat enemies were, in fact, flesh and blood-men—just boys, in reality.

An initial interrogation of the prisoners was conducted at Charleston by officers from the Navy's Anti-submarine Warfare Unit. Next the Germans were handed over to a U.S. Marines Provost Marshall, who immediately transported them to a permanent Detention Camp at Fort Bragg.

At Fort Bragg, the U-boat men were further questioned by officers from the Foreign Section of the Office of Naval Intelligence (ONI) and a Royal Navy Officer with first-hand experience dealing with German POWs. Three months later, 26 of the U-*352* survivors, including Rathke, were transferred to Fort Hunt in Fairfax County, Virginia, which had recently been turned into an ultra-secret military intelligence facility for interviewing prisoners of war known as "P.O. Box 1142." By then, Rathke had thoroughly drilled his men as to what they could say or not say. Still, the interrogators were able to extract some information, including a good description of what transpired inside the U-boat while it was being attacked by the *Icarus*:

U-*352* survivors marched to temporary detainment at Charleston NOB.

"Prisoners stated that they heard a hail of depth charges, some of them extremely close. The first explosions destroyed the periscope and killed an officer in the conning tower. Gauges and glasses were smashed in the control room. The deck was littered with broken gear. Lockers burst open. Crockery and other loose objects were flung about the boat. The crew was shaken up. All lights except the emergency system failed. There is evidence that the electric motors failed – perhaps the greatest injury the boat suffered."

The special interrogators admitted that they had been unable to gather much information useful for anti-submarine warfare from Rathke or his men, who were described as being well-disciplined and strictly security conscious. They did learn that the concussions affecting the U-*352* during the depth-charge attack must have been accentuated by the relatively shallow, sandy sea floor. During his interrogation Rathke said that he had estimated that the *Icarus* had dropped 60 depth charges on the U-boat. The inventory of ordinance expended by the *Icarus* revealed that 11 depth charges were actually dropped. Rathke was also forthcoming in stating that he had intentionally grounded his U-boat in the approximate location of swirling sand and mud caused by the explosion of the failed torpedo, in order to hide from the cutter's anti-submarine devices. As it turned out, it was a clever but unlucky tactical decision as it was the very spot where Lt. Jester commenced his attack. Rathke also said, for good reason, that he did not like operating in the shallow water off the American coast. Additional intelligence cobbled together during

Kplt. Hellmut Rathke (2nd from left) and unidentifed officer with U.S. Navy Intelligence.

interviews with the 33 survivors from the U-*352* included minor facts about previous war cruises, the crew's favorite bars at various French ports, and their personal attitudes toward the Japanese and Russians.

However, two items of information proved to be especially noteworthy. In the "Final Report of Interrogation of Survivors from U-*352* Sunk by USCGC *Icarus*," submitted to Admiral King on August 31, 1942, ONI concluded: "U-*352* seems to have arrived in American waters about May 2, a week before her destruction. Misfortune plagued her. As far as can be learned from the crew, she sank nothing. When on the surface, lookouts had to be put on the alert constantly for aircraft. They crash-dived several times to elude patrol planes." When Admiral Andrews received his copy of the report and read this statement, it must have brought him a great deal of satisfaction—it confirmed what he already knew and was precisely the result he and his staff had been striving for since January, when U-*123* arrived and Operation Paukenschläg began.

The second intelligence item of interest was that the U-*352* crewmen admitted that they had been patrolling the waters around Cape Lookout specifically waiting for a convoy. Had they not been sunk by the *Icarus*, they might have found what they were waiting for. A coastal convoy—the long-awaited and first of the war—was on its way in a matter of days.

CHAPTER 23

A K-type U.S. Navy airship flies over an Atlantic convoy.

THE TIDE TURNS

*"This is the first convoy to be sighted
on the American coast."*

Admiral Dönitz, KTP May 1942

Depending on the military commander's perspective—German or American—the U-boats' prospects for achieving operational successes in United States waters in the spring of 1942 were either improving or soon coming to an end.

Admiral Dönitz, in spite of acknowledging that he had probably lost his second U-boat off the coast of North Carolina in a month, was encouraged that the average number of ships sunk in United States waters, per U-boat per day, had risen every month since January. The admiral noted in his KTB: "Attacking conditions in the American area continue to be very good. [American] anti-submarine activity has increased, but its fighting power, its concentration, its determination to attack and destroy are small." One of Dönitz's skippers who had observed close at hand the American defenses—presumably the Hooligan Navy and the Civil Air Patrol— briefed the admiral on his return to France: "Those who fight are not sailors, but people who are being paid for their presence in the area endangered by U-boats." Dönitz wrote that all of his commanding officers returning from the western Atlantic were saying the same thing: "Namely that the American area will remain a highly favorable area for attacks for some months to come and that a high percentage of successes can be scored with very few losses."

Dönitz was also looking to the coming months with optimism because of the deployment of the Ubootwaffe's Type XIV Milchkühe boats, which were expected to extend the range and increase the operational days of U-boat patrols. A trial rendezvous of Atlantic front boats and a Milchkühe in April 1942 east of Bermuda was considered by Dönitz to be a tremendous success. Ten U-boats heading out on sorties had their fuel bunkers topped off, and two U-boats returning to France were supplied with desperately needed diesel oil and provisions. As more Type XIV U-boats were built and deployed, Germany would soon be able to increase the frequency of attacks off the Mississippi River Delta, the Panama Canal, and the petroleum terminals of northern South America.

Two other special U-boat operations were eagerly anticipated by Dönitz. On May 19, three Type VII U-boats—U-87, U-373, and U-701—departed France for the purpose of laying mines at the entrances to Boston harbor, the Delaware Bay, and the Chesapeake Bay, something that the German Kriegsmarine had wanted to do since the United States entered the war.

The second anxiously awaited special U-boat operation was the launching of Operation Pastorius and the planned landing of eight saboteurs on American soil. Sealed orders from Dönitz labeled "Most Secret" went out with U-202 and U-584 when the U-boats departed France in May with the saboteur-agents aboard. The agents' duties, outlined by Dönitz in the orders, included: "Sabotage attacks on targets of economic importance for the war; to stir up discontent and lower fighting resistance; to recruit fresh forces for these duties; to re-establish disconnected communications; and to obtain information." For the landing of its agents, U-202 was given three potential locations: near Seaside Park or Ocean City, New Jersey, or near East Hampton, New York. U-584 was given two suitable locations for its landing: either at Oak Island near Southport, North Carolina, or off the coast near Jacksonville, Florida. In each instance, the latter location was selected. Were the two teams of saboteurs to succeed, there is little doubt that Germany, much like in the aftermath of Operation Paukenschläg, would have been emboldened to increase the landings of enemy agents by tenfold.

On the negative side of the balance sheet for Dönitz's U-boats were the longer days and pleasant weather of the season. Persistent high pressure systems typical of spring weather off the mid-Atlantic states produced calm, smooth seas. Calm seas combined with increased hours of daylight and bright, moonlit nights resulted in excellent opportunities for spotting U-boats on the surface. Consequently, these conditions combined with constant sea and air patrols made it nearly impossible for U-boats to spend any time at all on the surface. If a U-boat was unable remain surfaced every 24-hour period at least for a few hours, it could not run its diesel engines, and therefore, it could not charge its batteries or refresh the oxygen levels inside the boat. Many U-boat commanders operating in United States waters in May and June 1942 were frustrated by their inability to operate on the surface. For example, on April 29, U-201 observed ship traffic off Cape Hatteras but was unable to commence an attack and reported the following to Dönitz: "Could not proceed on the surface day or night because of strong air patrol and bright full-moon nights."

U-boat crews returning to the American coast for their second patrols also sensed something else was different. Along the mid-Atlantic and northeast states, the bright glow of shore lights was lessened, and on the darkest nights when no moon was visible, the silhouettes of ships were no longer easy to see. More masters of merchant vessels diligently adhered to the Navy's blackout restrictions and zig-zag orders. However, in the heavily traveled sea lanes of the Florida Straits abreast of Miami and its adjoining communities, the glitzy glow of nightlife continued to betray merchant mariners offshore.

The other change to the situation off the American coast noted by Dönitz was first observed on May 9, 1942, by Kapitänleutnant Günther Krech of U-558. Krech was one of Dönitz's top aces, and U-558 was chosen by the admiral to be one of the U-boats to participate in the first Milchkühe refueling operation off Bermuda in April. Krech's U-boat took on 35 cubic meters of fuel[31] and then headed for the North Carolina coast. Southeast of Cape Hatteras, Krech encountered a small convoy consisting of a Coast Guard cutter, two gunboats, four tankers, and three steamers. U-558 missed its chance to attack the convoy when it disappeared into the notorious Gulf Stream fog. Upon receiving Krech's radiotelegraph report later that night, Dönitz noted in his KTB: "This is the first convoy to be sighted on the American coast. These are probably convoys [that] only round the dangerous area around Hatteras and then disperse again." Dönitz's interpretation of the intelligence was wrong on both counts. It was not the first true convoy, which had yet to sail, but one of Admiral Andrews's Bucket Brigades; and the Bucket Brigades were not then being formed only to navigate around Cape Hatteras. Merchant ships were, by late April and early May, being escorted the entire distance from Key West to New York (at least those ships capable of similar speeds). In one sense, though, Dönitz's intuition was correct that Cape Hatteras was an area of considerable danger for Allied ships that troubled Naval authorities—the departures and arrivals of all future convoys were going to be timed so that the convoys passed Cape Hatteras in daylight hours.

In contrast to the German perspective of the U-boat situation, U.S. Navy commanders like Admiral King and Admiral Andrews were optimistic about the coming months because the concentration of Allied forces on the sea and in the air were finally reaching levels that would permit fully escorted coastal convoys within the Eastern Sea Frontier. The commencement of true coastal convoys and the hoped-for corresponding drop in the numbers of merchant ships sunk by U-boats in American waters was awaited nervously by Roosevelt, Churchill, the petroleum industry, shipping companies, and insurance underwriters. Even the U.S. Army could see that the Navy's success against U-boats off the East Coast had a direct bearing on the future of the war. It was not until June that he made his feelings known when General George C. Marshall, chief of staff of the U.S. Army, wrote the following to King: "The losses by submarines off our Atlantic seaboard and in the Caribbean now threaten our entire war effort... I am fearful that another month or two of this will so cripple our means of transport that we will be unable to bring sufficient men and planes to bear against the enemy in critical theaters to exercise a determining influence on the war." By the time Marshall wrote to King, however, Germany's U-boat offensive in United States waters was already being repelled.

On May 14, 1942, 19 ships departed Hampton Roads in the first coastal convoy of the war. Designated KS 500, the southbound convoy headed for Key West. National flags of the vessels in the fleet included seven American, six British, four Norwegian, one Dutch, and one Panamanian. All 19 ships arrived safely at Key West five days later, including the 11,237-ton tanker *Esso Williamsburg* and the 13,797-ton British whale factory ship *Hek-*

toria. The two enormous vessels were safe for the time being, but both would be sunk in the north Atlantic by U-boats four months later.

On May 15, KN-100, a northbound convoy of just one ship departed Key West bound for Norfolk, but by the time *Sophocles* and its escorts reached the Florida Straits, four other ships unofficially joined the parade. That convoy, too, reached its destination unmolested.

For the remainder of 1942, 165 convoys were conducted off the U.S. East Coast between Norfolk and Key West or New York and Galveston. On average, 22 ships participated in each convoy escorted by six warships, including a combination of U.S. Navy destroyers, British armed trawlers, Coast Guard cutters, and 83-foot patrol boats. During that seven-and-a-half month period, only three Allied merchant vessels were sunk and one damaged by U-boats while the ships were in convoy. The number of convoy ships sunk by U-boats equaled the number of vessels sunk by the U.S. Navy's mined anchorage at Cape Hatteras.[32] The resounding success of coastal convoys proved that the British were right all along. Sounding somewhat like a politician, Admiral King portrayed himself as an ardent supporter of coastal convoys when he replied to General Marshall's scathing letter of June 19. King wrote: "Escorts are not just one way of handling the submarine menace; it is the only way that gives any promise of success."

"The convoy system that the U.S. Navy organized in May 1942 dramatically changed the condition of the U-boat war," said historian Michael Gannon. "This was something Admiral King very belatedly and reluctantly came to an understanding of—the importance of convoy. Prior to his establishment of convoys, he argued that an inadequately defended convoy is worse than no convoy at all. And this was against all of the experience that the British had acquired in two years of opposing U-boats. And when [King] finally established convoys in May, there was a noticeable drop in sinkings. Too bad he came to that conclusion too late, after the loss of so much steel and flesh."

In April, a total of 24 Allied ships had been sunk and 274 people killed by U-boats off the North Carolina coast. In May, sinkings and casualties inflicted by U-boats dropped markedly to just four ships sunk and 120 people killed. In June, while the number of sinkings increased to 10, the number of deaths dropped to only 12.

Military historians often cite escorted coastal convoys as the primary factor for deterring U-boat attacks in United States waters. The official statistics from the government and the analysis of historians, however, often fail to recognize the decisive role of air cover in the safe transport of coastal convoys. Bomb- and depth-charge-equipped aircraft were the one enemy of U-boats against which a U-boat could not engage, unlike the destroyer, which was touted by the Navy as the traditional foe of the U-boat. The daily logs of U-boats and Admiral Dönitz's KTB reflect that continuous aircraft patrols—Navy and Army bombers, lighter than air blimps, and the "yellow bees" of the Civil Air Patrol cursed by many a U-boat commander—were as much or more of a threat and deterrent to U-boats as surface vessels with guns. Later in the war, the victory over German U-boats in the Battle of the Atlantic was due in large measure to the extended range of Allied aircraft and the closure of the mid-ocean air gap. In the Bay of Biscay approaches to the French harbors at Lorient, Brest, La Rochelle, and St. Nazaire, British and American aircraft attacks made it nearly impossible for U-boats to safely sail to or from their home ports, which, in effect, killed the hornets at their nests.

Admiral Dönitz's hopes for his U-boat's successes in the American theater of operations in the late spring and summer of 1942 had mixed results. Operation Pastorius unravelled and failed with stunning rapidity and discouraged similar efforts until another desperate and futile attempt to infiltrate saboteurs was made in 1944. In November of that year, two agents were landed on the coast of Maine in what was named Operation Elster. Both agents were arrested in New York a month later.

The special operation in June 1942 to lay mines at harbor entrances fell far short of Dönitz's expectations. As in the failure of Operation Pastorius, the limited success of the mine-laying operation discouraged further efforts by the Germans. None of the mines laid by U-87 near Boston had any effect, but before it returned to France, the U-boat's torpedos did sink two ships off Cape Cod. A mine laid by U-373 at the entrance to Delaware Bay sank a steam tug and killed 10 of its crew members off Cape May, New Jersey.

Mines from U-701, the most successful of Dönitz's three special operations U-boats, sank a Royal Navy armed trawler and severely damaged two tankers off Cape Henry. The three vessels involved with the U-701's mines were part of a northbound convoy arriving at the entrance to the Chesapeake Bay on June 15. Before the convoy realized that it was in the midst of a German minefield, one of its escorts, USS *Bainbridge*, inadvertently detonated one of the mines during a depth-charge attack on the U-boat suspected of being nearby, which caused minor damage to the destroyer described as being "shaken from stem to stern." Just a few miles away, the catastrophe was witnessed by hundreds of appalled people enjoying the pleasant June weather on the beach and watching the parade of ships offshore. Two days later, after the sea lanes had been swept for mines by the Navy, one of the U-701's mines that had been missed by the minesweepers sank the departing coal freighter *Santore* as it was maneuvering into its assigned position for a southbound convoy.

After laying its mines off Cape Henry, U-701 moved southward into the waters off Cape Hatteras. Over the next 10 days, it used its deck gun to sink an American anti-submarine trawler, YP-389 and torpedoes to sink the 14,000-ton tanker, *William Rockefeller*. Two other ships were attacked and damaged by the U-boat.

Nearing the final days of its first war patrol in American waters, U-701 had sunk or damaged nine ships totaling an impressive 60,000 tons, making its skipper, 28-year-old Kapitänleutnant Horst Degen, a promising new star among Dönitz's commanders and a candidate for a Knight's Cross. Dönitz singled out Degen's success in the June 28 entry of his war diary. There was a good chance that at the end of the U-boat's patrol, a large crowd and festive military band would have been on hand to celebrate its triumphant return to Lorient, France. Degen's U-boat, however, never made it home.

CHAPTER 24

U-701 survivor arrives at Norfolk.

My Dear Admiral: A Cruel Fate Wrested the Weapon Out of My Hand

"You saw that airplane too late!"

Horst Degen, commander U-701

Since laying its mines and being given permission to hunt Allied merchant ships at will, U-701 had experienced frequent encounters with enemy aircraft, and it was bombed and depth charged repeatedly off Cape Hatteras. Interior lights would typically fail, bulbs shatter, and the glass of instruments would break, but damage was usually minor and repaired quickly. On a more serious encounter, the U-boat's main periscope and air scrubbing systems had been badly damaged, and repairs could only be made at its port in France. But instead of giving up the fight, Degen and his men refused to leave the fertile hunting grounds of Cape Hatteras as long as they had torpedoes aboard. They gamely continued to pursue their prey.

The frequent appearances of American air and sea patrols began to take a toll on the U-701's crew. The more the U-boat was forced to dive and remain submerged for lengthy periods, the more the air inside accumulated dangerous levels of carbon dioxide. Degen's men started getting sick—some complained of severe headaches or nausea, while others had difficulty simply breathing. In the early afternoon of July 7, Degen had no choice but to take a chance and surface his U-boat in order to draw in fresh air by using the conning tower hatch as the air intake for the boat's diesel engines.

Knowing that they were in a precarious location frequented by convoys and their escorts, and patrolled by their most-feared nemesis—aircraft—Degen personally supervised the watch on the U-boat's bridge. The commander had two men with him that he trusted, Lt. Bazies and Warrant Quartermaster Günter Kunert. Degen had one man on watch whom he did not trust, his executive officer Oberleutnant zur See Konrad Junker. Degen

reprimanded Junker earlier that morning when the young officer was goofing around while on watch. Degen warned him: "You must pay more attention. You can't carry on like that."

Each man on deck was responsible for watching a 90-degree quadrant. Degen was reasonably comfortable with the fact that a lookout could usually spot an aircraft while it was six miles away, which gave the U-boat sufficient time to crash dive and escape. To conduct a crash dive, however, it was necessary to have a minimum number of men on deck in order to quickly clear the bridge.

Degen decided that 15 minutes was enough time to refresh the air in the U-boat, and he issued the order to prepare to dive. Kunert and Bazies were the first to descend through the hatch. Standing with his back to Degen as he scanned his sector off the stern of the U-boat, Junker suddenly shouted, "Airplane there!" Degen whipped around thinking he would see a distant aircraft rising above the horizon. Instead, a large bomber was diving toward them and was frighteningly close. Degen screamed, "Alarm!" Men tumbled down the conning tower ladder followed by Junker and then Degen. The U-*701* crash dived, as they had done countless times since arriving in American waters three weeks earlier. As the U-*701*'s planesmen angled the U-boat down steeply by the bow, Degen turned to Junker at the base of the ladder and snarled, "You saw that airplane too late!" Junker replied, "Yes, I did." Degen later remembered: "Two seconds later, 'Pfft!' came the bomb. Junker admitted he was to blame."

About 32 miles east of Cape Hatteras at 2 p.m. on July 7, as Degen and his men were inhaling the refreshing ocean air, a Lockheed A-29 Hudson bomber was flying northward at 1,500 feet through fluffy cumulus clouds that drifted lazily over the warm, moist air of the Gulf Stream. The plane was patrolling a sector north of Cape Lookout and had been airborne for about four hours since taking off from Cunningham Field (later named Marine Air Station Cherry Point). The plane's red-haired, blue-eyed pilot, 2nd Lt. Harry Kane of the U.S. Army Air Corps 396th Bombardment Group, was seeing the same thing he saw everyday for five hours or more—nothing but water. There were times when convoys or independently steaming ships appeared, but what he was looking for he never could seem to find. Kane later recalled how boring it would be flying that patrol.

On that Tuesday afternoon, Kane and his four-man crew cruised at 160 knots toward the northeast, using the low-lying clouds over the Gulf Stream to conceal their aircraft. West of the Gulf Stream the sky was clear and the ocean devoid of whitecaps—visibility was excellent. The A-29 Hudson would intermittently disappear into a cloud for a couple of minutes and then break out in the clear for 30 seconds before entering the next cloud. On one of the 30-second breaks, Kane peered out the left window and suddenly saw an unusual vessel on the surface about seven miles to the west, moving away perpendicularly from the plane's line of flight. The altitude and distance from the object made it difficult for Kane to see what it was so he asked his men to look the next time they emerged from the cloud cover. "I'd gotten everybody in the crew to try to help me decide what it was, and finally we thought, well, it might be a submarine," Kane said in a 1981 interview. "We weren't sure, so we turned to a heading of almost due west and stayed up in the clouds, and I remember that I throttled back the airplane to try to cut down on the noise."

U-boat photo from 5,000 ft.

What appeared to be a vessel with its decks awash was on a northwest course, heading roughly toward Hatteras Island in the vicinity of Little Kinnakeet Coast Guard Lifeboat Station. Kane maneuvered his bomber into a textbook position, directly behind the target, and when about five miles away, he began a gradual descent. The slender shape and minimal superstructure of the suspicious vessel added to Kane's confidence that it was, in fact, a submarine. When the vessel abruptly began to submerge, he no longer had any doubt. Kane shoved the A-29's throttles fully forward, and the aircraft's twin 1,200-horsepower Wright 1820-87 Cyclone engines revved-up with a high-pitched whine. Kane recalled: "I yelled at the bombardier to get down there underneath and get ready to go, and get the bomb doors open—all this excitement and everything—and we were moving pretty fast that time. I think in my report I said something like 225 miles an hour."

Swooping down upon the swirl of the submerging U-boat at 50 feet above the water, the A-29 dropped three Mark 17 depth bombs, calibrated to explode at 25 feet below the surface. The bombardier, Corporal P.L. Broussard, released the bombs so that the first dropped just short of the U-boat's stern, the second just aft of the conning tower, and the third just forward of the conning tower. As they raced overhead, Broussard could see

from his position in the aircraft's nose the bluish-colored outline of the U-*701* as it slowly slunk into the deep. Kane pulled back on the joystick and banked a hard turn to see the result of their attack. "I could see this terrific explosion," he said. "Might have been the last one of the three depth charges. It was like a great big enormous bubble, and I'm just going to guess that it was 50 feet high and, of course, at this time we knew it was a submarine, but we didn't know whether we'd definitely gotten it or not."

Fifteen seconds later, a great exhalation of air rose to the surface. Then, in the middle of the dome of air, the unmistakeable figure of a man popped to the surface—a sight no American pilot had yet to witness in the dozens of previous reports of U-boats sunk by aircraft in United States waters. Clearly, this was no ruse by the U-boat captain. A few seconds later, more men appeared on the surface. Remarkably, the men in the water seemed to be waving at the A-29. Kane's radioman, Corporal L.P. Flowers breathlessly called in the report: "Sub sunk position 393376." The phrase, despite its truthfulness, was not destined to become famous like Donald Francis Mason's specious "Saw Sub, Sank Same."

Seconds following Degen's reproach of Junker's gross negligence, a violent explosion aft of the control room rocked the U-*701*. The pressure hull was breached, and seawater began to pour into the U-boat in the area of the petty officers' quarters. Recognizing that the damage was fatal to his vessel, Degen shouted to his engineer to blow the ballast tanks and prepare to abandon the boat. The U-*701* stopped descending and for the moment seemed to be suspended at a depth estimated between 45 and 60 feet. A man scurried up the conning tower ladder and spun the wheel that sealed the hatch. The hatch opened easily. One after the other, 18 Germans escaped, including Degen. According to another account, almost all of the men were able to get out of the boat. Overhead, Kane reported seeing between 25 and 50 men in the water. A more accurate number—derived by piecing together various sources of evidence—is that as many as 28 of the U-*701*'s crew of 43 were able to leave the U-boat before it sank. The 15 men unaccounted for were likely stationed in the aft compartments and were killed or severely wounded by the depth charge blast.

Later analysis by Naval investigators reveals that it remained unclear just how the U-boat crew was able to successfully leave their vessel. An official report stated, "So swift was the end of the boat that no coherent account has been forthcoming. One torpedo man stated he was asleep in the bow compartment at the time of the attack. He said the main lighting failed, but the emergency lights were still on. He made his way to the control room to ask whether they were to abandon ship. He then struggled back to the bow compartment—perhaps to get lifesaving apparatus or some treasured personal possession—and when he again reached the control room water was waist deep."

The 18 men in Degen's group only had three escape lungs and one life preserver among them. The nearest point of land was more than 20 miles away. The men were in the western fringes of the Gulf Stream and even though they had no sensation of it, they were being carried away to the northeast at about 1.3 nautical miles per hour.

In a replay of the communications calamity of the rescue of the U-352 survivors, the A-29's radioman transmitted numerous calls for assistance in order for the German U-boat castaways to be rescued. Kane was concerned for the Germans in the water—for humanitarian reasons and because as POWs they would be useful for intelligence purposes—but no one beyond the aircraft seemed to care. After numerous calls by Cpl. Flowers there were no radio replies. As Kane circled the bomber overhead, Flowers transmitted again: "Please send other aircraft to 393376. We are running low on gas. There are men in the water. Send help." At 3:11 p.m., nearly an hour after the attack, Kane's men dropped to the U-boat survivors all four of the crew's life vests and a life raft. They saw at least one German grab one of the life vests, but for some reason the raft fell too far away to be reached by the men in the water.

Finally, an hour after the U-boat was attacked, a reply came over the radio barely audible through heavy static: "Send details of sighting and attack." Radio interference from other transmitters made communication with his base virtually impossible. In the meantime, Kane chased down a passing Panamanian-flagged freighter that acknowledged his signals but failed to comply with his request to follow his plane to the survivors in the water. When Kane returned to the scene, the Germans were no where to be found. The Army pilot and his crew valiantly continued their search as the plane's fuel gauge dropped to the minimum required for their return to Cunningham Field. They were unable to relocate the survivors. At 4:30 p.m., two and a half hours after sinking the U-boat, Kane left the area for the hour and 10 minute flight back to his base.

Degen did his best to remain in command of his men while they floated or treaded water. Even though their U-boat had been sunk, some of their comrades were dead or missing, and they were more than 20 miles from land, the men were said to be in good spirits and believed that they would be saved at an early hour. (So did thousands of Allied merchant sailors who found themselves in a similar predicament during the preceding months.) The plane that had bombed them had departed for awhile but later returned to the area, but it was obvious to the Germans that the American aviators could not relocate them in the choppy waves. Degen urged his men to stay close together. Sometime after the bomber flew off toward the mainland, Ensign Lange and Boatswain's Mate Hansel announced that they were going to swim to shore despite Degen's warning that it was too far away. After dark, it became more difficult for the men to stay in close contact. At 9:00 p.m., U-701 coxswain Etzweiler, who did not know how to swim, could no longer keep himself afloat and disappeared beneath the waves. "As darkness descended, we consoled ourselves with hope in the morrow," Degen later remembered. "A few of us were ready to give up, but these we cheered up, so that we were all still together when it became light again."

During their second day in the ocean, some of Degen's men became delirious from inadvertently swallowing seawater. Some called out for glasses of beer; others mumbled incoherently. At noon, a Coast Guard vessel passed within a little more than a mile from the men, but it failed to respond to their cries for rescue. The psychological impact on the exhausted swimmers was devastating. One by one they gave up and drowned as their help-

less shipmates looked on in shock. Degen later recalled that one of his men, before dying, said goodbye to him: "I'm taking leave of you. Please remember me to my comrades."

Six men drowned during the second day; two more perished in the middle of the night; before dawn three more died. When the sun rose on the third day, there were only four survivors in Degen's group. Overnight, one of the men miraculously found a coconut and lemon floating nearby. With considerable difficulty they were able to open the coconut and the remaining survivors shared a swallow of milk, a bite of the meat, and a suck of the lemon.

Onward, they drifted, seemingly alone on an immeasurable sea of irony—littered with debris and oil slicks of their own nation's making and crisscrossed by untold numbers of patrols boats, merchant ships, and aircraft that failed to spot them.

At the Eastern Sea Frontier headquarters in New York, the radio center received a message at 1:42 p.m. on July 9 from the 5th Naval District: Navy blimp just found five men in water—weak, naked, and bearded. Dropped life raft, food, water, blankets, and first aid equipment. Navy reported that search of 15 miles revealed five dead bodies in life jackets, many empty life jackets, and large sharks around." Other aircraft observers on the scene reported seeing bodies scattered over a 10-mile area.

When the K-8 airship from Elizabeth City Naval Air Station spotted the survivors in the water, only three were strong enough to climb into the life raft it dropped to them. Degen was not among them. He later recounted his experience:

> "As the sea was still like a pond, I kept up the practice of discarding my life preserver, saying that I would swim to shore. I assumed that with a few strokes I would feel bottom under my feet and would be able to stand up, but every time I tried this I went under. That would bring me to again, and I would swim back to the life preserver. This occurrence must have happened many times. Then I lost consciousness. I awakened as though I had been asleep when I suddenly heard myself called. About 30 meters away sat Kunert, Vaupel, and Grotheer making for me in a white rubber boat. I was taken into the boat as Kunert was about to open a can of pineapple with a knife. Out of a can already opened Grotheer gave me tomatoes to eat, and all the while a Zeppelin airship circled about us."

At 4:05 p.m., 49 hours after their U-boat was sunk, a twin-engine Hall PH-2 amphibious biplane flown by a U.S. Coast Guard pilot, Lt. Cmdr. Richard Burke, rescued Degen and his men. The plane first scouted the area and found three German sailors floating separately about five miles away who Burke rescued first. The pilot then taxied his plane over the smooth seas to the life raft containing Degen, Kunert, Vaupel, and Grotheer. Sometime after he was revived, the oil-stained, badly sunburned Degen told his rescuers, "All four of us were completely finished. We shall probably never forget this 49-hour endurance swim." Indeed, for the rest of their lives, the survivors would never forget their time spent off the North Carolina coast.

The U-701 survivors were landed at Norfolk Naval Operating Base where they were admitted to the hospital. According to Naval Intelligence documents, during the POWs'

Rescue of U-*701* survivors.

first 36 hours in the hospital, overzealous intelligence officers from the 5th Naval District used drugs and hypnosis to interrogate Kapitänleutnant Degen and Obersteuermann Kunert. Degen, who was still suffering from the effects of his ordeal, remembered that after being injected with what he thought was morphine, two men shouted questions at him regarding the date of his departure from France and the number of torpedoes his U-boat carried. Kunert recalled that on the first night a young officer came into his hospital room and ordered everyone out. The Navy man put his hand on his holstered pistol and proceeded to question Kunert about his U-boat. The next day, an older civilian entered his room and attempted to hypnotize Kunert. The German warrant officer decided to play along. Speaking German with what Kunert believed was "a Jewish accent," the man kept saying over and over: "Now just relax... you are relaxed... you are getting more tired... gradually you will be asleep." According to Naval documents, the hypnotist "lifted Kunert's arm, and the latter permitted it to drop limply. Kunert became interested in this performance and offered no opposition, but refused to answer when the man started to question him after he thought he had hypnotized Kunert. As he got no answer to his questions, Kunert's visitor soon left."

Once officers from the Special Intelligence Section of the Office of Naval Intelligence arrived on the scene, the overly aggressive interrogation methods were discontinued.

U-*701* survivors rescued by Hall PH-2 amphibious biplane.

There was concern, however, that what had already been done to Degen and Kunert was in violation of the Third Geneva Convention and could cause problems later. In a secret memorandum sent to the Director of Naval Intelligence, Cmdr. John L. Riheldaffer wrote: "The use of injections and the attempts to use hypnosis were confirmed from another member of the crew of the U-*701* in independent interrogation and without possibility of collusion. The use of such methods is, of course, contrary to existing treaty agreements and may cause repercussions at a later date."

Without the benefit of primary source documents to ascertain the motivation behind the 5th Naval District's unauthorized interrogation techniques, a reasonable supposition might be made that the capture of the U-*701* crew members just two and a half weeks after the sensational arrests of the Operation Pastorius saboteurs by the FBI might have had the various district offices of U.S. Naval Intelligence in a panic. There was likely widespread concern that other U-boats might land additional teams of saboteurs on remote beaches of the East Coast. During his second day of questioning at the hospital, Degen was informed that U-*701*'s departure from France at the same time as the two Operation Pastorius U-boats implicated him very seriously. Had it been proven that the U-*701* survivors aided and abetted spies, they might have been subject to execution rather than enjoy the benefits of prisoners of war. Degen must have understood his predicament and vigorously asserted that landing saboteurs was not his mission, but neither did he ever confess that his primary mission was to mine the entrance to the Chesapeake Bay, a fact not known to U.S. Naval Intelligence until after the war.

As the officers responsible for interrogating the U-701 POWs were to find out, drugs and hypnosis were not particularly necessary to encourage Kapitänleutnant Degen to talk—the subject of mines off Virginia's coast notwithstanding. Even though Degen and his men were described as being security minded, Naval Intelligence officers were able to amass a significant amount of information about the German Ubootwaffe and its operations from Degen. Reasons for the interrogators' success were due in part to Degen's "garrulousness, his independent interpretation of security, the swiftness of the sinking, and the prompt preliminary interrogation." No doubt, the implied threat that he could be treated as a transporter of spies also did much to loosen his tongue. The U-boat commander was described in documents as an "unusually exuberant type; he is endowed with a quick wit, is given to strong likes and dislikes, and has a great capacity for uninhibited companionship. He owes his life to the devotion with which he had inspired in his crew, as he was often unconscious during the 49 hours the seven survivors spent in the water following the sinking and was actually supported for long periods by his companions, notably the stalwart quartermaster, Kunert."

It was also observed that Degen was "a loyal German officer but is in no sense an ardent Nazi. He has expressed grave misgivings over the eventual outcome of the war, in view of America's vast reserves of men and matériel, and considers that Germany made a costly mistake in provoking American entrance into the conflict." Oddly, Degen did not recall the contribution the Japanese made in provoking America's declaration of war against the Axis powers.

Naval investigators also learned that before U-701 sailed for the American coast in May it left its homeport of Brest to take on fuel at the U-boat facility to the south at Lorient, which was not as exposed to air raids by British aircraft. There, Degen had an opportunity to meet Kapitänleutnant Reinhard Hardegen, who had just returned triumphantly from his second war patrol to Cape Hatteras. Degen confided to his interrogators details of his discussions with Germany's famous Knight's Cross commander about the situation off the coast of North Carolina and the tactics Hardegen used to sink ships there. Degen, who had already divulged to the enemy more intelligence than Admiral Donitz would have ever imagined, was apparently more worried that the gossip he had to share about Hardegen might somehow get back to the U-123 commander in Europe, so he whispered "in confidence, that neither he nor a number of other U-boat officers had a high opinion of Hardegen, whom they regarded as a braggart."

On Saturday, July 11, Degen was told to expect a special guest. The U-boat commander was momentarily confused when five U.S. Army soldiers marched into the room where he was seated in one of two chairs. The five men were led by a red-haired, blue-eyed lieutenant who introduced himself as Harry Kane. He told Degen, "I'm the guy who sank you." Kane remembered that the U-boat commander had been badly sunburned and was still weak. Degen, however, had recovered remarkably in two days and had shaved his

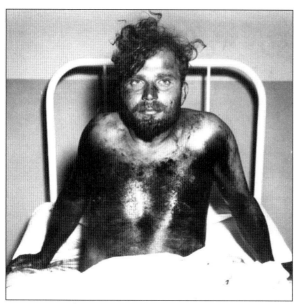

Obersteuermann Günther Kunert

beard into a goatee that would have been just as stylish in 2012. As soon as Degen realized who Kane was he stood up from his chair. Kane said in his 1981 interview: "He stood up the best he could and came to attention and threw me a salute and said, 'Congratulations; good attack!'" Kane replied that he and his crew were very sorry that they had been unable to rescue Degen and his men, but that their bomber was not made to land on water.

On Sunday, the U-*701* POWs were taken under heavy guard to Newport News where they boarded a train on which they were transferred to a detention facility at Fort Devens near Boston, Massachussetts. At his new home for the remainder of the war, Degen celebrated his 29th birthday on July 19. Prior to the loss of his U-boat, it never occurred to Degen that he might someday be a prisoner of war. Once he settled into his new surroundings and became adjusted to the American food (the Germans often complained about the quality of American white bread but were fond of American tobacco) and daily routine, he decided that it wasn't such a bad place to observe the progress of the war. He believed the Allies would eventually prevail. In a statement made on July 16, Degen said, "We shall now pass the days of our detention as prisoners of war. We are being correctly handled and receive good treatment. There is plenty of good food to eat."

When Degen got around to composing a letter to Admiral Dönitz, he did not make himself sound quite so contented: "My dear Admiral. Much to my regret it is not accorded me to report back to my Commander in the usual manner. A cruel fate, regrettably aroused by the personal fault and negligence of one of my watch officers, has wrested the weapon out of my hand. I assume that the few names of the survivors have been received by you through official Red Cross report. It is extraordinarily galling for us here to be prisoners of war while our comrades out there are continuing to do their duty."

Degen and his comrades were not at Fort Devens for very long. Once construction and technical preparations had been completed at "P.O. Box 1142," the ultra-secret POW interrogation facility at Fort Hunt, the U-*701* men were delivered there by train. Kapitänleutnant Rathke and his surviving crew members from the U-*352* were brought there two days later from Fort Bragg. For six weeks in August and September 1942, the survivors of two U-boats that were sunk near the beaches of North Carolina were interrogated by a secret unit known as MIS-Y.

In a previously untried experiment, men from the two different U-boat crews were

Capt. Harry Kane (seated left) meets Kplt. Horst Degen.

placed together in rooms containing hidden surveillance equipment. Military intelligence officers wondered if social interaction between the strangers from different U-boats would cause them to forget their secretiveness. Declassified documents describe the theory: "Introduction of a prisoner from another boat immediately causes curiosity to override caution, and it is in the exchange of experiences between such prisoners that vital facts are brought out. An excellent example can be given from our own experience. The U-352 had a crew that was very highly indoctrinated on security and a commanding officer who kept his men strictly to account. Relatively little was extracted from these men. When U-701 was sunk, the commanding officer was badly shaken by 49 hours in the water and talked freely. When he recovered, he continued to talk, partly in gratitude and partly because he is naturally loquacious and has an immense curiosity. When members of the U-352 were placed with him, a very large amount of valuable information was obtained from their conversations and reminiscences."

On September 21 and 22, the men of U-352 and U-701 were returned to Fort Bragg and Fort Devens for the remainder of the war.

CHAPTER: 25

THERE'S GOOD NEWS TONIGHT!

"Everyday at twelve, they'd listen to Gabriel Heatter to see how it was going."

Blanche Styron

O n Sunday afternoon, July 19, 1942, at his French chateau overlooking the harbor at Lorient, France, Admiral Dönitz dictated to a clerk a paragraph for entry into his Kriegstagebüch. The admiral uttered the following words with disappointment and reluctance: "Situation reports from boats in the American area show the following. In the sea area off Hatteras successes have dropped considerably. This is due to a drop in the traffic (formation of convoys) and increased defense measures. Of the boats stationed there in the recent period only two, U-*754* and U-*701* have had successes. On the other hand U-*701* and U-*215* have apparently been lost,[33] and U-*402* and U-*576* badly damaged by depth charges or bombs. This state of things is not justified by the amount of success achieved. The two remaining boats (U-*754* and U-*458*) will therefore be removed."

Thus ended the seven-month period, beginning with U-*66* and U-*123* in January, during which time Dönitz's U-boats waged unrestricted war on Allied vessels, sinking or damaging 93 merchant ships or U.S. Navy patrol vessels off the North Carolina coast and killing an estimated 1,710 people. In the larger sea frontiers defended by the U.S. Navy, staggering losses were inflicted by the Ubootwaffe. "During the first six months of 1942, 5,000 merchant mariners and some other non-merchant passengers were lost at sea along the American seaboard, the Caribbean Sea and the Gulf of Mexico—twice the number who were lost at Pearl Harbor," said historian Michael Gannon. "A total in six months of 397 vessels sunk in what has to be counted as one of the great maritime disasters of all time. And as the long time Professor of History at the University of

North Carolina Gerhard Weinberg has said, 'That maritime disaster has to go down as the greatest single defeat ever suffered by American Naval power.'"

Dönitz had not confirmed it at the time, but he had, only four days earlier, lost U-576 off the coast of North Carolina. On July 15, a day after being bombed and severely damaged by two Vought OS2U Kingfisher inshore patrol planes flown by U.S. Navy pilots out of Cunningham Field, U-576 audaciously attacked a southbound convoy off Cape Hatteras. After firing four torpedoes that sank one ship and damaged two others,[34] the U-boat was counterattacked while submerging by the U.S. Navy Armed Guard aboard the freighter SS *Unicoi*. Following the engagement, U-576 no longer transmitted any signals to France and was presumed lost off the North Carolina coast, making it the fourth U-boat sunk off the state. The U-boat has yet to be located.

For beach communities along the coast of North Carolina the summer of 1942 was nothing like the preceding winter and spring. No longer were the inhabitants of settlements and villages like Sea Breeze, Sea Level, and Seagull able to see towering over the ocean's horizon great billowing columns of oily black smoke rising from torpedoed tankers like monstrous tornados. Gone were the house-shaking, plaster-cracking, thunder-like rumbles of explosions offshore. There were still patches of thick gooey oil fouling the beaches, but absent were the many itinerant, empty, bullet-riddled lifeboats that washed up on shore or the infrequent but gruesome arrivals of corpses that seemed to have escaped their watery grave.

What occurred off the coast of North Carolina by late July was no less than a sea change of historic proportions—the German U-boats were gone. It happened abruptly after months of doleful and demoralizing devastation. For the civilians and servicemen living and working on the barrier islands and larger towns on the nearby mainland, the turn of events was dramatic, unmistakable, and heartening. Life began to return to normal—not the old leisurely normal, but a frenetic new normal. Thousands of servicemen continued to crowd the tiny beach communities. Construction of bases, airfields, ports, and piers continued at a breakneck pace (although, by the time it was all completed, many of the installations were no longer needed). With greater frequency, long freight trains rumbled back and forth on the rails supplying coal, fuel, and raw materials to the state's major ports. Post offices, drug stores, diners, and dance halls were crowded with new patrons, some with British accents. Every few days, island youths were able to sit in the dunes and see the ethereal mirages of what looked like long parades of ships slowly creeping southward or northward in convoys. Skies overhead hummed with the drone of patrols of Navy, Army, and Coast Guard aircraft and lighter-than-air dirigibles.

There was not, however, widespread relief that U.S. Armed Forces and its British and Canadian allies had finally managed to successfully defend American waters. During the peak of the hot and humid summer of 1942, German spy and saboteur mania preoccupied America as the startling news of the capture and trial of the Operation Pastorius agents and their collaborators was published in the daily papers. More landings were expected. Also attracting the attention of readers was news of the prosecution of the

Georg Nicolaus spy ring in Mexico, partly instigated the previous year by the former editor of the Raleigh *News & Observer*, U.S. Ambassador to Mexico Josephus Daniels. With the absence of marauding U-boats and frequent sinkings of merchant vessels, everyone's thoughts turned to the great Pacific conflicts at Coral Sea, Midway Island, and Guadalcanal; the furious desert battles of El Alamein over possession of the Suez Canal; and the Nazi offensive on the eastern front. Sobering news devastated many a North Carolina household when families learned that the war had claimed a loved one. World War II was no longer being fought off the beaches of North Carolina, but it was gradually gaining momentum elsewhere.

Throughout the year, a familiar routine was repeated in thousands of homes along the North Carolina coast. Each evening when supper was ended, dishes were cleaned and put away, and children were summoned from their outdoor fun, families gathered just in time to turn on the radio and hear the latest war news.

> Announcer: "Time for Gabriel Heatter and his up-to-the-minute news of the world brought to you by Forhan's Toothpaste. And now, Gabriel Heatter."
>
> Heatter: "Good evening everyone, there's good news tonight!"

Long before another famous newsman was revered with the title "the most trusted man in America," there was a broadcaster named Gabriel Heatter who would have qualified for the honor. Heatter was an American radio commentator who made a name for himself covering the trial of the suspected kidnapper of the Lindbergh Baby. During World War II, Heatter became better known for his opening line during his news broadcasts—"There's good news tonight!"—even when there was none. Heatter took it upon himself to brighten the spirits of Americans at a time when the future looked frightful. His optimism and ability to find a silver lining in a news day clouded with catastrophe made him extraordinarily popular among radio listeners. Heatter had his critics, however, like *The New Yorker* magazine's acerbic commentator Alexander Woollcott who once said, "Disaster has no cheerier greeter than gleeful, gloating Gabriel Heatter." (Woollcott, no doubt, was envious of Heatter's popularity.)

On the coast of North Carolina, people planned their days around Heatter's broadcasts. Ocracoke's Blanche Styron, who was 20 years old in 1942, remembers how the elders of the village spent their lunchtime on the porch of Amasa Fulcher's Community Store, whittling and talking. "Everyday at twelve, they'd listen to Gabriel Heatter to see how it was going," she said. "And then they'd talk about how it was in World War I and how different it was to this war."

The voices of other wartime commentators and reporters are still remembered on the islands, including the grave, measured delivery of Edward R. Murrow from the rooftops of London or the intense, rapid-fire news reading of Walter Winchell. Winchell would begin his radio broadcasts with the staccato sound of a telegraph key followed by his voice: "Good evening Mr. and Mrs. America, from border-to-border and coast-to-coast and all the ships at sea. Let's go to press." At his normal reading pace, Winchell could condense

about an hour's worth of news into a 30-minute broadcast.

Once the U-boats were gone and actual news was no longer occurring outside of his family's windows, Avon's Gibb Gray had a hard time tearing himself away from the family Ward's Airline radio that connected him to the latest world events. "I was listening all the time because my dad owned the store and that was a gathering place at night for the men, for the older men around here to talk about the war and the war news they heard that evening from Edward R. Murrow from England and all the other news commentators, Walter Winchell and Gabriel Heatter," Gray said. "They'd all discuss the war, and I'd just listen."

If Gray heard something new about which the older men were unaware, he enjoyed the empowering thrill of breaking the news. "Sometimes I would hear on the radio certain news, and I'd run and tell 'em in the store, but most of the time the elderly men did most of the talking," he said. "I was only about 15 years old. I was a listener. Gatherin' all the information I could."

On the evening of the one-year anniversary of Pearl Harbor, the Mutual Radio Network broadcast a special report featuring the ever-optimistic Gabriel Heatter.

> "Good evening, ladies and gentlemen. This is Gabriel Heatter inviting you on a journey prepared especially for you by WOR's War Services Division of the Mutual Network. One year after Pearl Harbor has brought vast and overwhelming change to millions of American homes. Millions of men have gone into uniform, and thousands of women are in uniform. More than half a million women are holding down war jobs. Vast overwhelming change rolls across America. We've had casualties, and we've avenged many. We've been taken by surprise, and we've surprised our enemies. We've been hit, and we've struck back. We're a long way from Berlin and Tokyo, but all men realize we're on our way."

Americans were indeed on their way to winning the war along with their allies. In the meantime, life at home went on. There were many inconveniences and sacrifices to endure in addition to rationing, darkening of shore lights, travel restrictions, and curfews.

Men who made their livelihoods from commercial fishing from docks at Harkers Island, Hatteras village, and Southport had to seek income elsewhere than from the ocean—oil-choked waters, minefields, submarine nets, and a seafloor littered with unexploded ordnance were hindrances not conducive to successful catches. Some men turned to the time-honored tradition of salvage.

The salvage industry was once an integral part of island life, but it had diminished considerably during the first half of the 20th century due to technological advancements in the shipping industry, improvements in weather forecasting, and wireless communications. Salvaging the dozens of hulks of partially submerged or derelict merchant ships, however, was not a legal occupation, as the vessels with sensitive navigational papers and secret routing instructions aboard from Naval authorities became the temporary property of the U.S. War Shipping Administration. That fact didn't always discourage destitute treasure seekers from impoverished fishing villages on the coast.

Earlier in 1942, before the U.S. Navy enveloped Cape Hatteras Bight with contact mines, the local fishing fleet would occasionally meander near some of the tankers and

Hatteras fishermen at wreck of M/V *Australia*.

freighters that protruded from the ocean surface surrounding Diamond Shoals. One especially calm day, some boats of the Hatteras fishing fleet were tied-up alongside the partially submerged hulk of the motor tanker *Australia*, about a mile and a half east of the Diamond Shoals bell buoy. The small boats surrounding the burned out tanker were unoccupied. The fishermen were aboard the ship hoping for a catch of a different sort, for it was well-known that the masters of merchant ships kept cash locked in safes in the vessel's wheelhouses. A story is told on Hatteras Island that a Coast Guard patrol approached the *Australia*, and the civilians aboard it quickly abandoned the ship and moved a safe distance away. The Coast Guard was there to retrieve the ship's secret documents, which the captain failed to throw overboard before he escaped. (Captain Martin Adler was later rescued by a vessel that delivered him and his surviving shipmates to Southport.) When the Coast Guardsmen found the open safe on the bridge, they called out to the nearby fishermen and told them what they were there to retrieve. "No questions asked," the Coast Guard men yelled, "But do any of you happen to have the ship's log?" Sheepishly, one of the fishing boats returned to the *Australia*, and a Hatteras man handed over the papers.

Sometimes even the Coasties got in on the act. "Yeah, *Harry F. Sinclair, Jr.*—that's the one I boarded," BM2c Theodore Mutro remembered. The tanker had been torpedoed in April by U-*203* near Cape Lookout. It burned but did not sink and drifted northward for the next four days. Mutro and his friend Mac Womac were part of a team sent out to the smoking derelict to see if it was a new victim of Torpedo Junction.

"I tried to go up to the pilot house because I knew they carried safes and that was where they kept the money," Mutro said. "Ain't no way in hell you could get up there—the damn deck was so hot. I could smell the rubber on my boots. So I uncovered the hatch and looked down. I waved to my boat, 'Hey, she's full of cases of motor oil—let's get it!'

Harry F. Sinclair, Jr.

As Mutro and his buddies were absconding with the motor oil, one of them spotted the unmistakable sight of the breaking bow wave of an approaching patrol vessel. It was one of Winston Churchill's 24 armed North Sea trawlers, the HMT *Senateur Duhamel.* "Someone said, 'Who the hell is that,'" Mutro recalled. "I said, 'I don't know, let's get the hell out of here.' So off we go, 'Putt, putt, putt, putt.' We didn't get no more than a quarter mile away from the *Harry F. Sinclair, Jr.,* when this British corvette shows up. So these Limeys with black flat hats call out, 'Did you pick up any of the survivors?' I said, 'No, we didn't.' They said, 'Do you think we can salvage the old boy?' I said, 'Don't know.' They told us to go ahead [and leave], they would take over." The Royal Navy Reserve sailors then began to try to douse the remaining pockets of fire on the stricken tanker. As Mutro, Womac, and the others departed the scene, a huge bang reverberated over the water. "Brooom!" Mutro exclaimed. "'What the hell?' I said to the others, 'I'm a son of a gun, they've turned their fire hoses with saltwater on that oil fire. Good thing we got away from it when we did. I don't know if they ever put it out or not." Mutro and his friends returned to Ocracoke with their disappointing treasure of motor oil. The British sailors did put the fire out, and the HMT *Senateur Duhamel* successfully towed the smoldering tanker back to Morehead City. The *Harry F. Sinclair, Jr.,* was later refurbished at Baltimore, and, despite the superstition that it brought bad luck at sea, the ship was renamed *Annibal.*

When Japanese forces captured the rubber tree plantations of the Dutch East Indies from where 90 percent of U.S. rubber was imported, the commodity became one of the first to be rationed in America. Everything made of rubber not in use was recycled—tires, inner tubes, rubber boots and shoes, garden hoses, and even bathing caps. Gas was also rationed, and a national Victory Speed Limit of 35 miles per hour was established primarily so that vehicle tires would last longer. Along with other commodities in short supply, the government mounted an all-out campaign to get Americans to scrounge their homes and farms for scrap materials that could supply the war effort. An emergency bulletin published in magazines by the Conservation Division of the War Production Board included this statement:

> "The rubber situation is also critical. Fortunately, the material exists in America's great 'mine above ground.' You may think, 'My little bit' won't help, but your

'little bit' multiplied thousands and millions of times can create a mountain of
raw material which can actually turn the tide."

The government's desperate need for rubber may have been ignored by some citizens
living on the Outer Banks where salvage of the sea's bounty was believed to be a God-giv-
en right. On December 16, 1942, the freighter *Louise* was caught in a winter blizzard off
Hatteras Island and was driven onto the lee shore north of Little Kinnakeet Coast Guard
Lifeboat Station. The small wooden vessel was loaded with a sizable cargo of military
truck tires and inner tubes that was government property before and after the tires and
tubes were disgorged up and down the Hatteras Island beach. The tubes, in particular,
were unusual and easily identifiable because of the long inflation stems typically found
on military vehicles. The Coast Guard did their best to recover as much of the cargo as
possible, and huge piles of tires were seen stacked behind the Little Kinnakeet station.
But not all of the highly prized rubber products were immediately found—tires and tubes
washed up on the beach for days. Even so, it was all government property, illegal for
civilians to possess. That didn't stop some Hatteras islanders.

"People would find them along the beach," remembered Gibb Gray of Avon. "We didn't
have any trucks around that could use them. Tires and tubes were rationed then, and
someone would find the tubes, but they would use them in these cars around here. The big
tubes had a long stem on 'em to pump the air in 'em. And when you would see a car going
down the road with that stem flopping and hitting the sand, you knew where it came from."

On September 14, 1944, the long-feared enemy assault on the islands of the coast of
North Carolina arrived in the form of a hurricane—the "far worst storm to ever strike the
island" according to residents of Ocracoke. Proving to be many times more destructive than
German U-boats or enemy saboteurs, "The Great Atlantic Hurricane" peaked as a category
4 storm with 140-mile-per-hour winds before weakening slightly as it passed near the Outer
Banks. A record low barometric pressure of 27.97 inches was recorded at Cape Hatteras.

Nature's deadly wrath rivaled Germany's most lethal U-boats. While still off the coast
of Florida, the storm sank the Navy destroyer USS *Warrington* with the loss of 248 officers
and men. Two Coast Guard cutters, *Bedloe* and *Jackson*, sank during the storm east of
Oregon Inlet with the loss of 47 men. At the Navy Auxiliary Air Station on Roanoke, a gust
of 125-miles-per-hour was recorded before the weather building was blown to the ground.

The village of Avon was among the places hardest hit by the hurricane. Residents
there counted dozens of houses that were lifted off foundations. Gibb Gray recalled that
his father had returned to his general store during the storm's eye only to be trapped
when the winds returned. His father had to jump into a nearby tree to avoid being swept
away. Gibb's father then watched in horror as his own house with his family inside
floated down the the street, finally coming to rest almost a mile away.

On Ocracoke Island, the storm warning was delivered throughout the village by
civilian Naval Intelligence Officer Aycock Brown, who had gotten word that the Miami
Hurricane Warning Office had designated the fast-approaching storm as one of the worst
it had ever tracked. The absolute stillness of the air and stifling heat didn't fool some of

Destruction caused by the Great Hurricane of 1944 at Ocracoke.

the old timers on the island who knew better, but many residents found it hard to believe that the storm was less than 24 hours away. "Aycock Brown, he was an intelligence officer," Blanche Styron recalled. "He goes around and tells everybody that we're having a big storm that night and to get their stuff together. So, anyway, nobody believed him because it was a beautiful night. The stars were shining, the moon was out, and everyone thought, well, Aycock's crazy. The next morning about 5, she hit, and it was the worst [storm] we ever had."

The wind-speed indicator on top of the water tower at the Ocracoke Naval Base (in 1944 it had been converted from a Section Base to an Amphibious Training facility) blew away after the winds went above 75 miles per hour. Long-time residents later estimated the winds at more than 100 miles per hour. When the winds shifted as the storm moved northward, the much-feared and more-destructive tidal surge out of the Pamlico Sound flooded the entire village. Some residents took refuge inside Ocracoke Lighthouse. The mailboat *Aleta* and many of the island's fishing boats were tossed like toys far from the shoreline of Silver Lake. Six homes and O'Neal's Store were completely destroyed. Perhaps saddest of all, the Pamlico Inn, the birthplace of SS *Caribsea* third mate Jim Baughm Gaskill, was also wrecked beyond repair.

The Wahab Village Hotel and Theatre, which had been a favorite gathering spot throughout the war for military personnel and their wives and girlfriends as well as island residents, had been inundated by water from the storm's torrential rains. After the hurricane had passed, it was noticed that the two-story wings of the hotel began to pull away from the center portion of the building, endangering the entire structure. Quickly, the Navy came to the rescue, and sailors engineered a resourceful repair by wrapping the entire hotel with steel cables and then winching the north and south wings back into place. The enduring and charming hotel has since been renamed Blackbeard's Lodge, and it still retains the 1944 "Navy winch in the attic."

For many of the residents of the Outer Banks, the 1944 Great Atlantic Hurricane made the turmoil and devastation of 1942 seem like an inconsequential and distant memory.

On May 7, 1945, radios across America and along the coast of North Carolina brought the news so eagerly awaited for so long—the report of Germany's surrender to Allied forces.

> "The National Broadcasting Company delays the start of all its programs to bring you a Special Bulletin: It was announced in San Francisco half an hour ago by a high American official, not identified, as saying Germany has surrendered unconditionally to the Allies—no strings attached."[35]

"I was in Ocracoke," Arnold Tolson remembered. "I was skipper of the 63-067 Air and Sea Rescue Craft, and we had one hell of a big party."

"Oh, I remember a group of us got in a jeep and rode up and down the island just whooping and hollering and having a great time," said Calvin O'Neal. "It was wonderful; the war was over. An awful lot of our young served in the war, and some didn't make it. I had a cousin that died in Germany. So it was a very joyous day for us. I still remember that."

Ocracoke resident Blanche Joliff also recounted the happy occasion while sitting on the same porch in 2000 where she heard the news 55 years earlier. "The Navy allowed the men to have a party on the beach, and I understood they furnished beer for them that day, but I only heard that—I can't say for a fact," the well-mannered Jolliff reported. "We were sitting on the porch—my mother and the lady that lived [next door]—and we were sitting here on the porch when we heard the news."

A 96-day national "brownout" order implemented by the U.S. War Production Board

"An economic lifeline"—the newly paved Highway 12.

to reduce fuel consumption when coal was in short supply in early 1945 was lifted on May 8 following President Harry Truman's official proclamation of the end of the war in Europe. The welcomed news was heard by coastal residents who were spellbound as the latest hourly developments were broadcast over their radios:

> "From Washington a moment ago we received this notice on the United Press that bright lights can be turned on throughout the nation with the blessing of the War Production Board. Edward Faulk, Director of War Utilities, revoked the brownout order, which had darkened shop windows, theater marquees, and out-door advertising signs in most of the nation for the past three months."

Before long, the once bustling Ocracoke Navy Base was decommissioned and dis-mantled. Barracks and buildings were torn down, dismantled for materials or moved to other spots in the village for civilian use. "When the base pulled out, some of the build-ings, like the recreation hall, they gave to the Methodist Church, and Captain Ben's Restaurant, too, was one of those Navy buildings they let people have," Blanche Styron remembered. "It was kind of lonesome when the base pulled out, you know."

At the top secret Loop Shack, the state-of-the-art submarine detection and tracking equipment had been removed about a year after the U-boats were called back by Admiral Donitz. The buildings remained for a couple of years, and today only the concrete foun-dations remain, hidden beyond the wall of cedars and wax myrtle alongside highway NC-12. Signs of the time when U-boats ravaged the shipping lanes off North Carolina's coast gradually disappeared. Out of public view, beyond the oil-stained beaches, the ocean bot-tom remained littered with unexploded torpedoes, artillery shells, depth charges, contact mines, and the detritus of more than 70 ships.

According to historian David Stick, it was not until the summer of 1946 when the stage curtain was drawn marking a new post-war period on the coast, beginning with the resumption of the popular outdoor drama "The Lost Colony." "New hotels, motels, restaurants, stores, cottages were open for business at Nags Head, Kill Devil Hills, and Kitty Hawk, and many more were being planned," Stick wrote in his book, *The Outer Banks of North Carolina*. Other major changes were on the way, including the official formation of the Cape Hatteras National Seashore, first envisioned by Stick's father, Frank, in 1933.

In a few years, an asphalt highway would wind its way south linking the Outer Banks villages south of Nags Head all the way to Ocracoke. The highway symbolized a ribbon of promise, an economic lifeline, a long-awaited signature of change. The islands would never be the same. For the first time since motor vehicles began driving the sands of the islands, driver's licenses were required, and a speed limit was enforced—a dawning of a new era of rules and regulations that would thenceforth restrain the wild, unbridled spirit of the residents of the once-isolated barrier islands.

Perhaps the most significant change, as it was for so many communities on the coast of North Carolina and across America, was that World War II cost Outer Bankers their innocence. "Things never got back to normal because we lost our innocence then," Calvin O'Neal said. "Because before [the war] we were not part of the rest of the world, isolated as we were. It did change things. Your outlook on life was different. You had experienced something close hand that normally would change your attitude, your life, your everything."

National address delivered by President Harry S. Truman from the Radio Room at the White House at 9 a.m. on May 8, 1945

"This is a solemn but a glorious hour. I only wish that Franklin D. Roosevelt had lived to witness this day. General Eisenhower informs me that the forces of Germany have surrendered to the United Nations. The flags of freedom fly over all Europe.

For this victory, we join in offering our thanks to the Providence which has guided and sustained us through the dark days of adversity.

Our rejoicing is sobered and subdued by a supreme consciousness of the terrible price we have paid to rid the world of Hitler and his evil band. Let us not forget, my fellow Americans, the sorrow and the heartache which today abide in the homes of so many of our neighbors—neighbors whose most priceless possession has been rendered as a sacrifice to redeem our liberty.

We can repay the debt which we owe to our God, to our dead, and to our children only by work—by ceaseless devotion to the responsibilities which lie ahead of us."

EPILOGUE

Burial of Michael Cairns at Cape Hatteras

Fallen
In the Cause
of the Free

"Your liberty was purchased with the lives
of good men; its price was too high that you
should squander it."

Sun Seaman's Memorial, Marcus Hook, PA

The large crowd of men, women, and children stood solemnly, gathered on an overcast morning at a tiny cemetery for an historic event. A breeze buffeted the gnarled limbs of a sprawling live oak tree as the melancholy melody of "Goin' Home," the spiritual rendition of Antonín Dvořák's 9th Symphony Largo, drifted skyward. A lone piper played, piercing the air with the harmonics of a Highland bagpipe's chanter and drones, and rending the hearts of listeners with sadness. The event took place on Friday, May 13, 2005, in the village of Ocracoke on hallowed ground known to many as a "corner of a foreign field that is forever England."

A row of dignitaries, including officers of the Royal Navy, Canadian Navy, United States Coast Guard, and Coast Guard Auxiliary faced the attendees with somber expressions. Nearby, a U.S. Coast Guard rifle party stood ready to fire a three-volley salute. Almost everyone's eyes were directed toward the white picket fence that surrounded the graves of four British sailors buried there 63 years earlier. Whispers were exchanged, and anticipation gripped the audience as a distinguished gentleman stepped forward wearing a British military service medal pinned to his civilian blazer. The surrounding landscape had changed over the years, but the location of the graves had not. Consequently, the participants and bystanders stood in the virtual footprints of their predecessors, and, like actors in a perpetual drama, they reprised a time-honored tradition.

The speaker and guest of honor at the podium, a 62-year-old retired commander in the Royal Naval Reserve, read the names and ages of the dead, his words expressed in a careful cadence, his voice wavering with emotion. "Perhaps, it is as well to remember

HMT *Bedfordshire* memorial service on May 8, 2009.

these young men in the verse of the poet Laurence Binyon from his poem, 'For the Fallen,'" he said as his blue-gray eyes averted downward and became teary with grief. "They shall grow not old, as we that are left grow old. Age shall not weary them, nor the years condemn. At the going down of the sun and in the morning, we will remember them."

And remember them, they still do—the intrepid sailors of the Royal Navy's armed trawler HMT *Bedfordshire*, torpedoed and sunk by U-*558* at 11:40 p.m. about 17 miles south of Cape Lookout. All 37 men aboard the patrol vessel perished in a cataclysmic explosion.

The short history of HMT *Bedfordshire* is well-known and was perhaps best told in L. VanLoan Naisawald's authoritatively written, *In Some Foreign Field: Four British Graves and Submarine Warfare on the North Carolina Outer Banks*. The 162-foot *Bedfordshire* was one of the 24 submarine-chasers dispatched to the United States by Winston Churchill in March 1942. Along with her sister ships, *Lady Elsa*, *Stella Polaris*, *Kingston Ceylonite*, *Coventry City*, *Norwich City*, *Hertfordshire*, and *Senateur Duhamel*, the coal-powered fishing boat named for the county north of London trawled the ocean waters of the 5th Naval District for German U-boats. She arrived later than the others but by April *Bedfordshire* was chasing elusive sound contacts, responding to distress calls and assisting the U.S. Navy in such services as delivering divers to the sunken U-*85* off Nags Head. Between Norfolk and Morehead City she went, steaming day and

"At the going down of the sun and in the morning, we will remember them."

night and performing her duties for God, king and country.

As the names of the *Bedfordshire*'s men were recited, the veil of time parted, and the past momentarily became the present.

Arnold Tolson was a mature, competent, and confident kid. In fact, he was so competent that a little more than two years after joining the Coast Guard at 17 years old, Tolson had attained the rating of chief petty officer and was put in command of men older than himself and an 83-foot patrol boat working the waters off Cape Hatteras. On Wednesday, May 13, the engines in Tolson's boat needed repairs—a few of the rocker arms on the Sterling-Viking motors needed to be replaced—so he and his crew put in at Ocracoke Coast Guard Station. The commander of the station at the time, Chief Petty Officer Homer Gray, asked Tolson if he would stand by for him for 24 hours. Gray then departed on the mail boat *Aleta* to go over to the mainland to have—as he told Tolson—some "teeth work done." Later that night, Tolson recalled hearing an explosion offshore. "It was awful; it shook the whole island," he said. (The explosion Tolson heard was not what he thought he heard, as no Allied ship was attacked within hundreds of miles of Ocracoke on the night of May 13-14. The concussion may have been depth charges being dropped or a destroyer's guns attempting to sink a lifeboat.)

CPO Arnold Tolson

Early the next morning, Tolson was curious if something might have washed up on the beach that would reveal the source of the explosion. He didn't become a chief petty officer at 19 by sitting on his hands, so he ordered a younger seaman to find the keys to the station's pickup truck so that they could drive up the island for an impromptu patrol. "We got to the beach and started riding north," Tolson recalled. "I saw this [body] in the surf so we stopped. I pulled off my shoes and [waded into the surf] and got him by the arm and pulled him on the beach. We put him in the truck and headed back over to the Coast Guard station."

On their return to the station, Tolson was flagged down by a civilian named Elwood Austin who breathlessly exclaimed that a second body was drifting in and out of the surf a little further down the beach where he had been fishing. "I asked him, 'Why didn't you pull him back?' He said, 'When he come in, I left.' We got [that body] and pulled him in and took him back to the station, too."

Over the years, variations of the story have been told so often that the facts have become somewhat distorted. One version describes the corpses as being naked without any identification as to who the men were or from which ship they might have come. Tolson, who possessed as much confidence in his memory in 2000 as he probably displayed in his ability to lead men in 1942, remembers the facts differently—primarily that the bodies were clothed and personal items were available to identify one of the men. "First one was a bearded gentleman; he was an officer and he had dungarees and a turtleneck on," Tolson said. "The other boy that we found, we didn't know his name until fingerprints were taken. [The officer] had a checkbook in his pocket where he had put some money in the bank a few days before in Morehead City. The ink wasn't even blotted off. And he had a newspaper with him, and the ink wasn't blotted off that." From where the bodies had come was still a mystery.

Later that morning CPO Gray returned from his dental appointment and put in a call to Aycock Brown, civilian agent for U.S. Navy Intelligence. Brown was a gung-ho, gangly, and gregarious character who made friends everywhere he went in the performance of his wartime duties in the 5th Naval District. His responsibilities included examining and identifying corpses and wreckage that had washed ashore with the purpose of learning the names of ships that had been destroyed before a distress signal could be sent. It was, at times, a ghastly task, but as far as Brown was concerned, a job was a job—in 1942, few Americans had the luxury of choosing their preferred line of work. Without any academic or formal training whatsoever, the irrepressible Brown was expected to perform the roles of forensic anthropologist and coroner unerringly. Like most Americans at the time, he did the best he could.

Aycock Brown

In April, Brown had been sent to investigate a corpse that had been recovered on the beach near the Cape Hatteras Lighthouse and moved to an equipment shed behind the Coast Guard Station. In an article for a 1955 issue of *Male* magazine, Brown wrote: "The man would most likely be one of three things—a member of the British or American military, a British or American seaman, or an enemy agent. I had to know which, and the subject himself couldn't tell me in his present condition."

Following a gruesome procedure described in his article titled, "I Wore a Dead Man's Hand," Brown succeeded in identifying the deceased through fingerprints as Michael Cairns, the 4th engineering officer from the torpedoed armed British tanker *San Delfino*, sunk on April 9 east of Rodanthe. Having been proven that he was not an enemy agent, Cairns' body was to be interred in a small plot near the Cape Hatteras Coast Guard Station. Brown insisted that the British sailor be buried with traditional military honors—it was the proper thing to do. However, without a British honor guard, rifle team, or bugler, the best that Brown could hope for was to find a British flag that could drape Cairns' roughly hewn pine casket.

Brown's quest for a British flag led him to the docks at the Morehead City shipyard where the HMT *Bedfordshire* was berthed while taking on coal and provisions for her next anti-submarine patrol. Upon stating the purpose of his visit at the vessel's gangway, Brown was directed to see the officer of the deck, the affable and handsome 28-year-old Thomas Cunningham, a sub-lieutenant in the Royal Navy Volunteer Reserve. Brown greeted the bearded Cunningham and informed the young officer what he needed. "I'd not only like to have a couple of flags, but if you could spare a few British seamen to represent His Majesty, I think that would be fine, too," Brown recounted in his 1955 article. "Terrible sorry, old man—terribly!" Cunningham replied. "The flags you may have. But

Sub-Lt. Thomas Cunningham

I can't let you have any men, because our orders are to sail as soon as we've filled our bunkers. But how's for a spot of something or another while I have the jacks brought up?" The hospitable Cunningham invited Brown to participate in an age-old Royal Navy tradition—the partaking of a daily ration of grog. Brown, who was known to nip from a bottle of bourbon at various times of the day—perhaps due to the pressures of war—was pleased to oblige. The two men retired to the officer's wardroom.

The happy Cunningham told Brown that he had good reason share in a toast. He had recently received a telegram from his wife, Barbara, informing him that the couple was expecting their first child in about seven months. The two sociable men—the dashing Brown (he bore a resemblance to the actor David Niven) and the ruggedly handsome Cunningham—sipped their rum and became instant friends. In his article, Brown reflected: "I wished that I could meet him again after the war. It's not very often that you make friends like him so quickly." The grog could have had a little to do with the convivial spirit in the wardroom—by the time their meeting had ended, the wicker-wrapped rum jug was empty. Brown asked if he could take it with him as a souvenir, and Cunningham was happy to comply. "I think they probably got to know each other pretty good," said Brown's son, Billy, in a interview years later while he cradled the jug symbolic of what would prove to be his father's folkloric friendship.

As they said their farewells, Cunningham handed Brown a stack of four Union Jacks that included two more than Brown had asked for. In his published recollections of the meeting—the only source for the words exchanged between the two men—Brown did not quote Cunningham with regard to the additional flags. It can only be speculated that Cunningham, perhaps, thought there might be a possibility that the bodies of more British sailors would wash up on North Carolina's beaches before the war's end.

Six weeks later, after being summoned to Ocracoke to investigate the corpses recovered by CPO Tolson, Brown arrived aboard a Grumman J4F-1 Widgeon amphibious aircraft. The bodies, wrapped in a tarpaulin, had been placed in a building that had once been the summer kitchen for the old life-saving station. Brown carried his fingerprint kit with him and was led to the little building by CPO Gray and CPO Tolson. In his retelling of the story, the ever-buoyant Brown wrote of the moment when the tarp was removed from the bodies: "As I looked at the faces of the two men, the strength seemed to flow out of my body." Brown turned to Gray and told him that without any further examination, he knew from where the dead men had come—HMT *Bedfordshire*. "I know this man," Brown told Gray. "He's Sub-Lieutenant Tom Cunningham." Of course, Tolson and Gray had already determined the identity of the bearded officer, but they did not know he had served aboard the *Bedfordshire*. Later, fingerprints taken from the second body confirmed the man's identity as the armed trawler's ordinary telegraphist, Stanley Craig.

When Brown placed a call to 5th Naval District Headquarters informing them that the HMT *Bedfordshire* must have been lost off Ocracoke, the Navy's first response was that it was unlikely—they were fairly sure they knew that the Royal Navy sub-chaser was still patrolling the waters around Cape Lookout. After checking with a British liaison officer in Norfolk who had not heard from *Bedfordshire* in a few days, the Navy reluctantly assumed that the brave little warship was lost. No one knew how it happened, however.

Neither the circumstances of the attack on the *Bedfordshire*, the location of the sinking, nor the identity of the U-boat that was presumed to have sunk the British vessel were known in 1942. Only after the war, when Kriegsmarine and Ubootwaffe records were captured by the Allies, was it deduced that U-558 was the only U-boat operating in the Cape Lookout area at the time. Commanded by Kapitänleutnant Günther Krech, U-558 had encountered the unsuspecting *Bedfordshire* passing south of Cape Lookout and sank it with a single torpedo. Admiral Dönitz's war diary for May 13 noted a radiotelegraph message sent by Krech that stated in cursory terms its accomplishments in North Carolina waters during the preceding days: "One patrol vessel sunk."

Brown and Tolson assumed the responsibility for properly burying the men. In response to Brown's inquiry, the Williams family of Ocracoke offered to provide two burial plots outside of their large, brick-walled cemetery. Tolson went in search of containers that could serve as caskets. (Island communities like Ocracoke, then as now, had to have caskets shipped over from the mainland for their funerals.) Tolson had to improvise quickly. "I went to see a fellow named Charlie Mack," Tolson said. "He always had some lumber around. I told him, 'I see you've got some battery boxes that look like could be used for coffins.' He said, 'Take them.'" (Battery boxes were floating duck blinds, alternatively called sink boxes, and were used by hunters to lay in while hunting in the shallow waters of the sound.) "I then got some sailors, and we went and dug the graves," Tolson added.

The burial of Lt. Thomas Cunningham, RNVR.

Meanwhile, Brown searched for the island's Methodist minister, Rev. W.R. Dixon, but was unable to locate him. In his place, church lay leader Amasa Fulcher agreed to lead a brief burial service. The bodies of Cunningham and Craig were wrapped in blankets, sealed within the watertight battery boxes, and taken by the Coast Guard Station International Harvester pickup truck to the burial site. Tolson, Theodore Mutro, Mac Womac, and Motor Machinist's Mate Chief Harvey Wahab served as pallbearers. Womac later recalled his feelings at the time: "Everybody was downcast and hoping that they could do something, but we couldn't do more than what we were doing. You just feel useless—which, you are." Tolson concurred. "Well, everybody's emotions were very high," he said. "You know, when you ride over to the beach and see men washing up, it was like somebody spit on you that you couldn't get back to."

Brown stood nearby to photograph the burial as he fought back tears and a bilious hatred of the nameless Germans who had killed his newfound friend. As he held his camera, he shook his head in disbelief at the irony—one of the two spare Union Jacks that Cunningham had given him now covered the Englishman's own casket. Brown snapped a photograph as Tolson, Mutro, Womac, and Wahab delicately lowered Thomas Cunningham into the sandy ground. Somewhere in England, Brown thought, there was a young widow—one of a countless many—expecting a child she would have to raise without his father.

Sixty-three years later, that child, Tom Cunningham, Jr., (photo p.281) stood in the

Memorial procession at Ocracoke on December 27, 1942.

faded footprints of Brown, Tolson, Mutro, and Womac before the large crowd of service-men, spectators and mourners, fighting back his own emotions while reading Binyon's words: "At the going down of the sun and in the morning, we will remember them." Seated in the front row of special guests was Theodore Mutro, the sole surviving member of the 1942 burial detail.

The tradition of the *Bedfordshire* memorial service originated in December 1942. When Barbara Cunningham had been notified of her husband's death, she wrote a letter inquiring if her husband, a practicing Roman Catholic, had been buried in accordance with the church's Rites of Burial. Since that was not possible under the time constraints that existed in May 1942, a promise was made to conduct a memorial service later that year with a Catholic chaplain, Lt. Cmdr. Donald Strange, co-presiding with Rev. Dixon of Ocracoke. On December 27, a large number of U.S. Navy sailors and U.S. Coast Guards-men reconvened at the small patch of sandy soil north of Silver Lake that marked the final resting place of Cunningham and Craig. There were two additional burials there, badly decomposed corpses found by Tolson and his men outside of Ocracoke Inlet when they finally got their 83-footer's engines working again in May. Neither of the two bodies could be identified but were presumed to have come from the *Bedfordshire*.

Four freshly painted crosses marked the graves. Under an overcast sky, Dixon and

Barbara Cunningham and Thomas Jr.

Strange took turns reading from Protestant and Catholic scripture. A rifle party of at least 17 sailors then fired a three-volley salute followed by a bugler who played taps. Brown was again present and took photographs. When the memorial was concluded and the dozens of servicemen marched away to rejoin the war against the Axis menace, the little cemetery and the memory of the men buried there gradually faded from the world's attention. The supreme sacrifice made by of the men of the *Bedfordshire* was in danger of being forgotten.

Ocracokers never forgot, however. A close and affectionate bond between the village and the Cunningham family was sustained by an abiding friendship between Ocracoke schoolteacher Fannie Pearl Fulcher and Barbara Cunningham. Over the years, a white picket fence was built around the graves, and the cemetery was kept free of weeds and vines by the island residents, but the typical visitor to the island would have hardly known it was there or what it represented.

In 1969, a group of Royal Navy sailors appeared unannounced to make repairs and erect a flag pole in order to fly a British flag over the historic cemetery. Every day for the next few years, a small Coast Guard detail from the nearby station faithfully went to the cemetery to raise and lower the Union Jack at dawn and dusk. One day in 1974, they went to lower the flag and found that it was missing—some small-minded, shameless miscreant had stolen it. Boatswain's Mate 2nd Class James Davis, Jr., of the Ocracoke Station was asked about the missing flag. "It sure made us mad," he said. "It's really sad that someone would do something like that. We'll get another one. It's funny, but we got to feel like we knew these guys [in the cemetery]. Brothers of the sea."

Davis agitated through his chain of command to acquire additional British flags in order to restore the tradition. Within a few weeks the cause inspired John Coit, the newly named state travel editor for the North Carolina Division of Travel and Promotion, to contact the British Embassy in Washington, D.C. In mid July, a letter arrived at the Ocracoke Coast Guard Station from Capt. K.C.D. Watson, a Royal Navy attaché to the British Ambassador. "The Commander British Navy Staff is most grateful for the interest shown by your Coast Guard personnel, particularly I understand, BM2C James H. Davis, Jr.,"

Watson wrote. He then informed the Ocracoke commander to soon expect a helicopter to arrive from the frigate HMS *Mohawk* (the "Mighty Mo"), which would anchor off Ocracoke in a few days on its way to Norfolk from the West Indies.

As promised, a Royal Navy helicopter descended at Ocracoke carrying Capt. Barry Wilson of the *Mohawk*, a small number of sailors, and a stack of Union Jacks. A joint military memorial ceremony was conducted in late July 1974 with members of the Royal Navy and U.S. Coast Guard present, as well as a few spectators and reporters. A British rifle team fired the customary three-volley salute, and the United Kingdom's Union Flag was restored to the flagpole. Wilson said to report-

Capt. John Gower, RN

er Jerry Allegood of *The News & Observer*: "A cemetery like this is a symbol of the very great friendship and liaison between the United States and Great Britain. This liaison is not a thing of history. It is something that is going on today."

Due to the tireless efforts of many dedicated people and organizations including Ocracoke Preservation Society, the Graveyard of the Atlantic Museum, and the United States Coast Guard Group Cape Hatteras, that liaison, the ceremony, and the memory of the *Bedfordshire*'s brave men endures to this day and will long into the future. Since 1976, when the property was transferred to the State of North Carolina, which subsequently leased the cemetery in perpetuity to the Commonwealth War Graves Commission, an annual memorial event has been conducted at the site on the Friday nearest to the anniversary of May 11.

At the memorial event on May 13, 2005, Royal Navy Capt. John Gower, representing the British Ambassador, spoke eloquently of Britain's perspective of the essence of the *Bedfordshire*'s story and the little cemetery on Ocracoke:

> "The story of the *Bedfordshire* highlights the deep affection felt by a group of Americans for the crew of an obscure little ship that scarcely rated being called a war vessel, though technically she was one. Only a few people had ever heard of HMT *Bedfordshire*, either in her homeports of Great Britain or in her temporary home in the United States.
>
> Her name would not find its way to the pages of World War II history books beside the names of such illustrious British men-of-war as HMS *Hood*, HMS *Prince*

HMT *Bedfordshire* cemetery at Ocracoke in December 1942.

of Wales, and HMS *Exeter*, and a score of others whose sheer size and flaming heavy guns earned them a place on the printed page. But she earned a different kind of memory—a most warm and personal one in the hearts of the people of North Carolina's Outer Banks—and her memorial is this small four-grave cemetery on Ocracoke Island, wherein one of her officers and three of her crew rest peacefully in the shade of overhanging live oak, juniper, and yaupon. The site is a spot beautiful in its simplicity, and the story of how it came into being is one of sorrow, of compassion, of kinship, of the appreciation one group of people felt for another they had never met. But the common bonds of the sea and of ancestry between the British seamen and the islanders of Ocracoke probably ensure that there will always be this warm feeling for the cemetery."

As the story of the ill-fated *Bedfordshire* is retold each year at the memorial on Ocracoke, more and more people will learn that the men of the little warship had no warning of the approaching torpedo—the resulting explosion was so abrupt and so violent that the *Bedfordshire*'s men were instantly killed. Decades later, when sport divers from Morehead City first discovered the remains of the armed trawler on the ocean bottom south of Cape Lookout, it was readily apparent by the expanse of the debris field that the men aboard never stood a chance. It would seem that during her brief couple of months of helping to defend America's shore against the evil of German U-boats, the brave little ship was never able to accomplish her mission.

There are some who, while listening to this story of the *Bedfordshire*, might wonder if Lt. Thomas Cunningham and his comrades had perished in vain. The truth is, their supreme mission—not issued to them verbally by their Allied commanders but silently by God—was not to sink German U-boats but to die in order to remind future generations of the incomparable, selfless sacrifices made by the millions of brave men and women who fought and died during World War II, the deadliest military conflict in history. In its own small way, the four graves of the *Bedfordshire* sailors on Ocracoke Island symbolically represent all of the estimated 40 million Allied military and civilians who lost their lives in defense of freedom. In the fulfillment of that mission and purpose, Cunningham and the *Bedfordshire*'s men were victorious. They have prevailed and live forever in our memory. Indeed, the brave never die.

> *As the stars that shall be bright when we are dust,*
> *Moving in marches upon the heavenly plain;*
> *As the stars that are starry in the time of our darkness,*
> *To the end, to the end, they remain.*

> Laurence Binyon, "For the Fallen"

W hen I was 17 in the summer of 1971, I set out on an adventure from a Morehead City dock in an outboard boat with a few high school friends to find and dive on the sunken and lost German U-boat U-*352* off Cape Lookout, North Carolina. We teenagers would not find the submarine because we were inexperienced, inadequately equipped, and terribly naïve (it was eventually located in 1975). We had no depth finder, no magnetometer, no side-scan sonar. We did possess a box compass, a chart, newly printed diving certifications, wrist depth gauges, and scuba tanks with double-hose regulators. We also had a fair amount of enthusiasm and daring. We knew the U-boat was out there somewhere—that's all that mattered. We never considered the fact that if we had somehow stumbled upon the U-*352*, we were unlikely to have ever been able to locate it again because we had no way to know where we were.

My curiosity about why German U-boats were sunk off North Carolina's coast never waned, however. Over the years, I found other ways to learn about the time World War II was fought within just a few miles of our coast. Much of my fascination, reading, and research culminated in the production of a three-hour television documentary I wrote and filmed in 2001 for the 60th anniversary of Pearl Harbor titled, *War Zone—World War II Off North Carolina's Outer Banks*. For that film, I had the privilege to meet and interview many of the people I have quoted in this book who endured this tumultuous time in American history. Sadly, in the 11 years since, many of those fascinating, gracious, and courageous folks have been lost to us and so has their colorful vision of the past. Also lost on the proverbial cutting room floor during the production of the documentary were innumerable anecdotes, facts, picturesque memories, and otherwise interesting information that was sacrificed for the sake of time. This book is my effort to tell a more complete story about this under-appreciated period in our history.

I foremost wish to recognize those people who shared their knowledge and personal stories with me so long ago: Michael Gannon, David Stick, Blanche Joliff, Theodore Mutro, Mac Womac, Calvin O'Neal, Gibb Gray, Blanche Styron, Carol Dillon, Ormond Fuller, Wallace Beckham, Manson Meekins, Charles Stowe, Owen Gaskill, Biff Bowker, Stocky Midgett, Ida O'Neal, Rhodes Chamberlin, Richard Rushton, Billy Brown, Russell Twiford, and Arnold Tolson. Jesse Roper Mohorovic was generous with his time and by sharing the records he had collected related to his birth.

I am especially pleased to express my heartfelt gratitude to Vicky Jarrett, the wise, insightful, and scrupulous editor of this book.

I will always appreciate and remember the assistance provided me for the production of the documentary film that formed the nucleus of this book by Joe and Melanie Schwarzer, Danny Couch, Dale Burrus, and Earl O'Neal.

I have enjoyed the friendship and benefited from the encouragement of Pat and Michael Mansfield, Ray and D.J. Midgett, Irene Nolan, and Erik Groves.

Some of the German translations in this book were made possible by my friends at Siemens AG: Michael Timme, Rita White, and Helene Condiff.

Others who have helped me along the way were James Davis, Jr., David Stick, Sarah Downing, Catherine Kozak, Philip Howard, DeAnna Locke, Doug Stover, Pat Stevens, Chip and Helena Stevens, Leon Reed, Mary Ellen Dedominicis Chestnut, David Stanley, Jerry

Allegood, Scott and Maggie Dawson, Capt. Horatio Sinbad, Ed Fox, Gee Gee Rosell, Belinda Willis, Jim Bunch, Gregg and Kathy Gelb, Bill Leslie, Sandy Quidley, Debbie and Butch Bryan, George and Betty Chamberlin, John Leys, Linda Malloy, and James Charlet.

My friends at Permanent Printing Limited of Hong Kong deserve the highest accolades for their peerless efforts to print fine quality books.

I am thankful for the support of the North Carolina Humanities Council and Carolyn Allen who makes it possible for me to speak to groups all around the state. The staff of the North Carolina Center for Advancement of Teaching, especially Dianne Lee, Henry Wong, and Renee Coward, have made it possible for me to present my programs to North Carolina teachers. June Dunleavy and the members of the New Bern Historical Society have been great friends. I am also honored to have the steadfast support of Martha Moye.

Our meeting was brief but I will always cherish my time with Thomas Cunningham, Jr.

Always there, working selflessly to support our household, providing strength and support, and attending to the demands of life, is my wife Susan, without whom my endeavors would not be possible.

Author's note: This book was written and published primarily for general readers and, although exhaustively researched, it is not intended to be considered an academic work. Consequently, not all of the sources consulted are listed. Whenever possible, primary source materials were utilized. As often as possible, sources were cited within the narrative.

Government and Military Primary Sources

Log of the United States Ship *Jesse Roper* (DD147).

Op-16-B-5 Memorandum: Summary Statements by Survivors, SS *City of New York*, April 16, 1942, Office of the Chief of Naval Operations.

Kriegstagebücher (KTB) & Stehender Kriegsbefehl, Des Führers/Befehlshaber der Unterseeboote (F.d.U./B.d.U.), Operational Archives Branch Naval Historical Center, Navy Yard, Washington, D.C.

U-*123* KTB: 7th War Patrol, Dec. 23, 1941-February 9, 1942; 8th War Patrol, March 2, 1942-May 2, 1942.

Monthly war diary of U.S. Navy Eastern Sea Frontier, 90 Church Street, New York, N. Y.

"Destruction of German submarine - Report of the Executive Officer, USS *Jesse Roper*." April 15, 1942.

"Report of Executive Officer, USCGC *Icarus*, on subject action 9 May, 1942, on Enemy Submarine." 15 May, 1942.

"Report of Interrogations of Survivors of U-*701*, Sunk by U.S. Army Attack Bomber." July 7, 1942.

"Final Report of Interrogations of Survivors from U-*352* sunk by USCGC *Icarus* on May 9, 1942 in Approximate Position Latitude 34.12.05 N., Longitude 76.35 W." Office of the Chief of Naval Operations.

U.S. Navy Harbor Defense Manual 1946 providing technical details of underwater magnetic indicator loops and installations.

Unpublished Sources, Manuscripts, and Private Collections

"The History of MIS-Y: U.S. Strategic Interrogation during World War II." Maj. Steven M. Kleinman, USAFR PGIP Class 2002. Unclassified thesis submitted to the Faculty of the Joint Military Intelligence College.

"Ultra and the Battle of the Atlantic." Authors: Patrick Beesly, former Deputy Chief, Submarine Plotting Room, the Admiralty; Jurgen Rohwer, Director of the Library of Contemporary History, Stuttgart, Germany; and Kenneth Knowles, former Head, Atlantic Section, Combat Intelligence, on the staff of the Commander-in-Chief, U.S. Fleet. Three papers presented at the Naval Symposium at the U.S. Naval Academy, Annapolis, MD, on Oct. 28, 1977. Document declassified by the National Security Agency, July 26, 2010.

Midgett Brothers Manteo-Hatteras Busline, from family files, interviews.

Jesse Roper Mohorovic—private files shared and communications with author.

James Davis, Jr.—documents provided related to Ocracoke British Cemetery.

Published Sources

Bunker, John. *Heroes in Dungarees: The Story of the American Merchant Marine in World War II*. Naval Institute Press, 1995.

Churchill, Winston. *The Second World War*, Vols. 1-4. Boston: Houghton Mifflin Company. 1948-1950.

Friedman, Norman. *U.S. destroyers: an illustrated design history*. Naval Institute Press, 2004.

Gannon, Michael. *Operation Drumbeat: The Dramatic True Story of Germany's First U-boat Attacks Along the American Coast in World War II*. New York: Harper Perennial. 1991.

Hoyt, Edwin P. *U-boats Offshore—When Hitler Struck America*. New York: Stein and Day. 1978.

Moore, Capt. Arthur R. *A Careless Word, a Needless Sinking*. American Merchant Marine Museum, Kings Point, NY. 1983.

Morrison, Samuel Eliot. *History of the United States Naval Operations in World War II, Vol. 1, The Battle of the Atlantic September 1939-May 1943*. Little, Brown and Company, Boston. 1964.

Naisawald, L. VanLoan. *In Some Foreign Field*. North Carolina Division of Archives and History, 1997.

Noble, Dennis L. *The Beach Patrol and Corsair Fleet—The U.S. Coast Guard in World War II*. U.S. Coast Guard Historian's Office, 1992.

O'Neal, Calvin; Rondthaler, Alice K.; Fletcher, Anita. *The Story of Ocracoke Island*. Hyde County Historical Society, 1976.

Sebag-Montefiore, Hugh. *Enigma—The Battle for the Code*. John Wiley & Sons, Inc., New York, 2000.

Stick, David. *The Outer Banks of North Carolina*. Chapel Hill: The University of North Carolina Press. 1958.

Stick, David, editor. *An Outer Banks Reader*. Chapel Hill: The University of North Carolina Press. 1998.

Wechter, Nell Wise. *Taffy of Torpedo Junction*. John F. Blair Publishers, 1957.

Periodicals and Weblogs

"U-boat attack still fresh to lone survivor." Michael Homans. *Savannah News-Press*. January 19, 1992.

"Ocracoke's Artists' colony." Philip Howard. Ocracoke Island Journal, November 29, 2008.

"My Experiences Off Cape Hatteras." Sarah King. "The Methodist Woman" June 1942.

"Union Jack is Raised over Gravesites." Jerry Allegood. Raleigh *News & Observer*, July 1974.

"Heroes in Hollywood—They come and conquer stars." *Life* magazine, Time Inc. publisher, July 13, 1942.

"I Wore a Dead Man's Hand." Aycock Brown (with Ken Jones). *Male* Magazine 1955.

NOTES

1. (p.35) Not all of the Outer Banks islands had ferry service on the eve of World War II. For example, Ocracokers at the time might have been inclined to replace the words ferry boat with mail boat, as regular ferry service to the island would not begin until 1950.

2. (p.100) The 100-foot-high sand dune, tallest in the eastern United States, was originally known to 18th-century mariners as "the Nag's head[land]," which is how the beach town got its name.

3. (p.124) Pemmican is a paste of dried and pounded meat mixed with melted fat and other ingredients.

4. (p.126) Between 1936 and 1950, the familiar barber-pole-striped lighthouse had been decommissioned and was not functioning as a lighthouse but was used by the Coast Guard as a lookout tower.

5. (p.130) Officially titled: Foreign Affairs/Defence Office of the Armed Forces High Command.

6. (p.138) The spy name Hans Haas has been suggested by Cape Hatteras residents. There was a well-known Austrian of that name who was once suspected of being a Nazi spy on the Caribbean island of Bonaire prior to the war. This Haas was a diving enthusiast who pioneered the use of underwater photos and movies. The diver Hans Haas left Bonaire and was in Germany when the Cape Hatteras spy Hans Haas was supposedly arrested in New York.

7. (p.140) Cullen's superior in charge of his station in the absence of their commanding officer who was on temporary leave was Boatswain's Mate second class Carl R. Jennette, ironically a native of the Outer Banks village of Avon.

8. (p.142) As a point of comparison, some al-Qaeda terrorists have been in U.S. custody for nearly 10 years.

9. (p.145) Dönitz's Kriegstagebücher or War Diary lists four U-boats operating off the East Coast of the United States during the last half of July 1943—U-66, U-190, U-230, and U-566. On July 22, U-66 was 600 miles east of the Bahama Islands; U-190 was more that 700 miles from Kure Beach and was on its way back to France; U-230 and U-566 were both more than 1,000 miles east of Virginia.

10. (p.153) This statement echos the words of UB-151's First Watch Officer Friedrich Körner who described seeing the American coast during the first world war in May 1918: "Far away from the battlefields, [at night] they sailed merrily with gleaming position lights, just like in peacetime."

11. (p.155) The first "happy time" occurred between June and October 1940 when Germany's U-boats sank more than 270 Allied ships.

12. (p.158) Before King assumed command of U.S. Naval forces on Dec. 30, 1941, his predecessor's office had been designated CINCUS, but King thought that COMINCH sounded less like an invitation to destroy his fleet.

13. (p.161) It has been often erroneously stated by writers that the USS *Jesse Roper* carried only five-3" guns but the ship was one of 27 destroyers refitted with six-3"/50 caliber guns after December 6, 1940. *U.S. Destroyers: An Illustrated Design History*, Norman Friedman, p.56 Naval Institute Press, Annapolis, 2004.

14. (p.171) USS *Jesse Roper* (DD-147) was named for Lieutenant Commander Jesse M. Roper, commanding officer of USS *Petrel* (PG-2), who died during the Spanish-American War while rescuing his crew.

15. (p.190) The German U-boat's 88mm deck gun fired a projectile 12mm larger in diameter than the U.S. Navy's *Wickes*-class destroyer's 3"/50 caliber gun.

16. (p.199) Helmut Schmoeckel is the author of *Menschlichkeit im Seekrieg* (*Humanity in the War at Sea*), which describes various acts of humanity performed by U-boat crews when they helped shipwrecked enemies during the war.

17. (p.201) Sport divers who have been systematically salvaging artifacts from the U-boat off Nags Head since the 1960s claim that no human remains have ever been found in or around the U-85. Of course, "human remains never found" does not mean that human remains have not been in the U-boat previously, or, are not there now. An urban legend has persisted that a rubber raft full of German U-boat men landed on an Outer Banks beach after the sinking of the U-85, but that could hardly have been possible considering the number of aircraft flying overhead in the early morning hours following the event.

18. (p.213) The figure for U-boats bombed—57—also seems suspect in light of the fact that a total of only 58 U-boats were documented to have operated in recorded engagements against Allied vessels in U.S. and Canadian waters between January and the end of August 1942.

19. (p.220) In the same month, an Army general in charge of the Department of War Plans wrote in his diary: "One thing that might help win this war is to get someone to shoot King." The hostile remark was made by none other than Dwight D. Eisenhower.

20. (p.221) Southbound ships were to be protected by aircraft—blimps, Vought OS2U Kingfishers, PBY Catalinas, and, of course, the intrepid Civil Air Patrol.

21. (p.222) As many as six anchorages surrounded by minefields from Cape Hatteras to Florida were thought to be warranted, but Cape Hatteras was given top priority with the anchorage west of Cape Fear considered second in importance.

22. (p.223) It has been sometimes stated in error, including by the U.S. Department of Interior, that the Norwegian motor vessel *Tamesis* was also sunk by a mine in the Cape Hatteras minefield. The ship had, in fact, been torpedoed by U-*701*, and it sought refuge within the anchorage. The ship was later towed to New York where it was repaired. However, a year later the unlucky *Tamesis* collided with another ship and sank 200 miles northeast of Bermuda.

23. (p.225) People familiar with the island today would hardly recognize the terrain between the village and the beach ramp near the airport as it appeared in 1942. There were no bushes, trees, grass, and few dunes between the village and the beach.

24. (p.225) Most civilians mistakingly called it Loop Shack Hill because of the circular antenna atop one of the buildings that was part of the high-frequency direction finding function of the installation.

25. (p.227) The Cape Lookout station had been in operation since 1935 (cisupa.proquest.com/ksc_assets/catalog/11221.pdf). The Poyners Hill station had been in operation since December 1939 (www.navyctfhistory.com/CI_Stations_past_and_present_alphabetical_4.html). The Navy had a number of problems with the reliability of the Poyners Hill station due to blowing sand and frequent storms (*Top Secret Studies on U.S. Communications Intelligence during World War II*, Part 3, Organization and Administration, Robert E. Lester, Editor, University Publications of America.

26. (p.228) Naval records reflect that none of the underwater indicator loops installed within United States territorial waters recorded the infiltration of a German U-boat during World War II.

27. (p.235) Capt. Henry Coyle was later assigned to command the USS *General William Mitchell*, a troop transport ship that made five trips to North Africa to deliver soldiers in the troop buildup prior to the Allied invasion of Europe. Coyle's command of the General William Mitchell, named for Gen. Billy Mitchell, was a strange connection of two military figures who became well-known on Ocracoke and Hatteras islands. Gen. Billy Mitchell used Hatteras village as his base of operations during his bombing demonstrations of the USS *Virginia* and USS *New Jersey* off Cape Hatteras in 1923. Coyle died in Norfolk in 1953 at the age of 64.

28. (p.243) The U-boat rose so rapidly by the force of the depth charge that the survivors described experiencing intense head pain from the rapid increase in air pressure.

29. (p.243) An inventory taken after the engagement of ordinance expended listed 350 machine gun bullets fired and 14 shells from the 3" gun.

30. (p.245) In recognition of sinking the U-*352*, Jester was promoted to Lieutenant Commander and was awarded the Navy Cross. Jester's citation read: "The President of the United States takes pleasure in presenting the Navy Cross to Maurice D. Jester, Lieutenant Commander, U.S. Coast Guard, for extraordinary heroism and distinguished service in the line of his profession as Commanding Officer of the U.S.S. ICARUS (WPC-110) during a successful action on 9 May 1942, with an enemy German submarine. The conduct of Lieutenant Commander Jester throughout this action reflects great credit upon himself, and was in keeping with the highest traditions of the United States Naval Service." Jester died in 1957 at the age of 68.

31. (p.251) 35 cubic meters equals 9,246 U.S. gallons of diesel fuel.

32. (p.252) Source: United States Naval Administration in World War II, History of Convoy Routing, Headquarters of the Commander in Chief, United States Fleet, Vol. XI, Appendix F, Summary of Principal Convoys Arriving in Calendar Year 1942.

33. (p.267) U-*215* was sunk on July 3, 1942, about 125 miles southeast of Nova Scotia.

34. (p.268) The two ships damaged by U-*576* were the steam freighter *Chilore* and the motor tanker *J.A. Mowinckel*. These were the two vessels that sought safety in shallow water south of Cape Hatteras and became ensnarled in the Cape Hatteras minefield, which precipitated the closure of the protected anchorage.

35. (p.275) Germany's surrender was ordered by Reich President Karl Dönitz who was elevated to the position following the suicide of Adolph Hitler.

Looking Glass Productions

*Books, Documentary Films,
Historical Research, New Discoveries*

Books

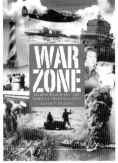

$24.95

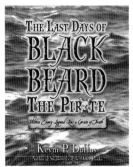

$24.95

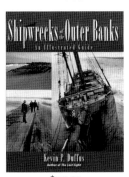

$24.95

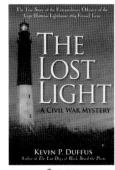

$19.95

DVDs

$19.95

$19.95

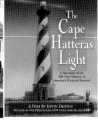

$19.95

$19.95

To order DVDs or personalized, signed copies of books:

ABOUT THE AUTHOR

Kevin P. Duffus is an award-winning filmmaker, researcher, and investigative journalist of historical events. In 2002, he solved the 140-year-old Civil War mystery of the lost Cape Hatteras Lighthouse Fresnel lens.

In 2008, after completing years of research, Kevin Duffus published **The Last Days of Black Beard the Pirate**, a detailed examination of the famous seafaring rogue's final six months in North Carolina. The controversial book presents stunning contradictions to traditional historical accounts about Black Beard's origins, his travels and motivations as a pirate, his death, and the identity and fate of his most trusted crew members.

He is the author of **The Lost Light—A Civil War Mystery** and **Shipwrecks of the Outer Banks—An Illustrated Guide**. Duffus presents informative, entertaining lectures on maritime history throughout the U.S. He lives in North Carolina.

Kevin Duffus is available to speak to groups of 50 people or more on "Shipwrecks of the Outer Banks," "World War II Off North Carolina's Outer Banks," "The Mystery of the Lost Hatteras Fresnel Lens," and "The Last Days of Black Beard." Send E-mail requests to: looking_glass@earthlink.net.

write:
Looking Glass Productions, Inc.
P.O. Box 98985
Raleigh, NC 27624-8985

call:
1-800-647-3536

web:
www.thelostlight.com